NORM DYNAMICS IN MULTILATERAL ARMS CONTROL

EST. 75 YEARS 1938
THE UNIVERSITY OF GEORGIA PRESS 2013

STUDIES IN SECURITY AND INTERNATIONAL AFFAIRS

NORM DYNAMICS IN MULTILATERAL ARMS CONTROL

Interests, Conflicts, and Justice

edited by Harald Müller and Carmen Wunderlich

The University of Georgia Press
Athens and London

Athens, Georgia 30602
www.ugapress.org

Set in 10/14 Minion Pro by Graphic Composition, Inc.
Manufactured by Sheridan Books, Inc.
The paper in this book meets the guidelines for permanence and durability of the Committee on Production Guidelines for Book Longevity of the Council on Library Resources.

Printed in the United States of America
17 16 15 14 13 P 5 4 3 2 1

Library of Congress Cataloging-in-Publication Data
Norm dynamics in multilateral arms control : interests, conflicts, and justice / edited by Harald Müller and Carmen Wunderlich.
pages cm. — (Studies in security and international affairs)
Includes bibliographical references and index.
ISBN-13: 978-0-8203-4422-5 (hardcover)
ISBN-10: 0-8203-4422-2 (hardcover)
ISBN-13: 978-0-8203-4423-2 (paperback)
ISBN-10: 0-8203-4423-0 (paperback)
1. Arms control. I. Müller, Harald, 1949 May 13–
JZ5625.N67 2013
327.1'74—dc23
2012048320

British Library Cataloging-in-Publication Data available

CONTENTS

ACKNOWLEDGMENTS

This book is the final product of a multiyear research project in which many more people participated than figure as authors here—and this number alone is considerable. The research was first funded by the German Research Association (DFG), then by the Cluster of Excellence "The Formation of Normative Orders" at Goethe University Frankfurt. We are grateful for this support.

The book would not have been possible without the work of our many student assistants who contributed hard work at different phases of the project: Hanif Aroji, Jean Backhus, Elizabeth Boshold, Sebastian Dietrich, Markus Friedrich, Helena Esther Grass, Marcus Jurk, Enrico Klotter, Jan Krauss, Philipp Langer, Christian Lebherz, Malte Lohrberg, Stephan de la Peña, Kaspar Pflaum, Christoph Reissfelder, Steffen Schiklenk, and Liza Torres. Without the meticulous editorial work and the tireless effort of Annabel Schmitz it would have never taken shape. Our thanks also go to Matthew Harris and Jane M. Curran for language editing the individual chapters.

Partial results of the project have been presented and constructive comments received on numerous conferences, notably several ISA and ECPR panels. We thank summarily all those who participated in these discussions and provided food for thought that helped shape the final manuscript. Two members of the PRIF Scientific Advisory Board, Nina Tannenwald and Richard Price, helped us with highly valuable observations to improve the quality of our work. We also like to thank the two anonymous reviewers for very useful suggestions for improvement. The unswerving encouragement by the editor of the University of Georgia Press series, Gary K. Bertsch, helped us to push forward with the book project. Finally, Nancy L. Grayson, the former executive editor, and John Joerschke, the project editor, have been wonderful partners in an extraordinarily smooth and efficient cooperation throughout. We thank all those who proved supportive on the long road to this volume. In the end, the responsibility for what is in it rests with the authors and the editors.

ABBREVIATIONS AND ACRONYMS

ABM	Antiballistic missile
ACDA	Arms Control and Disarmament Agency
AG	Australia Group
AHG	Ad Hoc Group
AL	Arab League
ANC	African National Congress
AP	Antipersonnel
AP I	Additional Protocol I
APEC	Asian-Pacific Economic Cooperation
APM	Antipersonnel mine
Art.	Article
ATM	Antitank mine
ATT	Arms Trade Treaty
AU	African Union
BK 90	Bombkapsel 90
BMS	Biennial meetings of states
BTWC	Biological and Toxin Weapons Convention
Bush 41	George H. W. Bush
Bush 43	George W. Bush
BW	Biological weapons
BWC	Biological Weapons Convention
CBM	Confidence-building measure
CBW	Chemical and biological weapons
CCM	Convention on Cluster Munitions
CCW	Convention on Certain Conventional Weapons
CD	Conference on Disarmament
CFE	Conventional Armed Forces in Europe
CFSP	Common Foreign and Security Policy
CMC	Cluster Munitions Coalition

CND	Campaign for Nuclear Disarmament
COARM	Council Working Group on Conventional Arms Exports
CODUN	Council Working Group on Disarmament in the UN
CONOP	Council Working Group on Non-Proliferation
CSCE	Conference on Security and Co-operation in Europe
CSI	Container Security Initiative
CSP	Conference of the States Parties
CTB	Comprehensive Test Ban
CTBT	Comprehensive Nuclear-Test-Ban Treaty
CTBTO	Comprehensive Nuclear-Test-Ban Treaty Organization
CTR	Cooperative Threat Reduction
CW	Chemical weapons
CWC	Chemical Weapons Convention
DC	Disarmament Commission
DDR	Disarmament, demobilization, and reintegration
DFAIT	Department of Foreign Affairs and International Trade Canada
DPRK	Democratic People's Republic of Korea
EC	European Commission
ECOWAS	Economic Community of West African States
EEAS	European External Action Service
ESS	European Security Strategy
EU	European Union
EURATOM	European Atomic Energy Community
FARC	Revolutionary Armed Forces of Colombia
FMCT	Fissile Material Cut-off Treaty
FOA	Swedish Defence Research Establishment (Försvarets forskningsanstalt)
FOI	Swedish Defence Research Agency (Totalförsvarets forskningsinstitut)
FRM-II	Research reactor Munich II (Forschungsreaktor München II)
G11	Vienna Group of Eleven
G36	Heckler & Koch Gewehr 36 (assault rifle)
G8	Group of Eight
GIF	Generation IV International Forum
HEU	Highly enriched uranium
IAEA	International Atomic Energy Agency
IALANA	International Association of Lawyers against Nuclear Arms

IANSA	International Action Network on Small Arms
ICAN	International Campaign to Abolish Nuclear Weapons
ICBL	International Campaign to Ban Landmines
ICBM	Intercontinental Ballistic Missile
ICF	Inertial confinement fusion
ICJ	International Court of Justice
ICRC	International Committee of the Red Cross
IDDS	Institute for Defense and Disarmament Studies
IDSA	Institute for Defence Studies and Analyses
IGO	International governmental organization
IHL	International humanitarian law
IHR-60	Hungarian anti-infantry directed territory defense weapon
IMS	International Monitoring System
INESAP	International Network of Engineers and Scientists against Proliferation
INF	Intermediate-Range Nuclear Forces
INFCE	International Nuclear Fuel Cycle Evaluation
INPRO	International Project on Innovative Nuclear Reactors and Fuel Cycles
IO	International organization
IPCS	Institute of Peace and Conflict Studies
IPPNW	International Physicians for the Prevention of Nuclear War
IR	International Relations
IRI	Islamic Republic of Iran
IT	Information technology
ITI	International Tracing Instrument
IUEC	International Uranium Enrichment Center
JACKSNNZ	Japan, Australia, Canada, Republic of Korea, Switzerland, Norway and New Zealand
JCS	Joint Chiefs of Staff
JNU	Jawaharlal Nehru University
KEDO	Korean Peninsula Energy Development Organization
LEU	Low-enriched uranium
LTBT	Limited Test Ban Treaty
MANPADS	Man-portable air defense systems
MBT	Mine Ban Treaty; also Ottawa Convention
MCF	Magnetic confinement fusion

MIIS	Monterey Institute of International Studies
MIRV	Multiple independently targetable reentry vehicle
MITL	Man-in-the-loop
MOX	Mixed oxide
MSP	Meeting of States Parties
MTCR	Missile Technology Control Regime
NAC	New Agenda Coalition
NAM	Non-Aligned Movement
NATO	North Atlantic Treaty Organization
NBC	Nuclear, biological, and chemical
NGO	Nongovernmental organization
NLW	Nonlethal weapons
NMD	National missile defense
NNWS	Nonnuclear weapon states
NP	Nonproliferation
NPT	Nuclear Non-Proliferation Treaty
NRA	National Rifle Association
NSA	Negative security assurances
NSD-A	Non-self-destruct alternative
NSG	Nuclear Suppliers Group
NTI	Nuclear Threat Initiative
NW	Nuclear weapons
NWC	Nuclear Weapons Convention
NWFZ	Nuclear-weapon-free zone
NWS	Nuclear weapon states
OAS	Organization of American States
OCPF	Other chemical production facilities
OPCW	Organisation for the Prohibition of Chemical Weapons
ORF	Observer Research Foundation
OSCE	Organization for Security and Co-operation in Europe
P5	The five permanent members of the UN Security Council
PGA	Parliamentarians for Global Action
PNI	Presidential nuclear initiative
PoA	UN Programme of Action on Small Arms and Light Weapons
PPNN	Programme for Promoting Nuclear Non-Proliferation
PrepCom	Preparatory Committee

PSI	Proliferation Security Initiative
PTBT	Partial Nuclear Test Ban Treaty
PTT	Power transition theory
PVC	Polyvinyl chloride
R&D	Research and development
RADAM	Remote Area Denial Artillery Munition
RevCon	Review Conference
S&T	Science and technology
SACBL	South African Campaign to Ban Landmines
SADC	Southern African Development Community
SALT	Strategic Arms Limitation Talks
SALW	Small arms and light weapons
SAS	Small Arms Survey
SIPRI	Stockholm International Peace Research Institute
SLBM	Submarine-launched ballistic missile
SORT	Strategic Offensive Reductions Treaty
SSOD	Special sessions on disarmament
START	Strategic Arms Reduction Treaty
TAN	Transnational action network
TAPM	Taser Anti-Personnel Munition
TRAD	Taser Remote Area Denial
TRIPS	Agreement on Trade-Related Aspects of Intellectual Property Rights
UN	United Nations
UNDC	UN Disarmament Commission
UNGA	United Nations General Assembly
UNIDIR	United Nations Institute for Disarmament Research
UNMOVIC	United Nations Monitoring, Verification and Inspection Commission
UNOG	United Nations Office Geneva
UNSC	United Nations Security Council
UNSCOM	United Nations Special Commission
UNSC Res	United Nations Security Council Resolution
UNSG	United Nations Secretary-General
USCBL	United States Campaign to Ban Landmines
VERPROG	Verification Research Programme

VERTIC	Verification Research, Training and Information Centre
WEOG	Western European and Others Group
WFSA	World Forum on the Future of Sport Shooting Activities
WMD	Weapons of mass destruction
WMDFZ	Weapons of mass destruction free zone

NORM DYNAMICS IN MULTILATERAL ARMS CONTROL

INTRODUCTION

Where It All Began

Harald Müller

WHILE AT THE UNITED NATIONS General Assembly Hall in New York City in April 1995, I was sitting on the backbench of the German delegation to the Review and Extension Conference of the parties to the Nuclear Non-Proliferation Treaty (NPT), proudly serving as an "expert advisor" on my country's negotiation team. Listening to the general debate, the first phase of the conference, it suddenly occurred to me that at every turn delegates were speaking of morals.[1] The Irish delegate protested the profoundly inhumane character of nuclear weapons. The South African speaker, taking the moral high ground, appealed to the nuclear weapon states to emulate his country's example and finally follow through with their obligation to lay down their nuclear arms. The representative from Nigeria complained bitterly about the unequal compliance of nuclear and nonnuclear weapon states with their mutual obligations under the NPT, making the status quo unjust. Egypt's statement condemned the unfairness of the situation in the Middle East, where Israel, not being an NPT party, was at liberty to add to its nuclear arsenal without being pressured by the great powers to disarm. There was no doubt: these seasoned representatives of their nation-states, known to pursue hard-nosed, cool-headed interest policies, could find no better use for their allotted speaking time than appealing to the sense of morals and justice of their audience—which consisted of the same brand of politicians and diplomats as those at the lectern.

Why, I asked myself. At that time, my theoretical home was more in the functionalist/rationalist camp: regimes were created to serve the interests of their creators, as compromises between functionally converging preferences of otherwise competing states (Keohane 1984). Over time, these preferences might change through habitualization of regime norms and rules. Still, I began to find this position unsatisfactory. If habitualization could shift the weight of interests, why would we assume that when regimes were formed in the first place, protagonists would meet one another in a Robinson-like way, in "first encounters," when in reality they were all embedded in what the English school had called "international society," that is, a dense system of norms in which all states but those with recent revolutions and sudden elite shifts have been acculturated for years, decades, even centuries (Bull 1995)?

Would it not make more sense to take seriously norms, and notions of justice, and not just as rhetorical fig leaves for the more pedestrian pursuit of material interests (Krasner 1999; Schimmelfennig 2003)? For why would audiences be moved by moral arguments when the entire world was populated only by rationalist utilitarians? And why would diplomat-utilitarians bother to employ such moral arguments when they had to reckon with an unmoved audience consisting of people just as utilitarian as themselves (Müller 2004)?

Having considered this line of thinking largely in the abstract sphere of academics, there I sat in the General Assembly Hall, listening to diplomats exchanging moral arguments in earnest and sounding quite authentic at that. From that moment on, I was determined to look at the issue in greater empirical depth. It took a while until I had the resources and brought together the large team of researchers needed to do so at the required scale, covering a variety of fields of arms control policy—nuclear, biological, chemical, and humanitarian—and cases for comparison.

This book is the final realization of the ambition that sprung up in New York. It tries to find answers to the questions that have been bothering researchers for a while (see the discussion of the state of the art in chapter 1): What is the relation between "norms" and "interests," that is, what autonomous quality of moral content is intrinsic to norms? How do moral considerations interact with other factors in influencing norm dynamics, including structural changes? What, in particular, is the impact of justice concerns on the way in which norms evolve? And what is the role of agency in driving norm systems forward?

ARMS CONTROL, DISARMAMENT, AND NONPROLIFERATION AS NORMATIVE GOVERNANCE SYSTEMS

Anarchy creates the security dilemma (Booth and Wheeler 2008), forcing states into self-help. Multiple self-help actions make the security dilemma worse: all feel less secure at the end of each turn of the spiral in the ensuing arms race. Arms control, disarmament, and nonproliferation are attempts to create consensual, norm-regulated systems to stop the spiral; they serve the purpose of common security governance. The three terms depict different modes of governance. *Arms control* aims primarily at stability, *disarmament* at eliminating certain types of weapons, and *nonproliferation* at preventing the spread of arms. For reasons of simplicity, we use the term *arms control* in this volume to refer to all three modes at once.

We can look at such cooperative security regimes as the outgrowth of mere interest convergence. Yet the degree to which moral formulas have intruded into those regimes is striking, especially in their preambles, which give the reasons why these regimes were created. The notion of inhumane weapons, for example, is found in all the regimes, as is the responsibility of the parties to these treaties toward all mankind to avoid war, or at least wars posing the risk of irreversible destructiveness.

At first sight, traditional goals emphasized by arms control theory (e.g., Bull 1965) offer a utilitarian picture: preserving *stability for avoiding war* is, of course, utilitarian in the sense of preserving one's own life, limb, and property. *Lowering the costs of defense* is utilitarian in that it enhances the wealth and freedom of action of the states concerned. *Limiting damage* in the case of war is utilitarian in diminishing the loss of property and personal misfortune that might otherwise occur.

Establishing arms control regimes with a view to prevent collective bads from emerging and to procure collective goods is, from this vantage point, a typical case of functionalist-driven governance that can be fruitfully analyzed with the instruments of rational choice theory. Agreed rules lengthen the "shadow of the future" and create the necessary information and communication to dissuade participating states from unilaterally maximizing their utility, attempts that inevitably lead to suboptimal if not catastrophic outcomes for all. They are typical governance structures in that they emerge in a political environment lacking superior authority to enforce rules, and rely on the services of intergovernmental organizations (as channels of communication and agencies for verification and dispute solution) as well as nongovernmental organizations or committed state officials/individuals (for agenda setting, information and advice, blaming and shaming of dissident actors).

At the same time, these governance structures have intrinsic moral purposes: *Avoiding war* prevents the taking of innocent life that is war's usual collateral. *Lowering the costs* of defense is moral in that it enables governments to divert resources from the unproductive activity of preparing for killing to more worthy purposes such as saving the environment or combating poverty.

Limiting damage is moral as it will save human life by reducing casualties and, notably, "collateral damage." The boundaries between utility and values are blurred.

Cooperative security regimes are thus normative governance systems of a primarily prescriptive and prohibitive character, that is, located in the realm of regulative norms. But they have, over time, two constitutive effects domestically and internationally. Domestically, once a state has become party to a regime and has transformed its obligations duly into domestic rules and concomitant habits, attitudes, and routines of procedure, complying becomes part of what is appropriate to do for the actors (politicians, diplomats, officials, businesspeople, etc.). As these actors represent the state, complying becomes part of the state's identity; the norms have a constitutive effect on what the collective actor believes it is all about. A striking example is Germany's transformation from NPT resister to NPT proactivist in the space of less than a generation (Müller 2003).

Internationally, a cooperative security norm, if close to universality, can become the defining standard for how a good international citizen should behave. It is striking how in the 1980s and 1990s scores of formerly reluctant states were flocking to NPT membership, notably after change in the national system of rule and particularly in the course of democratization processes: turning unequivocally nonnuclear or confirming nonnuclear status became the "right thing to do" (Rublee 2009; Müller and Schmidt 2010). Likewise, a considerable number of states, while abstaining from membership in the Ottawa Convention that prohibits antipersonnel landmines, observe the rules of this treaty to which by now more than two-thirds of the world community subscribe: a decent state just does not use or transfer antipersonnel mines (Price 1998). Compliance, then, becomes strictly coupled to status in the international community (Towns 2012).

The way in which regulative norms have come to assume a constitutive effect when it comes to defining the essence of a morally upstanding state is a reformulation of Finnemore and Sikkink's "tipping point" concept (Finnemore and Sikkink 1998), the "pull" effect of a significant number of states having joined a regime on the determination of outsiders to join as well: beyond formal membership, there is a "tipping point" effect concerning internalization (Price 1998); beyond that point, states come to observe the norm not out of calculations about loss of reputation or the risk of sanctions but because governments now regard compliance to be appropriate behavior.

Normative systems of cooperative security impose normative obligations on the membership. The attitude of "I do" and "I want to" that characterizes defense policy under the conditions of unregulated anarchy gives way to "I ought to" in a normatively regulated armament environment. Most, though not all, cooperative security regimes are treaty based. The "I ought to," the appropriateness of norm-compliant behavior, thus assumes the strong form of a legal obligation. That should not divert attention from the basic moral character of the norm that is always part of its normativity. A legal norm can be regarded as a moral obligation in the form of law. This is not to say that a legal norm cannot collide with a moral one. Clearly, the norm of non-intervention can come into conflict with the norm of humanitarian compassion. Yet it would be wrong to see this as the collision between the legal and the moral: non-intervention is a norm meant to prevent war; this has a deep moral content, because war, as argued above, inevitably has immoral consequences, even if fought for justifiable reasons. Thus, it is of little use to maintain a categorical distinction between legal and moral norms; rather, we must think of all behavior under the logic of appropriateness as unequivocally having a moral component, whether legally codified or not.

NORMS AND JUSTICE

The notion of "embeddedness" or "nesting" was developed during the early stages of work on regimes: normative systems are not free-standing but are integrated within hierarchies of increasing abstraction and comprehensiveness. Hence, we distinguish between "ordinary" norms, with the scope of a single or a few policy fields, and "metanorms" (Wiener 2008, 66-67; Sandholtz and Stiles 2009, 17). A metanorm, in our understanding, is normative in that it implies an "ought to," like all norms. It is, however, distinct from ordinary norms as it applies in *all* fields of policy. Sometimes metanorms are called "principles." This use, however, does not indicate its intrinsic normativity: the implication that it *should* be realized, supported, and defended and the expectation that people should act with those duties in mind.

One of these metanorms identified very early on was "reciprocity" that existed comfortably on the borderline between consequential and appropriate logics (Keohane 1989). Later on, Christian Reus-Smit (1997) rediscovered the treatment of large-scope (meta)norms in the English school, where Hedley Bull (1995) had done considerable work to understanding the workings of the international system as guided by a set of such umbrella norms that overarch more field-specific rules (Reus-Smit 1997).

A metanorm holding particular potential for conflict is *justice*, which had resounded so powerfully in the General Assembly Hall in 1995. Although justice has been the subject of empirical research on international relations (IR) only relatively rarely (e.g., Welch 1993; Albin 2001; Mayer 2006), there is enough evidence from these few studies to justify devoting more attention to it: justice has been discussed as a basic human need (Burton 1990), as an intercultural constant (Küng 1993), and as a basic issue in all political orders (e.g., Shapcott 2001; Forst 2002; Pogge 2003). David A. Welch has demonstrated its potential for escalating conflicts into violent conduct (Welch 1993), and Cecilia Albin (2001) has proven its omnipresence in international negotiations. Justice is thus a metanorm with considerable potential for contentiousness: while people generally agree that justice is a good thing, they tend to disagree over what precisely justice means in general—justice principles range from transcendental commands down to the utilitarian notion of the greatest utility for the largest number of people; and even if they agree on the justice principle to be applied, they might still dispute what it means in a specific situation.

It is for this reason that we follow Welch's (1993) lead and start from the principle that "justice is in the eye of the beholder." Justice enters international relations when actors raise justice-related claims. A claim is justice-related, according to Welch, when actors do not just express a desire but justify the claim with an entitlement: they want something that is their due, and denying this "something" constitutes a situation of injustice that has to be redressed. Such claimed entitlements might relate to the distribution of goods, to the right to participate in the shaping of events, and to the demand to be recognized in a certain capacity, that is, accorded a certain status valued by the actor (Fraser 2009).

The expectation that justice might be of particular salience in arms control relates to the nature of this policy field. Arms control deals—most of the time—with asymmetric relations. Asymmetries may concern brute, material strength, technological advancement, geopolitical differences, strategic choices, and the like. All these relations create inequalities in distribution, participation, and recognition that lend themselves easily to claims that a state of injustice exists and that justice should thus be created. This sort of claim becomes particularly relevant when a normative system contains inherent inequalities such as the NPT.

If norm contestation is a permanent feature of any normative system (Wiener 2008) and serves as a powerful engine to drive the process of norm dynamics (see below), then justice claims are a particularly salient type of contestation. They lead to two different, but equally explosive, conflicts over norms: first, whether the status quo, or change thereof, satisfies an agreed standard of justice and, second, what valid justice standard should be applied. The first one is a type of "practical judgment" about which people might disagree. Subsuming a particular case under a more general normative standard is all but self-executing: many lawyers make a living from it! The second conflict is a moral-philosophical dispute; positions are connected to broader worldviews and ethical beliefs. As the international realm is populated by actors from all cultures, ideologies, and theories, we must not be surprised when we see clashes over justice claims in diplomacy where the protagonists disagree profoundly on what justice means in the first place (Cohen 1997). "Cross-cultural differences" impact upon the decision-making style of political actors and thus the configuration of the international arms control agenda (see Krause 1998); justice belongs in the realm of domestic factors that set the parameters of what can and cannot be achieved during international negotiations, but it may also be that a group of state actors clusters around the same or similar justice claims.

To be sure, this book is *not* built on the belief that justice is the *only* norm that counts. There are also other norms of importance in arms control to which we devote our attention. Nevertheless, the neglect of justice in IR is a rationalist-based impoverishment that leads to underrating the emotional content of conflicts (Hall 2011) and to overlooking important measures required to address justice concerns lest conflicts cannot be managed or settled. Justice claims, we assume, are more than a smokescreen for the "real" interests that states are supposedly pursuing.

NORMS AND INTERESTS

National interest is one of the central categories in IR. A project that puts its focus on the impact of ethics on actors' behavior, and of justice concerns in particular, is obliged to clarify how it conceptualizes the relation between norms—the metanorm of justice included—and interests. In mainstream IR theory, interests (or "preferences") are intuitively given priority. Norms are frequently used to explain the "residual variance" for which interests cannot account. There is no scientific logic in this sequence. At first glance, it could as well be the other way around: norms dominate behavior, and only a residual remainder is explainable by the free pursuit of interest (in the same way that only a small portion of human behavior is unequivocally instinctive).

Nevertheless, both attempts to establish hierarchy suffer from the same shortcoming: the notion that norms and interests could be analyzed as if they belonged to absolutely divorced realms, different spheres of social nature, so to speak. This is implausible. What counts as an interest is obviously socially constructed. Cultural factors made up of domestic sociocultural attitudes and decision-making styles influence strongly the way "national interests" are defined and presented (Krause 1998). In most of modern society, status is not defined by counting a man's slaves. Consequently, it is not in men's interest to collect slaves. It is thus very hard to conceive of interest as a separate and independent variable untouched by social context. For centuries, emperors of the Holy Roman Empire attempted desperately to control upper Italy. Modern German political leaders showed no such intentions at all. The reason was that the Holy Roman Empire was constructed as the successor of Rome, and this implied, in the first place, control over Italy and the Holy City itself, which necessitated control over Northern Italy as a springboard; German leaders in the last two centuries, in contrast, viewed themselves as running an ethnonational state confined to the area north of the Alps. Interests vary with time for the same actors, and they vary with the socionormative environment in which actors operate.

It is a truism of considerable triviality that some interests are invariable and natural: survival, security, power, and economic welfare. Yet, at that level of abstraction these terms lose any substance; they become "empty signifiers" whose meaning can be negotiated by actors in a highly arbitrary way. Whether the term *survival*, for example, means to cede a piece of territory to a dissatisfied neighbor or to grab territory to expand strategic depth, whether it means preserving a dynasty in power because the king is identified with the land, or deposing an obnoxious leader in order to pacify relations with great powers, is very much in the eye of the beholders. We cannot fathom the "interests" of a state without learning how the (leading) people tick, how they understand their identity, and in what they believe. At that point, the border line between the interest-related and the normative becomes very much blurred.

The same can be said, vice versa, about norms (see chapter 1). It may well be that many norms originally grew from rationalist-utilitarian considerations; for example, religious hygienic and dietary prescriptions and proscriptions out of the need to protect the health of a community, or sexual rules out of the will to establish and anchor patriarchal hegemony against any remaining traces of matriarchal rule.

Norms and interests are thus no opposites. Many norms in modern society empower people to pursue "interests" that have been designed as legitimate. Parties are encouraged to compete for power in elections. Politicians are entitled—that is, normatively empowered—to compete for power within parties. Lawyers bear the *duty* to make the case for their clients no matter what. Diplomats are *obliged* to foster the "interests" (defined as explicit policy goals) of their countries. All these examples concern the normatively legitimated pursuit of interest. All actors quoted would be seen as not behaving appropriately if they failed to act in an interest-oriented way.[2] And yet, because appropriateness empowers them to behave in an ostensibly self-interested way, rationalism can well account for patterns of action within the scope of this type of appropriateness (Müller 2004).

We must thus expect that norms and interests penetrate each other and depend on each other. When we use the separate terms throughout this volume in the traditional way, it is to facilitate the reading of the book. But authors as well as readers are to be aware that this is not an ontological statement. It is not the objective of the book to understand under which circumstances *norms* or *interests* prevail. Rather, we want to know how the two co-evolve in the overall process of norm dynamics.

TWO-LEVEL NORM DISCOURSES/TWO-LEVEL INTEREST GAMES

The decision to look at norms and interests as two interrelated social factors rather than as two separate or even opposed phenomena can muster another important argument once we leave the level of the state as a unitary actor and look at its internal processes of identity building and decision making. What may look like the pursuit of interests by the representatives of a state from an "outside" perspective might appear as behavior following the logic of appropriateness once we analyze it from the perspective of a principal-agent relationship. This type of relations is usually characterized by bonds of duty. Agents are supposed to work with a mandate from their principals and to do their utmost to fulfill the mandate. The examples of politicians, advocates, and diplomats discussed in this book largely represent such principal-agent relations.

Robert Putnam and colleagues (Evans, Jacobson, and Putnam 1993) have analyzed this relation from a rationalist perspective as a "two-level *game*," whereby the agents have to engage in bargaining both with their international interlocutors in order to achieve agreement, and with their principals in order to achieve sufficient compromise to give their consent to the agreement. From an ideational perspective, the same set of relations can be described as a two-level discourse (Müller 2004). Establishing international norms for regulating a field of policy implies a debate of agents over the right set of norms with a view to securing broad legitimacy for the system of governance to be established. Almost as a matter of course, this means bringing together norms emerging from different cultural settings (see Krause 1998); usually, in the absence of strong hegemony, no actor will be capable of pushing their own norm set through such negotiations. This, in turn, will create problems for domestic acceptance. Agents may at times stretch the interpretability of the new international norm set to the extreme in order to gain domestic assent.

NORM DYNAMICS

Here may lie the roots of an important source of norm dynamics. As international norms are embedded in a broad range of highly varied national norms with which they fit more or less well together, there will always be tensions and differences among national interpretations of what an internationally agreed norm entails. These tensions reverberate back to the international level and give rise to repeated if not perpetual disputes over the meaning of the norm, in general and as applied to particular cases. These disputes may lead to a change of the shared meaning over time. The domestic politics related to international norms have a significant impact on norm robustness and development.

Much of the existing research on norms has been devoted to their creation and to how and why states comply with them. Both issues are aspects of a broader field, that of the dynamic development of norms. How a norm system changes once it has been established was in the focus of empirical research to a lesser degree (see chapter 1). This issue constitutes the core question of this volume.

Constructivism has been frequently criticized for a structuralist bias that obviates insights into the process of change and the role of agency therein (e.g., Sending 2002). This would be a horrible shortcoming for the theory putting so much emphasis on ideational factors, for it is so obvious that normative systems betray both, perseverance *and* change of an incremental and at times also a revolutionary character: while they possess a certain structural stability, they are never carved in stone. What norms mean is always negotiated from the beginning of the norm-setting process onward and is subject to change by agency—understood in this sense, it is precisely the vagueness and contestation of norms that accounts for them being diffused internationally (Krook and True 2012). This aspect of norm change is what we understand by the term "norm dynamics." While it cannot be denied that some of the early empirical studies applying constructivist metatheory to the field of IR are more comfortable with structure than with change, this is not intrinsic to constructivism: constructivism emphasizes agency as much as structure, and agency has the triple potential to confirm existing normative structures by just reproducing them, to change them incrementally by hardly noticeable shifts in emphasis and interpretation, and to revolutionize them by turning to radically different practices (Giddens 1984; Wendt 1987; Dessler 1989).

This insight necessitates an understanding of what circumstances might be responsible for agents to engage in such change. The answers fall into two different categories: intrinsic and extrinsic factors. Intrinsic change relates to the very nature of norms, given by their existence in human language and their ensuing contestability (Krook and True 2012). Extrinsic factors concern changes in the sociopolitical environment in which the norms are embedded.

Intrinsic reasons for change lie in how norms can be fundamentally interpreted and are thus subject to dispute (Wiener 2008); they do not impact the established normative system from outside but result from its internal contradictions and conflicts. One important aspect is the interplay between a given, policy-field-specific norm system and the metanorm of justice. We do not see normative change result solely from disputes on the application of an agreed norm to a specific situation, and thus we do not believe in normative change following a uniform pattern of "cycle" (Sandholtz and Stiles 2009, 3). Intrinsically rooted contestedness gains additional momentum through the two-level discourse structure, as the occasions for contention and interpretative change multiply. We can speak about "norm conflicts" as a constellation that pushes norm dynamics in either a constructive or destructive direction (on different norm conflicts see below and also chapter 1).

Extrinsic factors comprise major processes and events outside the norm system that influence its internal stability and development (Sandholtz and Stiles 2009, 11). Such reasons may lie in a shifting material basis of policy:

technological change or change in the power relations between the major actors in the world. Obviously, *new technologies* create a new reality; insofar as existing norm systems were designed to regulate the policy field on the basis of the old "technological reality," they have to be adapted in order to do their job. Technological innovation thus opens windows of opportunity for norm entrepreneurs by posing challenges as well as offering tools for solutions.

Seminal changes in the distribution of international power might lead to adjustments in the normative order with a view to accommodating the priorities of rising powers at the cost of declining ones. Recognizing the importance of this factor does not obviate the constructivist orientation of our research. The ideational and the material levels interact; actors have to cope with the conditions in which they find themselves. "Coping" expresses the nondeterministic character of this relationship.

Salient events change the way major actors look at their security environment (such as the end of the Cold War or 9/11). Old conflicts may quickly end; new threats suddenly appear. They may not really affect the *material* basis of policy, but they affect the way the world is seen by actors and thus influence the normative framing of the world these actors deem necessary and desirable.

Finally, *domestic shifts* in important countries can affect the international normative system. Revolutionaries tend to wish to invent the world anew. Standing outside of, and often opposed to, the established normative system, they want to turn the domestic norms upside down, and this usually has some consequences for their international interactions (Armstrong 1999). It is striking that since the American and French Revolutions, the norm of sovereignty has been challenged repeatedly and increasingly under the banner of individual rights and standards of good governance of which democracy has been the most important aspect (Sandholtz and Stiles 2009, 19–24). The Bolshevik and the Iranian-Islamist revolutions have brought their own challenges to international normative order. The neoconservative conquest of power in the United States has led to an attack on existing international law, while the rise of quasi-neoconservative prime ministers in Australia (John Howard), Canada (Stephen Harper), and Sweden (Fredrik Reinfeldt) has deprived the international community of some of its best norm builders, at least temporarily. Domestic shifts may lead to sources of resistance to the existing norm system and to efforts to reform or even replace it by something else; these are addressed when we analyze specific state actors (see part 3 of the book).

We have to distinguish between three distinct phases of norm dynamics: first, the establishment of a new norm (or a new regime); second, the further development of a norm (or a new regime) once it has been established and recognized by a critical mass of actors; and third, norm degeneration and decay, a neglected aspect of norm research in IR, but nevertheless highly relevant. Most of this book is devoted to the second phase.

In each phase, norms do not change automatically. The factors just discussed do not work like forces in physics, such as impulse, pressure, or gravity. They need human agency to gain social meaning and take effect. Intrinsic regime conflicts need active protagonists for the opposite positions that constitute the conflict to do their work for change. For domestic upheavals, this is obvious as well: the identity of the actor changes, and the quasi-newborn actor translates the momentum of domestic change into norm-changing efforts. But agency is also needed for the other extrinsic forces to take effect. Technology needs actors to use it for challenging an existing regime, for stimulating norm-guided responses, or for translating its potential into strengthening a norm, such as verification. Power change has different consequences when an emerging power devotes its energy to strengthen an existing order or to disrupt it. Salient events are almost completely uncertain as to how they are interpreted, and thus they become translated into regime-related activities. It all depends on the way actors deal with such events. There is no norm dynamics without intentional agency. This is why we devote a major part of the book to norm entrepreneurs.

PLAN OF THE BOOK

In chapter 1, Carmen Wunderlich introduces the state of the art of international research on norms. She presents what authors perceive the term *norms* as meaning in the context of the book and what we know about the process of norm creation and norm development. She also addresses the key concepts of norm conflicts and norm contestedness. This leads to a look at agency, with the concept of "norm entrepreneurs" as the focal point. Finally, Carmen Wunderlich cautions us against a normatively biased approach toward norms. There are norms that have beneficial consequences for people, but there are also some that may cost people life and limb (such as the norms of heroism or blood revenge). What is "good" and "bad," however, is most of the time a matter of judgment and not easily determined "objectively." Thus, there might be norm entrepreneurs with whom we feel compelled to sympathize, but there may be other actors whom we loathe, but who are norm entrepreneurs nevertheless. She thus emphasizes the approach taken here: to analyze norms and norm conflicts through an *actor's perspective*, not by a normative standard imposed by the authors.

In the first part of the book, we look at the structure of regimes—that is, systems of related norms—in arms control, at the conflicts residing in these structures, and at the dynamic processes in which these conflicts are worked out. This part consists of two chapters. Chapter 2, by Harald Müller, Una Becker-Jakob, and Tabea Seidler-Diekmann, deals with regimes addressing weapons of mass destruction (WMD), centered on the NPT, the Chemical Weapons Convention (CWC), and the Biological Weapons Convention (BWC). These are usually seen as the most relevant normative orders in international security. Chapter 3, by Simone Wisotzki, analyzes three conventional weapons norm systems: small arms and light weapons, antipersonnel mines, and cluster munitions. Of these three, the Ottawa Convention banning antipersonnel mines and the Cluster Munition Convention are full-fledged treaty regimes. The Oslo Convention, which prohibits cluster munitions, is hardly two years old at the time of writing, while the UN Programme of Action on Small Arms and Light Weapons (PoA) is a "soft norms" system that has not yet achieved legal status. The different objects of regulation as well as the variation in time horizon permit interesting comparisons across cases. All authors in this part of the book participated for some years in the German delegations to the various regime meetings and can thus supplement their readings with firsthand observation experiences.

Each chapter in part 1 opens with a general description of the fields. The motivation that compelled the international community to seek normative regulation is established, and the stability of the existing or emerging regimes is assessed. The second section of the chapters enumerates the normative structures in these regimes and notes the changes that have occurred during the period of investigation, which varies depending on regime history. The third section of the two chapters addresses conflicts within and about the normative order in each field. The authors present the contested issues and assess the contribution of "interests" and "norm conflicts" to these disputes. Particular attention is devoted to the impact of justice concerns: under scrutiny are both conflicting justice claims and opposed ideas of what just order means in the given field. The main protagonists of these conflicts are identified. The fourth section assesses the impact of these conflicts on the changes that have been observed during the research period. The final section compares conclusions across the fields: What impact do norm conflicts have on norm dynamics? Are they conducive to an evolutionary strengthening of the normative structure, or are they destructive? And what is the impact of justice concerns?

Part 2 deals with the impact extrinsic factors have on norm dynamics. In chapter 4, Elvira Rosert, Una Becker-Jakob, Giorgio Franceschini, and Annette Schaper ask how technological change influences the evolution of norms in the respective regimes. The cases concern proliferation resistance, nuclear testing, the dual-use potential of biotechnological development, and "alternative" landmines. The beginning of each section of the chapter elaborates the normative demands directed toward technology as conceptualized, for example, in blueprints for "technology assessment." In the second section, the opportunities and challenges emerging from technological change are discussed: technology is treated here as "independent," and arms control as a "dependent" variable. The third section inverts the perspective: how does arms control influence technological change? The comparison across the cases emphasizes the way actors frame technology in the light of both normative orientations and "interests," and whether justice concerns, apparently remote from the material world of technology, may account for, and remedy, asymmetries in technological capabilities or the effects technology has on different actors.

Chapter 5 (Harald Müller, Marco Fey, and Carsten Rauch) is devoted to exogenous events as norm triggers (or killers). The first event type concerns incremental power change—a shift in the polar structure of the international system. The second event type concerns power change over a couple of years: we assess the impact of the end of the Cold War. The third type is a sudden shock: 9/11. Each part starts with an analysis of the specific event under scrutiny. An empirical exploration of arms control developments follows, with a view to estimating continuity and change. Finally, the influence of the events on the arms control policy of selected actors is assessed.

Part 3 then turns to agency, focusing on norm entrepreneurship in arms control. Having screened the literature, and based on our knowledge about identifying "candidates," we end up with four types of entrepreneurs. Chapter 6 deals with *great powers*, the United States (Marco Fey) and Russia (Friederike Klinke), which are assumed to be status quo oriented, and "rising great powers," namely China (Andrea Hellmann and Franziska Plümmer) and India (Carsten Rauch), which we expect to be proponents of norm change. Chapter 7 turns to examples of *good international citizens:* Canada (Una-Becker Jakob), Germany (Harald Müller and Gregor Hofmann), and Sweden (Carmen Wunderlich), three countries that have been identified in previous research as "arms control proactivists" (Becker, Müller, and Wisotzki 2008). Chapter 8 deals with nonaligned countries that are expected to work for norm change. We distinguish between supposed *norm reformers* Egypt (Daniel Müller) and South Africa (Judith Reuter) and *revolutionaries* Iran (Carmen Wunderlich) and North Korea (Hans-Joachim Schmidt and Andrea Hellmann).

We briefly characterize all of these actors (identity, role in international relations, interests, and values) and then analyze the motivations for their activities, including the search for justice claims. All chapters use a standardized codebook for hermeneutic, qualitative content analysis for answering this research question.[3] We estimate the relationship of "interests" to "normative goals" and clarify the effects of norm entrepreneurship on norm dynamics. These chapters, dealing with nation-states, also take note of internal change or domestic shifts that may influence the actors' behavior toward cooperative security norms.

Chapter 9 looks into the activities of both nongovernmental organizations (NGOs, Simone Wisotzki) and international organizations, focusing on the European Union (Alexis Below) and the United Nations (Harald Müller). The chapter considers the empirical norm entrepreneurship potential of these collective entities vis-à-vis both realist skepticism and cosmopolitan enthusiasm.

In the conclusion Harald Müller compares the relationship between the intrinsic and extrinsic "independent variables" and their relative impact on the dynamics of norm development in the field of arms control. The interface between these structural factors and the agency of the various norm entrepreneurs is analyzed, as are the relationships between "interest" and normative orientations, and the weight of the justice issue. Finally, the findings are compared critically with alternative explanations for norm dynamics offered by other theoretical approaches. Suggestions for further research on the issue conclude the book.

Notes

1. Following Habermas, we use the term morals for value-based demands, assessments, or norms with a claim to universal validity, ethics for such demands, assessments, or norms that are founded on particularistic systems of values.

2. Space is too limited to discuss the consequences of identity or role conflicts. See Müller (2004) and Becker, Müller, and Wisotzki (2008).

3. Our data sample comprised a huge amount of statements uttered by country repre-

sentatives at the review conferences to the treaty regimes as well as to the UN First Committee and the Conference on Disarmament. Reasons of space, however, allow for a selective reference to statements only.

References

Albin, Cecilia. 2001. *Justice and Fairness in International Negotiation*. Cambridge: Cambridge University Press.

Armstrong, David. 1999. "The Diplomacy of Revolutionary States."In *Innovation in Diplomatic Practice*, edited by Jan Melissen, 43–59. Basingstoke: Palgrave Macmillan.

Becker, Una, Harald Müller, and Simone Wisotzki. 2008. "Democracy and Nuclear Arms Control: Destiny or Ambiguity?" *Security Studies* 17 (4): 810–54.

Booth, Ken, and Nicholas J. Wheeler. 2008. *The Security Dilemma: Fear, Cooperation, and Trust in World Politics*. Basingstoke: Palgrave Macmillan.

Bull, Hedley. 1965. *The Control of the Arms Race: Disarmament and Arms Control in the Missile Age*. New York: Praeger.

———. 1995. *The Anarchical Society: A Study of Order in World Politics*. London: Macmillan.

Burton, John, ed. 1990. *Conflict: Human Needs Theory*. Basingstoke: Macmillan.

Cohen, Raymond. 1997. *Negotiating across Cultures: International Communication in an Interdependent World*. Washington: United States Institute of Peace Press.

Dessler, David. 1989. "What's at Stake in the Agent-Structure Debate?" *International Organization* 43 (3): 441–73.

Evans, Peter B., Harold K. Jacobson, and Robert D. Putnam, eds. 1993. *Double-Edged Diplomacy: International Bargaining and Domestic Politics*. Berkeley: University of California Press.

Finnemore, Martha, and Kathryn Sikkink. 1998. "International Norm Dynamics and Political Change." *International Organization* 52 (4): 887–917.

Forst, Rainer. 2002. *Contexts of Justice: Political Philosophy beyond Liberalism and Communitarianism*. Translated by John M. M. Farrell. Berkeley: University of California Press.

Fraser, Nancy. 2009. *Scales of Justice: Reimagining Political Space in a Globalizing World*. New York: Columbia University Press. PDF e-book.

Giddens, Anthony. 1984. *The Constitution of Society: Outline of the Theory of Structuration*. Cambridge: Polity Press.

Hall, Todd H. 2011. "We Will Not Swallow This Bitter Fruit: Theorizing a Diplomacy of Anger." *Security Studies* 20 (4): 521–55.

Keohane, Robert O. 1984. *After Hegemony: Cooperation and Discord in the World Political Economy*. Princeton: Princeton University Press.

——. 1989. *International Institutions and State Power: Essays in International Relations Theory*. Boulder: Westview Press.

Krasner, Stephen D. 1999. *Sovereignty: Organized Hypocrisy*. Princeton: Princeton University Press.

Krause, Keith R., ed. 1998. "Culture and Security: Multilateralism, Arms Control and Security-Building." Special Issue, *Contemporary Security Policy* 19 (1).

Krook, Mona Lena, and Jacqui True. 2012. "Rethinking the Life Cycles of International Norms: The United Nations and the Global Promotion of Gender Equality." *European Journal of International Relations* 18 (1): 103–27.

Küng, Hans. 1993. *Projekt Weltethos*. Munich: Piper.

Mayer, Peter. 2006. *Macht, Gerechtigkeit und internationale Kooperation: Eine regimeanalytische Untersuchung zur internationalen Rohstoffpolitik*. Baden-Baden: Nomos.

Müller, Harald. 2003. "Germany and WMD Proliferation." *Nonproliferation Review* 10 (2): 1–20.

——. 2004. "Arguing, Bargaining and All That: Communicative Action, Rationalist Theory and the Logic of Appropriateness in International Relations." *European Journal of International Relations* 10 (3): 395–435.

Müller, Harald, and Andreas Schmidt. 2010. "The Little-Known Story of Deproliferation: Why States Give Up Nuclear Weapons Activities." In *Forecasting Nuclear Proliferation in the 21st Century*, vol. 1, *The Role of Theory*, edited by William C. Potter and Gaukhar Mukhatzhanova, 124–58. Stanford: Stanford University Press.

Pogge, Thomas W., ed. 2003. *Global Justice*. Oxford: Blackwell.

Price, Richard. 1998. "Reversing the Gun Sights: Transnational Civil Society Targets Land Mines." *International Organization* 52 (3): 613–44.

Reus-Smit, Christian. 1997. "The Constitutional Structure of International Society and the Nature of Fundamental Institutions." *International Organization* 51 (4): 555–89.

Rublee, Maria Rost. 2009. *Nonproliferation Norms: Why States Choose Nuclear Restraint*. Athens: University of Georgia Press.

Sandholtz, Wayne, and Kendall W. Stiles. 2009. *International Norms and Cycles of Change*. Oxford: Oxford University Press.

Schimmelfennig, Frank. 2003. *The EU, NATO and the Integration of Europe: Rules and Rhetoric*. Cambridge: Cambridge University Press.

Sending, Ole Jacob. 2002. "Constitution, Choice and Change: Problems with the 'Logic of Appropriateness' and Its Use in Constructivist Theory." *European Journal of International Relations* 8 (4): 443–70.

Shapcott, Richard. 2001. *Justice, Community and Dialogue in International Relations*. Cambridge: Cambridge University Press.

Towns, Ann E. 2012. "Norms and Social Hierarchies: Understanding International Policy Diffusion 'From Below.'" *International Organization* 66 (2): 179–209.

Welch, David A. 1993. *Justice and the Genesis of War*. Cambridge: Cambridge University Press.

Wendt, Alexander E. 1987. "The Agent-Structure Problem in International Relations Theory." *International Organization* 41 (3): 335–70.

Wiener, Antje. 2008. *The Invisible Constitution of Politics. Contested Norms and International Encounters*. Cambridge: Cambridge University Press.

CHAPTER ONE

Theoretical Approaches in Norm Dynamics

Carmen Wunderlich

THIS CHAPTER ELABORATES our understanding of "norms," introduces the concept of "norm dynamics," and establishes the central role of norm contestedness/contestability for the dynamic evolution of norms and regimes. We deal with individual norms here, but even more so with regimes as "sets of principles, norms, rules and decision-making procedures" (Krasner 1983, 2), because multilateral arms control norms are usually embedded in such regimes.

We are interested in understanding the process of how norms—and thus regimes—develop, that is, how they emerge, diffuse, become internalized, and, once established, become subject to change resulting in their strengthening, weakening, or even erosion. This is what is called *norm dynamics*.[1] We regard the evolution of norms as triggered by three driving forces: intraregime norm conflicts, exogenous factors, and—as a necessary condition—norm entrepreneurs who seize windows of opportunity that emanate from these factors and set out to alter the prevalent normative structure. As our focus is on states as norm entrepreneurs, drastic domestic changes within states are also regarded as inducing norm change as in the case of major political upheavals or revolutions.[2]

Thus we are trying to contribute to research on norms in three ways:

- Starting from the fundamental contestedness and ambiguity of norms (see Sandholtz 2007; Wiener 2008), we highlight the role of intraregime norm conflicts for the path regimes and single norms take once they are established. We thus transcend mainstream norm studies that tend to treat successful internalization as the end point of a norm's career (see also Sandholtz and Stiles 2009; introduction to this volume).
- Recognizing the—frequently criticized (Elgström 2000; Sending 2002)—static-structuralist bias of constructivist research on norms, we place the

emphasis on change as driven by agency, inquiring into the role of norm entrepreneurs not only in initiating norm establishment but also in norm maintenance and change.

- Noting the focus of mainstream (liberal-inspired) research on norms on supposedly "good" norms and amiable norm entrepreneurs, we also look at the possibility of ("oppositional") norms promoted by not so liberal, radical norm entrepreneurs.

NORMS AND THE LOGICS OF ACTION

The social sciences generally approach norms via two paradigms: Whereas *cognitivist* approaches (constructivists and poststructuralists) focus on the normativity of norms as setting standards of appropriateness, *rationalists* treat norms as emerging from actors' rational preference-based calculations (Axelrod 1986, 1097; Thomson 1994, 79–80). Both modes of access are linked to different logics of action[3]: the first one emphasizes that norms regulate actors' behavior due to a *logic of appropriateness*, while the second one sees a *logic of consequences* at work. Embedded in rationalist theorizing, proponents of the latter logic constrain the role of norms to the instrumental implementation of exogenous interests: actors observe norms motivated by their utilitarian cost-benefit calculations when they perceive the benefits of compliance as outweighing the costs of norm adherence (Axelrod 1986). It is mainly to *regulative* norms that rationalist-institutionalist approaches refer; rationalist regime theory usually confines the term *norms* to "institutional device[s] to facilitate interaction" (Gehring 1994, 374; see also Keohane 1989).[4] While treated as intervening variables in rationalist-institutionalist theory, norms are ostensibly rejected by realists: at best, norms are regarded as dependent variables that reflect the interests of the major powers (Mearsheimer 1994/95, 13). "Hegemonic norms" (Goertz and Diehl 1992, 640) are used by powerful actors to preserve their superiority. Rationalist approaches explain norm adherence by actors who do not benefit from the respective norms as resulting from material incentives (sanctions), coercion, or social pressure (loss of reputation). Hence, states abide by norms because it is in their interest to do so, or because they are forced into compliance (Krasner 1999).

Invoking a *logic of appropriateness* instead, constructivists attribute to norms *explanatory power* for actors' behavior as they influence both the formation and change of actors' preferences and identities. By describing common understandings of appropriate behavior and providing corresponding rules, norms enable orientation in a complex social environment: they serve as "rules of the road" (Kratochwil 1989, 24), coordinating behavior and facilitating cooperation in constellations of conflicting interests. Beyond regulative effects, constructivists attribute to norms a *constitutive* function. As the "cement of society" (Elster 1989), they not only constrain the actors' scope of action but constitute their identities and interests in the first place (March and Olsen 1998, 951–52). Norm adherence results not from external sanctions or coercion but from a feeling of obligation and "oughtness" (Finnemore and Sikkink 1998, 891)—actors follow normative prescriptions because their identity tells them to do so. Empirical evidence supports the constructivist proposition that norms are more than the corollary of rationalist calculations (e.g., Klotz 1995; Finnemore 1996; Katzenstein 1996a; Finnemore and Sikkink 1998; Risse, Ropp, and Sikkink 1999).[5] We support the constructivist approach and also adopt the conventional definition of *norms* as "collective expectations for the proper behavior of actors with a given identity" (Katzenstein 1996b, 5; see also Klotz 1995, 14; Jepperson, Wendt, and Katzenstein 1996, 54; Finnemore and Sikkink 1998, 891).

FUNCTIONS AND CHARACTERISTICS OF NORMS

Constructivist research on norms basically focuses on three distinguishing features (see, e.g., Finnemore 1996, 22–23; Florini 1996, 364): First, norms provide standards of appropriateness for actors with a common, shared identity—that is, they have an *intersubjective character*. Second, norms generate *regular patterns of behavior* for actors with a shared identity. And, third, they contain a "prescriptive (or evaluative) quality of '*oughtness*' that sets norms apart from other kinds of rules" (Finnemore and Sikkink 1998, 891; emphasis added). In terms of more detailed characteristics, conceptual frictions abound. While some authors see *morality* as inherent to norms (e.g., Nadelmann 1990; Price 2008), others identify mere functional norms in addition to moral ones (e.g., Bull 1977, 53; Elster 1989, 89–90). In our understanding (see also the introduction to this volume), norms inevitably carry ethical content, albeit with varying intensity depending on the type of norm (social, legal, moral; see Deitelhoff 2006), as even mere functional norms are tied to a higher normative order, and supporting or defying a norm thus carries a positive or negative ethical value because each non-observance might imply defying the prevailing order per se. Another contested attribute relates to the relationship between *norms* and *interests*. At times, following a logic of appropriateness might indeed conflict with pursuing one's own interests. As argued in the introduction to this volume, however, even self-interest has an underlying normative underpinning, and thus, in reality, norms and interests stand in a dialectical relationship to each other: norms express institutionalized interests, whereas, conversely, interests are defined by norms (Jepperson, Wendt, and Katzenstein 1996, 54; Müller 2004). Norms vary widely with regard to the distinctiveness of their prescriptions or their scope (local, national, regional, societal, etc.) as well as the degree of importance attached to them. Norms placed high in the hierarchy of a normative system may be usefully distinguished from ordinary norms as *metanorms* (Kelsen 1967; Fastenrath 1993; Frost 1996) lending validity to all other norms; one example is justice (see the introduction to this volume).[6] The exact meaning of and the rules emanating from metanorms are a matter of interpretation and thus subject to contestation, as is true for all norms (Wiener 2008; Sandholtz and Stiles 2009).

The contestedness of both the meaning and relative importance of single norms within a norm system have so far been insufficiently acknowledged by norm research. We address this lacuna by focusing on the dynamic interplay of single norms and regimes as systems of norms, paying tribute not only to competing norms and continuing negotiation and interpretation processes about their meaning but also to consequences that emanate from complex normative systems and their perception by actors. Norms not only provide public goods, but they also distribute benefits, costs, and participation opportunities, thereby rendering norm creating and maintaining processes justice-laden (Gehring 1994, 366) and power-laden endeavors (Epstein 2012; Towns 2012; Widmaier and Park 2012).

TAKING STOCK: THE RESEARCH ON NORM DYNAMICS IN INTERNATIONAL RELATIONS

The last two decades have witnessed the evolution of a constructivist-inspired research program on norm dynamics in International Relations (IR) that proceeded in two waves (Cortell and Davis 2000, 66; Hoffmann 2010).[7] The next section summarizes the main characteristics of both phases, putting emphasis on "critical" approaches that emerged in the course of second-wave norm studies and to which we also subscribe.[8]

From Demonstrating Effectiveness to Accounting for Norm Diffusion

During the early stages in the 1990s, norm studies were mainly occupied with defining boundaries vis-à-vis rationalist approaches by empirically demonstrating "that norms matter" (Checkel 1997, 473). Norms were conceptualized as independent variables, affecting actors' preferences and identities by establishing intersubjective standards of appropriateness (Klotz 1995; Finnemore and Sikkink 1998). In order to demonstrate the *effectiveness* of norms, a huge body of empirical studies emerged covering the full spectrum of international relations from security policy (Katzenstein 1996a; Price 1997; Tannenwald 1999) to human rights (Sikkink 1993; Klotz 1995; Risse, Ropp, and Sikkink 1999), foreign aid (Lumsdaine 1993), and environmental policy (Keck and Sikkink 1998). A major objective of these initial studies was to trace the process of *norm diffusion* through socialization processes, as a result of which a given norm spreads from one community to actors outside this community (Risse, Ropp, and Sikkink 1999; Checkel 2001). The mechanisms identified largely converged with those at work in norm emergence processes—that is, the transformation from ideas to norms—and include coercion, persuasion, learning, and emulation processes.

First-wave norm studies, for pragmatic reasons, treated norms as stable and constant phenomena and were thus stuck to a structuralist perspective, leaving only marginal space for the mutually constitutive effect of agency on norm dynamics. The impact of norms was conceptualized as a one-way street, simplifying the complex process of norm dynamics to "the structuring power of norms and their influence on state behavior in world politics" (Wiener 2009, 179) leading to progressive evolution. Feedback loops and the possibility of norm decay were dynamic aspects left out of mainstream research. By "freezing" (Hoffmann 2010, 5413) norms, early constructivist norm studies failed to provide comprehensive accounts of norm emergence and norm change in particular (Sending 2002). Subsequent studies thus shifted the focus to understanding norms as products of strategic social construction (Widmaier and Park 2012) and highlighted the role of agency in norm diffusion processes. Agency-based explanations emphasized the role of "norm entrepreneurs" who use ideational as well as material resources for their norm-initiating or norm-promoting activities (e.g., Ikenberry and Kupchan 1990; Nadelmann 1990; Haas 1992; Finnemore and Sikkink 1998, 896–901; Risse 2000; Payne 2001; Müller 2004). Still, however, these accounts predominantly adhered to a linear, unidirectional understanding of norm diffusion and conceptualized norm entrepreneurs as norm transmitters, leaving out the interactive aspect of norm dynamics.

A prominent example is the norm life cycle model according to which norms go through a three-stage process—a "patterned 'life cycle'" (Finnemore and Sikkink 1998, 888)—that develops from norm emergence to norm cascade and finally to norm internalization. Norm entrepreneurs are identified as the driving force for the emergence of new norms as they mobilize other actors to adopt a "norm candidate" framed as the solution to a salient problem. As soon as the (new) norm is accepted by a "critical mass" of actors, the "tipping point" (Finnemore and Sikkink 1998, 901) is reached, and a "norm cascade" starts.[9] As the socialization process wears on, and more and more states acknowledge the validity of the emerging norm, the norm assumes a "taken-for-granted quality" (Finnemore and Sikkink 1998, 895) and is no longer challenged.

In a similar vein, Risse, Ropp, and Sikkink (1999) elaborated a "spiral model" that highlighted the interplay between the domestic and transnational/international spheres in bringing about norm compliance. The authors suggest that norm diffusion processes are mainly initiated by nonstate transnational networks putting pressure on norm-violating governments through naming and shaming strategies. Faced with public attention, the target state will at first deny the accusations but ultimately enter a phase of tactical concessions by cautiously incorporating "norm talk" into the domestic discourse. Over time the norm-violating state may find itself rhetorically entrapped in its own (norm-abiding) rhetoric (Risse and Sikkink 1999, 25–28). In a final stage, the norm is internalized through processes of national implementation and institutionalization.[10]

In contrast, evolutionary models of norm diffusion take a structural approach instead. Florini (1996) draws an analogy between processes of norm development and Darwinian evolution, claiming that norms and genes share three characteristics[11]: both are instructive to their hosts, are transmitted from one individual to another through biological (genes) and cultural (norms) inheritance, and are in constant competition with their peers, which renders them subject to natural selection. Norms emerge through reproduction processes as a result of which some norms prevail while others decline. As causes of success she suggests initial norm prominence, being promoted by norm entrepreneurs, fitting the existing norm pool, conducive attributes of the norm itself (legitimacy, coherence, and consistency), and favorable environmental conditions. She distinguishes between a vertical reproduction mechanism that is the persistence of a norm over generations and horizontal reproduction through emulation of successful behavior of others. Because genetic evolution is a process in which intentions play no role, while norm dynamics involve a variety of intention-driven actors, applying a Darwinist analogy does not strike us as germane to our field and is thus not given consideration in this study.

Norm Contestation and Norm Change

During the last decade, scholars have begun to develop detailed insights into the complex process of *norm dynamics*. Norms stopped being treated as stable, fixed entities evolving in sequential/linear stages; instead, attention shifted over to grasping the dynamics and contestation of norms (Sandholtz 2007; Wiener 2008). The "second wave" (Cortell and Davis 2000, 66) of constructivist research on norms launched extensive intraconstructivist debates on concepts of and conditions for norm diffusion and compliance. Scholars aspired to demonstrate "when/where norms matter and how/when/why *norms themselves* change to a greater extent" (Hoffmann 2010, 5415; emphasis added). Recently, this insight culminated in what has been described as "critical constructivist research on norms" (Wiener and Puetter 2009): norms are understood as emanating from "interactive processes of 'strategic social construction'" (Wiener 2004, 194). Shifting the focus to the "dual quality of norms . . . as both structuring and socially constructed through interaction in a context" (Wiener 2007, 49), this approach made explanations for norm change and variation in norm compliance possible (Finnemore and Sikkink 2001, 397). The stabilizing function of norms (and thus their structural character) is not called into question per se, but instead their contingent, inherently ambiguous and indeterminate nature is stressed, leaving them "in constant state of dynamism and flux. Norms are born anew every day as actors instantiate them through their beliefs and actions" (Hoffmann 2010, 5419). Norms need to be interpreted by actors in order to be translated into concrete behavior (Sandholtz 2007; Wiener 2008). Even actors with a shared identity may hold varying views about the prescriptions and proscriptions contained in norms, opening up a multitude of possible interpretations (March and Olsen 2004, 8) without, however, leading to complete arbitrariness.

While second-wave research on norms must be given credit for tackling a range of theoretical gaps, an unfortunate "bias to focus on successful cases of norm diffusion" (Checkel 1999, 86; see also Finnemore and Sikkink 2001, 403; Rosert and Schirmbeck 2007, 253) still exists. Norms are usually regarded as "problem solving devices" (Kratochwil 1989, 69) which become institutionalized and codified in international law and eventually result in internalized standards for appropriate behavior. Mainstream approaches thus tend to conceptualize norm change as an evolutionary path resulting in the emergence of new norms or the replacement of obsolete norms by new ones, with a tendency toward the continuous improvement of norm systems and their efficiency over time. The possibility of norm degeneration or erosion has been acknowledged only recently (Rosert and Schirmbeck 2007; McKeown 2009; Heller, Kahl, and Pisoiu 2012; Lantis 2011a, 2011b); however, comprehensive models of norm erosion processes are still absent. In addition, norm studies have not provided convincing explanations of why and under what circumstances some norms survive while others decay (Risse-Kappen 1994, 187).[12] As a byproduct of their belief in progress, norm studies neglected the developments that occur *after* a norm has been established or become internalized. The discovery of norm contestedness gives leverage to inquiring about norm change in this later phase (Sandholtz 2007; Sandholtz and Stiles 2009). This volume devotes considerable attention to this aspect of norm evolution and contestation.

PHASES OF NORM DYNAMICS

Norm dynamics fall into three distinct phases: initially, the *establishment* of a new norm or regime and, second, its *further development*, which may possibly lead to a third phase, norm *degeneration* or decay. Within these phases, both structural and agency-oriented forces drive norm change: while norm entrepreneurs are indispensable for the occurrence of norm change, intrinsic and exogenous factors present windows of opportunity for their agency.

Phase 1: The Establishment of a New Norm or Regime

Constructivist norm studies continue to focus on comprehensive explanations for norm emergence. Especially in first-wave empirical works, scholars tend to treat norms as "unexplained sources of the exogenously given preferences of actors" (Florini 1996, 363). Underlying this custom is the observation that "norms are rarely (if ever) created de novo" (Kowert and Legro 1996, 469n37) but emerge out of (collectively held) ideas (Björkdahl 2002a, 58). Most explanations thus seem to equate norm genesis with the process of how ideas gain the status of binding norms (Patrick 2001, 137). Though the congruity of an emerging norm with the existing norm pool has been identified as beneficial for its further evolution (e.g., Finnemore and Sikkink 1998, 897; Price 1998, 628), the proposition that new norms emerge out of existing ones—for example, are deduced from norms of a higher order or result out of normative interaction processes—opens up the danger of circular reasoning (Kowert and Legro 1996, 470). Rationalist approaches offer a functionalist, demand-driven explanation for the origin of norms: norms are intentionally invoked if seen as beneficial for bringing about cooperation or as solutions to coordination problems (Ullmann-Margalit 1977; Opp 1982). A need for new regulation mechanisms may also arise in the course of exogenous shocks or crisis situations (Berger 1996, 331; Kowert and Legro 1996, 470–74; Finnemore and Sikkink 1998, 909) or be a consequence of domestic political upheavals, technological developments (Sandholtz 2007, 269), or shifts in the power structure of the international system (Farrell 2001, 83).[13] The bulk of norm emergence processes, however, are "supply-driven," that is "in most of these processes actors are playing an important role, and on a general level the interaction between structures and actors is the primary driving force in norm evolution" (Björkdahl 2002b, 16–17). Norm entrepreneurs figure as key driving forces for norm development by identifying *new* ideas as problem-solving devices. Norms originate from, and evolve within, controversial discursive negotiation processes among actors in the course of which mutual understandings may result in new norms or new understandings of old ones (Kowert and Legro 1996, 474–75; Elgström 2000). It is precisely the ambiguous quality of norms that enables norms to be diffused globally (Krook and True 2012, 105).

Phases 2 and 3: The Further Development of Norms and the Possibility of Norm Degeneration

In contrast to the theoretical models presented above, we do not conceptualize norm development as a teleological process resulting in norm internalization.[14] Recognizing the contestedness and interpretability of norms, we assume that norms have a dynamic character (see also Sandholtz 2007; van Kersbergen and Verbeek 2007; Krook and True 2012). This includes the possibility that even internalized norms may be weakened, lose their taken-for-granted status, or eventually decay (Rosert and Schirmbeck 2007; McKeown 2009; Heller, Kahl, and Pisoiu 2012). Similarly, Gehring (1994, 368–69) notes that "normative expectations commonly accepted at a given time are continuously confirmed and renewed, while outdated ones are abolished."[15] Norm diffusion should therefore be perceived as "an ongoing negotiation process" (Elgström 2000, 459) in the course of which norm entrepreneurs continually have to work for the consolidation of the norm they propagate and the meaning that they attach to it and to defend it against norm challengers. Following this assumption we expect conflicts, which emanate from ambiguous and competing norms, to have a substantial impact on how a norm or system of norms evolves.[16] Five directions of norm development are conceivable: a norm may become *obsolete*, leading to its eventual abolition; it may be *replaced* by another (new) norm; it may be *adapted* or reformulated to satisfy altered demands; it may be *further differentiated* and gain more clarity or coherence; or it may simply be *maintained* as it is.

DRIVING FORCES FOR NORM DYNAMICS

While we dismiss evolutionary approaches to norm diffusion, we conceptualize norm dynamics as driven by both structural and agency-oriented forces. Norm change may be induced by intrinsic and extrinsic structural factors constituting windows of opportunity for norm entrepreneurs, who are deemed indispensable for norm change to materialize (see also Krook and True 2012 for a similar approach). The following section briefly discusses recent explanations of norm change as proposed by second-wave norm studies. As *structural* drivers of norm change have been dealt with extensively in the previous chapter, the focus here will be on norm entrepreneurs as drivers in the role of *agency* for bringing about change.

Change from Within and Without: Norm Conflict and Exogenous Events

While there is disagreement on whether norm change occurs incrementally over a long period of time (e.g., Goertz and Diehl 1992, 645) or rapidly in a short time span (e.g., Axelrod 1986, 1096), the mechanisms causing change resemble those at work in norm emergence. Second-wave norm studies no longer consider norm change to be an evolutionary process in which a degenerated (local) norm is replaced by a new (international) one. Although this possibility is not precluded in principle, it is postulated that "studies of norm dynamics should account for a range of responses to new norms, from constitutive compliance to outright rejection, and evolutionary and path-dependent forms of acceptance that fall in between" (Acharya 2004, 242).

Recent approaches try to account for what happens with norms beyond the stage of their formal adoption and point to *intrinsic sources* of norm change. Such approaches hint at the ambiguity and interpretability common to language phenomena such as norms. Acharya (2004) demonstrates that the diffusion of international norms in local contexts depends on how local "norm-takers" interpret those norms, adapt them to local normative structures, and thereby rephrase their original meaning.[17] In a similar vein, Liese traces the contestation of international human rights norms in national contexts after their formal acceptance and warns not to "[equate] the text of law with the meaning of norms" (2009, 37) but rather to deduce the latter from the discourse surrounding norm evolution (including stages *after* formal norm acceptance). Therefore, norms are always subject to interpretability and consequently contestedness. Norm conflicts may arise either regarding differing understandings of a norm's meaning, its formal validity, or its application in a given social context (Wiener 2008, 37–58) but also result from competing norms. Variations in compliance may then result from different interpretations of the implications emerging from them.

The principle of norm contestation also lies at the core of Sandholtz's (2007, 9–23; see also Sandholtz and Stiles 2009) cyclic model of norm change. According to this, disputes over the context-dependent application of norms are inevitably due to the indeterminacy and contradictions inherent in norms. Norm change, however, does not come automatically but is thought to be triggered by disputes arising from applying the norm to a specific situation or in reaction to triggering events or acts.

Indeed, norm change, like norm emergence, might be triggered by *extrinsic events*, such as shocks or other exogenous crisis situations (Berger 1996, 331; Kowert and Legro 1996, 470–74; Finnemore and Sikkink 1998, 909). Concurrently, such salient events upset the existing international order, which may render normative commitments obsolete and pave the way for the establishment of new or the remodeling of existing norms. Norm change can also be caused by new or altered norms arising in the course of scientific or technological innovation or from transformations in the international distribution of power (e.g., Ullmann-Margalit 1990, 765–766; Klotz 1995, 23; Kowert and Legro 1996, 473; Farrell 2001, 83–85; Acharya 2004, 247; Sandholtz and Stiles 2009, 325).

Intrinsic and extrinsic factors, however, only provide windows of opportunity: agency is needed for norm change to take place.

Norm Entrepreneurs as Main Drivers of Norm Dynamics

It is norm contestedness and exogenous events where the relationship between agency and structure is most salient: contestedness is not a mechanical process but is the product of agency. In general, structures create opportunities and constraints for action, and agency handles opportunities and constraints to produce change or maintain the status quo. Such agency is epitomized by the role model "norm entrepreneur." The chapter explains why we feel the necessity to go beyond the usual suspects to fulfill this role script. Similarly, exogenous events of major importance affect structures but do not determine response. It is, once more, agents' perception, situation analysis, goal setting, and intentional action that decide in which way external change affects a regime and its norms.

Research on norm diffusion has given close attention to agency-centered approaches when reviewing the role of norm entrepreneurs (e.g., Florini 1996; Finnemore and Sikkink 1998). Although the term immediately gained a foothold in constructivist research on norms, it took some time before it became subject to more detailed conceptualization. The first effort to combine the isolated assumptions and theoretical underpinnings surrounding the concept of norm entrepreneurship was made by Björkdahl (2002a) from whom this section borrows.

The origin of the concept of norm entrepreneurship can be traced back to sociology; Becker coined the term *moral entrepreneur* (1963, 147–76) to characterize individuals committed to the establishment and enforcement of rules against deviant behavior. He identified two kinds of actors: rule creators, bringing about new prohibitions, and rule enforcers, working to enforce prohibitions already in place. As "crusading reformer[s]" (Becker 1963, 147), rule creators held an absolute ethic and were keen to combat threatening social evil by all necessary means. Interpreting their mission as a holy one, "they truly believe that their cause is just, and pursue it with fervent self-righteousness" (Muzzatti 2002). Though the notion of a *moral entrepreneur* has gained entry into political science vocabulary (see Nadelmann 1990), the term *norm entrepreneur* was coined by the legal scholar Sunstein, who applied it to "people interested in changing social norms" (1996, 909). Finnemore and Sikkink (1998) drew upon his work when they revitalized the concept in research on norms. They highlight the "ideational commitment" of norm entrepreneurs, that is "[their belief, CW] in the ideals and values embodied in the norms, even though the pursuit of the norms may have no effect on their well-being" (Finnemore and Sikkink 1998, 898). Empathy and altruistic motivation are depicted as the key elements of a norm entrepreneur's personality. Nevertheless, as Jacobsen notes, "entrepreneurs do not descend from Mount Olympus; they are usually interested actors who benefit when their ideas are adopted" (1995, 291n30). In reality, an actor may be motivated by a complex mix of self-interest and norms (Klotz 1995, 13); both may coincide, which is the case for most of the small state norm entrepreneurs, who undoubtedly promote norms that lie in the collective interest of the international community, but at the same time "create a niche for themselves in international politics" (Björkdahl 2002a, 48). Some authors, though, directly link impartiality and the absence of direct self-interest to the legitimacy attributed to a norm entrepreneur (e.g., Björkdahl 2002a, 49).

The concept's application in social sciences closely captures the French origin of the term *entrepreneur* as someone who undertakes a project, "for instance, agenda setters, policy innovators, morally committed actors as well as epistemic communities" (Björkdahl 2002a, 45). Usually, these actors are seen as committed to a certain idea or cause (Johnstone 2007, 126). Having identified problems within the existing normative framework and the need for new ways to cope with them, they eagerly devote themselves to resolving these grievances. For this purpose, norm entrepreneurs try to mobilize support for their cause: they bring a problem to public attention, search for norm followers, and struggle to get their idea accepted as a new standard for behavior. Sjöström describes norm entrepreneurs as "actors who break away from the established" and "advocate alternative ideas about appropriate behaviour" (2010, 180). Björkdahl sees them as "agent[s] of social change with an ability to shape the collective behaviour of others," or as "problem-solver[s]" (2002a, 45). As Pozen correctly emphasizes, "policy entrepreneurs are in this sense active rather than reactive" (2008, 301). Descriptions such as "proselytizing mission" (Johnstone 2007, 126), "moral proselytism" (Nadelmann 1990, 481), or "moral crusades" (Becker 1963, 148) are used to describe their high sense of commitment to changing the existing normative order—and already indicate the normative connotation linked with the concept.

Although most often located at the first stage of the "norm life cycle," norm emergence, norm entrepreneurs do not necessarily have to work for the initiation of *new* norms. The term *norm-maker*, which is synonymously used by Björkdahl to describe "the agents behind norm diffusion" (2002a, 45) is misleading. She nonetheless correctly remarks that "norm entrepreneurs may frame old ideas in new ways or revive an old norm, in order to build a norm candidate" (2002a, 49).

Types of Norm Entrepreneurs The concept of norm entrepreneur is applied to individuals as well as collective actors, although emphasis has been put on individuals and nonstate actors. Henry Dunant, the founder of the International Committee of the Red Cross, serves as the prototype; he became a norm entrepreneur out of his strong personal engagement in securing appropriate treatment for medical personnel and combatants wounded in war (Finnemore 1996, 73–85; Finnemore and Sikkink 1998, 896–97). Time and again individuals stand out as committed to their cause, advocating the establishment of a certain norm. Recent research has turned its attention increasingly to individual norm entrepreneurs serving in international organizations, like the UN Secretary General (Johnstone 2007) or state officials or bureaucrats (Blavoukos and Bourantonis 2011). Transnational advocacy networks such as nongovernmental organizations (NGOs), political foundations, trade unions, the churches (Klotz 1995), and epistemic communities (Haas 1992) are another norm entrepreneur archetype (Keck and Sikkink 1998). A more recent development is the inclusion of private-sector actors such as transnational corporations into the universe of norm entrepreneurship (Flohr et al. 2010).

Only in the last decade has research shifted its attention to *states* as norm entrepreneurs (Björkdahl 2002a; Ingebritsen 2002; Reich 2003; Job 2006); prior to that, states were predominantly depicted as norm *receivers*. There is still a lack of detailed case studies, although initial studies have been able to show that certain types of national identities can benefit norm entrepreneurial activities of states. Above all, such works highlight the role of middle powers that, in order to live up to their reputation as good international citizens, intentionally function as international norm entrepreneurs (Björkdahl 2002a, 2002b; Job 2006). However, the possibility of great powers acting as norm entrepreneurs as well should not be precluded (Florini 1996, 375; Johnstone 2007, 126). Due to the resources at their disposal, major powers are more likely to compel other states to adopt a norm through persuasion and coercion (Florini 1996, 375)—which qualifies them to take on the role of norm enforcers, and they may also have an interest in reinforcing or challenging the existing normative order. In a similar vein, Lantis (2011a, 2011b) highlights the role of elite agency in bringing about norm change by challenging the legitimacy of prevailing norms (or their meaning) and suggesting alternative redefinitions. Ultimately, this may lead to bandwagon behavior by other governmental actors and norm substitution.

"Good" and "Bad" Norms and Their Highly Different Entrepreneurs Past overemphasis on small states as norm entrepreneurs adds another research desideratum, as does the strong focus on apparently "good" actors in general. While mainstream norm research tends to overemphasize the problem-solving capacity of norms for stabilizing the prevalent normative order (Kratochwil 1989, 69; Checkel 1998),[18] poststructuralist and critical constructivist approaches acknowledge the downside of norms as reifying prevalent power structures (e.g., Price and Reus-Smit 1998; Epstein 2012; Towns 2012; Widmaier and Park 2012). Consequently, constructivist norm studies tend to focus on inherently "positive" norms and the respective actors. This ignores the fact that not all norms are inherently positive: viewed from today's perspective, there are historical examples of "negative" norms (such as apartheid). By focusing on norms deriving largely from a Western, liberal-democratic body of thought, mainstream research on norms tends to neglect the existence of oppositional normative concepts of order.

We try to overcome this bias by arguing that what is "good" or "bad" is not an objective given but a matter of judgment. We thus suggest analyzing norms through the lens of the *actors* involved. We transcend a major shortcoming of recent norm studies that have focused exclusively on ideal-type norm entrepreneurs committed to promoting supposedly "good" norms. By focusing only on those norm entrepreneurs who are committed to the promotion of norms deemed positive in helping to stabilize or incrementally reform the prevalent structure, research neglects revolutionary actors. Analogous to the prototype norm entrepreneurs as identified by the literature, such revolutionary norm entrepreneurs are expected to champion the promotion of a fundamentally alternative normative order. Their norm entrepreneurship exceeds mere resistance against the prevalent order, although sharing its disregard of existing rules. Norm entrepreneurship then comes in two slightly different forms. It might, first, be embedded within the prevalent normative structure aiming at its modification in the sense of adapting to changed external demands or the return to its original meaning (in the view of the actor involved). Such an understanding could be covered by the *prototype* concept of norm entrepreneurship. *Revolutionary* norm entrepreneurship, on the other hand, is marked by strong opposition to the prevalent normative order, aiming at overthrow of the existing system and the establishment of a new order that clearly defines boundaries separating it from the overthrown order.[19]

Domestic Change and Norm Entrepreneurship As the expression *revolutionary norm entrepreneurship* indicates, norm change effected by norm entrepreneurs might be due to domestic change within the entrepreneurial state: a state adopts a new set of values that is incompatible with the international normative structure and then attempts to change that structure in order to make it compatible with domestic normative preferences (Armstrong 1993). Domestic change creates an imbalance in the two-level discourse structure (see the introduction to this volume), giving momentum to the search for a new balance. Domestic change might emerge from a true revolution at home (Armstrong 1993; Sandholtz and Stiles 2009), as in the case of Iran. It might be the consequence of a shift in government in polities with a deeply split political culture (Müller and Wolff 2006), as in the United States, where the emergence of neoconservatism altered the mode and direction of US norm entrepreneurship considerably. In this volume we present other examples of sudden or incremental internal change (e.g., Germany, Russia, South Africa), and in each case the impact on the direction of norm entrepreneurship is critically reviewed in detail. That assumption ties in with newer research inquiring how domestic processes and social psychological traits affect agency (Shannon 2000; Widmaier and Park 2012; for the nuclear field see Hymans 2006; Rublee 2009; Solingen 2007).

Strategies and Stages of Norm Entrepreneurship Recent scholarly work generally locates norm entrepreneurial activities within the process of norm emergence. Indeed, the bulk of norm entrepreneurs become active during this stage of the norm diffusion process; above all, this applies to nonstate actors such as transnational advocacy networks or committed individuals who see the need to create a new norm and therefore start drawing public attention to a perceived problem. In this regard, norm entrepreneurs function as "teachers of norms" (Finnemore 1993) who raise awareness of a problem, signal need for action, and provide information and expertise as well as problem-solving strategies. These strategies may, however, also be applied in other phases of a norm's life cycle: norm entrepreneurs engage not only in norm creation but also in maintaining, ensuring, protecting, promoting, and enforcing norms. Johnstone tries to capture the full spectrum of norm entrepreneurs' tasks by using the term *managerial functions* (2007, 124); others point in the same direction by using terms such as *norm advocates* (Deitelhoff 2006, 252) or *norm transmitters* (Rublee 2008, 426) to refer to a broader understanding of norm entrepreneurship. Norm entrepreneurs may *initiate* a new norm or a reinterpretation of an existing one; they may *promote* norms to attract an increasing number of supporters and followers; they may struggle to *maintain* a contested or otherwise endangered norm and enhance its strength, or they may engage in *enforcing* a norm violated by a defecting actor.

In order to recruit followers and change the prospective norm receivers'—mostly states—preferences in the direction of the propagated norm, norm entrepreneurs engage in processes of strategic social construction and resort to a multitude of instruments such as "strategic use of information, symbolic politics, leverage politics and accountability politics, issue framing and shaming" (Finnemore and Sikkink 2001, 401). Drawing on social psychology, Rublee (2008, 426–27) discusses two main mechanisms through which norm advocacies attempt to influence decision makers: norm entrepreneurs first and foremost embark upon *linking* strategies by framing issues so that they are not only applicable to the existing normative context but even in a way that calls attention to the immediate need for change (Payne 2001, 43; Björkdahl 2002a, 52). Because of the fundamental contestation and ambiguity of all norms, whether established or proposed ones, and the fact that there may be competing norms principally applicable in a given situation, norm entrepreneurs also engage in *activating* one norm over another. Activation may imply advocating one particular meaning of a norm by simple "naming," may take the form of dramatizing by using more striking language or creating scandals, and may even include blaming and shaming strategies (Keck and Sikkink 1998; Finnemore and Sikkink 1998; Risse, Ropp, and Sikkink 1999; Adut 2004).

Success or failure of norm advocacy ultimately hinges on the strategies chosen and instruments used, but also on the degree of consistency shown by the norm entrepreneurs (Rublee 2008, 427) which may be enhanced through institutionalizing commitments. Often, norm entrepreneurs thus draw on "some kind of organizational platform from and through which they promote their norms" (Finnemore and Sikkink 1998, 899). Transnational advocacy networks established for the sake of norm promotion, as well as international or transnational organizations and regimes, provide information channels but also structural resources such as money, bureaucratic structures, or sanctioning mechanisms to expose pressure on noncompliant states (coercion or shaming strategies). Of course, states as norm entrepreneurs also make use of those resources. International organizations are crucial for the institutionalization—that is, codification—implementation, monitoring, and enforcement of norms (Finnemore 1993, 595; Finnemore and Sikkink 1998, 899–900). Moreover, institutionalized settings do not only offer the possibility of forming networks or coalitions of allies (Koh 1998; Björkdahl 2002a, 50), they also serve as arenas for governmental norm entrepreneurs to engage in communicative action that—according to the logic of arguing—may eventually lead to the breakthrough of the "better argument" (Deitelhoff 2009). Shaming and blaming strategies—that is, public criticism or denunciation of norm-breaking states—also benefit from institutional structures. Both strategies are, however, applied at the second stage of the norm life cycle—in other words, after a (new) norm has achieved critical mass by being successfully adopted in a sufficient number of states.

While they pursue goals not out of utilitarian motivation but instead while following a logic of appropriateness, norm entrepreneurs are, of course, fully capable of strategic action in order to achieve their objectives. They use "an eclectic mix of persuasive and instrumentalist tactics" (Finnemore and Sikkink 2001, 401) for their norm-advocating activities. However, norms also set limits to what strategies they feel entitled to use. Strategic action in this sense is not incompatible with the logic of appropriateness.

Taking the definition of norm entrepreneurs as put forward by Björkdahl (2002a, 46) as a starting point,[20] we define norm entrepreneurs as follows: norm entrepreneurs are characterized as actors who set out to alter the prevalent normative order according to certain ideas or norms that they deem more suitable as compared to the existing ones. In order to persuade the audience of the appropriateness and necessity of the propagated norm(s) and to recruit norm followers, they engage in processes of strategic social construction using ideational as well as material resources. The behavior of norm entrepreneurs is characterized by proactivism: their actions show a considerable degree of consistency, strength of purpose, and intentionality, are future-oriented, and show a continuously high level of activism. The strategies and means employed to achieve their aims are overall constructive, anticipatory, active rather than reactive, and marked by innovation. Continuous, occasionally altruistic, engagement for a certain cause does not preclude, but rather requires, tactical and strategic action. Proactivism does not assume focusing on norms perceived as inherently good from a certain perspective but involves all kinds of norms, including ones opposed to the established pattern. Understood in this sense, the concept may also be applied to actors who are not regarded as prototypical norm entrepreneurs but as advocates of an oppositional normative order.

CONCLUSION: A PIVOTAL ROLE FOR AGENCY IN DRIVING NORM DYNAMICS

The role of norms and systems of norms such as regimes that serve as pillars of international order is by now well established. Constructivist research has enriched the findings of previous work on international regimes considerably over the last twenty years. Our own study is grounded in that tradition while also seeking to push the agenda forward. We want to understand how regimes change over time—for better or for worse. With that goal in mind, we study the impact of regime conflicts—typifying the eternal condition of norm contestability and contestedness—on regime dynamics, inevitably looking into the decisive role of protagonists in these conflicts as norm entrepreneurs who struggle to initiate new norms, to confirm, maintain, or strengthen a given norm, or alternatively to change, amend, or replace it. We want to understand how the interests of such actors interact with their ethical orientations, in particular their concerns about distributive consequences, participatory opportunities, and the recognition afforded to them that the regimes entail; all three aspects touch on concerns about justice. We also investigate how relevant exogenous factors impact on regimes through the actors' use of the opportunities that such changes in the political or technological environment offer. At the end of the day, we hope to have enriched the state of the art of norm and regime studies in one important aspect, that of norm dynamics.

Notes

1. The dynamic nature of norm evolution is acknowledged by a range of other scholars (see, e.g., Sandholtz 2007; van Kersbergen and Verbeek 2007; Wiener 2008; Krook and True 2012).

2. In a similar vein, albeit using the slightly differing expression "norm dynamism," Krook and True (2012) highlight the role of "internal"—debates over their meaning—and "external" sources of a norm's life cycle—the normative context, consisting of other norms. We share with them an understanding of norms as being continuously subject to (re)negotiation and an emphasis on the role of agency in interpreting and thus giving meaning to norms. However, our model also accounts for exogenous driving forces

and presents a more comprehensive model of how structural and agency-oriented driving forces interact in bringing about, keeping alive, and at times also hampering norm dynamics.

3. Other than Deitelhoff (2006), we treat communicative action as a specific form of the logic of appropriateness.

4. According to Krasner, regimes are "implicit or explicit principles, norms, rules, and decision-making procedures around which actors' expectations converge in a given area of international relations. Principles are beliefs of fact, causation, and rectitude. Norms are standards of behavior defined in terms of rights and obligations. Rules are specific prescriptions or proscriptions for action. Decision-making procedures are prevailing practices for making and implementing collective choice" (Krasner 1983, 2).

5. For a comprehensive account of research on norms in International Relations (IR) see Finnemore and Sikkink (2001); Björkdahl (2002b); Hoffmann (2010); and most recently Widmaier and Park (2012).

6. Other examples of such foundational norms may include reciprocity, universality, or individual dignity; see Gouldner (1960); Keohane (1986); Keck and Sikkink (1998). As Sandholtz and Stiles put it, "arguments that are grounded in one or more of these foundational norms are difficult to oppose, and therefore carry persuasive weight" (2009, 17).

7. Similarly, Widmaier and Park (2012) differentiate between first-, second-, and third-generation constructivist research, focusing on structural factors, strategic social construction, and affective or sentimental factors inherent to norms respectively.

8. Underlying this line of research are an understanding of norms as emanating from "interactive processes of 'strategic social construction'" (Wiener 2004, 194) and an impetus to critically engage with "mainstream" approaches to norms by challenging their basic epistemological assumptions (e.g., Epstein 2012).

9. The authors do not, however, indicate a concrete number of states but point to empirical findings according to which this critical mass comprises one-third of all states.

10. The authors, however, emphasize that not all countries necessarily have to go through each stage, as well as that processes of norm diffusion are not successful by nature (Risse, Ropp, and Sikkink 1999, 34).

11. Evolutionary models of norm emergence are also advanced by Axelrod (1986); Eyre and Suchman (1996); and Patrick (2001).

12. Though lacking theoretical underpinnings, *norm robustness*—that is, the factors contributing to which norms will be influential—is commonly accounted for by intrinsic characteristics of the norm in question (its validity/legitimacy and specificity/determinacy), the level of norm compliance (concordance, commonality), its promotion by "prominent" or conspicuous actors, and the degree to which the norm matches the existing normative environment (coherence) (Chayes and Chayes 1993; Florini 1996, 376–77; Legro 1997, 33–34; and Finnemore and Sikkink 1998, 906). In a similar vein, regime

theorists tie the survivability of regimes to the level of compliance and noncompliance of member states (Müller 1995).

13. Behaviorist approaches furthermore conceptualize norms as unintended consequences of uncoordinated actions. Accordingly, norms emerge spontaneously out of habitualized social interaction processes between actors. A nonteleological understanding of norm emergence is also presented by Florini's (1996) biological analogy. However, evolutionary explanations for norm emergence have been criticized for disregarding the diversity and concomitance of norms as "some compete, some are synergistic, some are cooperative or symbiotic, some die of their own accord" (Björkdahl 2002a, 56). These approaches are not investigated further here.

14. In fact, Finnemore and Sikkink (1998, 895) acknowledge the possibility that a norm cascade may come to a halt before the final stage of norm internalization is reached. The possibility of norm degeneration is, however, not broached. Similarly, Risse, Ropp, and Sikkink (1999, 33–34) concede that norms may be weakened in the course of their diffusion. They do, however, restrict this possibility to the very early phases of their spiral model.

15. McKeown (2009) conceptualizes norm degeneration as a three-stage process analogous to Finnemore and Sikkink's "norm life cycle" model (1998). Accordingly, in the first stage, norm revisionists tacitly challenge the prevalent normative order by "secretive" changes in practice or discourse. The prescriptive status of the norm in question, however, remains intact. Only if the challengers achieve public resonance can the norm enter a reverse cascade. Finally, if the challenge is "sufficiently echoed by other respected members of the system" (McKeown 2009, 12), the norm expires.

16. A similar approach is outlined by Sandholtz (2007) and Sandholtz and Stiles (2009), who depict norm change as a cyclic process primarily caused by ongoing disputes over the meaning and applicability of norms.

17. Others refer to the sociocultural background or context of the potential norm-takers (resonance with local cultures) (Legro 1997; Checkel 1998); for the influence of local institutional procedures and structures, see Cortell and Davis (2000); and for the role that bureaucratic structures of international organizations play in the diffusion of international norms, see Chwieroth (2008).

18. Normative orders are conceptualized as "a complex of norms and values, legitimizing the basis of society" (Forst and Günther 2010, 7). Of course, there is no single such order, but a diverse field of contesting normative orders.

19. The scope of an actor's actions with respect to norms transcends the dichotomy of *prototype* vs. *revolutionary* norm entrepreneurship. Indeed, the following behavioral patterns regarding a state's behavior with respect to (international) norms are conceivable: norm adherence, norm entrepreneurship, norm destruction/negation.

20. "By identifying or creating opportunities, actors committed to a particular idea

set out to change the existing normative context and alter the behavior of others in the direction of the new norm"(Björkdahl 2002a, 46). Our definition of *norm entrepreneurs* adds further elements and transcends Björkdahl's focus on norm-initiating processes.

References

Acharya, Amitav. 2004. "How Ideas Spread: Whose Norms Matter? Norm Localization and Institutional Change in Asian Regionalism." *International Organization* 58 (2): 239–75.

Adut, Ari. 2004. "Scandal as Norm Entrepreneurship Strategy: Corruption and the French Investigating Magistrates." *Theory and Society* 33 (5): 529–78.

Armstrong, David. 1993. *Revolution and World Order: The Revolutionary State in International Society*. Oxford: Clarendon Press.

Axelrod, Robert. 1986. "An Evolutionary Approach to Norms." *American Political Science Review* 80 (4): 1095–111.

Becker, Howard S. 1963. *Outsiders: Studies in the Sociology of Deviance*. New York: Free Press.

Berger, Thomas. 1996. "Norms, Identity, and National Security in Germany and Japan." In Katzenstein 1996a, 317–56.

Björkdahl, Annika. 2002a. *From Idea to Norm: Promoting Conflict Prevention*. Lund: Department of Political Science, Lund University.

———. 2002b. "Norms in International Relations: Some Conceptual and Methodological Reflections." *Cambridge Review of International Affairs* 15 (1): 9–23.

Blavoukos, Spyros, and Dimitris Bourantonis. 2011. "Chairs as Policy Entrepreneurs in Multilateral Negotiations." *Review of International Studies* 37 (2): 653–72.

Bull, Hedley. 1977. *The Anarchical Society: A Study of Order in World Politics*. London: Macmillan.

Chayes, Abraham, and Antonia Handler Chayes. 1993. "On Compliance." *International Organization* 47 (2): 175–205.

Checkel, Jeffrey T. 1997. "International Norms and Domestic Politics: Bridging the Rationalist-Constructivist Divide." *European Journal of International Relations* 3 (4): 473–95.

———. 1998. "The Constructivist Turn in International Relations Theory." *World Politics* 50 (2): 324–48.

———. 1999. "Norms, Institution, and National Identity in Contemporary Europe." *International Studies Quarterly* 43 (1): 84–114.

———. 2001. "Why Comply? Social Learning and European Identity Change." *International Organization* 55 (3): 553–88.

Chwieroth, Jeffrey M. 2008. "Normative Change from Within: The International

Monetary Fund's Approach to Capital Account Liberalization." *International Studies Quarterly* 52 (1): 129–58.

Cortell, Andrew P., and James W. Davis Jr. 2000. "Understanding the Domestic Impact of International Norms: A Research Agenda." *International Studies Review* 2 (1): 65–87.

Deitelhoff, Nicole. 2006. *Überzeugung in der Politik: Grundzüge einer Diskurstheorie internationalen Regierens*. Frankfurt am Main: Suhrkamp.

———. 2009. "The Discursive Process of Legalization: Charting Islands of Persuasion in the ICC Case." *International Organization* 63 (1): 33–65.

Elgström, Ole. 2000. "Norm Negotiations: The Construction of New Norms Regarding Gender and Development in EU Foreign Aid Policy." *Journal of European Public Policy* 7 (3): 457–76.

Elster, John. 1989. *The Cement of Society: A Study of Social Order*. Cambridge: Cambridge University Press.

Epstein, Charlotte. 2012. "Stop Telling Us How to Behave: Socialization or Infantilization?" *International Studies Perspective* 13 (2): 135–45.

Eyre, Dana P., and Mark C. Suchman. 1996. "Status, Norms, and the Proliferation of Conventional Weapons: An Institutional Theory Approach." In Katzenstein 1996a, 79–113. New York: Columbia University Press.

Farrell, Theo. 2001. "Transnational Norms and Military Development: Constructing Ireland's Professional Army." *European Journal of International Relations* 7 (1): 63–102.

Fastenrath, Ulrich. 1993. "Relative Normativity in International Law." *European Journal of International Law* 4 (3): 305–40.

Finnemore, Martha. 1993. "International Organizations as Teachers of Norms: The United Nations Educational, Scientific, and Cultural Organization and Science Policy." *International Organization* 47 (4): 565–97.

———. 1996. *National Interests in International Society*. Ithaca: Cornell University Press.

Finnemore, Martha, and Kathryn Sikkink. 1998. "International Norm Dynamics and Political Change." *International Organization* 52 (4): 887–917.

———. 2001. "TAKING STOCK: The Constructivist Research Program in International Relations and Comparative Politics." *Annual Review of Political Science* 4: 391–416.

Flohr, Annegret, Lothar Rieth, Sandra Schwindenhammer, and Klaus Dieter Wolf. 2010. *The Role of Business in Global Governance: Corporations as Norm-Entrepreneurs*. Basingstoke: Palgrave Macmillan.

Florini, Ann. 1996. "The Evolution of International Norms." *International Studies Quarterly* 40 (3): 363–89.

Forst, Rainer, and Klaus Günther. 2010. "Die Herausbildung normativer Ordnungen: Zur Idee eines interdisziplinären Forschungsprogramms." Normative Orders Working Paper 1/2010, Cluster of Excellence, The Formation of Normative Orders,

Goethe-Universität, Frankfurt am Main. http://publikationen.ub.uni-frankfurt.de/volltexte/2010/8073/pdf/ForstGuentherDie_Herausbildung_normativer_Ordnungen._Zur_Idee_eines_interdisziplinaeren_Forschungsprogramms.pdf.

Frost, Mervyn. 1996. *Ethics in International Relations: A Constitutive Theory*. Cambridge: Cambridge University Press.

Gehring, Thomas. 1994. *Dynamic International Regimes: Institutions for International Environmental Governance*. Frankfurt am Main: Lang.

Goertz, Gary, and Paul F. Diehl. 1992. "Toward a Theory of International Norms: Some Conceptual and Measurement Issues." *Journal of Conflict Resolution* 36 (4): 634–64.

Gouldner, Alvin W. 1960. "The Norm of Reciprocity: A Preliminary Statement." *American Sociological Review* 25 (2): 161–78.

Haas, Peter M. 1992. "Introduction: Epistemic Communities and International Policy Coordination." *International Organization* 46 (1): 1–35.

Heller, Regina, Martin Kahl, and Daniele Pisoiu. 2012. "The 'Dark' Side of Normative Argumentation—The Case of Counterterrorism Policy." *Global Constitutionalism* 1 (2): 278–312.

Hoffmann, Matthew J. 2010. "Norms and Social Constructivism in International Relations." In *The International Studies Encyclopedia*, vol. 8, edited by Robert A. Denemark, 5410–26. Oxford: Wiley-Blackwell.

Hymans, Jacques E. C. 2006. *The Psychology of Nuclear Proliferation: Identity, Emotions, and Foreign Policy*. Cambridge: Cambridge University Press.

Ikenberry, G. John, and Charles A. Kupchan. 1990. "Socialization and Hegemonic Power." *International Organization* 44 (3): 283–315.

Ingebritsen, Christine. 2002. "Norm Entrepreneurs: Scandinavia's Role in World Politics." *Cooperation and Conflict* 37 (1): 11–23.

Jacobsen, John Kurt. 1995. "Much Ado about Ideas: The Cognitive Factor in Economic Policy." *Word Politics* 47 (2): 283–310.

Jepperson, Ronald L., Alexander Wendt, and Peter J. Katzenstein. 1996. "Norms, Identity, and Culture in National Security." In Katzenstein 1996a, 33–75.

Job, Brian L. 2006. "International Peace and Security and State Sovereignty: Contesting Norms and Norm Entrepreneurs." In *The Iraq Crisis and World Order: Structural, Institutional and Normative Challenges*, edited by Ramesh Thakur and Waheguru Pal Singh Sidhu, 57–74. Tokyo: United Nations University Press.

Johnstone, Ian. 2007. "The Secretary-General as Norm Entrepreneur." In *Secretary or General? The UN Secretary-General in World Politics*, edited by Simon Chesterman, 123–38. New York: Cambridge University Press.

Katzenstein, Peter J., ed. 1996a. *The Culture of National Security: Norms and Identity in World Politics*. New York: Columbia University Press.

———. 1996b. "Introduction: Alternative Perspectives on National Security." In Katzenstein 1996a, 1–32.

Keck, Margaret E., and Kathryn Sikkink. 1998. *Activists beyond Borders: Advocacy Networks in International Politics*. Ithaca: Cornell University Press.

Kelsen, Hans. 1967. *The Pure Theory of Law*. Translated from the 2nd rev. and enl. German ed. by Max Knight. Berkeley: University of California Press.

Keohane, Robert O. 1986. "Reciprocity in International Relations." *International Organization* 40 (1): 1–27.

———. 1989. *International Institutions and State Power: Essays in International Relations Theory*. Boulder: Westview Press.

Klotz, Audie. 1995. *Norms in International Relations: The Struggle against Apartheid*. Ithaca: Cornell University Press.

Koh, Harold H. 1998. "The 1998 Frankel Lecture: Bringing International Law Home." *Houston Law Review* 35 (3): 623–82.

Kowert, Paul A., and Jeffrey Legro. 1996. "Norms, Identity, and Their Limits: A Theoretical Reprise." In Katzenstein 1996a, 451–97.

Krasner, Stephen D. 1983. "Structural Causes and Regime Consequences: Regimes as Intervening Variables." In *International Regimes*, edited by Stephen D. Krasner, 1–22. Ithaca: Cornell University Press.

———. 1999. *Sovereignty: Organized Hypocrisy*. Princeton: Princeton University Press.

Kratochwil, Friedrich V. 1989. *Rules, Norms and Decisions: On the Conditions of Practical and Legal Reasoning in International Relations and Domestic Affairs*. Cambridge: Cambridge University Press.

Krook, Mona Lena, and Jacqui True. 2012. "Rethinking the Life Cycles of International Norms: The United Nations and the Global Promotion of Gender Equality." *European Journal of International Relations* 18 (1): 103–27.

Lantis, Jeffrey S. 2011a. "Irrational Exuberance?" *Nonproliferation Review* 18 (2): 389–409.

———. 2011b. "Redefining the Nonproliferation Norm? Australian Uranium, the NPT, and the Global Nuclear Revival." *Australian Journal of Politics and History* 57 (4): 543–61.

Legro, Jeffrey W. 1997. "Which Norms Matter? Revisiting the 'Failure' of Internationalism." *International Organization* 51 (1): 31–63.

Liese, Andrea. 2009. "Exceptional Necessity: How Liberal Democracies Contest the Prohibition of Torture and Ill-Treatment When Countering Terrorism." *Journal of International Law and International Relations* 5 (1): 17–47.

Lumsdaine, David H. 1993. *Moral Vision in International Politics: The Foreign Aid Regime, 1949–1989*. Princeton: Princeton University Press.

March, James G., and Johan P. Olsen. 1998. "The Institutional Dynamics of International Political Orders." *International Organization* 52 (4): 943–69.

———. 2004. *The Logic of Appropriateness*. ARENA Working Papers 09. http://www.sv.uio.no/arena/english/research/publications/arena-publications/workingpapers/working-papers2004/wp04_9.pdf.

McKeown, Ryder. 2009. "Norm Regress: US Revisionism and the Slow Death of the Torture Norm." *International Relations* 23 (1): 5–25.

Mearsheimer, John J. 1994/95. "The False Promise of International Institutions." *International Security* 19 (3): 5–49.

Müller, Harald. 1995. "Regime Robustness, Regime Attractivity and Arms Control Regimes in Europe." *Cooperation and Conflict* 30 (3): 287–97.

———. 2004. "Arguing, Bargaining and All That: Communicative Action, Rationalist Theory and the Logic of Appropriateness in International Relations." *European Journal of International Relations* 10 (3): 395–435.

Müller, Harald, and Jonas Wolff. 2006. "Democratic Peace: Many Data, Little Explanation?" In *Democratic Wars: Looking at the Dark Side of Democratic Peace*, edited by Anna Geis, Lothar Brock, and Harald Müller, 41–73. Basingstoke: Palgrave Macmillan.

Muzzatti, Stephen L. 2002. "Moral Panic." In *Encyclopedia of Crime and Punishment*, vol. 3, J–R, edited by David Levinson, 1076–79. Thousand Oaks: Sage.

Nadelmann, Ethan A. 1990. "Global Prohibition Regimes: The Evolution of Norms in International Society." *International Organization* 44 (4): 479–526.

Opp, Karl-Dieter. 1982. "The Evolutionary Emergence of Norms." *British Journal of Social Psychology* 21 (2): 139–49.

Patrick, Stewart. 2001. "The Evolution of International Norms: Choice, Learning, Power, and Identity." In *Evolutionary Interpretation of World Politics*, edited by William R. Thompson, 133–74. New York: Routledge.

Payne, Rodger A. 2001. "Persuasion, Frames and Norm Construction." *European Journal of International Relations* 7 (1): 37–61.

Pozen, David E. 2008. "We Are All Entrepreneurs Now." *Wake Forest Law Review* 43 (1): 283–340.

Price, Richard M. 1997. *The Chemical Weapons Taboo*. Ithaca: Cornell University Press.

———. 1998. "Reversing the Gun Sights: Transnational Civil Society Targets Land Mines." *International Organization* 52 (3): 613–44.

———. 2008. "Moral Limit and Possibility in World Politics." In *Moral Limit and Possibility in World Politics*, edited by Richard M. Price, 1–52. Cambridge: Cambridge University Press.

Price, Richard M., and Christian Reus-Smit. 1998. "Dangerous Liaisons? Critical International Theory and Constructivism." *European Journal of International Relations* 4 (3): 259–94.

Reich, Simon. 2003. "Power, Institutions, and Moral Entrepreneurs." ZEF—Discussion

Papers on Development Policy, no. 65, Center for Development Research, Universität Bonn, Bonn. www.zef.de/fileadmin/webfiles/downloads/zef_dp/zef_dp65.pdf.

Risse, Thomas. 2000. "'Let's Argue!': Communicative Action in World Politics." *International Organization* 54 (1): 1–39.

Risse, Thomas, Stephen C. Ropp, and Kathryn Sikkink, eds. 1999. *The Power of Human Rights: International Norms and Domestic Change*. Cambridge: Cambridge University Press.

Risse, Thomas, and Kathryn Sikkink. 1999. "The Socialization of International Human Rights Norms into Domestic Practices: Introduction." In *The Power of Human Rights: International Norms and Domestic Change*, edited by Thomas Risse, Stephen C. Ropp, and Kathryn Sikkink, 1–38. Cambridge: Cambridge University Press.

Risse-Kappen, Thomas. 1994. "Ideas Do Not Float Freely: Transnational Coalitions, Domestic Structures, and the End of the Cold War." *International Organization* 48 (2): 185–214.

Rosert, Elvira, and Sonja Schirmbeck. 2007. "Zur Erosion internationaler Normen: Folterverbot und nukleares Tabu in der Diskussion." *Zeitschrift für Internationale Beziehungen* 14 (2): 253–88.

Rublee, Maria Rost. 2008. "Taking Stock of the Nuclear Nonproliferation Regime: Using Social Psychology to Understand Regime Effectiveness." *International Studies Review* 10 (3): 420–50.

———. 2009. *Nonproliferation Norms: Why States Choose Nuclear Restraint*. Athens: University of Georgia Press.

Sandholtz, Wayne. 2007. *Prohibiting Plunder: How Norms Change*. New York: Oxford University Press.

Sandholtz, Wayne, and Kendall W. Stiles. 2009. *International Norms and Cycles of Change*. Oxford: Oxford University Press.

Sending, Ole Jacob. 2002. "Constitution, Choice and Change: Problems with the 'Logic of Appropriateness' and Its Use in Constructivist Theory." *European Journal of International Relations* 8 (4): 443–70.

Shannon, Vaughn P. 2000. "Norms Are What States Make of Them: The Political Psychology of Norm Violation." *International Studies Quarterly* 44 (2): 293–316.

Sikkink, Kathryn. 1993. "Human Rights, Principled Issue-Networks, and Sovereignty in Latin America." *International Organization* 47 (3): 411–41.

Sjöström, Emma. 2010. "Shareholders as Norm Entrepreneurs for Corporate Social Responsibility." *Journal of Business Ethics* 94 (2): 177–91.

Solingen, Etel. 2007. *Nuclear Logics: Contrasting* Paths in *East Asia and the Middle East*. Princeton: Princeton University Press.

Sunstein, Cass R. 1996. "Social Norms and Social Roles." *Columbia Law Review* 96 (4): 903–68.

Tannenwald, Nina. 1999. "The Nuclear Taboo: The United States and the Normative Basis of Nuclear Non-Use." *International Organization* 53 (3): 433–68.

Thomson, Janice E. 1994. "Norms in International Relations: A Conceptual Analysis." *International Journal of Group Tensions* 23 (1): 67–83.

Towns, Ann E. 2012. "Norms and Social Hierarchies: Understanding International Policy Diffusion 'From Below.'" *International Organization* 66 (2): 179–209.

Ullmann-Margalit, Edna. 1977. *The Emergence of Norms*. Oxford: Clarendon Press.

———. 1990. "Revision of Norms." Ethics 100 (4): 756–67.

Van Kersbergen Kees, and Bertjan Verbeek. 2007. The Politics of International Norms. *European Journal of International Relations* 13 (2): 217–38.

Widmaier, Wesley W., and Susan Park. 2012. "Differences beyond Theory: Structural, Strategic, and Sentimental Approaches to Normative Change." *International Studies Perspective* 13 (2): 123–34.

Wiener, Antje. 2004. "Contested Compliance: Interventions on the Normative Structure of World Politics." *European Journal of International Relations* 10 (2): 189–234.

———. 2007. "The Dual Quality of Norms and Governance beyond the State: Sociological and Normative Approaches to 'Interaction.'" *Critical Review of International Social and Political Philosophy* 10 (1): 47–69.

———. 2008. *The Invisible Constitution of Politics: Contested Norms and International Encounters*. Cambridge: Cambridge University Press.

———. 2009. "Enacting Meaning-in-Use: Qualitative Research on Norms and International Relations." *Review of International Studies* 35 (1): 175–93.

Wiener, Antje, and Uwe Puetter. 2009. "The Quality of Norms Is What Actors Make of It: Critical Constructivist Research on Norms." *Journal of International Law and International Relations* 5 (1): 1–16.

Part I
Norm Conflicts and Norm Dynamics

CHAPTER TWO

Regime Conflicts and Norm Dynamics

Nuclear, Biological, and Chemical Weapons

Harald Müller, Una Becker-Jakob, and Tabea Seidler-Diekmann

EFFORTS TO CONTROL the spread of and eventually eliminate biological (BW), chemical (CW), and nuclear weapons (NW) are referred to under the general heading "weapons of mass destruction" (WMD) regimes. Although the effects of and the opportunities to defend against these types of weapons differ widely, the global discourse has lumped them together as indiscriminate, cruel, treacherous, and having long-term consequences for survivors. Existing regimes prohibit BW and CW, but not NW. The Nuclear Non-Proliferation Treaty (NPT) and the Chemical Weapons Convention (CWC) have sophisticated verification regimes while the Biological and Toxin Weapons Convention (BWC) lacks any. The CWC has its own regime-specific organization (Organisation for the Prohibition of Chemical Weapons, OPCW), while the NPT has been using the services of an existing organization, the International Atomic Energy Agency (IAEA); the BWC, after many years, has only been provided with a very small administrative unit.

The NPT, the core of the multilateral regime concerning NW, is more than forty years old. The BWC is four years younger. By contrast, the CWC came into force only in 1997. Despite their different ages and features, efforts have been made over time within all regimes to develop their original normative settings further. These efforts have been only partially successful. The present chapter looks into the dynamics of the regimes and exposes conflicts and their consequences for regime development.

THE NUCLEAR (NONPROLIFERATION) REGIME

Why the Regime?

The destructive potential of NW was demonstrated in Hiroshima and Nagasaki. The inhumane consequences, the survivors' long suffering from radiation, and the intangibility of radioactivity all added to the horrors of the blast and firestorm. This experience motivated early attempts to control the spread of NW. They culminated in the Baruch-Lilienthal-Acheson plan of 1946, which proposed subjecting all nuclear activities to international ownership and control but fell victim to the nascent Cold War. More than twenty years later, the international community, stimulated by an Irish initiative and then under the leadership of both superpowers, negotiated the NPT. The Cuban Missile Crisis of 1962 had driven the world to the brink of a nuclear catastrophe; the United States and the Soviet Union were aware how much more dangerous the situation might have become if more nuclear armed states had been involved. With the number of nuclear weapon states (NWS) having risen to five in the meantime, and many more states engaged in nuclear research and energy production, the time had come to prevent the further spread of NW.

The NPT was negotiated from 1966 to 1968, opened for signature in 1969, came into force in 1970, and received its verification system in 1971. Initially valid for twenty-five years, it was extended indefinitely in 1995 without a vote by the Review and Extension Conference. The NPT is the core of the nuclear nonproliferation regime, which also includes nuclear-weapon-free zones (NWFZS) in Antarctica, Latin America, the South Pacific, Africa, Southeast Asia, Central Asia, and Mongolia as a "single-state zone," two supplier arrangements for coordinating export controls (the Zangger Committee and the Nuclear Suppliers Group, NSG), security assurances by nuclear weapon states to nonnuclear weapon states, and many activities of the IAEA (D. Fischer 1997).

The Normative Structure of the Regime

The NPT was the result of hard negotiations (Shaker 1980). The first draft by the two superpowers contained only the prohibition norm for nonnuclear weapon states (NNWS) barring them from pursuing a NW program (Art. II). The targets of this norm struck back: without some reciprocity they were not willing to renounce a right that was, after all, part and parcel of their sovereignty. The final compromise based the NPT on three pillars: nonproliferation, everybody's right to enjoy the peaceful uses of nuclear energy and the duty of all parties to cooperate in this field as far as possible (Art. IV), and an effort by all parties to negotiate on nuclear disarmament parallel to other disarmament measures (Art. VI). This commitment remained relatively vague compared with the undertakings of the NNWS. Beyond this, there was the duty of the NWS not to help NNWS to acquire NW (Art. I).

The NNWS also tried to include in the treaty guarantees that NWS would not attack or threaten them with NW and that they would be assisted if such a threat or attack ever occurred. They were only partly successful: security guarantees were not included in the NPT but were provided only by unilateral declarations of the NWS, which were then noted in a UN Security Council (UNSC) resolution (Bunn and Timerbaev 1993) and confirmed in a second resolution in 1995.

The only vaguely formulated disarmament norm and nonlegalized security assurances made the inherently asymmetric treaty even more unequal. The prohibition norm for NNWS was not only clearer than the disarmament norm for NWS but was also bolstered by "safeguards," that is, IAEA verification measures of all peaceful nuclear activities of NNWS; these measures became more stringent over time (Art. III, 1). The verification modalities are codified in two documents. These model agreements contained in IAEA Information Circulars INFCIRC/153 of 1970 and INFCIRC/540 of 1997 (W. Fischer 2000) were negotiated under IAEA auspices. NWS tolerate safeguards on their peaceful nuclear activities on a voluntary basis, but the IAEA is reluctant to take up their offers because of the costs involved.

All states were forbidden to export special nuclear materials and technology to other NNWS without the IAEA verifying that these items were to be used for peaceful purposes only (Art. III, 2); this requirement affected nuclear importers more than the NWS who were already technology holders. More stringent details of export policies were worked out by the Zangger Committee (Schmidt 2000) and the NSG (Strulak 1993; Cupitt and Khripunov 1997), with most exporters of nuclear and nuclear-related items collaborating in the latter.

An important norm, universalization, is found only in the preamble, but not in the operative articles of the NPT. The treaty was meant to attract eventually all states in the world. NPT review conferences (RevCons) have regularly emphasized this goal and looked for ways and means of coming closer to it. The treaty reached a critical stage in the late 1990s when all states had acceded with the exception of three (after North Korea's withdrawal, four), all of which possessed NW capabilities. By then, universalization could no longer be achieved by incremental growth of the membership, but only by tackling the hard cases; this, so far, has proved futile.

Some peculiarities in the legal structure of the NPT deserve attention. First, in Art. IX, 3 the treaty defines a NWS as "one which has manufactured and exploded a nuclear weapon or other nuclear explosive device prior to 1 January, 1967." Legally, this has the odd consequence that a state like the UK could not become a NNWS under the treaty even if it were to dismantle its entire nuclear arsenal, while India could not accede as a NWS. Second, while the NPT confirms the right of sovereign states to withdraw from the treaty, withdrawal must be announced ninety days in advance to all NPT parties and to the UNSC, stating the reasons for withdrawal (Art. X, 1); this gives the UNSC the chance of contesting the validity of the reasons stated. Third, the NPT is virtually unamendable: amendments can enter into force only after a majority of all NPT parties approve them, including all NWS and all parties sitting on the IAEA Board of Governors at the time the amendment is circulated (Art. VIII, 2). Fourth, the NPT provided for holding a RevCon five years after it entered into force; this practice has continued ever since the first conference in 1975. RevCons provide a forum for the further development of regime norms (Müller, Fischer, and Kötter 1994; Simpson 2001; Dhanapala 2005; Johnson 2005, 2010; Müller 2011).

Regime Conflicts

Priority Conflicts All conflicts in the NPT are connected to the inequality of NWS and NNWS. The basic dispute concerns the relative importance of the three pillars. One school of thought, embraced by NWS, maintains that the treaty is essentially about nonproliferation and that peaceful uses and disarmament are secondary objectives of lesser weight (Krause 2007; Rühle 2007). As a consequence, throughout the history of the treaty, NNWS have complained that the nonproliferation norm was observed by the vast majority of the parties while the NWS were not complying with their basic obligation to disarm. The refusal by the NWS to give legally binding security assurances was seen as further disadvantaging the have-nots. This complaint became louder when disarmament stagnated (late 1970s and early 1980s, and the years of the George W. Bush administration), and less audible in phases of successful arms control and disarmament (early 1970s, late 1980s, and early 1990s, and since President Barack Obama entered office). Unequal compliance/noncompliance by the two groups of states has been a source of acrimonious conflict. The front line was largely between the NWS and the Non-aligned Movement (NAM). With few exceptions (Canada, Norway, and occasionally Australia), allies of the NWS did not emphasize disarmament with the same fervor as the developing and some neutral countries. They had a conflict of interest between becoming equal through disarmament and retaining extended deterrence by being loyal to their nuclear patrons.

Disarmament Disagreements over disarmament prevented the adoption of a consensual final document at three out of eight review conferences: 1980, 1990, and 2005. The discussion of this issue consumed the most time and energy. RevCons achieved increasing specification of the disarmament norm's meaning. In 1995, parties adopted a document, "Principles and Objectives," as the prerequisite for accepting indefinite extension. The meaning of Art. VI was interpreted as including the prompt conclusion of the Comprehensive Nuclear-Test-Ban Treaty (CTBT), from the beginning the disarmament measure most intensely demanded by the NAM, as well as the immediate commencement of negotiations on a fissile material cut-off treaty (FMCT) and systematic steps for the further reduction of nuclear arsenals (Dhanapala 2005). In 2000, the RevCon adopted "Thirteen Steps" for disarmament, including reduction of tactical NW, enhanced transparency, the irreversibility of disarmament measures, and an "unequivocal commitment" of the NWS to eliminating their arsenals (Simpson 2001). In 2010, the conference updated this list in an "Action Plan" that included constraints on the development of new nuclear warheads and a recommendation to close facilities for the production of fissile weapons material, and asked for talks on security assurances, not excluding the possibility of a legal instrument. Also, transparency for the NWS was specified as including regular, systematic reporting on their arsenals and disarmament steps (Johnson 2010; Müller 2011). Thus, since 1995, RevCons have established an emerging norm of NWS accountability for their compliance with Art. VI. The conflict, while at times acrimonious, has proved productive.

Cooperation and Civilian Nuclear Technology Development The next important conflict concerns perceived attempts to restrict the "inalienable right" of NNWS to enjoy the peaceful uses of nuclear energy and related international cooperation. In this conflict, a remarkable shift of front lines has taken place. Initially, it was a contest between Western NWS and Western NNWS that had started to use nuclear energy or were planning to do so in the near future. They were confronted with attempts to prevent them from building national facilities for enrichment and reprocessing and using plutonium in mixed oxide (MOX) fuel or from building fast breeder reactors. In the 1970s, the United States had become increasingly concerned that all these technologies would be a source of nuclear proliferation. Since their advanced allies were moving in this direction, they were the first targets of related unilateral American policies, in which Congress was even more adamant than the Carter administration about forcing allies into compliance with America's well-intentioned demands. The conflict also covered export controls. In 1978, the United States turned to the principle of "full scope safeguards" as a condition for all nuclear and nuclear-related exports. This implied that nuclear items could only be transferred to countries where all nuclear activities were under IAEA verification, the equivalent of NPT membership. Export-minded countries such as Germany, Belgium, and Switzerland opposed these constraints on their international business. Another contested area concerned the extension of export controls beyond special nuclear items to dual-use goods and intangible technology transfer. These US demands were supported by a group of nonproliferation-minded Western NNWS that since 1980 have been working in the "Vienna Group of Ten" to strengthen the NPT. However, export-ready Western countries deemed these demands undue impediments to their foreign trade. Lastly, Western NNWS using nuclear energy were initially also averse to stricter verification measures that might put their own nuclear industries at a competitive disadvantage vis-à-vis those of the NWS. They negotiated hard to keep the original verification system (INFCIRC /153) at a minimum, and resisted attempts at improvement—despite calls by the IAEA—until the eve of the 1991 Gulf War (Bunn 1992; see also chapter 4).

The front line crumbled when Germany, the most obstinate nuclear energy user, reversed its stance in 1990. Germany adopted a full-scope safeguards export policy that included dual-use goods and intangible technology transfers. Following this, the rest of the industrialized world fell into line. Germany fought its last campaign as a nuclear user during the negotiations on changes in the verification system in the mid-1990s that led to the Additional Protocol (Loosch 2000). Appropriate provisions of the Additional Protocol were supposed to be applied to the NWS as well, a justice claim that reflected fears about competitive disadvantages. With the decreasing popularity of nuclear energy in Germany, Belgium, and other Western countries, this front line evaporated (Müller 2003).

In the meantime, major NAM states became interested in nuclear energy. The activities of the NSG, which had produced a sophisticated system of rules to guide export policies, awakened distrust in the developing world that this was an exporters' cartel designed to prevent developing countries from enjoying the fruits of advanced technology (Gualtieri 2003; Joyner 2005). Misgivings about perceived undue constraints on international cooperation pursuant to Art. IV became mixed with concerns about the unsatisfactory compliance of the NWS with their disarmament obligations. Increasingly, this dissatisfaction was also directed against America's allies that enjoyed extended deterrence and some of which hosted US NW on their territories. This was seen by critics as violating the undertakings of both NATO NWS and NNWS under Arts. I and II. As long as nuclear disarmament was not pursued, the NAM maintained, there was no reason to accept additions to the nonproliferation toolbox (including, during the last decade, proposals to make withdrawal from the NPT more difficult). As a consequence, since 2000 the NAM has opposed making the Additional Protocol the obligatory verification standard, accepting NSG guidelines as the export control standard (Hirsch 2004) and moving toward multilateral fuel cycle arrangements as a substitute for new national enrichment and reprocessing facilities (Yudin 2010). The opposition hardened further in reaction to attempts by the Bush administration to explicitly constrain Art. IV rights by preventing the building of fuel cycle facilities in countries that did not already have them.

These conflicts over the relative weight of the nonproliferation versus the peaceful uses/cooperation norm have had various results. The conflicts inside the industrialized world have propelled normative developments in the areas of export controls and verification measures through years of, at times, very acrimonious but in the end productive negotiations. The conflicts between the industrialized world and the NAM have not prevented this normative development but have hindered its acceptance as binding (Johnson 2005, 2010; Müller 2011).

Universalization and Unequal Standards A third major conflict relates to universalization. While this norm is accepted in principle by all parties, it is given varying emphasis: Western states, Russia, and China tend to weigh their overall relations with non-NPT parties against their interest in persuading them to accede to the NPT as NNWS, a proposition that is given poor prospects in the short term (and short of global nuclear disarmament). Major NAM countries regard the nuclear weapon status of India, Israel, and Pakistan with disdain because they see their own status diminished by this new inequality. Arab countries are even more insistent on universalization because they do not accept Israel as a de facto NWS, and they are critical of what they see as the unjust double standard applied by the West (Fahmy 2006; Kadhim 2006). For this reason, Egypt pushed the Middle East resolution through in 1995, obliging the NPT depositaries, Russia, the UK, and the United States to foster the creation of a nuclear-weapon-free zone (NWFZ) in the Middle East. After nothing had happened fifteen years later, Egypt succeeded in getting the United States to accept the proposal for a conference on this subject in 2012 and the appointment by the UN secretary-general of a facilitator to prepare this conference. This proposal was grudgingly accepted by the Obama administration at the end of the 2010 RevCon (Johnson 2010).

The universalization conflict took a different turn with regard to India. The Indian nuclear explosion in 1974 stimulated the strengthening of the export control norm that culminated in the adoption by the NSG in 1992 and by the NPT Review and Extension Conference in 1995 of the norm of full-scope safeguards as a condition for nuclear supply. The same norm was rescinded by the NSG in 2009 when it acceded to a US demand to grant an exception for India without major concessions. This led to bitter complaints and accusations by the NAM leadership at the 2010 RevCon that NPT nonparties were privileged compared with NNWS parties (Chari 2009).

So far, it appears that this conflict is tending to establish the norm of a special responsibility of the depositary powers to work for universalization of nuclear nonproliferation in the Middle East. At the same time, the depositaries are trying to dilute the notion of their strong responsibility (as maintained by the Arab states) and to replace it with the notion of weak responsibility (implemented by the appearance of action more than by serious activities).

Procedural Disputes The final regime conflict regards procedural inequalities. NAM states are concerned that decisions crucial for norm development, implementation, and enforcement are made in institutions where the developing world is insufficiently represented. Export control norms are established and adapted by the NSG in which only a few developing countries (South Africa, Brazil, and Singapore) participate; consequently, the NAM has repeatedly called for negotiation of a universal legal instrument on export controls. Verification and important enforcement issues are in the hands of the IAEA Governing Board, where industrialized countries are disproportionally represented. The ultimate enforcer of the NPT is the UN Security Council with an overrepresentation of the industrialized world, including four out of five permanent members with veto rights (Burroughs 2007). That the five NWS are charged with supervising the abstinence of the rest is resented by many. This adds to their solidarity with the few wrongdoers: NAM states are usually no friends of tough enforcement.

Norm Dynamics in the Nuclear Nonproliferation Regime

The most salient aspects of norm development are a strengthening of verification and export controls and a significant specification of the disarmament obligations of nuclear weapon states, including a distinct norm of accountability. The conflict over disarmament has driven norm specification and the imposition of accountability on NWS. The intra-Western conflicts on peaceful uses have contributed to the development of export control norms, while the conflict between the industrialized world and the NAM over the same issue has blocked norm development for a decade. The conflict over universalization has had limited impact so far. There were ad hoc compromises in 1995 and 2010. The norm of responsibility by the depositary states for universalization with a special focus on the Middle East is still weak. Procedural conflicts have not led to much more than a token presence of developing countries in the NSG but have impeded stronger enforcement activities.

A pervasive factor in all conflicts is justice concerns (Rathbun 2006; Müller 2010). The pivotal importance of this factor results from the inequality inherent in the NPT, which can only be overcome by disarmament and universalization. Justice concerns influenced the misgivings of NNWS (the NAM in particular) about disarmament and opposition by Western users of nuclear energy as well as developing countries to discrimination against peaceful nuclear energy use; resentment about inequality combines with a material interest in avoiding economic disadvantages. Justice claims are also inherent in NAM and Arab states' resentment of unequal standards and of a lack of opportunities to participate in decision-making procedures. Thus, justice drives norm dynamics in the nuclear nonproliferation regime, for better or worse.

THE BIOLOGICAL WEAPONS CONTROL REGIME

Why the Regime?

Biological weapons (BW)—living (micro)organisms or their products used to inflict sickness or death on humans, animals, or plants—are nondiscriminatory in their effects.[1] Once released, they are hard to control. Their use can have devastating physical, environmental, material, and psychological effects. Little military utility has been attributed to BW (Zilinskas 2000, 1), the number of known and suspected BW possessor states or aspirants has decreased (US Department of State 2005, 2010; Wheelis, Rózsa, and Dando 2006), and there have been few incidents of nonstate actors' use of BW (Tucker 2000). Yet, the potential consequences make disarmament and prevention of production and use of BW imperative. Biology and biotechnology are among the most rapidly growing areas of technology and science and have a dual-use character: many benign research activities, developments, materials, and applications, for example, in genetic engineering or synthetic biology, could be misused—not only in state-run BW programs, but also by criminals or terrorists. This risk could increase in proportion to continuing growth in research and industry.

An international disarmament regime has existed in this field for forty years with the 1972 BWC at its center.[2] The basic norm against BW, in particular against their use, is solid. The regime has proven dynamic and resilient, most recently in 2001–2 when a breakdown was prevented and a degree of stability regained. Nevertheless, the regime suffers from weaknesses such as insufficient transparency and inadequate compliance mechanisms, lack of verification measures (e.g., Chevrier 2000), and the nearly complete lack of institutional support (e.g., Sims 2006).[3]

The Normative Structure of the Regime

The norm against BW *use* dates back to the end of the nineteenth century and was codified in the Geneva Protocol of 1925. Being considered customary international law (Boserup 1973; Sims 2009, 21), it is by now universal. The BWC prohibits, inter alia, BW production, possession, and retention in a comprehensive and nondiscriminatory way. The BW taboo rests on a solid normative basis, a few known treaty violations notwithstanding (Wheelis, Rózsa, and Dando 2006). Additional norms include the obligation of biological disarmament (Art. II) and nonproliferation (Art. III), of national implementation, of assistance in the case of BW use against a state party (Art. VII), and of international cooperation in the exchange of biotechnology and the promotion of related development (Art. X). Initially, the regime did not contain any provisions for transparency and for ensuring compliance beyond the vague obligation of state parties to "consult one another" on problems arising in the context of the convention (Art. V) and the right to lodge a complaint with the UN Security Council in cases where treaty violations are suspected (Art. VI). More recently, ensuring biosafety and biosecurity has emerged as an important concept. Biosafety entails the prevention of accidental release of dangerous pathogens, whereas biosecurity consists of measures to protect against illegitimate access to such agents.

The BW regime represents a case of simultaneous dynamism *and* stasis. The BW taboo and implementation norm have been strengthened over time. The transparency in the regime was supposed to be improved by adopting, in 1986 and 1991, a set of politically binding confidence-building measures (CBMs), but participation, and hence the transparency norm, remain weak (Hunger and Isla 2006). Moreover, there is no verification; if suspicions regarding compliance arise, states can only follow the procedures described above. Efforts to add a legally binding compliance protocol and to establish a verification norm foundered in 2001 after years of negotiations, largely due to US resistance (Littlewood 2005).

Treaty members then created a new series of annual meetings between RevCons in order to save the regime and maintain multilateral dialogue, but also to tackle problems that had hitherto received little attention: effective national implementation, improved safety and security of laboratories, inter alia, and awareness raising among bioscientists of the potential misuse of their work. The topics covered in these intersessional meetings indicate a shift of emphasis; attention moved away from state-based problems toward nonstate actors and biological risks and threats in general. While this is not the primary focus of the BWC, the measures discussed are widely thought to help mitigate this threat (Sims 2009, 82–85). The emphasis of the intersessional process is on national measures and voluntary international cooperation; there is no mandate to negotiate collective recommendations, let alone binding instruments. Verification and multilateral, legally binding compliance measures have been off the (official) agenda since, but remain contentious. Hence, the initial weaknesses and problems remain, despite efforts to redress them.

The concept of biosecurity, which the United States introduced after 2001, was initially met with skepticism and resistance, which may in part have been due to confusion over the meaning of the term. Moreover, there were linguistic misunderstandings since the distinction between biosecurity and biosafety does not translate well into many languages (Guthrie et al. 2004, 664; Guthrie 2008). Yet, the discussion of this topic in the intersessional process led to an understanding of the concept and of its utility in the BW context that is by now widely shared.

In recent years, increasing attention has been devoted to issues related to the international cooperation and development norm (Art. X). In particular in the intersessional topic of 2010—responses to BW use including assistance to affected countries—greater convergence of BW concerns with public and international health issues became obvious. However, not all states are keen on pushing this change further, and it remains to be seen whether such change will constitute a permanent alteration in the regime's normative setting. If so, the disarmament and nonproliferation dimension might be placed alongside a reinforced health and preparedness component. This would move the BW regime closer to international regimes on world health and biosafety but would not create an entirely new normative setting: related activities could fall under BWC Arts. X and VII. Emphasis would shift away from the regime's classic interstate security functions and state-to-state interaction on weapons and biodefense policies and would probably involve new actors and new forms of governance. This might also have implications for the contested balance between disarmament and nonproliferation obligations on the one hand and international cooperation on the other.

Regime Conflicts

Nonproliferation vs. Technological Exchange and International Cooperation Norm conflicts in the BW regime exist in two areas. The first concerns the tension between the obligation to prevent the proliferation of the proscribed weapons, which includes controls on the transfers of (potentially) sensitive technologies (Art. III), and the obligation to foster the peaceful use of the respective technologies, including by promoting development and the "widest possible" technological exchange (Art. X).[4] The validity of either norm is not contested, but it is disputed whether they are of equal relevance, as members of the NAM claim, or whether the security aspect embodied in Art. III has priority, as many members of the Western European and Others Group (WEOG) maintain.[5] This conflict becomes especially notable given the importance of biotechnology to the improvement of public health.

At first glance, this could be read as a classic conflict of interests: industrialized countries could be reluctant to share their technological advantage with poorer states and therefore emphasize security concerns to justify trade barriers. Developing countries, in turn, could be eager to gain better access to biotechnology research and markets and hence discredit the industrialized countries' export controls as hampering their development. Moreover, for some actors this conflict serves as proxy for other political disputes and objectives. However, these are only some of several possible readings. In many developing countries there is a pressing need for improved capabilities for fighting infectious diseases through affordable medication and other forms of treatment or vaccines. The material interest in enhanced capabilities for providing medical care coincides with a claim to equal access to and a fairer distribution of such capabilities and the moral necessity to satisfy basic human needs. Experience with Western reluctance to comply with transfer obligations in other regimes such as the Convention on Biological Diversity and the limits placed on biotechnology transfer by the Agreement on Trade-Related Aspects of Intellectual Property Rights (TRIPS)(Dhar 2002) provide grounds for developing countries to generally mistrust "the West."[6] Finally, there is a normative component to the perceived entitlement to technological and economic development that also extends to the biotechnology sector (Becker-Jakob 2011, 7).

Western countries, on the other hand, may indeed have been reluctant to give up their (bio)technological advantage and may also maintain an interest in securing potential export markets; but they also harbor compliance concerns vis-à-vis some NAM countries and, given the reluctance of some NAM members to provide more transparency through confidence-building measures (CBMs), were unwilling to abandon export controls as coordinated through the Australia Group.[7] They see the BWC's security functions as the primary objective and the developmental aspects as secondary to it; hence, many Western states are not willing to assign technological exchange the same normative importance as BW nonproliferation or the national implementation of the BWC. Even though several Western countries frequently quote the relevance of BWC Art. X or point out how they promote the exchange of knowledge and equipment (e.g., statements by Ekéus 1986; Lowitz 1986a, 1986b; Moher 1996; Westdal 2001; Sano 2001; Gröning 2006), and though there seems to be a growing readiness to discuss this issue in more concrete terms, Western approaches to dealing with it lack the normative and justice-related components attached to this issue by many NAM members.

Verification and Compliance A second set of norm conflicts centers on compliance and verification. Differing points of view over the desired form of interaction, including agenda-setting powers, arose from this set of conflicts. The origins of disagreement lie in the weakness of the BWC's compliance mechanism and the lack of verification. In 1980 and 1982 Sweden proposed an amendment to the BWC to include a "nondiscriminatory" compliance procedure independent of UNSC decisions and actions that would not allow for a veto and would provide equal access to a complaint procedure for all BWC members regardless of their position in the UNSC or their affiliation with any of the "Permanent Five" (Sims 1988, 168–212). Its discriminatory nature was considered one of the key problems inherent in the existing mechanism; many small and middle-sized states supported the Swedish proposal.

The 1991 RevCon mandated the initiation of a process intended to strengthen the BWC through a verification system and culminating in negotiations on a legally binding compliance protocol between 1995 and 2001. During these negotiations conflicts with varying line-ups emerged. On the surface, conflicts revolved around the details of a future protocol, including export controls and the exact design and intrusiveness of the verification system (Littlewood 2005), but they were also affected by different attitudes toward verification of the BWC and by fundamental political disputes. It is difficult to assess the influence of normative, justice-related considerations on these conflicts and attitudes: demands for nondiscriminatory measures (by NAM members) and for equal burden-sharing (Western states) permeated the negotiations (Littlewood 2005). However, apart from the normative component that such claims contain, because they assume *equal rights and obligations* of all states parties, the former also served the NAM's interest in gaining better access to biotechnology, while the latter was intended to ease the Western bio-industry's burden in the event that a verification system were to be established.

After the collapse of negotiations in 2001, conflict lines re-emerged mainly along a Western-NAM divide, with the Western Group split between the United States and the rest. Contentious issues remained unresolved; that the negotiations were first stalled and then ended by a single state, the United States, added a new dimension to the conflict. A group of like-minded NAM states that had previously been skeptical about the draft protocol (Sims 2009, 67–68) now called for a return to protocol negotiations and for the conclusion of a legally binding instrument, but the sincerity of this demand might be questioned given their previous positions (Littlewood 2005, 212). The United States remained opposed to a return to the protocol approach. The other Western countries, while maintaining their support for a verification system as a "long-term objective," refrained from pushing the issue lest the United States retreat even further from the BWC.

The proposal for a new intersessional process was designed as a way out of the 2001–2 impasse; it envisaged annual meetings that would discuss, though not negotiate, a set of predefined issues. This set reflected a list of US priorities published in 2001 (Bush 2001; Tucker 2004, 30). Many parties were angered and frustrated by the fact that the United States, despite carrying the biggest responsibility for the crisis, was able to dictate the terms of the regime's changed setup, at least indirectly, while the concerns of others were not reflected. Many also resented the proposal for an intersessional process being presented as a "take it or leave it" package with no room for alterations or negotiations. This reinforced another dimension of the norm conflict(s) over verification: procedural justice. Owing to the success of the first intersessional process (Khan 2007) and the inclusion of NAM concerns in the agenda of the second, this conflict has abated somewhat, although the continuing calls for a return to the protocol negotiations might represent a holdover of the situation in 2001–2.

This norm conflict still contains elements of the notions of a nondiscriminatory compliance system and of a strengthened disarmament regime, but it has also come to epitomize regime conflicts more generally. Justice-related arguments can be found mainly in the original debate from the 1980s and again in the early 2000s regarding agenda-setting and the intersessional process. For the protocol negotiations, justice appears mostly in references to equal burden sharing and to a holistic, balanced approach, with the latter owing more to the norm conflict over technological exchange, cooperation, and development than to that over verification.

Norm Dynamics in the Biological Weapons Control Regime

This first norm conflict, the NAM's insistence on giving Art. X more prominence and the West's reluctance to do this, has long impeded progress in the regime. Efforts to strengthen the BWC often failed because of political bargaining or because they were accompanied by irreconcilable interpretations of BWC norms.[8] Changes unrelated to this conflict may have a mitigating effect, however. An increased recent willingness of Western countries to deal with Art. X–related issues may reflect the realization that strengthening of the regime can be achieved only if NAM concerns are addressed. It may also have been fueled by the shift of attention to bioterrorism and more broadly defined biological risks and by recognizing that the prevention of illegitimate access to and accidental release of dangerous pathogens, as well as the effective combating of infectious diseases, whatever their origin, require international cooperation and capacity building in developing countries. The inclusion of Art. X–related topics in the intersessional work program of 2009 and 2010 and again for 2012–15 (BWC 2011, 21) reflects these changes. It forced NAM members to concretely discuss their demands and needs that had hitherto been voiced as abstract claims. Moreover, due to the expansion of their domestic biotechnology sector, some NAM members may become potential suppliers rather than recipients; a number of developing and threshold countries have introduced export controls and other legislation and regulations in recent years, in part due to the requirements of UN Security Council Resolution 1540 (2004) and its successor resolutions 1673 (2006), 1810 (2008), and 1977 (2011), in part also due to the insight that such measures improve their own national security. This has rendered strident criticism of similar measures in Western countries less credible.[9] As international cooperation is being discussed more pragmatically, different approaches of various NAM countries (e.g., political objectives, practical needs) are becoming more and more visible. Nevertheless, this conflict remains one of the major political problems in the regime.

Virtually all major regime developments were connected to the conflict over verification. Some stemmed from the desire to mitigate problems resulting from the weak compliance mechanism and lack of verification measures. The intersessional process was initially designed to save the regime from collapse but proved more useful than many had anticipated, as it allowed states parties to tackle a number of practical problems in a less politicized way (Khan 2007; Sims 2009, 46). Moreover, regular interaction improved the working atmosphere. The norm conflict over verification thus had an ambivalent effect: though it brought about one of the most positive changes in the regime, the intersessional process, this process had to be created in response to the most severe crisis of the regime, a crisis this norm conflict had caused in the first place.

As a nondiscriminatory treaty, the BWC does not contain any obvious inherent "injustices." Justice-related claims emerge over its interpretation and the potential nature of additional instruments to enhance BW control. These claims can be grouped into the categories of distributive justice (regarding equal access to biotechnology and its products) and procedural justice (concerning nondiscriminatory compliance procedures, export control measures, and equal chances of determining the agenda). Generally, normative claims to fair distribution and to equal opportunity for participation combine with material interests.

THE CHEMICAL WEAPONS CONTROL REGIME

Why the Regime?

The world first experienced the horrifying effects of chemical warfare in World War I (Tucker 2006, 9–23).[10] In the 1980s, the Iran-Iraq war served as a reminder that the then valid norm, the Geneva Protocol, which prohibits the use but not the production or possession of CW, was not sufficient. In addition, the specter of chemical terrorism has been widely discussed, although actual incidents rarely occurred, despite the spectacular release of sarin by the Aum Shirinkyo sect in the Tokyo subway. Presently, no CW are being employed in armed conflict. Yet the risk of their use, notably against unprotected civilian populations, remains a terrifying thought. The need for a new norm was also seen as urgent because of the spread of the chemical industry and its use of many toxic chemicals for legitimate civilian purposes.

The CWC, today the core of the regime against CW, entered into force on April 29, 1997, after more than twenty years of negotiations (e.g., Robinson 1998; Kenyon 2007, 7–15).[11] The OPCW came into being at the same time. It consists of the Technical Secretariat, which is charged, inter alia, with verification activities, the Executive Council, with forty-one periodically rotating seats, and the annual Conference of States Parties (CSP). Five regional groupings guarantee a balanced representation in the Executive Council (Art. VIII, C. 23). Although the 188 states parties to the CWC represent close to 98 percent of the world's population, some states, notably North Korea, Syria, Israel, and Egypt, have not acceded (Feakes 2008). However, the core norm of the CWC, the prohibition norm, has gained almost universal acceptance. It is bolstered by the drastic reduction in CW stockpiles pursuant to the CWC's disarmament norm and the intention of states parties to eliminate those stockpiles completely. Nevertheless, the problem remains that the two largest CW holders, the United States and Russia, did not complete the destruction of their arsenals by the prescribed target date, April 2012.[12]

The Normative Structure of the Regime

The CWC prohibits its parties from developing, producing, acquiring, stockpiling, retaining, transferring, and using CW or assisting, encouraging, or inducing anyone in prohibited activities (Art. I, 1). This core prohibition norm has established a "CW taboo" (Price 1997). The disarmament norm (Art. I, 2–4; Art. III; Art. IV; Art. V; Verification Annex) applies to weapons stockpiles and to their production facilities. Additional norms enable and constrain the handling of toxic chemicals and their precursors. They may only be used for "purposes not prohibited" (Art. VI; Art. II, 9). In addition, states parties have undertaken to facilitate the "fullest possible exchange of chemicals, equipment and [. . .] information" for purposes not prohibited and to refrain from maintaining restrictions among themselves on trade and research in chemistry for peaceful purposes (Art. XI; Art. VI, 11). Parties receive and provide assistance through the OPCW in case of CW threat or use (Art. X). The Technical Secretariat implements these provisions (Art. X; Art. XI) through international cooperation and assistance activities. The CWC contains complex and detailed verification provisions. Certain toxic chemicals and their precursors, as well as certain facilities, must be declared and are verified in specific ways. Chemicals to be declared are listed in three "Schedules," that is, lists, distinguished by the risk they pose to the objective and purpose of the CWC (Art. VI; Annex on Chemicals; Verification Annex). In case of suspected noncompliance, a challenge inspection can be requested in addition to other clarification procedures (Art. IX; Verification Annex). Scientific and technological developments that might affect the operation of the CWC are to be reviewed (Art. VIII, 21 (h)). All states parties are obliged to pass laws and regulations required to implement the CWC and to inform the OPCW accordingly (Art. VII).

Verification applies to the destruction of CW stocks; routine inspections are also conducted in industrial and military facilities. The OPCW enables the membership to review the functioning of the convention regularly. This relieves the RevCons, which take place at five-year intervals, from mission overload. So far, two such conferences have taken place, the third is scheduled for 2013. The first called for action plans on universalization and on implementation of Art. VII. These plans were formally adopted during the Conference of States Parties in 2003. The action plan for universalization led to the accession of nearly thirty new member states. Implementation has improved, although gaps remain (Tabassi 2007).[13]

The second RevCon (April 2008) showed less progress. Differences between developing countries emphasizing disarmament and Western industrialized states intent on strengthening nonproliferation blocked adaptations of the verification system (Meier 2008). This North-South confrontation restrains actual regime developments. Many Western states put their focus on nonproliferation and verification issues (Art. VI) and on national implementation (Art. VII), whereas developing states often highlighted international cooperation in the peaceful use of chemistry under Art. XI.

Regime Conflicts

The Dispute over the Disarmament Norm Even though all states recognize the disarmament norm, disputes exist. During the negotiations within the Conference on Disarmament (CD) there were already lengthy discussions on the timetable for the destruction of the arsenals. The temporary desire of the United States not to disarm completely until all CW-capable states had ratified the CWC was controversial (Manley 2007, 142–43). Under the CWC, states parties are responsible for the expenses of destroying their own CW stockpiles, including verification, unless the Executive Council decides otherwise (Art. IV, 16; Art. V, 19). However, some states did not reimburse the OPCW for its inspection efforts (Smithson 1998, 46–48). The organization's financial crisis of 2001 resulted partly from CW possessors' either failing to make or falling behind with their payments (Kelle 2004, 228–29).

The countries with the largest CW stockpiles, Russia and the United States (which together declared about 68,577 metric tons [Walker 2010] of the total of around 71,195 metric tons of Schedule 1 chemical warfare agents declared to the OPCW), did not complete destruction by April 2012 despite their efforts. In a precedent, Albania was not able to comply with its target date in 2007 because of technical problems and completed destruction of its CW stockpiles two months late. The Executive Council and the states parties solved the problem unanimously (Walker 2010). However, the volume of stockpiles held by the United States and Russia is greater by several orders of magnitude; the United States will reportedly be late by nine years and Russia anticipates missing the target date by three years (Walker 2010). Parties found a solution in 2011 by determining that the remaining CW possessors are to continue the destruction with a number of additional requirements (CSP 2011b). However, not all states parties were satisfied with this result, and it is unclear whether and how this might still affect the future of the CWC.

In this conflict, positions differed about what behavior is appropriate and still in compliance with the convention. While Western states recognized the situation as problematic, NAM states maintained that compliance with the target date is essential for the "credibility and integrity of the Convention" (NAM and China 2008). Iran, retaliating for being pressured in the nuclear nonproliferation regime, defined missing the target date as a "clear and serious case of non-compliance" (Ziaran 2008); it was also the only country that did not join consensus on the compromise solution in 2011 (Horner 2012). The African Group, in contrast, although associating itself with the NAM position, uttered more moderate statements (Horner 2011; e.g., African Group 2008, 2011).

More Verification or More Cooperation? The most basic conflict concerns the priority of nonproliferation versus civilian cooperation. Many Western states emphasize strengthening the verification norm in order to ensure transparency and confidence building, while developing states focus on improved economic and technological cooperation.

Developing countries expected economic and technological advantages from joining the CWC (Shah 2001, 10). Consequently, it was important for completing the CWC negotiations that the Australia Group declared its willingness to rescind restrictive measures on trade for CWC parties in good standing (Kenyon and Kisselev 2007, 251–52; Shah 2001, 11). During the work of the Preparatory Commission for the OPCW the demands by developing countries were not unanimous. They agreed in principle that there should not be export controls beyond the provisions of the CWC, but they differed on the time when the Australia Group regime should be abolished and what arrangement should replace it. These national positions depended on bilateral relations with industrialized states and on how much states were affected by the Australia Group's policies (Kenyon and Kisselev 2007, 253–54).

Over time, this dispute developed into an amalgam of hard interests and unfulfilled justice claims. Some NAM states feel unjustly discriminated against by the continued existence of the Australia Group (e.g., Khoshro 2003; Cuba 2008). In contrast, Australia Group members deem the group as indispensable for fulfilling their own nonproliferation undertakings and maintain that this position is fully compatible with Art. XI (Australia Group 2007). This conflict proved a barrier to agreeing on a decision on implementation of Art. XI during the Conference of the States Parties until 2005 (Trapp 2007, 286; see e.g., CSP 2005).

While many member states, plus the OPCW, have enhanced their efforts to implement Art. XI (OPCW 2008, 70–81), some developing countries resent what they believe is still insufficient international cooperation by the industrialized states to support their development. In order to achieve a "full and equitable implementation of all provisions of the Convention," for several years they have been demanding an action plan to implement Art. XI (e.g., African Group 2008). In 2011, the CSP decided on several measures intended to enhance Article XI implementation (CSP 2011a).

Today, chemical facilities producing unscheduled discrete organic chemicals (other chemical production facilities; OCPF) that have to be reported to the OPCW only above a high production threshold are increasingly located in developing countries and emerging economies, especially in China and India. Only a small portion of these facilities is covered annually by the OPCW's routine inspections, although many of them could be diverted for the production of CW agents (Tucker 2009/2010, 18). While many Western states are proponents of increasing the number of inspections at those facilities and request that selection be based on the specific risk posed by each facility, some NAM states insist on limiting inspections largely to facilities that produce scheduled chemicals. In their view this would follow the "hierarchy of risk" they see stipulated in the convention (Art. II, 2). Some more advanced developing countries seem to be reticent to bear an increasing verification burden in the future (Tucker 2007).

Another conflict concerns challenge inspections. Routine inspections cover only declared facilities. Challenge inspections can be conducted at any site. They are essential to uncover breaches of the rules by clandestine activities. The United States had introduced the idea of challenge inspections based on the "anytime, anywhere" principle in the mid-1980s but later developed second thoughts about its erstwhile initiative (Stock 1995, 21–22).[14] While many Western states argue that challenge inspections are no means of last resort and could establish confidence building as well as security, NAM states treat them as a mechanism for determining a supposed breach of the convention only after consultations have failed (e.g., NAM and China 2008; EU 2008). Different notions of sovereignty underlie this dispute that has weakened the verification norm. Because the political barrier was too high, not a single challenge inspection took place, although several states parties to the CWC have been publicly accused of having breached their commitments (Tucker 2009/2010, 7–8; see, e.g., Rademaker 2003).

Norm Dynamics in the Chemical Weapons Control Regime

The CW regime is not challenged by basic opposition to core norms, but by their different weighting and interpretation. The CWC gives equal rights and duties to all members. Some NAM states, however, feel discriminated against by the existence of the Australia Group. They claim a case of procedural injustice and demand the installation of a "truly representative body" (Nasseri 1997) within the CWC. Many developing countries maintain that due to export restrictions, they cannot truly enjoy economic and technological cooperation, which they perceive as resulting in an unjust distribution of benefits. While they achieved equitable representation in the Executive Council, they now demand the same for staff positions in the Technical Secretariat (e.g., African Group 2008). In seeking equality the NAM stance brings together the quest for justice with a material interest in industrial development; most Western standpoints are nearly devoid of justice concerns and instead focus on regime efficiency, whereas the United States is noteworthy for the emphasis it places on its exceptional national security and economic interests.

These differences cause conflicts strong enough to block improvements of the regime regarding a) adapting verification to technological change and b) promoting cooperation in economic and technological development of member states. Nevertheless, the CWC possesses a verification system that has proven effective in numerous routine on-site inspections (Trapp 2007, 274). Cooperative activities of several member states as well as the OPCW have increased and intensified, e.g., through various workshops convened by the organization or exchanges between member states and other relevant actors such as the chemicals industry. While this process has led to moderate regime development, it has not yet developed or specified particular norms.

The conflict over the disarmament norm has hindered regime development as well. Several Conferences of States Parties became deadlocked when Iran attempted to insert condemnations of the destruction delay into the final documents; however, Tehran has become more and more isolated within the NAM.

Conclusion: Countervailing Interests, Normative Concerns, and Their Influence on WMD Norms

The three regimes show both significant norm dynamics and exasperating norm stagnation. Dynamic development rests on most members' interest in preventing the spread of WMD and eliminating existing ones. This interest is often bolstered by a moral revulsion against the nature of these weapons and the inhumane effects of their use. At the same time, countervailing interests (hedging, superior military postures, and economic development and benefits) and countervailing normative concerns (justice and equality) produce conflicts, some of which lead to, and some of which hinder, norm development.

Certain conflicts permeate all three regimes (see table 2.1). The most obvious one is the claim by NAM countries that cooperation, civilian use, and sharing the respective technologies are of equal rank to, or of higher priority than, the nonproliferation objective. This implies a justice claim based on principles of need, compensation, and equal opportunity, which the developing world propagates with a view to previous deprivations.[15] In the past, this conflict frequently blocked improvements of the nonproliferation toolbox, verification, compliance, and enforcement. In the NPT, and more recently in the CWC and BWC, it has also led to moderate adjustments, notably increased cooperation activities in the BWC and CWC and outreach and cooptation activities by the NSG in order to counter the accusation of discrimination against developing countries. This dynamic notwithstanding, the conflict appears to have impeded rather than fostered improvement of the normative setting.

Verification has played an ambivalent role. In the chemical and nuclear regimes, the NAM treated verification as part of the demanding obligations that must be compensated for by enhanced cooperation (in the nuclear regime, some industrialized countries initially displayed the same attitude), thereby framing it in justice terms. In the BW regime, in contrast, many NAM states have joined most Western parties in asking for a verification regime, while the United States is blocking such progress. Generally, the United States asks for verification of the activities of others while exempting itself on the grounds of industrial and security interests.

The conflict over disarmament obligations exists in the CWC and, with more prominence and from a different angle, dominates in the nuclear

Table 2.1. Norm conflicts in the WMD regimes

NPT	BWC	CWC
Disarmament		Disarmament
Proliferation vs. peaceful use	Proliferation vs. peaceful use	Proliferation vs. peaceful use
Universalization		
Procedural inequalities	Procedural inequalities	Procedural inequalities
Compliance, enforcement, verification	Compliance, enforcement, verification	Verification

nonproliferation regime. The justice aspect—achieving equality between "haves" and "have-nots"—has been a driving motivation. In the CWC, it concerns the failure to meet the time limit for the destruction of Russian and American arsenals, but it is pursued most strongly by Iran as a compensation for being under pressure in the nuclear nonproliferation regime and has had little effect on norm development. In the NPT it proved to be repeatedly disruptive at RevCons but has also led to norm development in two directions, the increasing specification of what disarmament means and the emerging norm of NWS accountability for what they do with their nuclear arsenals. In the BWC, the lingering doubts about Russia's compliance with its disarmament obligation and the ambivalent nature of the US defense research program after the anthrax attacks in the fall of 2001 (Wheelis and Dando 2003) did not lead to a comparable controversy. This regime has been troubled by the complex basic conflict concerning verification and compliance that is absent from the other regimes.

Procedural conflicts are common to the three regimes. Institutional positions and power resources are distributed asymmetrically, limiting the opportunity for weaker (developing) parties to exert influence. Decisions on export controls and on enforcement are most relevant. Developing countries demand equal opportunity to participate, a classic procedural justice claim.

Justice conflicts are most virulent in the nuclear context, where the regime provides for asymmetrical rights and duties. Equality of rights and duties mitigates conflicts in the two symmetric regimes, but development and power differentials and the legacy of the past, notably the experience of colonial rule, make the developing countries much more justice-sensitive, while developed countries put more emphasis on regime efficiency.

Three basic attitudes have been observed toward regime norms: regime efficiency (guiding policies of many Western states), security and economic interest (endorsed by all parties, with particular weight in the US case), and moral/justice concerns. The latter are frequently mixed up with material interests (distributive claims by NAM states in particular), and the resulting amalgam appears impossible to disentangle.

Notes

1. The author is grateful to Nicholas Sims for helpful comments on this and the following sections.

2. For analyses of the BW regime see Chevrier (2000); Kelle (2003); Sims (2001).

3. In 2006, a small secretariat-style unit was founded, but its mandate is limited and subject to renewal.

4. For a useful discussion of the impact of the NPT on this conflict see Sims (2009, 12).

5. Work in the BW regime is still organized in the Cold War group structure: Western European and Others Group (WEOG), Eastern European Group, Group of the Non-Aligned Movement and Other States Parties (NAM). The inactive Eastern European group is not considered in this analysis.

6. The author owes this point to Thilo Marauhn.

7. Between 2000 and 2005, of all states having submitted CBMs, fewer than 10 percent were NAM members for each given year (EU 2006, 10–11). The Australia Group is an informal grouping of forty countries and the EU Commission that coordinates its export control policies designed to prevent the transfer and proliferation of dual-use chemical and biological items and materials; see http://australiagroup.net.

8. One example was the failure of the sixth RevCon to agree on an action plan on national implementation (Becker 2007, 28; Sims 2009, 58–65).

9. The author owes these observations to Volker Beck.

10. The author is grateful to Jonathan B. Tucker for helpful comments on this and the following sections.

11. For an analysis of the CW regime see Kelle (2004); on norm development see, e.g., Price (1997).

12. Libya, Iraq, India, South Korea, and Albania also have declared CW stockpiles; the latter three have completed their destruction activities.

13. By 2011, 46 percent of states parties had adopted the necessary national implementation legislation (Üzümcü 2010, 11), about 6 percent more than before the Action Plan was adopted (Pfirter 2003, 5).

14. The US Senate's implementation legislation permits the president to reject the request for a challenge inspection if he or she determines that US national security might be compromised, and it prohibits the transport of samples taken in the United States to laboratories abroad. Samples may be analyzed only in the United States (Smithson 2001, 25).

15. In the nuclear nonproliferation regime this point was initially raised by a group of industrialized nonnuclear weapon states.

References

African Group. 2008. Statement on Behalf of the African Group of States Parties to the 2nd CWC RevCon, The Hague, April 7.

———. 2011. Statement on Behalf of the African Group of States Parties to the CWC at the 16th Session of the CSP. C-16/NAT.29. The Hague, November 28.

Australia Group. 2007. "Relationship with the Chemical Weapons Convention." Australia Group. www.australiagroup.net/en/cwc.html.

Becker, Una. 2007. *Light at the End of the Tunnel? The Sixth Review Conference of the Biological Weapons Convention.* PRIF Report no. 79. www.hsfk.de/fileadmin/downloads/prif79.pdf.

Becker-Jakob, Una. 2011. "Notions of Justice in the Biological Weapons Control Regime." PRIF Working Paper no. 09–2011. Peace Research Institute Frankfurt, Frankfurt am Main. www.hsfk.de/fileadmin/downloads/arbeitspapier0911k.pdf.

Boserup, Anders. 1973. *CBW and the Law of War: The Problem of Chemical and Biological Warfare.* Vol. 3. Stockholm: Almqvist & Wiksell.

Bunn, George. 1992. *Arms Control by Committee: Managing Negotiations with the Russians.* Stanford: Stanford University Press.

Bunn, George, and Roland M. Timerbaev. 1993. "Security Assurances to Non-Nuclear-Weapon States." *Nonproliferation Review* 1 (1): 11–21.

Burroughs, John. 2007. "The Role of the UN Security Council." In *Nuclear Disorder or Cooperative Security? U.S. Weapons of Terror, the Global Proliferation Crisis, and Paths to Peace: An Assessment of the Final Report of the WMD Commission and Its Implications for US Policy,* edited by Michael Spies and John Burroughs, 35–43. New York: Lawyers Committee on Nuclear Policy.

Bush, George W. USA. 2001. Statement on Strengthening the International Regime against Biological Weapons, November 1. www.gpo.gov/fdsys/pkg/WCPD-2001-11-05/pdf/WCPD-2001-11-05-Pg1580.pdf.

BWC (Biological Weapons Convention). 2011. "Final Document, Part III, Decisions and Recommendations." 7th BWC RevCon. BWC/CONF.VII/7, Geneva, December 5–22.

Chari, P. R. 2009. "Introduction: The Indo-US Nuclear Deal." In *Indo-US Nuclear Deal: Seeking Synergy in Bilateralism,* edited by P. R. Chari, 1–17. London: Routledge.

Chevrier, Marie I. 2000. "Strengthening the International Arms Control Regime." In *Biological Warfare: Modern Offense and Defense,* edited by Raymond A. Zilinskas, 149–76. Boulder: Lynne Rienner.

CSP (Conference of the States Parties). 2005. Decision on the Full Implementation of Article XI. C-10/DEC.14. The Hague, November 11.

———. 2011a. Decision on Components of an Agreed Framework for the Full Implementation of Article XI. C-16/DEC.10. The Hague, December 1.

———. 2011b. Decision on the Final Extended Deadline of 29 April 2012. C-16/DEC.11. The Hague, December 1.

Cuba. 2008. Position Paper Submitted by the Delegation of the Republic of Cuba on Behalf of the Member States of the NAM CWC States Parties and China to the 2nd CWC RevCon. RC-2/NAT.17/Rev.1. The Hague, April 15.

Cupitt, Richard T., and Igor Khripunov. 1997. "New Strategies for the Nuclear Suppliers Group (NSG)." *Comparative Strategy* 16 (3): 305–15.

Dhanapala, Jayantha. 2005. *Multilateral Diplomacy and the NPT: An Insider's Account.* With Randy Rydell. Geneva: United Nations, UNIDIR.

Dhar, Biswajit. 2002. "The Global Patent Regime: Implementing Art. X." In *Biological Warfare and Disarmament: New Problems/New Perspectives*, edited by Susan Wright, 391–410. Lanham: Rowman & Littlefield.

Ekéus, Rolf. Sweden. 1986. Statement to the 2nd BWC RevCon. BWC/CONF.II/SR.7. Geneva, September 22.

EU (European Union). 2006. "Enhancement of the Confidence-Building Measure (CBM) Process." Working paper. Submitted by France on Behalf of the EU to the 6th BWC RevCon. BWC/CONF.VI/WP.4. Geneva, October 20.

———. 2008. Statement to the 2nd CWC RevCon. RC-2/NAT.13. The Hague, April 7.

Fahmy, Nabil. 2006. "An Assessment of International Nuclear Nonproliferation Efforts after 60 Years." *Nonproliferation Review* 13 (1): 81–87.

Feakes, Daniel. 2008. "Getting Down to the Hard Cases: Prospects for CWC Universality." *Arms Control Today* 38 (2): 12–17.

Fischer, David. 1997. *History of the International Atomic Energy Agency: The First Forty Years*. Vienna: IAEA.

Fischer, Wolfgang. 2000. "Nuclear Non-proliferation and Safeguards: From INFCIRC/153 to INFCIRC/540 and Beyond." In *Tightening the Reins: Towards a Strengthened International Nuclear Safeguards System*, edited by Erwin Häckel and Gotthard Stein, 9–22. Berlin: Springer.

Gröning, Friedrich. Germany. 2006. Statement to the 6th BWC RevCon. Geneva, November 20.

Gualtieri, David S. 2003. "The System of Non-Proliferation Export Controls." In *Commitment and Compliance: The Role of Non-binding Norms in the International Legal System*, edited by Dinah Shelton, 467–86. Oxford: Oxford University Press.

Guthrie, Richard. 2008. "The 2008 Meeting of Experts: Biosecurity and Education." MX Report no. 1, BioWeapons Prevention Project, Geneva. www.bwpp.org/documents/MX%20Report1.pdf.

Guthrie, Richard, John Hart, Frida Kuhlau, and Jacqueline Simon. 2004. "Chemical and Biological Warfare Developments and Arms Control." In *SIPRI Yearbook 2004: Armaments, Disarmament and International Security*, 659–96. Oxford: Oxford University Press.

Hirsch, Theodore. 2004. "The IAEA Additional Protocol: What It Is and Why It Matters." *Nonproliferation Review* 11 (3): 140–66.

Horner, Daniel. 2011. "CWC Members Debate Inspection Distribution." *Arms Control Today* 41 (1): 50–52.

———. 2012. "Accord Reached on CWC's 2012 Deadline." *Arms Control Today* 42 (1): 38–40.

Hunger, Iris, and Nicolas Isla. 2006. "Confidence-Building Needs Transparency: An Analysis of the BTWC's Confidence-Building Measures." *Disarmament Forum* 2006 (3): 27–36.

Johnson, Rebecca. 2005. "Politics and Protection: Why the 2005 NPT Review Conference Failed." *Disarmament Diplomacy* 80. www.acronym.org.uk/dd/dd80/80npt.htm.

———. 2010. "Assessing the 2010 NPT Review Conference." *Bulletin of the Atomic Scientists* 66 (4): 1–10.

Joyner, Daniel H. 2005. "The Nuclear Suppliers Group: History and Functioning." *International Trade Law and Regulation* 11 (2): 33–42.

Kadhim, Abbas. 2006. "The Future of Nuclear Weapons in the Middle East." *Nonproliferation Review* 13 (3): 581–90.

Kelle, Alexander. 2003. "Strengthening the Effectiveness of the BTW Control Regime—Feasibility and Options. *Contemporary Security Policy* 24 (2): 95–132.

———. 2004. "Assessing the Effectiveness of Security Regimes—The Chemical Weapons Control Regime's First Six Years of Operation." *International Politics* 41 (2): 221–42.

Kenyon, Ian R. 2007. "Why We Need a Chemical Weapons Convention and an OPCW?" In Kenyon and Feakes 2007, 1–19.

Kenyon, Ian R., and Daniel Feakes, eds. 2007. *The Creation of the Organisation for the Prohibition of Chemical Weapons: A Case Study in the Birth of an Intergovernmental Organisation*. The Hague: T.M.C. Asser Press.

Kenyon, Ian R., and Sergei Kisselev. 2007. "Cooperation in Peaceful Uses: Article XI." In Kenyon and Feakes 2007, 249–60.

Khan, Masood. 2007. "The 2006 BWC Review Conference: The President's Reflections." *Disarmament Diplomacy* 84: 13–16.

Khoshro, G. Ali. Iran. 2003. Statement to the 1st CWC RevCon. The Hague, April 30.

Krause, Joachim. 2007. "Enlightenment and Nuclear Order." *International Affairs* 83 (3): 483–99.

Littlewood, Jez. 2005. *The Biological Weapons Convention: A Failed Revolution*. Aldershot: Ashgate.

Loosch, Reinhard. 2000. "From 'Programme 93+2' to Model Protocol INFCIRC/540: Negotiating for a Multilateral Agreement in the International Atomic Energy Agency." In *Tightening the Reins: Towards a Strengthened International Nuclear Safeguards System*, edited by Erwin Häckel and Gotthard Stein, 23–66. Berlin: Springer.

Lowitz, Donald. USA. 1986a. Statement to the 2nd BWC RevCon. BWC/CONF.II/SR.3. Geneva, September 18.

———. USA. 1986b. Statement to the 2nd BWC RevCon. BWC/ONF.II/SR.10. Geneva, October 1.

Manley, Ron G. 2007. "Preparing for Disarmament: Articles III, IV and V." In Kenyon and Feakes 2007, 139–78.

Meier, Oliver. 2008. "CWC Review Conference Avoids Difficult Issues." *Arms Control Today* 38 (4): 32–35.

Moher, Mark. Canada. 1996. Statement to the 4th BWC RevCon. Geneva, November 26.

Müller, Harald. 2003. "Germany and WMD Proliferation." *Nonproliferation Review* 10 (2): 1–20.

———. 2010. "Between Power and Justice: Current Problems and Perspectives of the NPT Regime." *Strategic Analysis* 34 (2): 189–201.

———. 2011. "A Nuclear Nonproliferation Test: Obama's Nuclear Policy and the 2010 NPT Review Conference." *Nonproliferation Review* 18 (1): 219–36.

Müller, Harald, David Fischer, and Wolfgang Kötter. 1994. *Nuclear Non-proliferation and Global Order*. Oxford: Oxford University Press.

NAM and China. 2008. Joint Statement by Cuba on Behalf of the NAM CWC States Parties and China to the 2nd CWC RevCon. The Hague, April 7.

Nasseri, Sirous. Iran. 1997. Statement to the 1st Session of the CWC CSP. The Hague, May 8.

OPCW. 2008. Note by the Technical Secretariat, Review of the Operation of the Chemical Weapons Convention since the First Review Conference. RC-2/S/1*. The Hague, March 31.

Pfirter, Rogelio. 2003. Opening Statement by the Director-General to the CWC CSP at Its 8th Session. C-8/DG.7. The Hague, October 20.

Price, Richard M. 1997. *The Chemical Weapons Taboo*. Ithaca: Cornell University Press.

Rademaker, Stephen G. USA. 2003. Statement to the 1st CWC RevCon. The Hague, April 28.

Rathbun, Nina Srinivasan. 2006. "The Role of Legitimacy in Strengthening the Nuclear Nonproliferation Regime." *Nonproliferation Review* 13 (2): 227–52.

Robinson, Julian Perry. 1998. "The Negotiations on the Chemical Weapons Convention: A Historical Overview." In *The New Chemical Weapons Convention—Implementation and Prospects*, edited by Michael Bothe, Natalino Ronzitti, and Allan Rosas, 17–36. The Hague: Kluwer Law International.

Rühle, Michael. 2007. "Enlightenment in the Second Nuclear Age." *International Affairs* 83 (3): 511–22.

Sano, Toshio. Japan. 2001. Statement to the 5th BWC RevCon. Geneva, November 19.

Schmidt, Fritz. 2000. "NPT Export Controls and the Zangger Committee." *Nonproliferation Review* 7 (3): 136–45.

Shah, Prakash. 2001. "International Co-operation in Chemical Trade: Has the Chemical Weapons Convention Helped?" *OPCW Synthesis*, April: 10–12.

Shaker, Mohamed I. 1980. *The Nuclear Non-Proliferation Treaty: Origin and Implementation, 1959–1979*. London: Oceana.

Simpson, John. 2001. "The 2000 NPT Review Conference." In *SIPRI Yearbook 2001: Armaments, Disarmament and International Security*, 487–502. Oxford: Oxford University Press.

Sims, Nicholas A. 1988. *The Diplomacy of Biological Disarmament: Vicissitudes of a Treaty in Force, 1975–85*. New York: St. Martin's Press.

———. 2001. *The Evolution of Biological Disarmament*. Oxford: Oxford University Press.

———. 2006. "Strengthening Structures for the Biological and Toxin Weapons Convention: Options for Remedying the Institutional Deficit." *Disarmament Forum* 2006 (3): 17–26.

———. 2009. *The Future of Biological Disarmament: Strengthening the Treaty Ban on Weapons*. London: Routledge.

Smithson, Amy E. 1998. *Rudderless: The Chemical Weapons Convention at 1 ½*. Henry L. Stimson Center Report no. 25. www.stimson.org/images/uploads/research-pdfs/Rudderless.pdf.

———. 2001. "U.S. Implementation of the CWC." In *The Chemical Weapons Convention: Implementation Challenges and Solutions*, edited by Jonathan B. Tucker, 23–29. Washington: Monterey Institute of International Studies.

Stock, Thomas. 1995. *History of the Negotiations on the CWC—Short Overview*. SIPRI-Saskatchewan-Frankfurt Research Group on Implementation of the Chemical Weapons Convention. Paper no. 13.

Strulak, Tadeusz. 1993. "The Nuclear Suppliers Group." *Nonproliferation Review* 1 (1): 2–10.

Tabassi, Lisa. 2007. "National Implementation: Article VII." In Kenyon and Feakes 2007, 205–21.

Trapp, Ralf. 2007. "The First Ten Years." In Kenyon and Feakes 2007, 261–89.

Tucker, Jonathan B., ed. 2000. *Toxic Terror: Assessing Terrorist Use of Chemical and Biological Weapons*. Cambridge: MIT Press.

———. 2004. "The BWC New Process: A Preliminary Assessment." *Nonproliferation Review* 11 (1): 26–39.

———. 2006. *War of Nerves: Chemical Warfare from World War I to Al-Qaeda*. New York: Pantheon Books.

———. 2007. "Verifying the Chemical Weapons Ban: Missing Elements." *Arms Control Today* 37 (1): 6–13.

———. 2009/2010. "The Future of Chemical Weapons." *New Atlantis*, no. 26, 3–29.

Üzümcü, Ahmet. 2010. Opening Statement by the Director-General to the CWC CSP at Its 15th Session. C-15/DG.14. The Hague, November 29.

US Department of State. 2005. *Adherence to and Compliance with Arms Control, Nonproliferation and Disarmament Agreements and Commitments*. Washington: US Department of State, August. www.state.gov/t/avc/rls/rpt/51977.htm.

———. 2010. *Adherence to and Compliance with Arms Control, Nonproliferation and Disarmament Agreements and Commitments*. Washington: US Department of State, July. www.state.gov/t/avc/rls/rpt/170924.htm.

Walker, Paul F. 2010. "Abolishing Chemical Weapons: Progress, Challenges, and Opportunities." *Arms Control Today* 40 (9): 22–30.

Westdal, Christopher. Canada. 2001. Statement to the 5th BWC RevCon. Geneva, November 19.

Wheelis, Mark, and Malcolm Dando. 2003. "Back to Bioweapons?" *Bulletin of the Atomic Scientists* 59 (1): 40–46.

Wheelis, Mark, Lajos Rózsa, and Malcolm Dando, eds. 2006. *Deadly Cultures: Biological Weapons since 1945*. Cambridge: Harvard University Press.

Yudin, Yury. 2010. *Multilateralization of the Nuclear Fuel Cycle: The Need to Build Trust*. Geneva: United Nations, UNIDIR.

Ziaran, Bozorgmehr. Iran. 2008. Statement to the 2nd CWC RevCon. The Hague, April 7.

Zilinskas, Raymond A. 2000. "Introduction." In *Biological Warfare: Modern Offense and Defense*, edited by Raymond A. Zilinskas, 1–10. Boulder: Lynne Rienner.

CHAPTER THREE

Humanitarian Arms Control

The Anti-Personnel Mine Ban Treaty, the Programme of Action on Small Arms and Light Weapons, and the Convention on Cluster Munitions

Simone Wisotzki

THE DECADE OF "HUMAN SECURITY" was in many respects constitutive for humanitarian arms control in the 1990s (Shaw, MacLean, and Black 2006, 3). The change in security policy perspectives that unfolded during this period encouraged new forms of arms control and disarmament. The 1997 Anti-Personnel Mine Ban Treaty (MBT), also called the Ottawa Convention, the 2001 Action Programme on Small Arms (PoA), and the 2008 Convention on Cluster Munitions (CCM) were established. These instruments seek to limit illicit transfers of arms, restrict their indiscriminate use, and deal with the deadly consequences of war. The three regimes share certain characteristics that have permitted a form change in arms control and disarmament. This is particularly relevant following the end of the Cold War, as states had to adjust their security policies while new directions had yet to be defined.

Humanitarian arms control means the development of new norms in the field of landmines, small arms, and cluster munitions that were negotiated outside existing institutions of international humanitarian law. Humanitarian arms control was the consequence of the misuse of weapons against civilians in internal state conflicts, but also of the dissatisfaction of many states with the norms of international humanitarian law (Green 2000, 17). The difference between humanitarian and WMD arms control becomes obvious by comparison. WMD arms control, while in part also motivated by the inhumane nature and consequences of nuclear, biological, and chemical weapons, focuses on preventing war and easing tension between states by limiting damage in the event of interstate war, and reducing the cost of arms, whereas humanitarian arms control was developed as a consequence of the indiscriminate use of weapons in intrastate conflicts. This applies to cluster munitions as well, which, while largely in the arsenals of states rather than nonstate actors, have been excessively employed in conflicts and leave behind the same dangerous legacy as antipersonnel mines. Humanitarian arms control seeks to prevent and reduce tension between people and to reduce criminal violence in postconflict situations. It extends beyond preventive efforts and includes activities in peace building and postconflict reconstruction, thus including a broad societal component. While it focuses on peoples' suffering through arms misuse, it also aims to assist states in reforming the security sector. As humanitarian arms control developed in close relation with the discourse on "human security," it attaches importance to the protection of civilians and the rehabilitation of victims of armed violence. Though it was motivated by the horrors of intrastate conflict, it binds states. It presents a landmark shift in priorities: classical humanitarian law had subordinated the humanitarian objective to military efficiency if the two values were at odds with each other, applying the principle of "as human as possible, as militarily efficient as necessary." Humanitarian arms control at least partly reverses these priorities.

Nevertheless, the three regimes of humanitarian arms control exhibit certain differences when their norm generation processes, normative contents, conflicts, and norm dynamics are compared. The PoA remains the most inclusive, universalized regime; consequently, it reveals serious norm conflicts among states that influenced its norm dynamics. In contrast, norm-building efforts in the MBT and the CCM were placed outside the routine arms control institutions, such as the Conference on Disarmament (CD) or the UN. While these norm-building processes ensured effective regimes, in the case of the MBT with an impact seen beyond the treaty's parties, they both lack universality.

THE ANTI-PERSONNEL MINE BAN TREATY

Why the Regime?

Even though the number of wars and victims thereof is in decline, armed conflicts of the twenty-first century continue to exhibit severe violence and the indiscriminate use of weapons against, or even the intentional targeting of, noncombatants. The brutalization of conflicts and the tendency to direct violence strategically against civilian populations provided strong motives for seeking new forms of arms control (Vines 1998, 118). Landmines—in particular antipersonnel landmines—were increasingly deployed in intrastate conflicts. These weapons were originally developed as tactical defensive weapons for conventional interstate warfare to reduce the mobility of opposing armies. Despite this they have been more commonly used in intrastate conflicts for offensive purposes, primarily to force civilian populations to leave their communities, thereby violating principles of international humanitarian law (Gard 1998, 136). Humanitarian aid organizations working in conflict zones were increasingly confronted with the effects of the indiscriminate use of mines against civilians, which left a complex problem once the conflict had ceased. The long-term consequences of this indiscriminate use of mines have proven highly detrimental to postwar reconstruction efforts. The vast human suffering and the costs of rehabilitation and rebuilding provided the incentive for taking action. Nongovernmental organizations (NGOs) responded by developing the idea of an arms control initiative that went beyond existing standards of international humanitarian law (Williams and Goose 1998; Faulkner 2007, 115).

The Convention on Certain Conventional Weapons (CCW) and its five protocols restrict, or ban, the use of weapons that cause disproportional injuries or target indiscriminately. The first effort to control antipersonnel mines (at the CCW Review Conference process in 1995–96) failed to provide effective solutions to the humanitarian crisis. When more than 120 states signed the Convention on the Prohibition of the Use, Stockpiling, Production and Transfer of Anti-Personnel Mines and on Their Destruction (MBT) in December 1997, an unprecedented diplomatic process in the realm of arms control and disarmament was brought to a successful conclusion. The so-called Ottawa Process was initiated and orchestrated by a small number of like-minded states (Austria, Belgium, Germany, Norway, the Netherlands, Ireland, Mexico, the Philippines, and South Africa) under the leadership of Canada, which organized a process of collective action that aimed to produce a comprehensive ban on antipersonnel mines (Cameron, Lawson, and Tomlin 1998, 160). The small- and middle-power initiative came as a reaction to the mounting pressure of the International Campaign to Ban Landmines (ICBL), which succeeded in changing global rhetoric in favor of a humanitarian solution. Canada initiated the Ottawa Process in December 1996 when it announced negotiations for concluding a comprehensive ban on antipersonnel mines (APMS) within one year. In an unusual diplomatic process, this small- and middle-power initiative materialized in the final negotiation round in September 1997 in Oslo. The MBT was opened for signature from December 1997 and entered into force on March 1, 1999.

The Normative Structure of the Regime

The MBT bans the production, export, and use of this category of weapons. APMS are defined in Art. 2 as "designed to be exploded by the presence, proximity or contact of a person and that will incapacitate, injure or kill one or more persons" (MBT 1997). This definition distinguishes APMS from antitank mines (ATM) not covered by the text of the treaty, which includes ATMS with antihandling devices that explode when someone tries to remove them.

Art. 4 regulates the problem of the remaining APM stockpiles: they must be destroyed within four years of accession to the treaty. The aim of clearing all remaining APMS in the world's minefields appears even more ambitious: in Art. 5 member states commit to clearing all mines within ten years. In general, states parties must ensure the destruction of APMS in all mined areas under their jurisdiction within this time frame. If a state is unable to achieve these treaty obligations, it may request an extension of up to ten years. Art. 6 of the Ottawa Convention requests international cooperation and assistance. This should guarantee donor support for heavily mined countries. Each state party may seek and receive assistance, either in the form of mine clearance equipment or personnel and financial support; upon request additional support should be provided for destroying remaining APM stockpiles. Donor assistance can also be requested for care and for social and economic rehabilitation of mine victims, as well as for mine awareness programs. Art. 6 reflects the distinct humanitarian character where arms control and disarmament aims coincide with norms of cooperation and assistance.

For ensuring implementation, Art. 7 foresees transparency measures, such as providing information about stockpiles, location of mined areas, or suspected mined territories. Contrary to other arms control and disarmament regimes, there is no solid verification system. If parties wish to clarify matters of compliance, Art. 8 provides for the possibility of requesting information through the UN secretary-general. In serious disputes, a special meeting of states parties can be convened that should make every effort to reach decisions by consensus. If further clarification is needed, either a meeting of states parties or a special meeting can authorize a "fact-finding mission" to visit the territory of the requested party. Art. 8 further specifies the rules under which foreign experts may ensure compliance through fact-finding missions. Furthermore, compliance is checked by other "soft" forms of verification: states parties must provide annual reports on the status of implementation, which are supplemented and put into a civil society perspective by the ICBL's annual "Landmine Monitor" (e.g., ICBL 2011).

Under Art. 20, the APM Convention foresees the possibility to withdraw from the convention. States involved in armed conflict cannot abandon the treaty as long as violence continues. This norm is to ensure that states do not break international humanitarian law by using APMs.

Regime Conflicts

Norm-binding efforts to ban APMs had pursued various venues until the MBT was signed in December 1997. Questions of procedural justice loomed large between the participating states. Critics of negotiations outside the UN system feared that their concerns would not be taken seriously, and that aspects of fairness would be subordinated to other considerations, such as effectiveness. A conflict also emerged over whether to achieve universality through compromise or effectively negotiate a total ban on this weapon category at the expense of certain states not joining the treaty. States pursued different venues such as a strengthened Protocol II under the CCW, which failed to truly ban APMs. The unprecedented negotiating process that the like-minded states deliberately established outside the UN institutions was decisive for negotiating a comprehensive ban. The legitimacy of this process was not undisputed among the states: The United States, Great Britain, Australia, and France, together with a number of other states, initially tried to launch a negotiating initiative parallel to the Ottawa Process within the framework of the CD. Their aim was to establish a regime that would merely impose a ban on the transfer of antipersonnel mines, arguing that this would effectively remedy the problem of indiscriminate use of APMs in intrastate conflicts. This form of negotiations best suited their national security interests. The attempt failed due to the ongoing blockade on negotiations at the CD (IDDS 1997, 5).

Conflict over Defining Antipersonnel Mines The small- and middle-power initiative—together with the ICBL—aimed at negotiating a comprehensive regime for banning the production, stockpiling, transfer, and use of APMs (Rutherford, Brem, and Matthew 2003; Rutherford 2009). Nevertheless, the question of whether a universal ban might be worthwhile, or whether it would be wiser to accept limitations on its overall effectiveness, became a contested issue. Norm conflicts occurred over various other aspects. The Ottawa Process experienced intense conflict over the definition of the antipersonnel mines that were to be banned. Here, the tension between humanitarian moral concerns and military interests became virulent. While ATMs were exempted from the negotiations right from the start, the question of whether humanitarian concerns or national security interests would prevail reappeared in the definition issue. To the displeasure of the ICBL and affected states, antivehicle mines with antihandling devices, although they pose deadly risks to noncombatants—in particular, to children—were exempted from the ban. In addition, the periods established for the destruction of stockpiles and deployed mines were prolonged over the course of negotiations. The first Austrian draft envisaged one year for the destruction of stockpiles and five years for deployed mines; in the final negotiating round participants acknowledged the need for extended deadlines to realistically reflect the justice concern of need and proportionality expressed by mine-affected countries. They argued that the burden of cleaning the mine-infested territory would imply intense efforts by the international community over a longer period of time. Short-term deadlines overtax the resources of the—mostly very poor—states most affected by mines and could induce the international community to phase out assistance once the deadline had been reached. Either consequence would increase the burden on the victim states. In the end, compromises in effectiveness had to be made to reconcile states' national security interests with broader moral and humanitarian concerns.

Bargaining on Exemptions: The United States at the Oslo Negotiations The US attitude vis-à-vis the Ottawa Process can be characterized as ambivalent. While the United States initially favored negotiations at the CD, it eventually decided to participate in the final round of negotiations at Oslo. While President Bill Clinton and the State Department sympathized with the Ottawa Process, the Pentagon argued against joining a potential ban on APMs. The United States Campaign to Ban Landmines (USCBL), the national branch of the International Campaign to Ban Landmines, managed to lobby prominent members of Congress to support their campaign. The most influential leadership from Capitol Hill came from Senator Patrick Leahy (Democrat), who years before had already established a War Victims Fund to provide assistance to victims of landmines.[1]

In Oslo, US delegation chief Eric Newsom announced his sincere intention "of negotiating in good faith a treaty we will be able to sign" (IDDS 1997, 708.B.26). The US Joint Chiefs of Staff had agreed to participation subject to five conditions: 1) strengthening the verification provisions of the treaty, 2) an exception for the use of APMs on the Korean peninsula, 3) a transition period of nine years for entry into force during which technical alternatives to antipersonnel mines had to be developed, 4) a clause of withdrawal for "supreme national interest," and 5) an exception for antipersonnel mines used with antitank mines (US 1997). While having the United States be a signatory to an APM ban would have strengthened its universality, these far-reaching exemptions would have seriously diminished the effectiveness of the treaty and subordinated compassion for the victims to military expediency. The US position reflected national security and military interests; the majority of like-minded states and supportive countries meanwhile perceived the issue as one of humanitarian concern. Moral norms enshrined in the "new humanitarianism" had become a sort of standard of appropriateness for the majority of states. Nevertheless, Canada and Germany were at some point willing to grant the US exemptions in order to achieve universality. In contrast, the affected countries and NGO networks rejected the superpower's claim of corresponding special privileges and instead stressed the aspect of fairness in negotiations and the UN Charter principle of sovereign equality, a principle enshrined in emphasizing that all member states have to be treated alike (Simpson 2004, 27). Granting an exemption to allow for technical progress would have favored the technologically advanced countries over the less developed ones. In the end, the United States withdrew from the negotiations.

Norm Dynamics in the Anti-Personnel Mine Ban Treaty

The record of implementation is mixed. On the one hand, an emerging taboo on the use and export of APMs has been established that even guides nonparties: major outsiders appear to have ceased transferring APMs, too (Price 1998). Nevertheless, the MBT has not achieved universality. Crucial states, such as the United States, Russia, China, Israel, several Arab states, and South Korea, have not acceded to the treaty. In contrast, and significantly so, most states with formerly or currently intense intrastate conflicts have acceded.

Of the 157 signatory states, 83 have destroyed their stocks, totaling 41.8 million antipersonnel mines (ICBL 2008b; MBT 2008). The state of affairs with regard to mine clearance is less straightforward. A large number of states were to have cleared all antipersonnel mines on their territory by September 2011. Bulgaria, El Salvador, Swaziland, and Macedonia can report success. Heavily mined states such as Bosnia-Herzegovina, Croatia, and Mozambique have not been able to meet the deadline. Furthermore, a number of Western states have also been lax in enforcing the regulations, including Denmark and Great Britain, which still has to clear mines on the Falkland Islands (ICBL 2008a). Meanwhile, 24 states that are seriously affected by mines have stated that they will be unable to meet the ten-year deadline due to lack of international support, including Afghanistan, Burundi, Eritrea, and the Democratic Republic of Congo. While mine clearance is progressing, there is still a shortage of funds for victim rehabilitation (MBT 2012).

Overall, norm conflicts did not inhibit the course of implementation. Regime dynamics were owed to a strong and steadily growing group of member states together with an agenda-setting NGO community. NGOs had already become a stakeholder in the negotiations and provided assistance to the implementation process. Remarkably, this alliance was strong enough to create an international norm against the will of some of the most powerful states. Despite the lack of universality, a certain taboo on producing, exporting, and using antipersonnel mines has developed even among nonmember states (Price 1998). This development and the continued mine-clearing efforts are the most remarkable dynamics of the APM regime since its establishment. It was the strengthening of the normative framework rather than additional norms that characterized the form of the particular norm dynamics.

THE PROGRAMME OF ACTION ON SMALL ARMS AND LIGHT WEAPONS

Why the Regime?

Despite the reduction in the number of conflicts, the illicit proliferation of small arms and light weapons (SALW) remains a global problem with significant consequences for affected states and civil society.[2] The international community is faced with a tremendous task in view of an estimated 875 million SALW in illicit circulation worldwide (SAS 2011, 116). These weapons are the most important instruments of violence to terrorize civilians in intrastate conflicts. The deliberate misuse of SALW in armed conflicts and forms of criminal violence in postconflict situations violate international humanitarian law and core principles of human rights. Some 500,000 people die every year from bullet wounds, 300,000 are victims of intrastate conflicts, and a further 200,000 are victims of violent crime or kill themselves using pistols or rifles (SAS 2003).[3]

The illicit proliferation of SALW is not an immediate cause of conflict but provides the potential for escalating existing tensions. Weapons cross borders in the crisis regions of Africa due to poorly trained police, border guards, and custom agents and the lack of transfer and border controls, and pass from one zone of conflict to the next. Without postconflict disarmament, demobilization, and reintegration (DDR) programs, remaining SALW endanger human security, increase the risk of renewed fighting by up to 44 percent, and result in high levels of criminal violence and massive human rights violations (IANSA 2006). When huge numbers of SALW remain in societies, they hinder peace consolidation and obviate the objectives of successful development aid and cooperation. In regions of fragile statehood the correlation between state failure and large numbers of weapons has been observed (Byman and van Evera 1998). The problem of illicit trafficking of SALW can be related to demand and supply-driven determinants. The demand for arms control of SALW intensified in the aftermath of 9/11 because of the link between terrorism and small-arms proliferation: nonstate stakeholders in Afghanistan and Iraq repeatedly deployed man-portable air defense systems (MANPADS) against the allied forces (Wisotzki 2009a). MANPADS also pose a threat to civilian air traffic.

Demand for SALW is stimulated primarily by the complex of fragile statehood, economic deprivation, conflicts over resources, and growing regionalization and transnationalization of armed violence. On the supply side, various forms of the globalized trade in small arms matter. A major part of the illicit trade of SALW, especially in sub-Saharan Africa, dates back to the Cold War when the United States and the Soviet Union supported their allies with military aid and weapons (Laurance 1998, 22). After 1989, following the reduction in conventional armies of the former Warsaw Pact and the North Atlantic Treaty Organization (NATO), surplus weapons reached conflict regions on direct or indirect routes (Volman 1998, 150–62). The global, legal state trade in SALW reportedly accounts for eight million small arms per year (SAS 2003, 98). The legal trade frequently turns into a supply channel for illicit trafficking, as the supply of Chinese SALW to Zimbabwe in April 2008 demonstrated.[4] Manufacturing states often grant licenses to states with lax export controls. Germany licensed G3 fabrication to Saudi Arabia, while the Libyan opposition identified newly produced G36 small arms in confiscated weapons stocks of former Gaddafi regime forces.[5]

The Normative Structure of the Regime

Due to legitimate security interests of states needing weapons for police and armed forces, a complete ban on SALW was never considered; this reflects the UN Charter that emphasizes the right to self-defense in Art. 51 and in Art. 2.7 exempts from interference "matters which are essentially within the domestic jurisdiction of any state" to which police matters belong. Nevertheless, the politically binding 2001 PoA sets out to tackle the problem of *illicit trafficking* of SALW through a variety of strategies (UN 1997, 1999). It was agreed by the UN General Assembly (UNGA), calling on states to establish preventive and reactive measures to stop the uncontrolled and unrestricted proliferation of SALW. The PoA combines measures of humanitarian arms control with legitimate security interests of states. In Art. III.1 the PoA recognizes that the primary responsibility for solving the illicit trade in SALW falls on all states. Nevertheless, Art. III states that the illicit proliferation of SALW also calls for civil society action, such as awareness programs and improved health and medical systems (see UNODA 2012).

The aim of the Action Programme is to tackle the causes of the demand for and supply of small arms. Measures for fighting illicit proliferation of SALW are pursued through various initiatives at the global, regional, and state levels, such as establishing national contact points and coordination agencies for facilitating interstate cooperation, particularly between donor and recipient countries. These norms are enhanced by assistance measures that are typical of humanitarian arms control. The PoA requests the provision of technical and financial aid to states that are particularly affected by SALW proliferation.

While the legitimate possession of SALW by police and military forces is acknowledged, the PoA calls on states to review state-owned stocks of SALW. Surplus stocks held by police and military forces are to be destroyed instead of being sold to third parties. Moreover, states are asked to improve stockpile security of their legitimately held SALW arsenals to prevent illicit trafficking and to adopt adequate laws, regulations, and administrative procedures to exercise effective control over the production and transfer of SALW. Weapons exports should include reliable end-user certificates. In cases of retransfer, the importing country should notify the state of the weapons' origin. Illegal SALW production, possession, trade, and transfer should be made punishable. National legislation should regulate activities of nonstate arms brokers and impose penalties on illicit brokering. Licensed manufacturers of SALW must apply reliable marking systems on the weapons produced. States should, furthermore, set up comprehensive record-keeping systems on the manufacture, holding, and transfer of SALW.

Regional cooperation should be improved. For example, national regulations governing the transfer of small arms should be coordinated and harmonized under regional arms control agreements. At the global level, the PoA stresses the need for all states to comply with UN arms embargoes. It highlights the importance of DDR processes in postconflict situations, including the destruction of SALW collected. The PoA has no verification mechanism. Compliance was originally monitored through an annual report; since 2010 a biannual reporting scheme exists as well as biennial meetings of states (BMS) parties, where the implementation status of participating states is evaluated. The states met in 2003, 2005, 2008, and 2010 to present a status report on the progress made in implementing the Action Programme (Kytömäki and Yankey-Wayne 2003; Garcia 2006). The first review conference (RevCon) on the PoA took place in 2006, and the second review conference, held in August/September 2012, concluded with a consensual outcome document (UN 2012).

The PoA contains certain justice elements. According to the principle of equality, all states must review their legal stocks of small arms, close legal gaps, and present regular reports on implementation of the Action Programme. In addition, the PoA takes into account the principle of proportionality and the varying needs of member states. Accordingly, it contains norms and rules for handling small arms in postwar processes: the focus here is on DDR programs. Weak states affected by the proliferation of small arms may receive assistance from donor countries.

Regime Conflicts

Norm-building efforts to control the illicit trafficking of SALW were impeded by states focusing on their legitimate security interests in producing, transferring, and using SALW. Coupled with these security interests were differences in the perception of justice concerns, mainly between Western states and countries from the Southern Hemisphere. This led to conflicts and continues to overshadow implementation. Norm conflicts also appeared due to the hybrid character of humanitarian and justice concerns, as well as the respective national interests of the participating states: in practice, justice concerns often intermingle with states' interests.

Questions of Definitions: Illicit and Legal Trade in SALW Conflicts arose over how best to define SALW and whether to include ammunition in the agreement. States quarreled about the term *illicit trafficking* in SALW and the related question of who is to be held responsible for the illegal proliferation of SALW. Questions over whether prevention of illicit trade should also cover legal, state-to-state transfers and whether this should result in a global norm on restricting SALW exports became particularly contested. The Non-Aligned Movement (NAM), particularly African members, stressed the responsibility of producing countries for restricting their legal trade and for refraining from arming nonstate actors with SALW. A group of states, led by the United States, countered that the legal trade in SALW, including to nonstate agents, had to be seen as a national prerogative.

Norm conflicts over the question of defining the term *illicit* also occurred among Western democracies. From a US perspective, global norms should not interfere with national security policy aims and not restrict arming oppositional forces in support of democratic regime change. In contrast, certain European Union (EU) states favored a broad definition that also included aspects of legal trade. Moreover, they supported norms on export controls, pointing to their 1998 Joint Action on SALW and the EU Code of Conduct on Arms Transfer as reference.

Justice Concerns vs. National Sovereignty Norm conflicts also occurred regarding Art. 51 of the UN Charter (the right to self-defense). In 2001, Arab states and also India, Pakistan, Iran, and Israel began to stress and continue to emphasize throughout the biennial meetings of states that states' rights to self-defense were of utmost importance. Norms that might infringe on that principle failed to gain their support. In BMS-4 in 2010 they blocked any attempts to formulate common, global border control standards to curb cross-border illicit SALW trafficking. Pakistan and Cuba argued on the same grounds against EU efforts to make the instrument on marking and tracing of SALW legally binding.

The United States refused to accept regulating the civilian possession of weapons, expressing domestic concerns over regulation of arms ownership that would be in violation of the Second Amendment to the US Constitution (Wisotzki 2009b). Due to the consensus principle, these norms and provisions were left out of the PoA. African states perceived this as unjust on substantive grounds since they identified civilian possession as a core source of illicit SALW trafficking. Therefore, they saw it as a serious weakness of the program, which is only politically binding. However, only the United States provoked norm conflicts during the negotiating processes. National interests also determined China's refusal to include in the PoA preamble a norm against the violation of human rights resulting from the misuse of weapons. The NAM states, on the other hand, insisted on emphasizing the connection between small arms disarmament and nuclear disarmament in the preamble to the PoA but failed in the face of opposition from the five permanent UNSC members (P5). Recipient countries often stressed their concern that the request for assistance was the prerogative of affected countries and should not be conditioned on certain criteria by the international donor community.

Remedying the PoA's Normative Weaknesses: Failure of the 2006 Review Conference Norm conflicts broke out again at the first RevCon in 2006 over the issue of tackling the program's normative weaknesses. Here too, the United States refused to agree to common standards of transfer controls, restrictions on arms transfers to nonstate actors, and the regulation of civilian possession of weapons. The future of the PoA was at stake when the United States also objected to further state meetings to continue implementing the program. In the end, the first RevCon closed without a final document, further undermining the Action Programme (Taylor 2006, 46; Wisotzki 2009a). However, the PoA process was re-established through an initiative of supportive states in the First Committee of the UN General Assembly. As demonstrated, norm conflicts in the case of the PoA exhibit hybrid characteristics of pursuing interests as well as justice-related motives.

Norm Dynamics in the Programme of Action on Small Arms and Light Weapons

Conflicts during negotiations on the PoA also affected its implementation and attempts at further norm generation. Despite normative loopholes in the PoA, states avoided renewed efforts to close the gaps such as insisting on norms for domestic gun control or banning transfer to nonstate actors. Norm conflicts during negotiations, notably US prioritization of domestic norms over international concerns, affected the norm dynamics of the PoA, as they inhibited further attempts at normative strengthening during the 2006 RevCon. Moreover, the breadth of the normative action program to tackle the illicit proliferation of SALW made it hard to identify priorities, time frames, and core aims for implementing the PoA. Over the course of the four biennial meetings of states, agreement among the stakeholders was reached to concentrate on certain thematic issues in order to achieve a better understanding of progress and deficiencies while implementing the action program. The implementation process nevertheless suffers from the overall weakness of the PoA. There is no obligation to act and no means to assess progress in implementation.

The discrepancies between the extensive reports (584) presented by states and the measures that they had actually introduced became apparent at the 2006 RevCon. For example, 102 countries stated that they were attending to the security of state stockpiles and had relevant standards and procedures. Yet only 30 states have reviewed or improved these standards. In weak states, poorly paid soldiers and police officers use stockpiles for financial gain; some of the national reports are obviously not reliable. The weaknesses of the PoA also became apparent in the field of transfer controls; global standards that could serve as a guide are absent. The number of disarmament processes appears inadequate as well: only 62 states have conducted SALW disarmament, 73 have destroyed surplus weapons (BtB 2007, 3). At BMS-4 in 2010, UN Institute for Disarmament Research (UNIDIR) and Small Arms Survey (SAS) studies revealed a serious implementation shortfall: of 151 national points of contact, only 51 could be verified.

On the other hand, the UN arena provided ample opportunities to address issues through expert panels or working groups. Recommendations, resolutions, or even new instruments to limit illicit trafficking in SALW were negotiated in parallel to the existing PoA, rather than opening the program itself for any further normative improvements. SALW arms control is evolving more and more as a gradually thickening network of different norms, rules, regulations, and institutions is being established at not only the global but also the regional and subregional levels. On December 5, 2005, the "International Instrument to Enable States to Identify and Trace, in a Timely and Reliable Manner, Illicit Small Arms and Light Weapons" (UNGA 2005) (International Tracing Instrument, ITI) was adopted. With the politically binding ITI, states have agreed to verify the implementation process for marking and tracing at the BMS of the

PoA (Parker 2010, 1). Also in 2005, a Group of Governmental Experts convened to consider further steps to enhance international cooperation in combating illicit brokering of SALW. They recommended a set of measures to strengthen national legislation and advance international cooperation. Two further groups of UN experts have been charged with preparing solutions to important subissues of uncontrolled small arms proliferation. The UN Group of Experts that is to draft recommendations for dealing with surplus conventional ammunition stockpiles met under German chairmanship in the first half of 2008. Incidents in Mozambique in March 2007 and in Albania one year later made it clear that munitions stockpiles represent a danger to civilians. In addition, current efforts to negotiate an Arms Trade Treaty emerged from the normative weakness of the PoA. Because covering the legal trade of SALW in the PoA had led to norm conflicts, only general provisions regarding legal transfers were included. Another UN Group of Experts deliberated over global standards for controls on the transfer of conventional weapons. After four Preparatory Commissions (PrepComs), final negotiations for a legally binding Arms Trade Treaty took place in summer of 2012 but did not manage to achieve a treaty by consensus.

Regional approaches to SALW control are also part of related norm dynamics. Two reasons for the increasing relevance of regional and subregional arms control can be noted: First, such efforts seek to address specific regional problems related to SALW such as criminal gang violence or domestic possession of SALW. Second, regional approaches close normative gaps the PoA is unable to address. The Economic Community of West African States (ECOWAS) Protocol on the Proliferation of Small Arms and Light Weapons banned the transfer of SALW to nonstate actors in the West African region, while the 2004 Nairobi Protocol also subjects the private possession of weapons to new legislative procedures in the Great Lakes region and the Horn of Africa.

THE CONVENTION ON CLUSTER MUNITIONS

Why the Regime?

Cluster bombs and cluster munitions have an indiscriminate effect similar to that of APMS but are usually deployed in interstate wars. Since the end of World War II, cluster munitions have been used in approximately twenty-five military conflicts—for example, by the United States in Vietnam, but also in wars in the 1990s and the early 2000s: in the Second Gulf War in 1991, by NATO forces in

Kosovo, as well as in Afghanistan. According to estimates, about two million cluster bomblets were dropped during the last Iraq War alone. Cluster bombs are an important means of tactical air warfare to avoid own-side casualties and are cost efficient. Their use contradicts core principles of international humanitarian law, as they cannot distinguish between combatants and civilians. The submunitions of cluster bombs have a 10 to 15 percent failure rate, making them a threat to people long after conflicts cease.

Cluster munitions are more deadly than antipersonnel mines. Even modern types of cluster munitions with a self-destructing mechanism can fail, as incidents in Lebanon have shown. In the 2006 war against Hezbollah, Israel dropped an estimated 2.8 to 4 million cluster bomblets over Lebanon—Hezbollah also used these weapons against Israel. In Afghanistan, the number of submunitions in the war against the Taliban is estimated at approximately 40,000 pieces of unexploded ordnance—this is a humanitarian catastrophe in a country that is also contaminated with antipersonnel mines. Nevertheless, vast media coverage of the two recent cases of intense cluster munitions usage has raised public awareness. This helped to accelerate momentum for norm-building efforts.

As in the case of the campaign against APMs, states had previously tried to establish legal provisions for the use of cluster bombs within the framework of international humanitarian law (IHL). The use of cluster munitions violates two core principles of IHL: the prohibition on inflicting unnecessary suffering as well as the prohibition on indiscriminate attack.

In principle, Protocol I of the 1949 Geneva Convention implies a ban on the use of cluster munitions. In November 2003, the parties to the CCW negotiated Protocol V on the marking and clearance of explosive remnants of war. This new international legal norm entered into effect in November 2006 and has in the meantime been ratified by twenty-three states. However, Protocol V does not include any general provisions banning the use of cluster munitions (Justen 2007, 1–4; van Woudenberg 2007, 455). Parallel to the Oslo Process that led to the CCM, efforts were made under the framework of the CCW to establish a negotiating mandate. Similar attempts had been made on several occasions in the preceding twenty-five years (Borrie 2009, 183). Such efforts served the interests of certain states that wished to indicate their humanitarian concern while refraining from a legally binding ban. This initiative finally failed in November 2011 when states were once again unable to reconcile their disputes over key elements of a draft protocol on cluster munitions (Zughni 2011).

The elements of success for the CCM are similar to those of the MBT: the international campaign against cluster bombs was initiated in November 2003 with the aim of initiating a ban.[6] The transnational NGO campaign lobbied for a ban and received support from the EU Parliament, which passed a resolution in October 2004 calling upon EU member states to observe voluntary moratoriums and to work for a global ban on cluster bombs. In late 2005, Belgium, Norway, and Austria were the first states to promote a ban. Following the disappointing results of the Protocol V negotiations in the CCW, Norway initiated the Oslo Process in February 2007. Like the MBT, negotiations on a cluster munitions ban were scheduled outside the scope of routine UN disarmament forums. A core group consisting of Austria, Ireland, the Holy See, Mexico, New Zealand, Norway, and Peru served as a steering committee for drafting the convention. To counter the bias toward Western industrialized nations, they organized regional meetings to universalize the normative effort. The initial Oslo Declaration had been signed by 46 states. After five rounds of negotiation, the process was brought to a successful end on May 30, 2008, when 107 states signed the convention in Dublin, Ireland. Meanwhile, 66 states have ratified the CCM, which entered into force on August 1, 2010 (Borrie 2009; CCM 2012b).

The Normative Structure of the Regime

The central provision of the CCM, Art. 1, stipulates that the production, stockpiling, use, and transfer of all cluster munitions are prohibited in all circumstances, including international conflicts and intrastate conflicts. It is also prohibited to assist, encourage, or induce anyone to engage in any activity forbidden by the convention. The ban on assistance makes it illegal for any financial institution to invest in companies that manufacture cluster munitions. Art. 2 of the CCM defines cluster munitions as conventional munitions designed to disperse or release explosive submunitions, each weighing less than twenty kilograms, and includes those explosive submunitions in the definition. The definition exempts weapons that have submunitions but are not considered cluster munitions, such as weapons with submunitions designed for smoke, flare, and electronic countermeasures. Art. 3 stipulates that stockpiles of cluster munitions should be destroyed as soon as possible but not later than eight years after entry into force of the convention. Clearance and destruction of cluster munitions remnants should be completed within ten years (Art. 4). States not able to reach this goal can ask for financial and technical assistance.

Like the MBT, the CCM took *individual* security into account by including an article on victim rehabilitation. The treaty included principles of justice: proportionality, recognition of particular needs, and compensation. For example, the "polluter pays principle" applies to the clearance of cluster munitions and the obligation to provide comprehensive assistance to states on whose territory these weapons were deployed. Moreover, donor countries are called upon to provide comprehensive technical and financial support and to take into account the socioeconomic rehabilitation of the mined areas.

Art. 7 stipulates transparency measures. Each state party should report to the UN secretary-general its national implementation measures and the total numbers and characteristics of cluster munitions in stock, including those produced before the convention entered into force. Information on cluster munition–contaminated areas and the national resources allocated to enhancing effective international cooperation are also to be provided. Art. 8 regulates facilitation and clarification of compliance issues; similar to the Ottawa Convention, the Oslo Treaty forgoes a detailed verification system. RevCons are held on the status of implementation at five-year intervals.

Regime Conflicts

The CCM was deliberately negotiated outside the UN system to facilitate a complete ban on certain categories of weapons (Borrie et al. 2009). While this process guaranteed an effective regime, it diminished the chances of universality and raised questions about fairness. Inter alia, China, India, Iran, Israel, Pakistan, Russia, and the United States shun the Oslo negotiations and have not joined the convention so far. Instead, they spared no effort to seek an alternative solution within the framework of the CCW. For the Oslo Process, these efforts have created complications and conflicts.

Defining Cluster Munitions The conflict between humanitarian views and tangible military interests came into focus in the dispute over definitions. At the beginning of the CCM negotiation process, Norway provided a broad definition of a ban on only those cluster munitions that cause unacceptable harm to civilians, leaving the decision about a more precise definition open until a later stage of the process. In the course of negotiations, certain like-minded states, such as Australia, Canada, France, Germany, Japan, the Netherlands, Sweden, and Switzerland, insisted that sensor-fused cluster munitions with a failure rate of less than 1 percent should not be banned. Some of these states relied on arguments underlining political equity (Borrie 2009, 214). They stressed that, contrary to the majority of states not possessing any of these weapons, their military forces relied on relatively "safe" cluster munitions; this argument implicitly favored technologically advanced countries. The issue of "good" versus "bad" cluster bombs also dominated the negotiations on an alternative protocol under the CCW.

At the meeting in Lima in May 2007 states at first agreed to exempt certain types of weapons with sophisticated submunitions using sensor-fusing technology. A new approach was taken at the next meeting in Vienna where cluster munitions were at first banned completely; yet when defining cluster munitions in greater detail under Art. 2, certain exemptions could be envisaged, although states had to make persuasive efforts to gain the support of others (Borrie 2009, 186). Nevertheless, the fifteen like-minded states seeking to exempt "smart" cluster munitions faced increasing opposition from developing countries and affected states, such as Lebanon. A study undertaken by the NGO network Cluster Munition Coalition on the M-85 cluster bombs used in Lebanon supported the view that submunitions with self-destruction mechanisms had a higher failure rate than officially acknowledged. The argument of "relative safety" was countered by the majority of states, as was the argument of "political equity." Some compromise was achieved in the final negotiation round at Dublin when a weight criterion was introduced that ensured banning cluster munitions with considerable humanitarian effect while exempting certain forms of sensor-fused munitions (Borrie 2009, 252). Paragraph 2c finally specified which types of cluster munitions are not covered by the ban: those containing fewer than ten explosive submunitions, any of which must weigh less than four kilograms and be equipped with an electronic self-destruction mechanism.

The Conflict over Interoperability Absent from the Oslo Process, the United States tried to influence the like-minded states. For US allies, interoperability caused concern and conflict. Whether parties can cooperate with nonmembers still using APMs in joint military operations had already become an issue under the MBT. While the APM ban included certain legal loopholes concerning the issue, the United States sought to ensure that a potential ban on cluster munitions would anticipate a norm regulating interoperability between members and nonmembers in military alliances. The United States, but also other allies such as Australia, Canada, Germany, Japan, and the United Kingdom, reiterated that cluster munitions were more likely to be used than APMs, as they were perceived as more relevant from a military point of view. A legally workable solution for interoperability became a relevant prerequisite for these states to join in supporting the ban. Norway (despite being a NATO member), the International Committee of the Red Cross (ICRC), and the Cluster Munition Coalition contested the assumption that cluster munitions continued to be of military utility despite the humanitarian harm they cause, or that exemptions should be allowed (Borrie 2009, 211).

At the final negotiation round in Dublin, a compromise was drafted under Swiss leadership in small-group and bilateral consultations. This nevertheless raised fairness concerns among the affected states that complained about the perceived exclusiveness of these talks. A new article, Art. 21/3, was introduced in the text. It stipulates that states parties may cooperate in military alliances with states not party to the convention, even though these activities may violate the rules of the CCM and involve the use of cluster bombs.

Norm Dynamics in the Convention on Cluster Munitions

The CCM is the latest treaty among the efforts of humanitarian arms control. Nevertheless, two meetings of states parties took place in 2010 in Laos and in 2011 in Lebanon where the implementation process was organized in greater detail, through common action plans, model legislation, and assistance provisions (see CCM 2012a). Similar to the MBT, NGOs assist in verifying the convention.[7]

Norm conflicts have not affected the implementation process of the CCM so far. While much has been learned about how to assist mine-infested countries through the implementation process of the MBT, similar problems, such as setting realistic time frames for clearing territories of the remnants of war, might only occur when the implementation process of the CCM proceeds further.

CONCLUSION: NORM DYNAMICS TRAPPED BETWEEN COSMOPOLITAN SOLIDARITY AND NATIONAL SOVEREIGNTY

In humanitarian arms control, regime dynamics follow different paths. In the case of antipersonnel mines and cluster munitions, conflicts over the adequate arena for negotiations dominated the agenda-setting stage. Once these were settled, additional conflicts arose mainly over definitions, membership, cooperation, and assistance. These conflicts nevertheless did not influence further evolution of the APM ban and the CCM and their implementation processes. In the end, the bans on mines and cluster munitions provided both regimes with unambiguous norms that facilitated the implementation process. The effectiveness of the two regimes is admittedly diminished by their lack of universality because important and powerful states have not yet become members. However, at least when it comes to the use and export of antipersonnel mines, a certain taboo has been established. Moreover, regime dynamics in both cases reflect characteristics of cosmopolitan solidarity up to a certain degree, as global efforts to clear mine-infested terrain have been considerably increased since the establishment of the MBT.

For SALW, the relationship between norm/regime conflicts and regime dynamics is more complex. On the one hand, conflicts over norms ended in deleting the contested proposals due to the consensus principle at the UN but moved efforts and initiatives undertaken at the regional level to control SALW forward. On the other hand, the PoA has become an Action Programme with considerable normative loopholes. Most importantly, normative weakness is intensified by a tenuous implementation process. The fragility of the PoA became apparent when the first RevCon ended in 2006 without a final document because of the tenacious resistance of the United States, led by John Bolton, which initially left the global arms control process at a precarious impasse. Regime dynamics in the case of the PoA also consist of global efforts to remedy normative weaknesses and close loopholes, such as the instruments on marking and tracing, brokerage, or ammunition control demonstrate. Moreover, regime dynamics are reflected in regional efforts to strengthen SALW arms control.

Generally speaking, justice concerns have played a prominent role in humanitarian arms control. Aspects of procedural justice addressing inclusiveness emerged in the Ottawa and Oslo Processes, respectively. While norm-building efforts at the CD or CCW would have been more inclusive and guaranteed increased fairness, such efforts would have failed in terms of effectively banning weapons without exemptions. Concerns about procedural justice also emerge in inclusive processes such as in the PoA. States complain that negotiations often take place in bilateral or small group consultations with the chairman in closed settings held in camera. While this procedure again furthers effectiveness, to a certain degree it compromises the legitimacy of the negotiation process. Concerns over substantial justice came to the forefront during debate over definitions, notably the issue of how burdens are to be distributed. Neither in the MBT nor in the CCM were exemptions made for "smart" mines or cluster munitions that would have favored industrialized states included in the treaty. In the case of the PoA, in particular the African, Latin American, and European states continue to insist that efforts aimed at curbing illicit trafficking in SALW must also encompass the legal trade. Whether this aspect of placing the burden of tackling the global trade equally on all states will succeed in the negotiations on an inclusive, comprehensive, and eventually even legally binding Arms Trade Treaty is yet to be determined.

Notes

1. Mary Wareham dates Leahy's engagement back to a personal experience with landmine victims during a visit to Honduras. See Wareham (1998, 213).

2. Small arms (and light weapons) are considered to be "any man-portable lethal weapon that expels or launches, is designed to expel or launch, or may be readily converted to expel or launch a shot, bullet or projectile by the action of an explosive" (UNGA 2005, 2). Whenever the term *small arms* is referred to in this chapter, the intended meaning is "small arms and light weapons."

3. These figures are based on estimates; reliable numbers are not available as a result of weapons traded illegally and gaps in the statistics on violent crime in numerous countries.

4. See "China's Arms Sales to Zimbabwe: Fact Sheet," Human Rights First, http://www.humanrightsfirst.org/wp-content/uploads/pdf/080428-CAH-china-zimbab-arms-fs.pdf.

5. Germany recently exported G36 to Egypt. Whether there is a connection between Egypt and the Libyan case has yet to be proved.

6. In the meantime the campaign includes more than 250 nongovernmental organizations from 70 countries (CMC 2012).

7. The Landmine and Cluster Munition Monitor is an initiative providing research for the International Campaign to Ban Landmines (ICBL) and the Cluster Munition Coalition (CMC). See www.the-monitor.org.

References

Borrie, John. 2009. *Unacceptable Harm: A History of How the Treaty to Ban Cluster Munitions Was Won.* Geneva: UNIDIR (United Nations Institute for Disarmament Research).

Borrie, John, Maya Brehm, Silvia Cattaneo, and David Atwood. 2009. "Learn, Adapt, Succeed: Potential Lessons from the Ottawa and Oslo Processes for Other Disarmament and Arms Control Challenges." *Disarmament Forum* 2009 (1–2): 19–25.

Brem, Stefan, and Kendall Stiles, eds. 2009. *Cooperating without America: Theories and Case Studies of Non-Hegemonic Regimes*. London: Routledge.

BtB (Biting the Bullet Project). 2007. "Global Implementation of the PoA." Biting the Bullet Project, International Alert, Saferworld and University of Bradford. http://web.archive.org/web/20080720081412/http://www.international-alert.org/pdfs/BtB_global.pdf.

Byman, Daniel, and Stephen van Evera. 1998. "Why They Fight: Hypotheses on the Causes of Contemporary Deadly Conflict." *Security Studies* 7 (3): 1–50.

Cameron, Maxwell A., Robert J. Lawson, and Brian W. Tomlin, eds. 1998. *To Walk without Fear: The Global Movement to Ban Landmines*. Oxford: Oxford University Press.

CCM (Convention on Cluster Munitions). 2012a. "The Convention on Cluster Munitions—CCM." www.clusterconvention.org/.

———. 2012b. "Convention Status." www.clusterconvention.org/ratifications-and-signatures.

CMC (Cluster Munitions Coalition). 2012. "Our Fight: The Cluster Munitions Coalition." www.clusterbombs.org/our-fight/la-coalition-internationale-contre-les-sous-munitions.

Faulkner, Frank. 2007. *Moral Entrepreneurs and the Campaign to Ban Landmines*. Amsterdam: Rodopi.

Garcia, Denise. 2006. *Small Arms and Security: New Emerging International Norms*. London: Routledge.

Gard, Robert G. 1998. "The Military Utility of Anti-Personnel Mines." In Cameron, Lawson, and Tomlin 1998, 136–57.

Green, Leslie C. 2000. *The Contemporary Law of Armed Conflict*. Manchester: Manchester University Press.

IANSA (International Action Network on Small Arms). 2006. Position Paper for the PrepCom for the UN Conference to Review Progress Made in the Implementation of the PoA. New York, January 9–20.

ICBL (International Campaign to Ban Landmines). 2008a. "Backgrounder: Impending Treaty Deadlines for Mine Clearance." ICBL News Articles, April 2. www.icbl.org/index.php/icbl/Library/News-Articles/Work/treaty-deadlines-bckgr.

———. 2008b. "Backgrounder: Stockpile Destruction." ICBL News Articles, April 2. www.icbl.org/index.php/icbl/Library/News-Articles/Work/SD-bckgr/.

———. 2011. *Landmine Monitor 2011*. www.the-monitor.org/index.php/publications/display?url=lm/2011/.

IDDS (Institute for Defense and Disarmament Studies). 1997. *Arms Control Reporter*. Cambridge.

Justen, Detlev. 2007. *Streumunition im Visier des Völkerrechts*, SWP-Aktuell 51. www.swp-berlin.org/fileadmin/contents/products/aktuell/2007A51_jst_ks.pdf.

Kytömäki, Elli, and Valerie Yankey-Wayne. 2003. *Implementing the United Nations Programme of Action on Small Arms and Light Weapons: Analysis of the Reports Submitted by States in 2003*. Geneva: United Nations, UNIDIR.

Laurance, Edward J. 1998. *Light Weapons and Intrastate Conflict: Early Warning Factors and Preventive Action*. A Report to the Carnegie Commission on Preventing Deadly Conflict. Washington: Carnegie Corporation of New York.

MBT (Mine Ban Treaty). 1997. *Convention on the Prohibition of the Use, Stockpiling, Production and Transfer of Anti-Personnel Mines and on Their Destruction*. www.apminebanconvention.org/fileadmin/pdf/mbc/text_status/Ottawa_Convention_English.pdf.

———. 2008. "Stockpiled Mines Destroyed by the States Parties." February 1. www.apminebanconvention.org/fileadmin/pdf/mbc/text_status/StockpiledMinesDestroyed-ByStateParty-Feb2008.pdf.

———. 2012. "Assisting the Victims." www.apminebanconvention.org/en/background-status-of-the-convention/assisting-the-victims/.

Parker, Sarah. 2010. "National Implementation of the United Nations Small Arms Programme of Action and the International Tracing Instrument: An Analysis of Reporting in 2009–10." Working Paper no. 8, Small Arms Survey, Geneva.

Price, Richard. 1998. "Reversing the Gun Sights: Transnational Civil Society Targets Land Mines." *International Organization* 52 (3): 613–44.

Rutherford, Kenneth. 2009. "The Anti-Personnel Landmine Ban Convention: A Non-Hegemonic Regime." In Brem and Stiles 2009, 123–46.

Rutherford, Kenneth R., Stefan Brem, and Richard A. Matthew, eds. 2003. *Reframing the Agenda: The Impact of NGO and Middle Power Cooperation in International Security Policy*. Westport: Praeger.

SAS (Small Arms Survey). 2003. "Insights and Mysteries: Global Small Arms Transfers." In *Small Arms Survey 2003: Development Denied*, 97–123. A Project of the Graduate Institute of International Studies, Geneva. Oxford: Oxford University Press.

———. 2011. "A Booming Business: Private Security and Small Arms." In *Small Arms Survey 2011: States of Security*, 101–33. A Project of the Graduate Institute of International and Development Studies, Geneva. Cambridge: Cambridge University Press.

Shaw, Timothy M., Sandra J. MacLean, and David R. Black. 2006. "Introduction: A Decade of Human Security; What Prospects for Global Governance and New Multilateralisms?" In *A Decade of Human Security. Global Governance and New Multilateralisms*, edited by Sandra J. MacLean, David R. Black, and Timothy M. Shaw, 3–18. Aldershot: Ashgate.

Simpson, Gerry. 2004. *Great Powers and Outlaw States: Unequal Sovereigns in the International Legal Order*. Cambridge: Cambridge University Press.

Taylor, Miles E. 2006. "UN Small Arms Conference Deadlocks." *Arms Control Today* 36 (7). www.armscontrol.org/act/2006_09/SmallArms.

UN (United Nations). 1997. Report of the Panel of Governmental Experts on Small Arms. A/52/298, August 27.

———. 1999. Report of the Group of Governmental Experts on Small Arms. A/54/258, August 19.

———. 2012. "Annex 1: Outcome Document: Programme of Action to Prevent, Combat and Eradicate the Illicit Trade in Small Arms and Light Weapons in All Its Aspects." RevCon. A/CONF.192/2012/RC/CRP.3/Rev.3. New York, September 7. http://www.poa-iss.org/RevCon2/Documents/RevCon-DOC/Rev1/Draft-Outcome-CRP3-Rev3.pdf.

UNGA (United Nations General Assembly). 2005. *International Instrument to Enable States to Identify and Trace, in a Timely and Reliable Manner, Illicit Small Arms and Light Weapons.* A/CONF.192/15.

UNODA (United Nations Office for Disarmament Affairs). 2012. "Small Arms." www.un.org/disarmament/convarms/SALW.

US (United States). 1997. US Proposal for the Diplomatic Conference on an International Total Ban on Anti-Personnel Land Mines. APL/CW 8, Oslo, September 1, 1–3.

van Woudenberg, Nout. 2007. "The Long and Winding Road towards an Instrument on Cluster Munitions." *Journal of Conflict and Security Law* 12 (3): 447–83.

Vines, Alex. 1998. "The Crisis of Anti-Personnel Mines." In Cameron, Lawson, and Tomlin 1998, 118–35.

Volman, Daniel. 1998. "The Militarization of Africa." In *What Women Do in Wartime: Gender and Conflict in Africa*, edited by Meredeth Turshen and Clotilde Twagiramariya, 150–62. London: Zed Books.

Wareham, Mary. 1998. "Rhetoric and Policy Realities in the United States." In Cameron, Lawson, and Tomlin 1998, 212–47.

Williams, Jody and Stephen Goose. 1998. "The International Campaign to Ban Landmines." In Cameron, Lawson, and Tomlin 1998, 20–47.

Wisotzki, Simone. 2009a. *Between Morality and Military Interests: Norm Setting in Humanitarian Arms Control.* PRIF Report no. 92. www.hsfk.de/fileadmin/downloads/PRIF_NO_92hp.pdf.

———. 2009b. "Negotiating with a Reluctant Hegemon: The Case of the Small Arms and Light Weapons Regime." In Brem and Stiles 2009, 21–43.

Zughni, Farrah. 2011. "Cluster Munitions Protocol Fails." *Arms Control Today* 41 (10). www.armscontrol.org/act/2011_12/Cluster_Munitions_Protocol_Fails.

Part II
External Drivers of Norm Dynamics

CHAPTER FOUR

Arms Control Norms and Technology

Elvira Rosert, Una Becker-Jakob, Giorgio Franceschini, and Annette Schaper

WAR IS, AS MARTIN VAN CREVELD (1991, 1) puts it, "completely permeated by technology and governed by it." Technological innovations, be it through increasing precision, lethality and range of weapons, or decreased defensibility against them, have led to an increase in the destructiveness of war that culminated in the "mechanised slaughter of the twentieth-century conflicts" (Monin and Gallimore 2002, 41). However, warfare has been affected not only by technological developments—international norms regulating and prohibiting the use and possession of certain weapons have accompanied it as long as has technological innovation. Especially in the second half of the twentieth century, weapon technological developments have been accompanied by the tightening and deepening of international arms control, so that today numerous international norms regulate and prohibit the use and possession of certain weapons, including prescriptions and proscriptions for stockpiling, transfer, production, destruction, and, rarely, weapons development. These norms fulfill three main functions: to prevent war by mitigating the security dilemma and assuring stability between opponents (Larsen 2002, 8) and, if prevention fails, to limit war damages and to reduce human suffering by specifying the legitimate means of combat (Oeter 2008, 119, 126).

However, a glance at the state of the art of military technologies reveals that while international norms have restrained the accumulation, proliferation, and use of *some* weapons, the development of new weapons and the modernization of existing warfare technologies continues. This puts existing norms under a constant challenge, as the pace of technological progress by far exceeds that of the normative (M. Smith 2009, 105). On the other hand, new technologies can and do strengthen existing norms as well—by creating new options for verifying their implementation, hampering the transfer of dangerous materials, or limiting the weapons' effects. But when does technology serve as a norm-threatening factor and when as a norm-promoting factor? To pursue this question, the chapter starts with some general considerations concerning the relationship of norms and technology and shows how new weapons technologies have affected the emergence of *new* norms. In the second part, we examine the influence of technological innovation on *existing* norms and regimes in four cases—biological weapons (BW), nuclear proliferation, nuclear testing, and antipersonnel landmines.

HOW TECHNOLOGY TRIGGERS NORM EVOLUTION

As the following section will show, historically, most arms control-related norms emerged as reactions to advances in warfare technology and thus can be seen as an effort to contain the constantly increasing levels of destructiveness (Croft 1996, 22). However, the project to humanize war was only partly successful, since not all advances in warfare technologies have led to the emergence of new norms—rather, only a few of them did (Price 1995, 73–74). Furthermore, some recent processes of norm setting were not directed against new weapons but against weapons that had been in use for a long time.

Major breakthroughs in warfare technology came with the Industrial Revolution bringing about magazine-loading firearms, machine guns, explosive bullets, mines and torpedoes, and, later, larger military hardware such as tanks, battle jets, steel-hardened battleships, and submarines (M. Smith 2009, 112–15). Most of these weapons still escape normative opprobrium. Nonetheless, the tremendous increase in the number of victims of war that some of these technologies had brought about in the nineteenth century led to the evolution of the international humanitarian law—a body of international law that regulates the protection of victims and the use of means and methods of combat. The latter's principles (discrimination between combatants and civilians, proportionality and avoidance of unnecessary suffering) and the norms derived from them were codified in several multilateral documents that usually followed the introduction of new warfare technologies: the St. Petersburg Declaration of 1868 prohibited the exploding bullets that the Russian military had introduced in 1863 (Schindler and Toman 1988, 101). This prohibition did not prevent the British Army from developing another weapon causing cruel wounds, namely the dumdum bullet—which, however, was prohibited at the Hague Peace Conference in 1899 (Prokosch 1995, 11–13). Moreover, the Hague Conventions of 1899 and 1907 prohibited the use of poisonous weapons, although this prohibition was also disregarded when various parties made massive use of chemical warfare in World War I. After this war, the desire to hedge the use as well as further development and proliferation of the respective technologies resulted in several norm-setting attempts: the Geneva Protocol of 1925 prohibited poisonous gases and bacteriological warfare. Since naval and aerial warfare had become major areas of concern due to their widespread uses in World War I and due to the foreseeable further progress in the respective technologies, the Washington Treaty of 1922 prohibited the destruction of merchant ships by submarines (Schindler and Toman 1988, 877–79), the Hague Rules of Air Warfare of 1923 prohibited the bombardment of cities (Cantrell 1977, 256), and the London Naval Treaties of 1931 and 1936 regulated the size of the naval forces, maximum gun calibers, and ship weights (Croft 1996, 26–29; Burns 2009, 67–69).[1]

The norm against chemical warfare was violated by Italy, which employed mustard gas against Ethiopians in 1936.[2] However, chemical weapons (CW) were not used on World War II battlefields, this non-use thus indicating the effectiveness of the Geneva Protocol. The prohibition of city bombing, on the other hand, was systematically disregarded, and counter-city-targeting became an essential part of combat strategy built on the conviction that "airpower was about bombing ordinary people" (Farrell and Lambert 2001, 317). Consequently, the development of bombing technologies was a military priority of that period (Murray 1996; Burns 2009, 68) that not only resulted in the production of conventional missiles such as the German V-1 and the use of napalm for firebombs against Japanese cities, but culminated in the invention of the atomic bomb (Aldrich and Chinkin 2000, 93). Overshadowed by its use and the accelerating nuclear arms race between the superpowers, none of the other new technologies used in World War II—such as napalm, air-delayed landmines, or fighter jets—triggered new norms; on the contrary, norms regulating the means and methods of combat were deliberately left out of the Geneva Conventions of 1949 because the Allied Powers feared criticism of their own warfare strategies (T. Smith 2002, 360; Oeter 2008, 122).

As the pursuit of technological progress became an essential feature of superpower confrontation during the Cold War (Gelber 1974, 522), bilateral nuclear arms control gained unique importance as an instrument for preventing the destruction of humankind by assuring strategic stability. For some decades, the focus on nuclear weapons diverted attention from other weapons (Tannenwald 2007, 46). But the first large-scale uses of cluster munitions and napalm in Southeast Asia brought conventional weapons back onto the table. After the Additional Protocol I (AP I) to the Geneva Conventions had rendered the general principles regulating the use of means and methods of combat legally binding in 1977, the Convention on Certain Conventional Weapons (CCW) was adopted three years later. This was the first treaty to address conventional weapons. The CCW also provided a framework for regulating the use of specific weapons through its attached protocols (Mathews 2001, 996). At the same time the convention only partially confirms the trend that norm setting follows technological breakthroughs: it has ignored several recent troubling technologies completely (cluster munitions, flechettes, and small-caliber projectiles [Prokosch 1995, 162]), prohibited an irrelevant one (weapons primarily designed to produce fragments undetectable by X-ray—which did not exist and were not planned [161]), addressed an old one (antipersonnel landmines), only seemingly banned one (incendiary weapons), and in 1995 banned another before its use (blinding laser weapons). The trend is also not reflected by the three recently adopted arms control treaties, since the Chemical Weapons Convention of 1993, the Anti-Personnel Landmines Convention of 1997, and the Cluster Munitions Convention of 2008 all deal with "old" technologies. Yet, they still reacted to current problems: the use of chemical weapons by Iraq against Iraqi civilians and Iran in the 1980s, the widespread use of millions of landmines, and several uses of cluster munitions during the last twenty years.

In the following section, we shift our perspective to existing norms that have been institutionalized in arms control regimes, namely the Biological Weapons Convention (BWC), the Nuclear Non-Proliferation Treaty (NPT), the Comprehensive Nuclear-Test-Ban Treaty (CTBT), and the Anti-Personnel Landmine Convention, and discuss how they have been affected by ongoing technological developments.

BIOTECHNOLOGY AND NORM DYNAMICS IN THE BIOLOGICAL WEAPONS CONVENTION

Biological warfare denotes any attempt to inflict death or disease on humans, animals, or plants by using pathogenic microorganisms, such as bacteria, viruses, or fungi or their products, such as toxins.[3] The related technologies can be as basic as extracting the toxin ricin from castor beans or as sophisticated as in the offensive weapons program of the Soviet Union that included highly dangerous genetically modified agents (Hart 2006). Bioweapons thus involve a whole range of relevant technologies and materials, including the agents themselves, as well as the technologies necessary for analyzing, multiplying, storing, modifying, and disseminating them.

The field of BW control is characterized by high dual-use potential—that is, many materials, processes, and technologies that have civilian and benign applications (e.g., in medicine or pharmacology) could be misused for harmful purposes. Moreover, it can be very difficult to distinguish between (legal) defensive and (illegal) offensive research and development through many stages of a research or production process, which in turn makes assessing a technology's desirability and inherent risks complex. This, and the fact that the agents in question occur naturally all around the globe, renders the simple prohibition of "dangerous" materials or technologies impracticable, as this would also impair benign medical or biological research.

Various fields of (civilian) science have been relevant for the development of BW, for efforts to prevent their spread, and for biodefense. The evolution of a more precise understanding of the mechanisms of disease transmission as well as the discoveries of bacteria and viruses in the nineteenth and early twentieth centuries changed the basics not only of medicine and pharmacology, but also of biological weapons and biodefense research (Davison 2005, 2–12). In fact, the first known offensive BW programs were initiated around this time by France and Germany, then the leading countries in terms of microbiological discoveries (Davison 2005, 9), followed by Canada, Japan, the UK, the United States, and the USSR in the first half of the twentieth century, and Iraq and South Africa in the second (Geissler and van Courtland Moon 1999; Wheelis, Rózsa, and Dando 2006). A number of other countries have been suspected of maintaining offensive BW programs (US DoS 2005, 2010).

After the basic discoveries of microbiology, the major advances in genetics and genetic engineering from the 1970s onward represented the next challenge for BW control and biodefense (Petro, Plasse, and McNulty 2003, 162; Zanders 2001, 370). For instance, the USSR expanded its offensive BW program, inter alia, by developing genetically modified organisms as BW agents, in violation of the BWC it had signed in 1972 (Hart 2006). More recently, rapid advances in various fields of science have raised concerns regarding their potential for malign misuse and consequent risks for the norms against BW (Bowman, Hughes, and Husbands 2011, 19; Zanders 2001, 371). Relevant developments in "new biology" (Wheelis 2004) have contributed to a better and more "detailed understanding of the physiology of living organisms" (Wheelis 2004, 6; see also e.g., Disarmament Forum 2005; Kelle, Nixdorff, and Dando 2006), which could allow for a more specific and targeted BW attack. Moreover, research in emerging scientific fields such as synthetic biology, bioinformatics, and systems biology as well as research on delivery methods for biological or biochemical substances could harbor covert misuse (e.g., Kelle, Nixdorff, and Dando 2006; Tucker and Zilinskas 2006; McLeish and Trapp 2011; National Research Council 2011). Finally, in several areas the distinction between biology and chemistry is becoming blurred (Tucker 2010)—another new challenge for BW control (Wheelis 2002; Kelle 2007, 7). In a more positive trend, technological advances have also contributed to improved biodefense—for example, in the areas of vaccines, protective equipment, and detection technologies (National Research Council 2011)—and they harbor a vast potential for the improvement of global health.

Almost a century after norm-setting efforts to place international legal restraints on chemical and biological warfare had begun, the BWC was opened for signature on April 10, 1972, and entered into force on March 26, 1975. Subsequently, a regime formed with the BWC at its center (see chapter 2), which comprehensively and nondiscriminately prohibits the development, production, stockpiling, acquisition, and retention of BW (Art. I) and assisting others in acquiring such weapons (Art. III). Moreover, the treaty obligates its members, inter alia, to facilitate the exchange of biotechnological material and know-how for peaceful uses and not to hamper development and cooperation in this field (Art. X). Advances in the biosciences would probably also facilitate the verification of compliance with the BWC; yet the last comprehensive stocktaking of the relevant technologies dates back to 1992–93 and would have to be thoroughly reviewed should the issue return to the BWC agenda.

Effects of Technological Progress on the Norms against Biological Weapons

Despite its potential relevance, the impact of technological change on regime norms has received little attention in the BWC regime: Unlike the Chemical Weapons Convention (CWC), for which a scientific advisory board provides regular information, the BWC regime has no institutionalized mechanism for monitoring scientific and technological developments (S&T). Although the convention tasked the first review conference explicitly with "[taking] into account any new scientific and technological developments relevant to the Convention" (Art. XII) and this task has been repeated for most of the subsequent five-year review conferences (BWC 1991, 14; see also, e.g., BWC 2006, 17), the issue has never been discussed systematically by states parties. States have been asked to provide reports on developments they consider relevant to the BWC, but until 2011 only a few such reports had been provided (Dando 2011, 2), and they have never prompted any follow-up action. While in 2006 some states unsuccessfully promoted the inclusion of S&T review in the new intersessional process for 2007–10 (Becker 2007, 24), in 2011 BWC members decided to discuss S&T annually until 2015 (BWC 2011, 21, 23–24). Before this, the only visible and consensual recognition of S&T developments was found in the additional understandings on BWC Art. I (BW prohibition) as recorded by the review conferences in their final declarations, which all aimed at reaffirming and strengthening the prohibition norm.

While the topic has been neglected in the regime itself, there are numerous pertinent publications by nongovernmental experts (see above). Yet, most of these are concerned with *potential* developments, not with past impact, which is indicative of the strength and resilience of the BWC's basic prohibition norm in the face of technological challenges. This resilience is grounded in the norm's scope, which is defined in such a way as to "immunize" it against any new and potentially harmful S&T developments. Instead of defining a list of prohibited agents and technologies, which could be outpaced by science, it is circumscribed by the so-called general purpose criterion. Art. I stipulates that each state party "undertakes never in any circumstances to develop, produce, stockpile or otherwise acquire or retain [m]icrobial or other biological agents, or toxins whatever their origin or method of production, of types and in quantities *that have no justification for prophylactic, protective or other peaceful purposes*" (emphasis added).

Nevertheless, subsequent review conferences saw the need to explicitly include scientific areas that seemed particularly threatening to the prohibition norm, such as microbiology, genetic engineering, and biotechnology in 1986 and 1991, and in addition molecular biology and "any applications resulting from genome studies" in 1996 (BWC 1986, 3; 1991, 3; 1996, 15; see also Kelle 2005, 11–12). In 2006 and 2011, however, instead of expanding a possibly contested list of scientific areas that could be viewed as exhaustive, the states parties emphasized that

> the Convention is comprehensive in its scope and that all naturally or artificially created or altered microbial and other biological agents and toxins, as well as their components, regardless of their origin and method of production and whether they affect humans, animals or plants, of types and in quantities that have no justification for prophylactic, protective or other peaceful purposes, are unequivocally covered by Article I.
>
> The Conference reaffirms that Article I applies *to all scientific and technological developments in the life sciences and in other fields of science relevant to the Convention.* (BWC 2006, 9; BWC 2011, 10, emphasis added)

The agreed reaffirmation renders the prohibition even more comprehensive and clearly states that no S&T development could ever be used to legally produce biological weapons (Sims 2009, 53–54).

This strength notwithstanding, regimes and norms are not carved in stone and might alter with changing circumstances. Several experts are concerned that developments in the life sciences such as those described above might threaten or undermine the prohibition of BW.

While this research is not primarily directed toward weapons development but driven by benign objectives, its new discoveries might endanger non-use and nonproliferation norms by altering previous assessments of the cost-benefit ratio or of the feasibility and military utility and effectiveness of certain BW. Hence, the weapons might become more attractive to some actors and, due to the rapid growth and geographical spread of biotechnology (Bowman, Hughes, and Husbands 2011, 19–20), more readily accessible. Such changes might prompt some offensive BW planning but more probably could induce enhanced biodefense efforts against potential new threats. Given the dual-use nature of the field and the lack of transparency in the BW control regime (see chapter 2), this might create new risks, cause mistrust, and, in the worst case, fuel a biological arms race (Wheelis and Dando 2002, 6). However, technology alone does not create a weapons program. New discoveries might enhance offensive or defensive capabilities of certain agents only if the actors show *the political will to employ them that way.* For a state-run BW program, which requires significant resources and the infrastructure to apply cutting-edge technologies to weapons research, a political decision to violate the strong international norm against biological weapons would have to be made. It is currently unlikely that terrorists could use state-of-the-art technology for weapons purposes without state support. However, Dando (2011, 8) cautions that since modern developments in the life sciences might make access to effective BW agents easier for substate groups too, a change in the practice of (non)use of BW by such actors might contribute to a slow erosion of a norm. Moreover, in conflicts different from traditional interstate military conflicts, BW and CW might appear attractive "particularly because they lend themselves to tactics such as terror, population displacement, and wider forms of social/economic destabilization" (McLeish and Trapp 2011, 534).

Another area of concern is the interest of some states in "nonlethal" (bio) chemical weapons, notably biochemical substances with incapacitating effects on humans (Dando 2011, 8). The "Moscow incident" of 2002, in which Russian authorities used a narcotic to free 830 hostages taken in a Moscow theater by Chechen terrorists but "accidentally" killed about 180 of the hostages in addition to the hijackers, fueled the debate about the legal and ethical implications of "nonlethal" (bio)chemical weapons and their legal status under the CWC and the BWC (see, e.g., Fidler 2005; Pearson, Chevrier, and Wheelis 2007). While the CWC explicitly permits the use of certain chemical substances for law enforcement and riot control purposes, there is currently debate about the extent to which "nonlethal" substances might weaken the norms against chemical weapons and whether developments in this area might also affect the BWC norms. Dando argues that if a broad agreement developed enabling law enforcement to be equated with "peaceful purposes," the use of *bio*chemical "nonlethal" agents could be construed as legal too under the BWC (Dando 2011, 8). Others have a more optimistic view of the BWC's scope regarding this problem, arguing that the formulation of Art. I includes "all of the biochemical products of the living body that in abnormal doses can be used as toxins, including bioregulators, neurotransmitters, and hormones" and should thus also cover "nonlethal" biochemical weapons (Wheelis 2002, 52; see also Meselson 2000, 18).

In a more generic development, the rapid advance of biotechnology since the 1980s has exacerbated the old conflict between the norms of nonproliferation and biotechnological cooperation, and hence between the industrialized and developing BWC members. On the one hand, the conflict intensified as demands for a more equitable distribution of scientific and technological knowledge and equipment, combined with an interest in the highly profitable biotechnology sector and with a particular need for enhanced capabilities for combating infectious diseases in the Global South have led countries of the Non-Aligned Movement (NAM) to place more emphasis on the implementation of Art. X. These demands have clashed with the Western-coordinated export controls of the Australia Group that serve nonproliferation goals but are considered by NAM states to hinder their own technological development (Becker-Jakob 2011, 5–9). In a more recent trend, however, conflict intensity is decreasing in part because of technological development and its geographical spread: some leading NAM members have come to appreciate the value of export controls, inter alia, because they have become threshold states in terms of their biotechnological capacities. However, as long as biotechnological disparities and certain political tensions between countries of the Global South and the West persist, the conflict between nonproliferation and cooperation norms is likely to remain.

Science and Technology Threat Awareness Strengthens the Norm

Until recently, interactions between the realms of biotechnology and the life sciences and the BWC regime have been scarce. On the positive side, S&T advances have had no significant negative effects on the prohibition norm of the regime. On the contrary, concerns about potential threats to the BWC have prompted states parties to reaffirm and even strengthen this norm. On the negative side, states parties have so far failed to equip the regime with a functioning mechanism to monitor and respond to relevant S&T developments. Moreover, the rapid growth of the biotechnology sector has intensified the existing norm conflict between nonproliferation and cooperation obligations.

The lack of awareness among life scientists of the weapons aspect and the potential for malign misuse of their work (e.g., Rappert, Chevrier, and Dando 2006) could lead to the assumption that the BWC norms have had no effect on the "science world" at all. However, given the fact that there have been only a few instances of "rogue scientists" conducting offensive BW programs or committing biocriminal or bioterrorist acts, it is also conceivable that the BW taboo as codified in the BWC has an effect even beyond the regime and the state level.

Proliferation Resistance: How a Norm Can Precede a Technology

Several norms that aim at preventing the use, possession, and further development of nuclear weapons are part of the nonproliferation regime. This includes, inter alia, international nuclear arms control treaties, national and international export control principles, and measures for protecting nuclear plants and materials. The nonproliferation norms have evolved over time, and many have taken effect. Examples are the norms not to conduct nuclear tests or not to pass on nuclear weapons to nonnuclear weapon states. In several cases, nonproliferation norms have prevented the development of a nuclear arsenal and induced states to renounce nuclear weapons (Müller and Schmidt 2010). There are also cases in which the nonproliferation regime at least complicated and delayed military nuclear developments, such as for India, Pakistan, Iraq, and North Korea.

The existing norms aim at the *military* use of nuclear energy. But proliferation problems are caused not only by specific nuclear weapons technology but also by their components, precursors, fabrication tools, and related knowledge that overlap with the technologies of *civilian* nuclear energy systems. This dual-use nature of nuclear energy is central to proliferation problems. The use of nuclear weapons can be banned—a norm that is largely in place—but the denial of civilian nuclear technology meets insuperable resistance and, furthermore, contradicts Art. IV of the NPT that explicitly states the right of all parties to the treaty to use it and to participate in technological exchange. Civilian nuclear use is on the rise and will probably not be reversed by the Fukushima nuclear accident, as the International Atomic Energy Agency (IAEA) (2011b) projects; this rise is both quantitative, as the rising numbers of the reactors under construction show (IAEA 2011a), but also qualitative, as many new reactor and fuel cycle concepts are being explored and developed. The work of the Generation IV International Forum (GIF)[4] is indicative of the innovative momentum in this field: six new nuclear reactor types are now the subject of research and development and are due to be deployed by 2030.

Development of the Norm of Proliferation Resistance

Several attempts to meet the challenge of complying both with the norm of nonproliferation of military nuclear technologies and with the norm of granting access to civilian nuclear technologies exist: one of these is the establishment of an international fuel cycle center that would offer enrichment and reprocessing services and replace the need for national acquisition of these technologies (Yudin 2009). Another is the promotion of high proliferation resistance of a nuclear technology as the appropriate criterion for choosing a particular type of power reactor: a widely accepted definition describes proliferation resistance as "that characteristic of a nuclear energy system that impedes the diversion or undeclared production of nuclear material, or misuse of technology, by

States intent on acquiring nuclear weapons or other nuclear explosive devices. The degree of proliferation resistance results from a combination of, *inter alia*, technical design features, operational modalities, institutional arrangements and safeguards measures" (IAEA 2003, 106). Hence, in addition to the external barriers provided by the nonproliferation regime, high proliferation resistance would also provide intrinsic technical features that minimize proliferation dangers. The earlier in the planning stage such intrinsic features are considered, the higher the proliferation resistance of a technology can become—the norm to produce proliferation resistance technologies would therefore demand assessments of emerging new nuclear systems already in the design phase, in particular of those fuel-cycle and reactor technologies that are more proliferation-prone than others.

This idea of norms already affecting civilian nuclear technology during the early stages of research and development in order to inhibit proliferation is not new. Alarmed by the Indian nuclear test of 1974, for which plutonium from an ostensibly civilian research reactor had been used, in 1977, the United States initiated the International Nuclear Fuel Cycle Evaluation (INFCE)—an IAEA-coordinated program that sought to channel civilian nuclear technology in a nonproliferation-friendly direction (Skjöldebrand 1980). The INFCE published a report in 1980 that, inter alia, recommended the development of new fuels to replace highly enriched uranium (HEU) because of the latter's potential to be directly used as material for nuclear explosives (INFCE 1980, 43, 137–80). The new norm of not using HEU fuels was established largely successfully. As new fuels containing only low-enriched uranium (LEU) and having the same properties for civilian use while being useless for nuclear explosives were developed, many research reactors could be converted to the new LEU fuels, and for about two decades no new HEU-fueled reactors were constructed. This new norm has been violated only once so far, by the construction of a new HEU-fueled research reactor (FRM-II) in Garching (Germany) during the 1990s, which was sharply criticized internationally (Schaper 1996). The strong criticism demonstrates that the norm exists. The example of phasing out HEU use shows the mutual dependence between technological and normative progress: the success of the norm was dependent on achievements in fuel development, but these would not have been possible without funding that was provided because of the political will to phase out civilian HEU use. While the norm against HEU use has been strengthened over the years, other elements of INFCE have proved abortive. The United States has tried to persuade other states to phase out the civilian use of plutonium—in vain, because some countries continued to engage in a closed fuel cycle.

A new effort to strengthen the proliferation resistance of nuclear technologies was undertaken by the IAEA in response to the "nuclear renaissance." In 2000, it created the International Project on Innovative Nuclear Reactors and Fuel Cycles (INPRO) that devised methodologies for assessing the proliferation resistance of new nuclear systems. The project's first report (IAEA 2003) suggests an assessment of several intrinsic features that result from the design of an innovative nuclear technology, such as the attractiveness of the fuel, the conversion time, the difficulty and detectability of diversion, the skills needed for and the complexity of abuse, and several extrinsic measures that result from political decisions such as access barriers and safeguards, conditions for trade, commitment to nonproliferation obligations, or international ownership. Subsequent INPRO reports apply the methodology and evaluate specific nuclear systems—hence, INPRO is an ongoing process, whereas INFCE was a unique event. The assessments yield quantitative and descriptive markers indicating the degree of proliferation resistance—the idea is that these assessments would result in the choice of the design with the highest ranking and its further optimization. Put differently, this methodology would assure the promotion of technologies that best comply with the norm of proliferation resistance. The effort has had some success already: evaluation methodologies similarly based on intrinsic features and extrinsic measures have also been adopted and applied by GIF (GIF 2006), not least because there is an overlap between the expert committees of INPRO and GIF. Many more scholars are now working with the methodology and are aiming at applying it to various nuclear and other energy systems.

However, the fact that INPRO's (and GIF's) catalogues of risk assessments also reflect other aspects beyond proliferation risks such as risks to safety, efficiency and economics, environmental and health, and waste management has the potential to create conflicts of priorities that might reduce the importance of nonproliferation as the attention to other risks might outweigh that of proliferation. Evaluations of different aspects of a given nuclear technology may result in very different ratings, and there will be no methodology for finding a balance between them for a comparison. Weighting the different aspects in their respective significance will always be a political judgment. The outcome of this, however, will depend on the strength of respective norms. This challenge arises out of the difficulty of devising reactor and fuel cycle concepts that reduce all risks—in fact, the inventors of innovative nuclear systems usually focus on one specific shortcoming of current technology but neglect other risks. For example, a research reactor using the new LEU fuels has higher proliferation resistance than one fueled with HEU; however, it produces slightly more waste. Some proposals pose even higher proliferation risks than traditional ones: The Gas-Cooled Fast Reactor, one of the GIF systems, minimizes long-lived radioactive waste and uses various fuels very efficiently, but fast neutrons can principally also be abused to breed weapon-grade plutonium. In a comparison, the once-through fuel cycle is much more proliferation-resistant than recycling. But several decision makers consider the minimization of waste as more valuable than the minimization of proliferation risks. Nevertheless, the proponents of the GIF systems claim high proliferation resistance for their proposals, which some critics call a hypocritical appeasement (Lyman 2006).

Technological and Normative Progress Go Together

The possibility of enhancing the proliferation resistance of nuclear technologies demonstrates the role technical properties can play in the strength of norms: the idea is that once proliferation resistance offers proven reactor technology, choosing reactors incorporating such technology will be seen as appropriate decision making by states pursuing the civilian use of nuclear energy. However, as the examples given above demonstrate, this norm competes with other norms, such as minimization of nuclear waste. Therefore, it is unlikely that the norm will become very strong. But what is new with the norm of enhancing the proliferation resistance of innovative nuclear technologies, in contrast to other nonproliferation norms, is its early timing: it aims at preceding the technology and influencing all its stages, namely research, development, implementation, and use.

A COMPREHENSIVE BAN ON NUCLEAR TESTS: THE SLOW EVOLUTION OF A GLOBAL NORM

Because the 1950s were a decade of an intense superpower nuclear arms race, high-yield atmospheric nuclear tests were carried out in large numbers by both the Soviet Union and the United States. Aside from political motives, these tests were carried out for a variety of reasons: to “certify” a new weapon, to assess the damage to living beings, buildings, and military equipment, and, a motive that is often overlooked, to validate the performance of an aging warhead (Franceschini and Schaper 2006). The demand to regulate nuclear testing started after a US thermonuclear test in 1954 "overshot" and led to widespread contamination of the nearby Marshall Islands and of a Japanese fishing boat, causing the immediate death of a fisherman and lasting sickness of the rest of the crew as well as of several inhabitants of the archipelago. As a consequence, a number of these islands had to be evacuated in ensuing years. Early attempts to stop these tests, consequently, focused on their environmental legacy and impact on public health.[5] In the ensuing debate, the United States and the Soviet Union came close to a comprehensive test ban, but agreement foundered on the issue of verification. The two countries then agreed on a Limited Test Ban Treaty (LTBT), which entered into force in 1963 and which prohibited all explosive nuclear weapons tests with the exception of underground tests. Although the LTBT succeeded in containing the adverse effects of testing on humans and the environment, it failed to curb or at least slow down the nuclear arms race: on the contrary, American nuclear testing "increased substantially after the LTBT was signed" (Fetter 1988, 10–11). Thus, the treaty merely shifted the arms race underground. Furthermore, it dampened the calls to end *all* nuclear tests and somehow stole the thunder from the political demand for a *comprehensive* test ban (CTB) for several decades. Promising CTB debate would only be resurrected in the context of post–Cold War détente.

In the CTB debate at the beginning of the 1990s a number of technological questions that had already been present in the LTB debate regained momentum: the most salient topics within this debate were the verifiability of a comprehensive test ban and the issue of stockpile confidence in the absence of testing. Also in 1963, the US Joint Chiefs of Staff (JCS) had made their approval of the treaty conditional upon a number of "safeguards" (such as efforts to attract first-class scientists to the nuclear weapon labs and strong investments in verification technologies). We find such quid pro quo arguments in the current US debate on the CTB, too: in order to "compensate" for the pending test ban, investments in the nuclear weapons complex—both in terms of new technologies and human capital—are deemed indispensable (Biden 2010). The main difference from the LTB lies in the fact that the CTBT—unlike the LTBT, which allows underground testing—prohibits *any* nuclear explosions (Schaper 1994). Thus, nuclear weapons possessors are compelled under a CTBT to find suitable "non-explosive" means of keeping their arsenals safe and reliable.

The Mutual Influence of the Norm against Nuclear Testing and Technological Progress

This verification of stockpile confidence represents the main challenge for nuclear weapons possessors under a CTB, as the other motives for considering a test—certification of a new weapon or damage assessment of an existing weapon—would be incompatible with the spirit of the treaty. Thus, while the CTB took shape in the 1990s, nuclear weapons possessors had to think about a maintenance strategy compatible with the regime—that is, one that would not have recourse to explosive tests. The solution was generally seen to lie in investing in new technologies and capabilities to replace nuclear testing. As a result a disarmament norm ironically led to increased funding for the nuclear weapons laboratories that were supposed to develop these new surrogate technologies (Mello 2010).

The science and technology campaigns that were started in the shadow of the CTBT aim at simulating the various stages of an exploding nuclear weapon, both on computers as well as in small- and large-scale experimental settings. For this purpose, highly expensive and sophisticated research programs were launched in major nuclear weapons states. At the center of these campaigns "virtual testing" carried out on ultrafast computer clusters ("supercomputers") replaces traditional explosive testing. The importance of these simulation capabilities was tangible in the American CTBT debate of the 1990s, where concerns were raised about the performance of supercomputers and where these doubts were central to the treaty's defeat in 1999 (Schneidmiller 2011). More than a decade later, supercomputing power in the US nuclear weapons labs has increased by more than an order of magnitude. According to Jeffrey Lewis, a senior US arms control expert, this massive leap "should resolve questions about nuclear blast modeling, surmounting another obstacle to US approval of the treaty" (quoted in Schneidmiller 2011). The supercomputers are fed with data from previous tests and from special experimental facilities that have been constructed in the CTBT context of "virtual testing": these facilities simulate both the primary stage of an exploding weapon (nuclear fission) and the secondary stage (nuclear fusion). For this purpose, nuclear weapons laboratories direct their attention increasingly to hydrodynamic tests (imaging of imploding—though subcritical—primaries) and inertial confinement fusion or ICF (simulation of secondaries). Both experiments are costly and based on cutting-edge technology, and it is doubtful that these experimental facilities would have been constructed without the CTBT. Furthermore, the ICF campaigns distort the technological trajectories of decades of civilian fusion research. Whereas the civilian fusion research budgets always favored other technologies for a future commercial fusion reactor, the massive funding of ICF research under weapons maintenance programs might boost the chances of an ICF-based civilian fusion reactor, maybe even ahead of the mainstream civilian technology based on magnetic confinement fusion (MCF).

A second set of test ban–related technologies concerns verification tools. Whether a CTBT would be verifiable has always been a contentious issue. Numerous studies by nuclear weapons scientists and by independent experts have been carried out on this issue. The results are complex because with the advancement of monitoring technologies potential clandestine nuclear weapons testers could also advance their knowledge of concealment strategies (Medalia 2008). Nevertheless, the establishment of the International Monitoring System (IMS) under the auspices of the Comprehensive Nuclear-Test-Ban Treaty Organization (CTBTO) has greatly contributed to worldwide acceptance of the CTBT. The gradual buildup of this impressive network of seismic, infrasound, hydroacoustic, and radionuclide measuring stations—unique in its size and scope in the world—has certainly bolstered the test ban norm simply by its capability to detect (and thus to deter) nuclear tests above and below ground as well as under water (Dahlman et al. 2011).

The verification regime of the CTBT had an impact on the evolution of some of the associated monitoring technologies: for example, it resuscitated research on infrasound, a technology that had almost died out since the 1960s. It also advanced (radionuclide) noble gas monitoring, which is fundamental in determining whether an explosion was conventional or nuclear. The paramount importance of radionuclide detection was visible after the two North Korean underground nuclear tests in 2006 and 2009. In the former case, radionuclides stemming from the blast were detected by the IMS two weeks after the explosion, but in the latter case the IMS could only register the seismic signal of the blast, but no trace of radioactive fallout. This setback might have repercussions in the US ratification debate, as the second North Korean test had a considerable yield (4kt), which was readily detected by the seismic network of the IMS (it is assumed that this network operates at an overall sensitivity of well below 1kt worldwide and—recently—even of 0.1kt in most parts of Asia). As the ultimate proof of a nuclear test is the detection of specific radioactive noble gases, the test norm would obviously benefit from corresponding advances in radionuclide detection capabilities, as the seismic signal alone could also be attributed to a conventional explosion.

While the future of the CTBT is still unclear, three further technological developments deserve attention. First, rapid advances in satellite technologies will soon provide an additional layer of defense against clandestine testing. Remote sensing satellites, although not formally part of the IMS, are permitted national technical means according to CTBT Art. IV, section A, paragraph 5, and may be used by the CTBT Executive Council to request an onsite inspection (CTBT Art. IV, section D, paragraph 37). These satellites, operating at different frequencies of the electromagnetic spectrum (optical, infrared, radar), may detect test preparation activities as well as ground deformations caused by underground tests (Hafemeister 2007). The corresponding images, which are available from commercial vendors at reasonable prices, may help ease some of the reservations about the verifiability of the CTBT and strengthen the treaty's verification regime. Second, in the US debate on stockpile maintenance and modernization, the issue of "warhead surety" (meaning the whole package of measures in the realm of safety, security, use control, and use denial) has gained momentum since the 9/11 terror attacks. As some experts claim that not all surety features can be applied to existing nuclear weapons without testing (Medalia 2008, 16–19), it remains to be seen how the United States will balance the need of highly safe and secure nuclear weapons—"useless for terrorists"—with an interest in maintaining a global test moratorium. Third, new insights into the migration of radioactivity through the geosphere might trigger secondary norm dynamics in favor of the CTBT: if adverse effects on humans and the environment stemming from *underground* nuclear explosions cannot be ruled out any longer, a global prohibition of nuclear tests might also benefit from the emerging precautionary and sustainability norms governing international environmental law (Tabassi 2009).

The Norm as Beneficiary and Trigger of Technological Progress

The relationship between the norm prohibiting nuclear testing and technological progress has always been complex and multilayered. On the one hand, progress in the field of monitoring technologies has sustained the process of establishing a universal test ban norm. At the same time, the prospect of a global nuclear test ban has unleashed a science and technology offensive in nuclear weapons complexes around the world in order to replace the "unacceptable" nuclear tests with "more acceptable" technologies. Thus, the rising test ban norm has benefited from technological advances and has triggered some of these advances itself: the ability to monitor a global test ban and the ability to perform "virtual" nuclear weapons tests are both prerequisites for and consequences of an evolving norm to end nuclear testing.

The CTBT is not in force at this writing in 2012, but the norm prohibiting nuclear tests is growing. Both the progress of and setbacks to the norm could be attributed to technological advances, mainly in the fields of verification and stockpile maintenance. Yet, it should not be forgotten that technological advances in the field of stockpile maintenance—first and foremost the ability to perform "virtual tests"—have distorted the original purpose of the CTBT, its disarmament and nonproliferation dimension that is clearly expressed in the treaty's preamble, which contains the word *disarmament* thirteen times. Maintaining nuclear weapons indefinitely and renouncing explosive testing alone was certainly not the goal of the norm entrepreneurs advocating global prohibition of nuclear tests.

ANTI-PERSONNEL LANDMINES TREATY: IS ITS EFFECTIVENESS ENDANGERED BY NEW TECHNOLOGIES?

Art. 2 of the Ottawa Treaty defines a mine as "a munition designed to be placed under, on or near the ground or other surface area and to be exploded by the presence, proximity or contact of a person or a vehicle." When used in defense, mines are meant to protect by shaping, delaying, and breaking up the movement of enemy forces or even by deterring an attack. When used in offense, mines are meant to depopulate areas and disrupt the enemy's logistics. Beyond tactical uses on the battlefield, landmines are also used strategically, for example, for the protection of facilities or borders.

The mass production of antipersonnel landmines arrived with World War I, triggered by one technological and one tactical development: the beginning of armored and of trench warfare (this section is based on McGrath 2000; Monin and Gallimore 2002; Youngblood 2006). Since battle tanks were difficult to disable with other weapons, antitank mines proved to be a feasible solution; as these mines were easy to detect and to lift, antipersonnel mines were planted to secure them against removal. Since the combatants in the trenches were relatively immune to small-caliber weapons, landmines were used for underground tunneling and to blow up trenches. In World War II, extensive laying of antipersonnel and antitank minefields became a common tactic to hinder the intrusion of enemy forces. Because mine clearance technologies progressed as well, efforts were made to make the detection of mines more difficult by constructing them from nonmetallic materials such as wood, glass, clay, and plastic. Two further major technological changes occurred with the deployment of the first air-dispersed mines and the development of the first self-destructing mines. Because remote delivery techniques meant that mine emplacement became less precise and minefields more difficult to locate and mark, self-destructing devices were supposed to protect one's troops from one's previously dispersed mines. The wars in Southeast Asia marked the emergence of a global landmine industry that provided for wide-scale proliferation of the weapon and introduced the indiscriminate use of landmines and their use by nonstate armed groups. As described in chapter 3, this human calamity led to the establishment of the antipersonnel mine ban enshrined in the Ottawa Convention.

Effects of Technological Progress on the Norm: The Challenge of Alternatives to Landmines

While the treaty has an exceptional compliance record, even of nonparties (see chapter 3), it has stimulated technological efforts to develop alternatives to landmines. Both the convention's nonsignatories (e.g., China, India, Pakistan, Russia, and the United States) and some of its signatories (e.g., Australia, Canada, France, Germany, Japan, and the United Kingdom) have shown interest in weapons providing the same capabilities for warfare while being compatible with the requirements of international humanitarian law (Doucet and Lloyd 2001, 115–16; NATO 2003a, IIi). Of 57 former and current antipersonnel (AP) landmine producers,[6] 27 have publicly announced interest in weapons that might replace landmines; 10 have given the lack of alternative weapons as a reason for their non-accession to the MBT. A total of 22 countries have conducted evaluative research to assess the potential of existing weapons to serve as alternatives and of ongoing weapons programs to result in such alternatives; 9 have commenced research and development (R&D) efforts to develop and produce alternative weapons, while 6 have ongoing programs with the potential to develop alternatives; 3 countries have announced production of a weapon that might serve as an equivalent to at least some functions of AP landmines.[7] However, no weapon has been developed that might fully replace the warfare capabilities of AP landmines.

As almost all NATO member states (except the United States and Poland) had joined the Mine Ban Treaty (MBT) and started to "actively consider alternative means of providing the capabilities that Anti-Personnel Mines (APMS) give to the warfighter" (NATO 2003a, 1), the Alliance's Research and Technology Board established a study group (SAS-023) consisting of forty-eight (military) state representatives to coordinate the efforts and to compile a list of possible alternative systems and concepts. While the group arrived at the conclusion that a one-to-one replacement "does not seem obtainable," it identified a number of weapons and weapons systems that might replace some APM functions while being compliant with the MBT as well as Protocol II of the CCW (NATO 2003b).

The R&D efforts envisaged two alternatives: lethal but nonvictim-activated weapons, or victim-activated but nonlethal weapons (NLW). The former, so-called man-in-the-loop (MITL) systems are supposed to eliminate the indiscriminate effect of antipersonnel landmines, as their activation requires identification by soldiers and their conscious decision to engage a target with a lethal mechanism. These systems include three components: a real-time surveillance system to automatically detect and classify objects, command and control systems to immediately react if the object has been identified as hostile, and precise firepower to hit the object (Doucet and Lloyd 2001, 41).[8] Contrary to such MITL systems, "nonlethal" or "less lethal" alternatives *are* victim activated—their indiscriminate effects are presented as acceptable because the victims are supposed to recover from the attack, because the weapons are "designed and developed to incapacitate or repel personnel, with a low probability of fatality or permanent injury, or to disable equipment, with minimal undesired damage or impact on the environment" (NATO 2006, sec. 1.2). While the activities of NATO and its members on nonlethal weapons predate the MBT (Davison 2007, 20) and include a broad range of weapons without being limited to antipersonnel landmine (APM) alternatives, these programs gained further importance with the adoption of the MBT, as some of the weapons under consideration were assigned functions similar to APMS, such as incapacitating individuals to impede them from entering an area, stopping vehicles, and controlling the movement of crowds (or forces). To produce these effects, several materials and instruments are taken into account: calmatives or obscurants that are released from a device after it has been stepped on, entanglements such as slippery substances and nets, acoustic mines incapacitating the victim with sounds, and electric weapons incapacitating the victim with electroshocks (Doucet and Lloyd 2001; NATO 2003b, 2006, G1–G7).[9]

While approving efforts to develop substitutes for nondiscriminatory APMS, humanitarian organizations have criticized the technologies developed in these projects for creating a number of problems with regard to the MBT. Generally, technological efforts were seen as subverting the status of APLs as a prohibited category: they draw a distinction between dumb and "smart" mines and obstruct the humanitarian impact of so-called alternatives because the label *landmine alternatives* suggests that these weapons do not cause the same problems as landmines (McGrath 2000, 17; Monin and Gallimore 2002, 199). Some MITL systems—for example, the US NSD-A (non-self-destruct alternative) munition and the US Spider XM-7 munition—announced as alternatives were reported to have a victim-activated mode incompatible with the treaty because of its indiscriminate effects. Other "alternatives"—systems combining antivehicle and antipersonnel mines such as the landmine system RADAM (Remote Area Denial Artillery Munition)—were criticized for blurring the distinction between APM and other weapons. The criticism proved effective as most of these programs were canceled or at least modified: funding for the NSDA program and for RADAM was canceled in 2002; it was announced in 2008 that the US Spider would be produced in a command-detonated version only (ICBL 2000, 2003, 2008). Nevertheless, doubts continue to exist whether man-in-the-loop systems can really pose a reliable solution to the problem of discrimination, since it may not always be possible for the commander operating remotely to identify and classify the intruding object. With regard to the label *nonlethal*, critics point out that it is not based on independent criteria but assigned by the manufacturers (Doucet and Lloyd 2001, 7); in some cases, so-called nonlethal weapons have caused lethal effects—while conventional weapons are not necessarily lethal for everyone but have a lethality rate of 20–25 percent (Coupland 1997). Target-triggered munitions such as nonlethal landmines would violate the principle of discrimination enshrined in international humanitarian law (IHL)—even if they do not kill, they inflict physical and psychological harm. By making it harder to determine what weapons belong in the category and by playing down the risks of the new weapons (Doucet and Lloyd 2001, 10–11) these technologies might restore the legitimacy of landmines by suggesting that the category itself does not deserve to be stigmatized.

A Strong Norm Impedes Technological Circumvention

MITL systems and NLW have posed challenges to the antipersonnel landmine norm, but with different results. While in the case of MITL alternatives the norm has prevailed, nonlethal alternatives still endanger it. As to the former, the power of the norm to restrict technological circumvention shows itself when the inclusion of victim-activated elements spurred criticism that led to the abandonment of the programs or at least to the elimination of this feature. The normative restriction also explains the limited output of these programs: R&D efforts have resulted in only a few weapons intended to replace antipersonnel landmines, namely the US Spider XM-7, the Australian Area Denial Weapon System, and the Hungarian IHR-60 system (ICBL 2004). Progress reports on the five ongoing programs (in China, Japan, Poland, Russia, and South Korea) have contained the same wording for years, which probably indicates only hesitant progress—yet, they still may result in new weapons. The case is different with nonlethal weapons as their use would contradict not only the core of the APM norm but also a fundamental norm of IHL—the prohibition against targeting civilians—by suggesting that indiscriminate weapons and indiscriminate targeting are acceptable as long as the consequences are reversible.

The overall picture gives reason for optimism, however: a weapon that has caused a humanitarian tragedy for decades has been banned, and while the weapons that may replace it are problematic in different respects, they are not comparable with antipersonnel landmines in their humanitarian impact.

CONCLUSION: NORMS AND TECHNOLOGY ARE MUTUALLY INFLUENTIAL

The cases discussed in this chapter provide insights into the relationship between technological and normative development. They show that this relationship is neither unidirectional nor uniform: norms and technology mutually influence each other, and each may serve as a trigger, promoter, or inhibitor of the other. While over the centuries technological change has usually preceded and triggered norm change, all our cases include examples of how norm change spurred technological developments after the establishment of initial norms, be it verification technologies, as in the cases of biological weapons and nuclear testing, substitutes for prohibited technologies, as in the cases of antipersonnel landmines and nuclear testing; clearance technologies, as in the case of landmines; or compliance-promoting technologies, as in the case of proliferation resistance.

As we have shown at several points, not all of these developments are exclusively positive—rather, they involve trade-offs and create new risks that may complicate the preservation of arms control, humanitarian, or environmental norms. Nonlethal weapons—be they biological, chemical, acoustic, or electric—may come to be used against civilians and thus undermine the norm of civilian immunity. Other aspects of more proliferation-resistant technologies may have economic drawbacks or other issues such as waste management; the norm against nuclear testing that strives toward nuclear disarmament has dramatically increased funding for nuclear weapons research, and, moreover, the shift to supercomputers may retrigger "real" nuclear testing by those parties lacking highly advanced simulation technologies.

Yet, the cases have also shown the robustness of norms against technological challenges. The equation that the prohibition of one weapon (or weapon development method) will lead to technological circumvention and the development of other weapons or methods is too simplistic. Technological progress does not take place in a vacuum but, rather, normative barriers restrict its trajectories. The norms against biological weapons have remained undisputed despite enormous biotechnological developments due to the wise decision not to become too specific but to reaffirm the BWC's comprehensive scope. The norm against antipersonnel landmines has halted the development of weapons that might possess similar features and expose civilians and soldiers to similar dangers. The norm against nuclear testing has halted physical nuclear testing and provided protection against its effects on humans and the environment.

However, while arms control norms do restrict technology and weapons development within their areas of regulation, we can still see that technological developments in weaponry in other, nonrestricted areas can continue in an unimpeded manner. This has occurred in the area of conventional weapons, while the world was troubled with WMD (Tannenwald 2007, 317–18), and might occur again in the area of nonlethal, cyber, and space weapons, inter alia. It is probable that the most momentous technology that could come to dominate weaponry and warfare in the future might be nanotechnology, with its possible military applications for unmanned vehicles, targeting systems, and satellite technologies (Altmann 2004). Another field that is intrinsically hard to control is the "Revolution in Military Affairs"—because it mainly concerns the utilization of information technology for enhancing the effectiveness of weapons and accelerating the speed of combat actions, it defies classic arms control methods such as regulation or prohibition of production or the use of certain weapons systems (Müller and Schörnig 2001). The risk emerging from such developments is that they might not only circumvent existing treaties but also stimulate new arms races by fueling the security dilemma and contributing to a feeling of technological inferiority.

Coming back to our initial question about when technology serves as a norm-promoting factor and when as a norm-threatening factor, we can thus conclude that it is neither the intrinsic features nor the very emergence of a technology that determines its impact but, rather, the political will of the actors. After all, it is they who initiate technological efforts, decide upon the military uses of new technologies, and react to these developments by interpreting them in the context of existing norms and, if deemed necessary, modifying the norms to assure their strength.

Notes

1. The London Naval Treaties did enter into force; the Washington Treaty could not because it lacked ratification by France; and the Hague Rules of Air Warfare were not even adopted but remained the suggestion of the Commission of Jurists that was in charge of drafting them.

2. In Nazi Germany, millions were killed in concentration camps with poisonous gases without, however, this being considered a breach of the norm because the Geneva Protocol only prohibited the use of chemical weapons in warfare.

3. See, e.g., the control list of the Australia Group; www.australiagroup.net/en/biological_agents.html#d.

4. The following are GIF members: Argentina, Brazil, Canada, France, Japan, the Republic of Korea, the Republic of South Africa, the United Kingdom, the United States, Switzerland, the People's Republic of China, the Russian Federation, and EURATOM.

5. The United States estimates that about 11,000 American deaths between 1951 and 2000 are attributable to atmospheric testing (CDC and NCI 2005). The global death rate—including future casualties—might well be of the order of several million (Sakharov 1990).

6. Fifty-one confirmed and six alleged producers (ICBL 2010, 14).

7. The data are based on country reports provided by the "Landmine Monitor" (ICBL 2000–2010).

8. Available examples of such weapons are the Australian Area Denial Weapon System, the Canadian Automatic Grenade Launcher, the French Moder, and the Dutch M-19 (National Research Council 2001, 115; NATO 2003b). One recently produced system is the US Spider XM-7 Network Command Munition, resulting from the US Department of Defense's three-track program to find APM alternatives. It achieved initial operational capability in June 2011 (DOT&E 2009, 93; 2010, 87–88; 2011, 89).

9. E.g., the electrical antipersonnel mine called Taser Anti-Personnel Munition

(TAPM) (also Taser Remote Area Denial, TRAD), causing neuromuscular incapacitation through electroshock, and the M5 Modular Crowd Control Munition, causing short-term incapacitation through polyvinyl chloride (PVC) balls (Davison 2007, 20, 31; Global Security 2011).

References

Aldrich, George H., and Christine M. Chinkin. 2000. "A Century of Achievement and Unfinished Work." *American Journal of International Law* 94 (1): 90–98.

Altmann, Jürgen. 2004. "Military Uses of Nanotechnology: Perspectives and Concerns." *Security Dialogue* 35 (1): 61–79.

Becker, Una. 2007. *Light at the End of the Tunnel? The Sixth Review Conference of the Biological Weapons Convention.* PRIF Report no. 79. Peace Research Institute Frankfurt. www.hsfk.de/fileadmin/downloads/prif79.pdf.

Becker-Jakob, Una. 2011. "Notions of Justice in the Biological Weapons Control Regime." PRIF Working Paper 09-2011. Peace Research Institute Frankfurt, Frankfurt am Main. www.hsfk.de/fileadmin/downloads/arbeitspapier0911k.pdf.

Biden, Joe. 2010. "The President's Nuclear Vision." *Wall Street Journal,* January 29.

Bowman, Katherine, Kathryn Hughes, and Jo L. Husbands. 2011. "Moving Forward: Trends in Science and Technology and the Future of the Biological Weapons Convention." *Bulletin of the Atomic Scientists* 67 (3): 16–25.

Burns, Richard Dean. 2009. *The Evolution of Arms Control: From Antiquity to the Nuclear Age.* Westport: Praeger Security International.

BWC (Biological Weapons Convention). 1986. "Final Document, Part II, Final Declaration." 2nd BWC RevCon. BWC/CONF.II/13/II, Geneva, September 8–26.

———. 1991. "Final Document, Part II, Final Declaration." 3rd BWC RevCon. BWC/CONF. III/23/part II, Geneva, September 9–27.

———. 1996. "Final Document." 4th BWC RevCon. BWC/CONF.IV/9/part II, Geneva, November 25–December 13.

———. 2006. "Final Document." 6th BWC RevCon. BWC/CONF.VI/6, Geneva, November 20–December 8.

———. 2011. "Final Document, Part III, Decisions and Recommendations." 7th BWC RevCon. BWC/CONF.VII/7, Geneva, December 5–22.

Cantrell, Charles L. 1977. "Humanitarian Law in Armed Conflict: The Third Diplomatic Conference." *Marquette Law Review* 61: 253–78.

CDC (Centers for Disease Control and Prevention) and NCI (National Cancer Institute). 2005. *Report on the Feasibility of a Study of the Health Consequences to the American Population from Nuclear Weapons Tests Conducted by the United States and Other Nations.* Vol. 1, Technical Report. www.cdc.gov/nceh/radiation/fallout.

Coupland, Robin M. 1997. "'Non-lethal' Weapons: Precipitating a New Arms Race: Medicine Must Guard against Its Knowledge Being Used for Weapon Development." *British Medicine Journal* 315 (7100): 72.

Croft, Stuart. 1996. *Strategies of Arms Control: A History and Typology*. Manchester: Manchester University Press.

Dahlman, Ola, Jenifer Mackby, Svein Mykkeltveit, and Hein Haak. 2011. *Detect and Deter: Can Countries Verify the Nuclear Test Ban?* Dordrecht: Springer.

Dando, Malcolm. 2011. "Advances in Neuroscience and the Biological and Toxin Weapons Convention." *Biotechnology Research International* 2011: 1–9. doi:10.4061/2011/973851.

Davison, Neil. 2005. "The Role of Scientific Discovery in the Establishment of the First Biological Weapons Programmes." Bradford Science and Technology Report no. 5. Department of Peace Studies, University of Bradford. www.brad.ac.uk/acad/sbtwc/ST_Reports/ST_Report_No_5.pdf.

———. 2007. *The Contemporary Development of "Non-Lethal" Weapons*. Bradford Non-Lethal Weapons Research Project (BNLWRP), Department of Peace Studies, University of Bradford. Occasional Paper no. 3. www.brad.ac.uk/acad/nlw/research_reports/docs/BNLWRP_OP3_May07.pdf.

Disarmament Forum. 2005. "Science, Technology, and the CBW Regimes." *Disarmament Forum* 2005 (1).

DOT&E (Director, Operational Test and Evaluation). 2009. *FY 2009 Annual Report*. Washington. www.dote.osd.mil/pub/reports/FY2009.

———. 2010. *FY 2010 Annual Report*. Washington. www.dote.osd.mil/pub/reports/FY2010.

———. 2011. *FY 2011 Annual Report*. Washington. www.dote.osd.mil/pub/reports/FY2011.

Doucet, Ian, and Richard Lloyd, eds. 2001. *Alternative Anti-Personnel Mines: The Next Generations*. Commissioned by Landmine Action and the German Initiative to Ban Landmines. www.landmineaction.org/resources/Alternative_APMs_report.pdf.

Farrell, Theo, and Hélène Lambert. 2001. "Courting Controversy: International Law, National Norms and American Nuclear Use." *Review of International Studies* 27 (3): 309–26.

Fetter, Steve. 1988. *Toward a Comprehensive Test Ban*. Cambridge: Ballinger.

Fidler, David P. 2005. "The Meaning of Moscow: 'Non-lethal' Weapons and International Law in the Early 21st Century." *International Review of the Red Cross* 87 (859): 525–52.

Franceschini, Giorgio, and Annette Schaper. 2006. *Nuclear Weapons Research and Modernization without Nuclear Testing: The CTBT in Danger?* PRIF Report no. 77. Peace Research Institute Frankfurt. www.hsfk.de/fileadmin/downloads/prif77_01.pdf.

Geissler, Erhard, and John Ellis van Courtland Moon, eds. 1999. *Biological and Toxin*

Weapons: Research, Development and Use from the Middle Ages to 1945. Oxford: Oxford University Press.

Gelber, Harry G. 1974. "Technical Innovation and Arms Control." *World Politics* 26 (4): 509–41.

GIF (Generation IV International Forum). 2006. "Evaluation Methodology for Proliferation Resistance and Physical Protection of Generation IV Nuclear Energy Systems." Prepared by the Proliferation Resistance and Physical Protection Evaluation Methodology Expert Group of the GIF, Revision 5, November 30. www.gen-4.org/Technology/horizontal/PRPPEM.pdf.

Global Security. 2011. "M5 Modular Crowd Control Munition." www.globalsecurity.org/military/systems/munitions/m5.htm.

Hafemeister, David W. 2007. "Progress in CTBT Monitoring since Its 1999 Senate Defeat." *Science and Global Security* 15 (3): 151–83.

Hart, John. 2006. "The Soviet Biological Weapons Program." In *Deadly Cultures: Biological Weapons since 1945*, edited by Mark Wheelis, Lajos Rózsa, and Malcolm Dando, 132–56. Cambridge: Harvard University Press.

IAEA (International Atomic Energy Agency). 2003. *Guidance for the Evaluation of Innovative Nuclear Reactors and Fuel Cycles: Report of Phase 1a of the International Project on Innovative Nuclear Reactors and Fuel Cycles (INPRO)*. IAEA-TECDOC-1362. Vienna: IAEA.

———. 2011a. "Under Construction Reactors by Country." Nuclear Power Plants Information. www.iaea.org/cgi-bin/db.page.pl/pris.reaucct.htm.

———. 2011b. "IAEA Projects Slower Nuclear Growth after Fukushima." IAEA News Centre, September 22. www.iaea.org/newscenter/news/2011/nuclgrowth.html.

ICBL (International Campaign to Ban Landmines). 2000. *Landmine Monitor 2000, Country ReportUSA*. www.the-monitor.org/index.php/publications/display?url=lm/2000/usa.html.

———. 2003. *Landmine Monitor 2003, Country Report USA*. www.the-monitor.org/index.php/publications/display?url=lm/2003/usa.html.

———. 2004. *Landmine Monitor 2004, Country Report Hungary*. www.the-monitor.org/index.php/publications/display?url=lm/2004/hungary.html.

———. 2008. *Landmine Monitor 2008, Country Report USA*. www.the-monitor.org/index.php/publications/display?url=lm/2008/countries/usa.html.

———. 2010. *Landmine Monitor 2010*. www.the-monitor.org/index.php/publications/display?url=lm/2010.

INFCE (International Nuclear Fuel Cycle Evaluation). 1980. *Advanced Fuel Cycle and Reactor Concepts: Report of INFCE Working Group VIII*. Vienna: IAEA.

Kelle, Alexander. 2005. "Science, Technology and the CBW Control Regimes." *Disarmament Forum* 2005 (1): 7–16.

———. 2007. Introduction to *The Changing Scientific and Technological Basis of the CBW Proliferation Problem*, edited by Alexander Kelle, 4–10. Bradford: University of Bradford.

Kelle, Alexander, Kathryn Nixdorff, and Malcolm Dando. 2006. *Controlling Biochemical Weapons: Adapting Multilateral Arms Control for the 21st Century*. Basingstoke: Palgrave Macmillan.

Larsen, Jeffrey A., ed. 2002. *Arms Control: Cooperative Security in a Changing Environment*. Boulder: Lynne Rienner.

Lyman, Edwin S. 2006. "The Global Nuclear Energy Partnership: Will It Advance Nonproliferation or Undermine It?" Paper presented at the annual meeting of the Institute of Nuclear Materials Management, Washington, July 19.

Mathews, Robert J. 2001. "The 1980 Convention on Certain Conventional Weapons: A Useful Framework despite Earlier Disappointments." *International Review of the Red Cross* 83 (844): 991–1012.

McGrath, Rae. 2000. *Landmines and Unexploded Ordnance: A Resource Book*. London: Pluto Press.

McLeish, Caitríona, and Ralf Trapp. 2011. "The Life Sciences Revolution and the BWC: Reconsidering the Science and Technology Review Process in a Post-Proliferation World." *Nonproliferation Review* 18 (3): 527–43.

Medalia, Jonathan. 2008. *Comprehensive Nuclear-Test-Ban Treaty: Issues and Arguments*. CRS Report for Congress RL34394.

Mello, Greg. 2010. "The Obama Disarmament Paradox." *Bulletin of the Atomic Scientists*, Web ed., February 4. www.thebulletin.org/web-edition/op-eds/the-obama-disarmament-paradox.

Meselson, Matthew. 2000. "Averting the Hostile Exploitation of Biotechnology." *CBW Conventions Bulletin*, no. 48 (June 2000): 16–19.

Monin, Lydia, and Andrew Gallimore. 2002. *The Devil's Gardens: A History of Landmines*. London: Pimlico.

Müller, Harald, and Andreas Schmidt. 2010. "The Little-Known Story of Deproliferation: "Why States Give Up Nuclear Weapons Activities." In *Forecasting Nuclear Proliferation in the 21st Century*, vol. 1, *The Role of Theory*, edited by William C. Potter and Gaukhar Mukhatzhanova, 124–58. Stanford: Stanford University Press.

Müller, Harald and Niklas Schörnig. 2001. "RMA and Nuclear Weapons—A Calamitous Link for Arms Control." *Disarmament Forum* 2001 (4): 17–26.

Murray, Williamson. 1996. "Strategic Bombing: The British, American, and German Experiences." In *Military Innovation in the Interwar Period*, edited by Williamson Murray and Allan R. Millett, 96–143. Cambridge: Cambridge University Press.

National Research Council. 2001. *Alternative Technologies to Replace Antipersonnel Landmines*. Committee on Alternative Technologies to Replace Antipersonnel Landmines. Washington: National Academy Press. PDF e-book.

———. 2011. *Trends in Science and Technology Relevant to the Biological and Toxin Weapons Convention: Summary of an International Workshop: Bejing, China, October 31 to November 3, 2010*. Washington: National Academies Press.

NATO. 2003a. *Alternatives to Anti-Personnel Landmines*. RTO Technical Report TR-040(I). Neuilly-sur-Seine: NATO. http://ftp.rta.nato.int/public//PubFullText/RTO/TR/RTO-TR-040-I///TR-040%28I%29-$$ALL.pdf.

———. 2003b. *Alternatives to Anti-Personnel Landmines. Annex A: sas-023 Country Participation & Representatives*. RTO Technical Report TR-040(I). Neuilly-sur-Seine:NATO. http://ftp.rta.nato.int/public//PubFullText/RTO/TR/RTO-TR-040-I///TR-040%28I%29-$$ALL.pdf.

———. 2006. *The Human Effects of Non-Lethal Technologies*. RTO (Research and Technology Organisation) Technical Report TR-HFM-073. Neuilly-sur-Seine: NATO. http://ftp.rta.nato.int/public/PubFullText/RTO/TR/RTO-TR-HFM-073/$$TR-HFM-073-ALL.pdf.

Oeter, Stefan. 2008. "Methods and Means of Combat." In *The Handbook of International Humanitarian Law*, edited by Dieter Fleck, 119–235. Oxford: Oxford University Press.

Pearson, Alan M., Marie I. Chevrier, and Mark Wheelis, eds. 2007. *Incapacitating Biochemical Weapons: Promise or Peril?* Lanham: Lexington Books.

Petro, James B., Theodore R. Plasse, and Jack A. McNulty. 2003. "Biotechnology: Impact on Biological Warfare and Biodefense." *Biosecurity and Bioterrorism* 1 (3): 161–69.

Price, Richard. 1995. "A Genealogy of the Chemical Weapons Taboo." *International Organization* 49 (1): 73–103.

Prokosch, Eric. 1995. *The Technology of Killing: A Military and Political History of Antipersonnel Weapons*. London: Zed Books.

Rappert, Brian, Marie Chevrier, and Malcolm Dando. 2006. "In-Depth Implementation of the BTWC: Education and Outreach." Bradford Review Conference Papers 18, Department of Peace Studies, University of Bradford. www.brad.ac.uk/acad/sbtwc/briefing/RCP_18.pdf.

Sakharov, Andrei D. 1990. "Radioactive Carbon from Nuclear Explosions and Nonthreshold Biological Effects." *Science and Global Security* 1 (3–4): 175–87.

Schaper, Annette. 1994. "The Problem of Definition: Just What Is a Nuclear Weapon Test?" In *Implementing the Comprehensive Test Ban: New Aspects of Definition, Organization and Verification*, edited by Eric Arnett, 26–47. Oxford: Oxford University Press.

———. 1996. *Der geplante Forschungsreaktor in Garching: Rückfall in alte Sünderzeiten deutscher Nichtverbreitungspolitik?* HSFK-Standpunkte 3/1996, Peace Research Institute Frankfurt. Frankfurt am Main.

Schindler, Dietrich, and Jiří Toman. 1988. *The Laws of Armed Conflicts*. Dordrecht: Martinus Nijhoff.

Schneidmiller, Chris. 2011. "As Obama Prepares to Push Nuclear Test Ban, Technological Basis Still Debated." Global Security Newswire, Nuclear Threat Initiative, July 20. www.nti.org/gsn/article/as-obama-prepares-to-push-nuclear-test-ban-technological-basis-still-debated.

Sims, Nicholas A. 2009. *The Future of Biological Disarmament: Strengthening the Treaty Ban on Weapons*, London: Routledge.

Skjöldebrand, R. 1980. "The International Nuclear Fuel Cycle Evaluation—INFCE." *IAEA Bulletin* 22 (2): 30–33.

Smith, Michael E. 2009. "Technology Change, Rule Change, and the Law of Armed Conflict." In *War, Torture and Terrorism: Rethinking the Rules of International Security*, edited by Anthony Lang and Amanda Russell Beattie, 105–24. London: Routledge.

Smith, Thomas W. 2002. "The New Law of War: Legitimizing Hi-Tech and Infrastructural Violence." *International Studies Quarterly* 46 (3): 355–74.

Tabassi, Lisa. 2009. "The Nuclear Test Ban: *Lex Lata* or *de Lege Ferenda*?" *Journal of Conflict and Security Law* 14 (2): 309–52.

Tannenwald, Nina. 2007. *The Nuclear Taboo: The United States and the Non-Use of Nuclear Weapons since 1945*. Cambridge: Cambridge University Press.

Tucker, Jonathan B. 2010. "The Convergence of Biology and Chemistry: Implications for Arms Control Verification." *Bulletin of the Atomic Scientists* 66 (6): 56–66.

Tucker, Jonathan B., and Raymond A. Zilinskas. 2006. "The Promise and Perils of Synthetic Biology." *New Atlantis* (12): 25–45.

US DoS (US Department of State). 2005. *Adherence to and Compliance with Arms Control, Nonproliferation and Disarmament Agreements and Commitments*. Washington: US Department of State, August. www.state.gov/t/avc/rls/rpt/51977.htm.

———. 2010. *Adherence to and Compliance with Arms Control, Nonproliferation and Disarmament Agreements and Commitments*. Washington: US Department of State, July. www.state.gov/t/avc/rls/rpt/170924.htm.

van Creveld, Martin. 1991. *Technology and War: From 2000 B.C. to the Present*. London: Brassey's.

Wheelis, Mark. 2002. "Biotechnology and Biochemical Weapons." *Nonproliferation Review* 9 (1): 48–53.

———. 2004. "Will the 'New Biology' Lead to New Weapons?" *Arms Control Today* 34 (6): 6–13.

Wheelis, Mark, and Malcolm Dando. 2002. "On the Brink: Biodefence, Biotechnology and the Future of Weapons Control." *CBW Conventions Bulletin*, no. 58 (December), 3–7.

Wheelis, Mark, Lajos Rózsa, and Malcolm Dando, eds. 2006. *Deadly Cultures: Biological Weapons since 1945*. Cambridge: Harvard University Press.

Youngblood, Norman. 2006. *The Development of Mine Warfare: A Most Murderous and Barbarous Conduct*. Westport: Praeger Security International.

Yudin, Yury. 2009. *Multilateralization of the Nuclear Fuel Cycle: Assessing the Existing Proposals*. Geneva: United Nations, UNIDIR (United Nations Institute for Disarmament Research).

Zanders, Jean Pascal. 2001. "Challenges to Disarmament Regimes: The Case of the Biological and Toxin Weapons Convention." *Global Society* 15 (4): 361–85.

CHAPTER FIVE

Winds of Change

Exogenous Events and Trends as Norm Triggers (or Norm Killers)

Harald Müller, Marco Fey, and Carsten Rauch

BOTH LONG-TERM TRENDS in the international system and individual events, shocks, or traumas of a certain magnitude hold potential for triggering norm change in arms control regimes. They might challenge dominant ideas and ideological paradigms, put new issues on the table that call for collective action, alter cost-benefit calculations of member states, or shake the international balance of power, and thus impact on both agency and structure. While scholars often invoke exogenous events as explanations for institutional change, such events can also inhibit change within a given normative structure: "Exogenous shock remains an indeterminate explanation" and thus cannot be used for forecasting (Legro 2000, 423). We analyze the impact of three exemplary significant international developments and events for their effects on international arms control: the current power shift from the transatlantic area to Asia, the end of the Cold War within half a decade, and the rise of the terrorist threat after the singular event of 9/11.

POWER TRANSITION AND ARMS CONTROL

Power Transition: What Does It Mean for Arms Control?

For two decades there have been signs of the rise of new powers, notably China and India. Their economies are growing at significantly higher rates than that of the United States (World Bank 2011a). While the United States will remain the dominant power for some time, a power transition is looming on the horizon.

Power transition theory (PTT) assumes a hegemonic international system as the normal state of affairs. The hegemon guarantees and protects the material and normative status quo it once created. Through its preponderance of power the hegemon and its allies maintain peace and stability against the efforts of dissatisfied actors (Kugler and Organski 1989, 173). When a rising dissatisfied power approaches parity with the hegemon, it starts to challenge the international status quo and tries to replace it by arrangements more favorable to its own desires. If the declining power does not cede its privileges voluntarily, this often results in international conflict or even war (Kugler and Organski 1989, 174). Conflict can be avoided if the declining hegemon respects the challenger's vital interests and invites it to participate in shaping and running the international order, granting it the degree of "ownership" that is functionally reasonable and meets its aspirations: in short, whether the hegemon can satisfy the rising power (Müller and Rauch 2011). The outcome of a power shift is thus not determined but is contingent. Applied to arms control, this consideration leads to two quite different scenarios.

First, and more in line with traditional thinking on PTT, power transitions can be expected to act as *regime killers*, essentially hampering or even destroying existing regimes. Two similar but distinct motivations could fuel this scenario. The first relates to freedom of action. A challenger that intends to overthrow the international order needs military strength. Likewise, a hegemon facing a rising challenger will want to defend *its* order by all necessary means. Both hegemon and challenger will thus wish to keep their scope of action as intact as possible by not joining or not complying with multilateral (arms control) regimes. Additionally, as already discussed, the challenger is implacably dissatisfied with the international order of which arms control regimes are an integral part. It thus appears likely that the challenger will oppose, and try to dismantle, existing arms control regimes.

Second, and less thoroughly explored in the existing literature, power transitions could also be expected to function as *regime boosters*, leading to the advancement of regimes by common action of hegemon and rising power. Again there are two underlying motivations, one focusing on the rising power and one focusing on the hegemon: an only partly dissatisfied challenger may try to use its increasing power to bargain successfully for changes within regimes without threatening the system as a whole and thus advance norm change. In turn, the dominant power may try to maintain its position or to smooth the transition by integrating the rising power into the existing normative framework as "cochair."

Whereas the *killer scenario* posits power transitions primarily as a structural phenomenon and as a determining factor, the *booster scenario* requires an effort by hegemon and rising power to *manage* a power transition, and therefore depends on agency.

US-Chinese Relations and Their Impact on Multilateral Arms Control Regimes

The perception of a power shift between the United States and China influences the defense policies of either side. The 2002 US National Security Strategy (US White House 2002) vowed to prevent any challenger from achieving equal superpower status with the United States, a doctrine unmistakably directed against China. And while the 2010 US National Security Strategy (US White House 2010) contained reconciliatory language, the quest to maintain conventional superiority is still a clear tenor of the document. This would make little sense if the United States accepted parity with the rising power.

China, on the other hand, suspects that Washington wants to prevent the rise of China to its deserved place as a world power (Goldstein 2005) and is taking measures to close the vast gap between the military power of the two states. Chinese defense expenditures in relation to the US defense budget accounted for less than 25 percent in 2009, even with estimated purchasing power parity included (IISS 2011, 31, 46, 198). Most Chinese weapons systems are technologically less sophisticated than US systems, and Chinese troops are not trained as well as US forces. But China's absolute defense budget has been increasing over recent years and is indicative of huge military modernization plans, even if expenditures stay at the same percentage level of its growing GDP (World Bank 2011b).

Three impacts of this rivalry on arms control concern the nuclear nonproliferation regime. First, the rivalry impedes nuclear disarmament. This adds to the regime conflict between nuclear weapon states (NWS) and (mainly NAM) nonnuclear weapon states (NNWS). The United States has been claiming superiority in all relevant military areas—to use the language of the Department of Defense, "full spectrum dominance" (2010, 149). This includes the capability to carry out precise, prompt long-range conventional strikes, national missile defense, and eventually, weaponry in space. China is concerned that its deterrent might be compromised. It is trying to develop robust antisatellite (Gill and Kleiber 2007) and cyberwar capabilities (Kanwal 2009, 14, 16; Sharma 2010, 38) in order to counter US strengths, and it does not accept limits to the (slow) growth of its nuclear arsenal as long as the dimensions of US national missile defense (NMD) and conventional strike options remain uncertain (Blumenthal and Mazza 2011, 2, 7; NTI 2011). China's plans (which lack transparency) to increase the size of its nuclear weapon stocks (in combination with its growing conventional capabilities) put curbs on Russia's and India's willingness to agree to strict overall limits on nuclear weapons, nonstrategic ones included (Sokov et al. 2009, 13). This reluctance by Russia has an impact on NATO's willingness to terminate the deployment of substrategic weapons in Europe (Woolf 2011, 13). This motivational chain betrays how a vague concern—retaining hegemony or achieving equal status—reverberates across strategic considerations with the result that disarmament is impeded. This, in turn, influences the degree of satisfaction with the Nuclear Non-Proliferation Treaty (NPT) by NAM states and their willingness to accept stronger nonproliferation measures (see chapter 2). China is also skeptical about demands for more transparency; it regards its ability to conceal its military assets as a necessary part of its minimum deterrence posture against the United States (Saalman 2009, 49; Sokov et al. 2009, 16).

Second, the strengthening of the nonproliferation toolbox suffers from China taking the side of the NAM. Like the NAM, China feels strongly about sovereignty and is deeply concerned that nonproliferation may impede development or impact detrimentally on its own capacity to import and export at will. This is especially true for fossil fuel from Iran (Garver 2011, 12). There is thus an inbuilt Chinese bias against bold steps to strengthen the instruments of nonproliferation. This, in turn, is frequently interpreted by the United States as a sign of bad faith and leads to pressure being applied to China that the Chinese perceive as hegemonic attempts to block its development (Medeiros 2007).

Third, the rivalry stands in the way of more determined norm enforcement. China regards its relations with North Korea (Shen 2006, 19, 27; Lee 2009, 57) and Iran as conducive to its own geopolitical standing (Lin 2010, 3). Iran, in addition, is also important for Chinese access to needed energy resources, an area where it feels inferior to the United States with its strong strategic position in the Middle East (Garver 2006, 264; Park 2010, 1). China does not promote proliferation and has agreed to UN sanctions against either country, while working to limit their severity. The continuation of Sino-Iranian cooperation in the fossil fuel sector (Park 2010, 3), despite concerns noted in UN Resolution 1929 that Iran might use its energy trade revenues and related technology imports to finance and support its nuclear program (UNSC 2010, 9), shows that strategic economic interests and energy security may take priority over nonproliferation objectives. In addition, China has tried to shape UN sanctions in a way that does not damage its trade relations with Iran too much (Garver 2011, 7). Chinese conduct, in turn, is seen by some in the United States as an attempt to build coalitions to bring down US hegemony (Kagan 2006). What China sees as unequal standards in US nonproliferation policy (Israel, India) reinforces this attitude (Foot and Walter 2011, 163–64, 169–70).

China acts in the nuclear regime—with regard to its relations with the hegemonic power—in four directions (for details see chapter 6): it resists initiatives that could compromise its minimum deterrence; it resists proposals that would obviate its quest for "equal security"; it promotes norms that are compatible with either objective and correspond to traditional stances; and, finally, China promotes changes that conform to the NAM agenda, such as those regarding peaceful uses and export controls. Yet, perhaps surprisingly, on the whole China has improved its overall norm compliance (Foot and Walter 2011, 157–61).

The United States is struggling to find ways of reconciling its own lust to retain primacy with the inevitability of accommodating the Asian power. Obama's *National Security Strategy* recognized Chinese (as well as Russian) concerns and expressed the desire to develop a mutual strategic partnership that would be built on common interests (US White House 2010, 11, 16). At the same time, the United States reserves the right to norm deviance if its government deems this necessary in order to live up to the exceptional "special responsibilities" of a hegemon (Foot and Walter 2011, 284). As the rise of China is the pivotal challenge to its hegemony, norm violations by the United States may continue to grow.

The effect of US-Chinese rivalry on norm development in international regimes appears to be less a function of the rivalry as such than of the US government's particular perception of the virulence of this rivalry as well as the importance of the regimes. Since this perception varies between the US Democratic and Republican Parties, the impact of the "rivalry" depends on the outcome of US elections. Domestic factors, not systemic ones, are the drivers.

US-Indian Relations and Their Impact on the Nuclear Nonproliferation Regime

Unlike China's rise in power, India's rise has been well received by the United States, even though New Delhi and Washington were at odds during the Cold

War. Now it appears they can be a kind of "natural allies," as some observers anticipate (Müller and Schmidt 2009). The United States welcomes India as a power that helps balance China's rise. India sees good relations with the United States as insurance, should China turn aggressive, while cultivating good relations with China as long as Beijing behaves peacefully. For example, India is watching with concern China's increasing naval presence in the Indian Ocean, where a barely concealed naval arms race between the two powers is under way.

US-Indo relations have developed rapidly in the last decade. As late as 1996, India felt locked into inferior status by the US push for indefinite extension of the NPT and a CTBT, and in 1998 the Indian nuclear tests interrupted an emerging process of mutual rapprochements when the United States sided with the other UNSC permanent members in issuing a harsh condemnation. Only one year later, however, Washington took New Delhi's side in the 1999 Kargil War with Pakistan. The ensuing improvement was further accelerated by the Bush administration's pressure on Pakistan after a series of Islamist terrorist attacks against India in 2001–2, even though, at the same time, the United States had to court Islamabad as an ally in the "war against terror."

Through the "nuclear deal"—finalized in 2008—the last barrier to close relations, America's nonrecognition of India's nuclear status and the decades-old sanctions against India's civilian nuclear development, was lifted. As part of this deal India agreed to subject all civil nuclear facilities to IAEA safeguards, and the United States resumed civil nuclear cooperation with India and removed national and (via the Nuclear Suppliers Group, NSG) international trade restrictions.

Political relations between two virtual allies in balancing China loom large in the background. The deal lacks any disarmament or nonproliferation commitments and is interpreted by most observers as a blow to the nonproliferation regime (Mian and Ramana 2006). India now shares most of the benefits that NPT membership offers, without bearing most of the obligations, such as full-scope safeguards on all nuclear facilities or the duty to work for nuclear disarmament (Rauch 2010, 3).

Thus while the agreement decreases Indian dissatisfaction, it could increase the dissatisfaction of other actors, most notably NAM states. India may feel less discriminated against, but for those states the deal means special treatment for New Delhi that leaves them discriminated against even more strongly than before.

For them and other NPT NNWS the message of the deal could furthermore be that a successful nuclear weapons program, after a brief period of sanctions and retributions, would lead to recognition by the international community. This might provide an incentive to consider clandestine nuclear weapons programs and to eventually withdraw from the NPT (Müller 2010, 192). Another factor that could damage the nonproliferation regime is potential US noncompliance with NPT rules, as the cooperation envisaged could indirectly help India to manufacture more nuclear weapons. In addition, the system of norms of the NSG, an important element of the regime outside the NPT, has been seriously compromised by US pressure for a singular exception in favor of India (Weiss 2007).

However, some features point to a more positive interpretation. India shares most of the norms and principles enshrined in the regime. Because of the NPT's rules, it cannot accede as a NWS and will not accede as a NNWS; yet, while actual universalization of the NPT may remain utopian, drawing India closer to the regime could lead to virtual universalization. Even though the deal does not put India under full-scope safeguards, it increases the number of facilities under, and therefore enhances the scope of, IAEA verification. India, which already has a good nonproliferation record, has also agreed to harmonize its export control legislation with NSG and the Missile Technology Control Regime (MTCR) guidelines. Moreover, reducing Indian dissatisfaction with the regime could also lead to a tougher Indian stance regarding noncompliance by regime members. Since then, India has several times voted for IAEA resolutions condemning Iran's actions (Bagchi 2009). Finally, as India grows in power and importance, the impact of India's dissatisfaction with the NPT and the nonproliferation regime in general may also have grown in importance. It is an open question whether the regime would be able to handle opposition from a dissatisfied India that is more active and powerful. The nuclear deal may contribute to saving the regime from this serious challenge (Rauch 2010, 6).

US-Indo cooperation offers a mixed bag of norm boosters and killers, but only as collateral effects of efforts by two great powers to adjust their relationship in the face of China's rise (Foot and Walter 2011, 153–54). It is not the result of intentional strategic action aimed at affecting the regime. This augurs ominously for periods when great power relations may be tenser than during the last two decades. However, as US-Indo reconciliation started under a Democratic administration (Clinton), received a boost under a Republican administration (Bush II), and has been sustained so far by a new Democratic administration (Obama), domestic factors on the United States side will probably not interfere to an important extent. In India the situation is rather different, as considerable explicitly anti-American sentiment still exists in some regions of the political spectrum (Rauch 2010, 9–11).

THE SMOOTH LANDING: THE END OF THE COLD WAR AND ARMS CONTROL

The long superpower confrontation engendered an arms race as well as several incidents that could have resulted in nuclear war. Its end could have triggered a boost for arms control as the United States and Russia no longer needed to prepare for large-scale nuclear war; the expectation of a peace dividend called for massive reductions in arsenals, too. The international environment after 1990 was favorable to multilateral regimes; new windows for cooperation opened up. But the end of the East-West conflict could also have rendered arms control less relevant, as some had seen it primarily as an instrument for reducing the risks and costs of a superpower confrontation. Moreover, the emergence of the United States as the hegemon could have dramatically reduced American incentives to engage in international cooperation, specifically in arms control.

The beginning of the end of the Cold War was heralded by a little-noticed event in 1986: Mikhail Gorbachev opened the Soviet Union for obligatory maneuver observation by NATO officers in the framework of the Helsinki confidence-building measures. This unprecedented concession to transparency by a hitherto secretive Soviet regime indicated changes ahead. This impression received a further boost by the Reykjavik meeting later that year, where Reagan and Gorbachev were only drawn back from the "abyss" of nuclear disarmament by unnerved staffers. In 1987 they agreed on eliminating the entire class of intermediate nuclear weapons and an unprecedentedly intrusive verification system. The Intermediate-Range Nuclear Forces (INF) Treaty was followed, in rapid procession, by the Treaty on Conventional Armed Forces in Europe (CFE), which reduced conventional forces in Europe, the START I (Strategic Arms Reduction Treaty), which cut strategic nuclear forces by about a third, and START II, which brought further reductions and prohibited heavy, multiple-warhead land-based intercontinental ballistic missiles, drastically reducing the warhead/target ratio and thus fostering strategic stability. The demise of the Soviet Union led to mutual unilateral reductions of substrategic nuclear weapons—that is, the elimination of several thousand warheads and whole categories of weapons such as nuclear landmines or antisubmarine charges, and US-Russian cooperation in minimizing the proliferation risk emerging from the decay of the Soviet Union. The indefinite extension of the NPT, the revamping of its verification system by the Additional Protocol (INFCIRC/540 of 1997) and the conclusion of the CTBT in 1996 completed the success story of nuclear arms control and disarmament.

The end of the Cold War opened the door to the introduction and improvement of transparency and confidence-building measures within the framework of the Biological Weapons Convention (BWC). This started at the second BWC Review Conference (RevCon) in 1986, and was refined by the third RevCon in 1991. These measures were followed first by expert work and later by negotiations aimed at complementing the convention with a transparency and compliance protocol. Negotiations on the Chemical Weapons Convention (CWC) were accelerated after 1990 and finalized in 1992. The construction of the Organisation for the Prohibition of Chemical Weapons (OPCW) started through a preparatory process and was completed by 1996 when the convention entered into force.

In a quite different sense, arms control was given impetus by the dissolution of the Soviet Union and the Warsaw Treaty organization. The risk of acquiring uncontrolled materials for weapons of mass destruction (WMD) led to unprecedented assistance to the Soviet Union to secure control over such fission materials. The proliferation of small arms and light weapons from Eastern bloc stocks motivated the international community to install new instruments to curb illicit trade in such weaponry.

The end of the Cold War made possible the most spectacular effort at enforcement: the disarmament of Iraq's weapons of mass destruction programs, which followed the UN-mandated repulsion of the Iraqi occupation of Kuwait, the result of unprecedented US-Soviet cooperation in the UN Security Council. The creation of the United Nations Special Commission (UNSCOM), a verification and dismantlement agency directed by the Security Council and working in step with the IAEA, set precedents for future enforcement actions by the world organization.

The golden decade of bilateral and multilateral arms control set off an unprecedented cascade of progress across all fields, surpassing the progress made during the first major period of arms control "détente" between 1968 and 1977. The trigger was a landmark change in Soviet foreign policy that accompanied far-reaching internal reforms. The neoconservative narrative that Moscow had been forced into surrender by the consistent pressure exerted by the Reagan administration and ensuing economic necessities is shown to be false by a counterfactual thought experiment: the Soviet elite could have returned to Stalinist practice, forcing the population to endure further hardship for the glory of the motherland. This is what Kim Il-Sung and his successor did to the North Koreans. That Gorbachev chose another path was not historical necessity, but an expression of agency: his mindset contained other preferences, including avoiding a nuclear war (Gorbachev 1996). On the other hand, the United States concluded that it was not a good option to just let the Soviets go down the drain. Ronald Reagan, George H. W. Bush, and Bill Clinton took change as an opportunity to create a dense, cooperative network of normative, partly legal and institutional relations at the bilateral and multilateral levels with the former enemy and rival (Baker 1995). Bush's concept of a "New World Order," and Clinton's 1994 "National Security Strategy of Engagement and Enlargement" (US White House 1994) included arms control and nonproliferation as essential elements of a cooperative security approach that was understood to foster US national security.

Arms control by the two superpowers did not progress in a vacuum. It was enabled by, and promoted in turn, momentous changes of policy, notably the tolerance by the Soviet Union of reforms in Eastern Europe, and its withdrawal from confronting the United States in geopolitical competition around the world, of which the settlement of conflicts in Africa and Central America was the main indicator (Evangelista 1995). These policy changes and arms control worked together in a positive feedback loop, each step enhancing mutual confidence by giving an indication of goodwill and peaceful, cooperative intentions, thereby opening opportunities for still more daring steps. If 1989–91 was the culmination of a landmark change in the global political structure, successful arms control both preceded and followed this moment, facilitating it and in turn becoming possible itself through it (Evangelista 2004). In this sense, the end of the Cold War was not just an independent variable pushing arms control, but as well a dependent variable influenced by arms control progress. Eventually, global regimes against nuclear, biological, and chemical weapons emerged in a significantly stronger shape.

The Sudden Shock: 9/11 and the Regimes

The terrorist attacks of September 11, 2001, were the most shocking event after the end of the Cold War.[1] While they did not shake the international balance of power, they transformed American threat perception and that of other major players. Transnational terrorist networks emerged as the preeminent danger for national security. The potential conjunction of terrorism and WMD had a profound impact on risk calculations. This could have led states to put more effort into strengthening the existing nonproliferation regimes in order to combat the new menace. At the same time, 9/11 could have induced more emphasis on unilateralism as a reassurance of governments' capacity to act. Thus, traditional bilateral or multilateral arms control could have been perceived as obsolete. Considerations like these have induced analysts to speak of a *watershed* or a *new world* that emerged from this unique event. Notably, high representatives of the Bush administration have made this point (Bush 2010, 151, 228–29; Cheney 2011, 10, 330–32). This subchapter maintains that this diagnosis is exaggerated. While some change is observable, it nevertheless remained relatively marginal for the development of the regimes.

Before September 2001, the nuclear nonproliferation regime was already under the shadow of increasing US aversion to disarmament and multilateralism. The Comprehensive Nuclear-Test-Ban Treaty (CTBT) had been rejected by the Senate, and the new administration was on record as not wanting to bring it back under consideration. START II was dead because of the Russian Duma's refusal to ratify it after the United States, and the National Missile Defense Act of 1999, had declared missile defense a national goal. Consequently, the Bush administration unilaterally withdrew from the Anti-Ballistic Missile (ABM) Treaty. The positive mood that had re-emerged during the 2000 NPT RevCon had gone with the Clinton administration (Walker 2012, chapter 6). The next years saw controversy and stagnation. The atmosphere during the preparatory process for the 2005 NPT RevCon grew more confrontational by the year. The RevCon could not even agree on an agenda until the last week and produced only a meager formal document that simply stated that the parties had met.

Meanwhile, some change could be observed as governments scrutinized potential threats that could emerge from terrorists' acquisition of a variety of weapons. Such considerations led to extra-regime activities that responded to the challenges of 9/11: the IAEA started a program against nuclear terrorism; the Group of Eight (G8) financed activities to secure nuclear facilities, materials, and radioactive sources through the Global Partnership Against the Spread of Weapons and Materials of Mass Destruction. In April 2004 the UN Security Council adopted S/RES/1540 which imposed binding obligations on all UN members to establish domestic controls to prevent the proliferation of WMD and their means of delivery, including appropriate export control laws. The Proliferation Security Initiative (PSI) emerged as a "coalition of the willing," with close to a hundred supporters today, and aimed at stopping the trafficking of dangerous contraband to and from state and nonstate actors. The Container Security Initiative (CSI) intended to identify and target cargo containers that pose a risk of terrorism and to improve international shipment security.

The 2010 NPT RevCon was a weaker repetition of the successful 2000 conference. Its consensus action plan contained a list of practical steps to be taken. The impact of the Bush years showed in the reluctance of the NAM to accept any significant strengthening of nonproliferation instruments. By and large, the regime appeared to be back to normal (Müller 2011).

The BWC came close to destruction when the United States marched out of the negotiations on a transparency and compliance protocol—three months *before* 9/11. Afterward, a new procedure, the intersessional process, was installed, which focused on biosafety and, more closely related to the terrorist menace, biosecurity: the Bush administration had discovered that cooperating within the framework of the BWC might be of some use in combating its main concern, WMD terrorism. As with the NPT, important developments in the biological weapons field took place outside the regime: combating the spread of biological weapons was also mainly addressed by S/RES/1540 and the PSI. The CWC did not witness confrontations like the two other regimes, but parties used the OPCW for new initiatives to prevent WMD terrorism. S/RES/1540 as well as the PSI did concern the CWC as well.

North-South tensions in all three regimes rose as new export control initiatives enhanced non-aligned concerns that their development in advanced technologies might be unduly impeded by efforts to curb the transfer of materials and technologies. US efforts to prohibit outright the further spread of fuel cycle technologies met strong resistance from leading non-aligned countries; disputes about the meaning and priority of Art. X, the cooperation norm, became more intense in the BWC; and demands to dissolve the Australia Group grew louder in the CWC at exactly the moment when Western states believed their export control coordination was more necessary than ever.

9/11 and the Policies of Key States

On the surface the end of the Cold War period and the post-9/11 period show significant differences, and we might be seduced into regarding the terrorist attacks as an independent variable driving both regime change and regime conflict. An analysis of governmental policies, however, refutes this simplistic view.

William Walker places the change in US policy toward the nonproliferation regime at around 1997 and traces it back to the increasing pressure by a conservative Republican majority in Congress, skeptical about arms control and deeply antithetical to multilateralism, on an increasingly compromising Clinton administration (Walker 2012, 135–39). Republican ideology was well encapsulated in policy publications by neoconservative think tanks (e.g., Donnelly 2000). The decline in US support for multilateral arms control started in 1996 when the Senate voiced reservations and added conditions to its resolution supporting ratification of the CWC that contradicted the mandatory language in the CWC concerning verification. It continued with the increasing reluctance of the US delegation to help the BWC protocol negotiations and culminated in the 1998 National Missile Defense Act and refusal by the Senate to consent to CTBT ratification in 1999.

The Bush administration entered office with a deep disdain for arms control and multilateralism, an attitude that was personified by the State Department's new undersecretary for arms control, John Bolton, who described the policy as follows: "We were simply rejecting inferior policies and agreements, and replacing them with greater American independence and fewer unnecessary constraints. It was just that there were so many unnecessary constraints that everywhere we turned there was something to eliminate" (Bolton 2007, 84). President Bush entered office determined to withdraw from the ABM Treaty and not to bring the CTBT back to the Senate; the US delegation derailed the BWC protocol talks in June 2001, well before 9/11. US policy afterward consistently followed the line already taken, confirming Levy's proposition that "learning" from events may mean that governments, applying their existing perceptive and evaluative schemes, see their views and policies confirmed or even reinforced (Levy 1994, 283, 290). What was new were the emphasis on the nexus of WMD/nonstate actors and some ensuing efforts to utilize international regimes for the "war on terror," or to establish new instruments (e.g., S/RES/1540, PSI, CSI, G8 Global Partnership) for that purpose. Somewhat surprisingly, the United States was one of the strongest blocking forces against efforts to establish stronger controls for small arms and light weapons (SALW), again already in July 2001 at the UN Conference on Small Arms and Light Weapons; reducing the flow of such weapons to places like Afghanistan, Somalia, Yemen, or Northern Africa could have helped curb the potential of Al Qaida and its allies to do harm. But US policy was in line with the demands of the National Rifle Association: the right of Americans to own arms must not be jeopardized by undue constraints. Domestic ideology was trumping conservative security priorities, and the United States brought the process of holding Review Conferences on the UN Programme of Action on Small Arms and Light Weapons (PoA) to an end in 2006 (Bolton 2007, chapter 3).

However, 9/11 and the failed terrorist attack against an El Al Airliner close to Mombasa Airport in 2002 motivated US efforts in multiple forums to mitigate the risks inherent in man-portable air defense systems (MANPADS) (Schroeder 2007). By definition, these weapons are included in the SALW PoA, but policies developed after 9/11 went beyond that instrument in order to prevent transfers that could end up in the hands of nonstate actors. The UN General Assembly adopted two resolutions (A/RES/59/90 in 2004, A/RES/60/77 in 2006) calling on member states to terminate the transfer of MANPADS to nonstate actors and to change national legislation accordingly. Establishing norms that prohibit such transfers and provide for secure storage and increased transparency on national policies was pursued by the G8 and in many regional settings. The most advanced set of norms is the Expanded Elements of Export Controls of the Wassenaar Agreement. Also active in norm setting were the EU Code of Conduct, the Organization for Security and Co-operation in Europe (OSCE), the Organization of American States (OAS), and the Asian-Pacific Economic Cooperation (APEC).

Russian and Chinese policies after 9/11 continued those of the pre-9/11 period, with some adaptation to the security challenges they were facing as a result of Bush's unilateralism and unfettered investment in military hardware and R&D (Hansell and Perfilyev 2009). They tried to maintain the regimes' basic structure and to emphasize principles of "stability and equal security for all," language that was meant to counter the US drive for unchallenged superiority. Russia managed to engage the Bush administration in concluding the Moscow Treaty but obtained a substantively meager result. It cooperated in bilateral threat reduction programs—in continuation of pre-2001 practice—and joined G8 activities to combat WMD terrorism. China further developed its adoption of multilateralism as part of a national security policy that had already begun in the 1990s.

Western states committed to multilateral arms control continued their proactivist stance and tried to save as much of the regimes as possible, such as the EU security and nonproliferation strategies worked out in 2003 (see chapter 9). In contrast to the 2002 US *National Security Strategy*, the EU documents emphasized the centrality of multilateral regimes, diplomacy as the first line of nonproliferation efforts, and the authority of the UN Security Council as enforcer against breaches of the rules. Countries such as Canada, Germany, and Sweden tried to mitigate conflicts between the West and the NAM over technology transfer and cooperation, to save the BWC from complete demise by devising the intersessional process as a way out of the 2001 impasse, and to restore the NPT review process after 2005. At the same time, they loyally supported US initiatives to focus on combating WMD terrorism. Canada and Sweden lowered their profile in the course of the years after 9/11. The reason, however, was not this event, but national elections that brought to power more conservative forces whose commitment to arms control did not match that of their centrist or center-left predecessors.

The non-aligned countries remained unimpressed by 9/11. Their policies did not change across the regimes. They pushed their justice claims as before, firmly opposed efforts to curb technology transfer in the name of combating proliferation and terrorism, and accepted a focus on terror only reluctantly under the condition that existing commitments would not be touched. Where this could not be granted, as in the 2005 NPT RevCon, they blocked consensus. A similar move was made against proposals for multilateralizing the nuclear fuel cycle as long as they believed this was a ploy to deny advanced technology to developing countries.

Thus, most of what seems superficially a sea change in regime developments before and after 9/11 on closer examination can be identified as the consequences of a policy shift clearly predating the event in the most powerful state, and of the reactions of other players to this policy shift. Domestic change and ideological orientations, not the terrorist attacks per se, triggered a shift in the regimes' trajectories. A broad opportunity had emerged for international cooperation, but the learning capacity of the Bush administration proved limited: it did not go beyond the insight that a small modicum of multilateralism might be useful for fighting Al Qaida's access to dangerous substances. Under Obama, so far, things have moved back in the direction of the pre-Bush era, with the addition of the antiterrorist activities that have been integrated into, or installed outside, the regimes.

CONCLUSION: DIFFERENT WINDS, DIFFERENT CHANGES?

The three cases are distinguished by the time factor. The power shift is a drawn-out process lasting for decades. The end of the Cold War happened over a period of about six years. 9/11 was a single discrete event, viewed through the looking glass of dramatic television pictures. The first two concerned the deep structure of the international system; indeed, we can look at the end of the Cold

War as the culmination of a "challenge to an established hegemony" that failed over time, to use the language of PTT. The impact of the third case on the structure has been frequently proclaimed a *watershed* event, but it may be asked whether such a profound shift really took place.

If we take the fate of multilateral arms control as an indicator of the intensity of change, the end of the Cold War reflects the powerful impact structures have on actors and the astonishing capability of actors to react to this challenge by carrying out profound structural reform in turn. Gorbachev, Reagan, and the elder Bush used opportunities that had been opened up by structural change, developing in a highly creative way a new, more cooperative structure that matched the new power relations.

With regard to the current global power shift, actors have pursued hedging policies rather than determinedly utilizing opportunities for arms control. We see neither a "killing" of arms control nor the triggering of a new spring but, rather, something in between. First, there was the Bush administration's bold attempt to preserve hegemony by unfettered military superiority and the concomitant effort at scrapping arms control institutions that threatened to constrain US freedom of action; the other global players took moderate countermeasures and tried to preserve the multilateral structures that constrained US power. More recently, the United States under Obama has shifted back to multilateralism and to a more accommodative approach toward global rivals, so far with no decisive results. Thus, it appears that either hypothesis on the impact of global structural change applies, depending on the choices by agents, for "structures do not come with an instruction sheet" (Blyth 2003).

The tragedy of 9/11 opened up opportunities for international cooperation that were only partially used. At the same time, it enabled a domestic US faction hostile to multilateralism to secure its hold over the course of US policy. The ripple effect through the regimes, however, proved limited as other actors tried to steer the previous course with some inevitable but minor adaptive shifts toward the destructive US practice. In some cases this tended to compound the damage resulting from the Bush administration's disdain for multilateralism, as in the NAM's outright rejection of efforts to strengthen the nonproliferation toolbox. Overall, however, the steadfastness of most states helped the regimes survive even in the era of hegemonic extremism.

Four conclusions emerge from these considerations. First, structural change may have deeper consequences than salient events. The sample under scrutiny is too small to corroborate such a hypothesis, but the findings are interesting enough to invite further research. Second, the effect of structural change, short-term and long-term, is highly ambivalent. Structural change does not determine the direction of its effects; it gives rise to opportunities and possibilities that did not exist before, but no more. Third, agency decides the direction of change; domestic and ideological factors play a pivotal role (Widmaier, Blyth, and Seabrooke 2007).

Finally, the success and failure of multilateral arms control mirrors the satisfaction of actors with how their justice claims are accommodated.[2] The willingness of the elder Bush and early Clinton administrations to treat the Soviet Union/Russia as a peer despite the growing power differential helped stimulate progress in arms control in the "golden decade." Their willingness to accommodate NAM's related demands (for a strong cooperation norm in the CWC and for fulfillment of Art. IV and VI of the NPT "bargain") was needed to reach agreements in 1992 and 1995, respectively. Renouncing the NPT bargain and violating the demand for "equal security for all" jeopardized the cooperative attitudes of America's partners during the George W. Bush presidency. Obama's shift back to recognizing existing claims as the basis for multilateral cooperation seems to have restored these attitudes to some degree at least.

Notes

1. Regime developments are only briefly mentioned here; see chapters 2 and 3 for more references.

2. This corroborates findings by Foot and Walter (2011) from their comparison of US and Chinese regime compliance.

References

Bagchi, Indrani. 2009. "India Votes against Iran at IAEA." *Times of India*, November 28. http://articles.timesofindia.indiatimes.com/2009-11-28/india/28074607_1_india-votes-iaea-resolution-nuclear-programme.

Baker, James A. 1995. *The Politics of Diplomacy: Revolution, War and Peace, 1989–1992.* With Thomas M. DeFrank. New York: Putnam.

Blumenthal, Dan, and Michael Mazza. 2011. "China's Strategic Forces in the 21st Century: The PLA's Changing Nuclear Doctrine and Force Posture." Nonproliferation Policy Education Center, April 6. www.npolicy.org/article_file/Chinas_Strategic_Forces.pdf.

Blyth, Mark. 2003. "Structures Do Not Come with an Instruction Sheet: Interests, Ideas, and Progress in Political Science." *Perspectives on Politics* 1 (4): 695–706.

Bolton, John. 2007. *Surrender Is Not an Option: Defending America at the United Nations and Abroad.* New York: Threshold Editions.

Bush, George W. 2010. *Decision Points.* New York: Crown.

Cheney, Dick. 2011. *In My Time: A Personal and Political Memoir.* With Liz Cheney. New York: Threshold Editions.

Donnelly, Thomas. 2000. *Rebuilding America's Defenses: Strategy, Forces and Resources for a New Century.* A Report of the Project for the New American Century. Washington. www.newamericancentury.org/RebuildingAmericasDefenses.pdf.

Evangelista, Matthew. 1995. "Transnational Relations, Domestic Structures, and Security Policy in the USSR and Russia." In *Bringing Transnational Relations Back In: Non-state Actors, Domestic Structures and International Institutions,* edited by Thomas Risse-Kappen, 146–88. Cambridge: Cambridge University Press.

———. 2004. "Turning Points in Arms Control." In *Ending the Cold War: Interpretations, Causation, and the Study of International Relations,* edited by Richard K. Herrmann and Richard Ned Lebow, 83–105. Basingstoke: Palgrave Macmillan.

Foot, Rosemary, and Andrew Walter. 2011. *China, the United States, and Global Order.* Cambridge: Cambridge University Press.

Garver, John W. 2006. *China and Iran: Ancient Partners in a Post-Imperial World.* Seattle: University of Washington Press.

———. 2011. "China's Current and Emerging Foreign Policy Priorities." Testimony before the U.S.-China Economic and Security Review Commission on "China's Current and Emerging Foreign Policy Priorities." April 13. www.uscc.gov/hearings/2011hearings/written_testimonies/11_04_13_wrt/11_04_13_garver_testimony.pdf.

Gill, Bates, and Martin Kleiber. 2007. "China's Space Odyssey: What the Antisatellite Test Reveals about Decision-Making in Beijing." *Foreign Affairs* 86 (3): 2–6.

Goldstein, Avery. 2005. *Rising to the Challenge: China's Grand Strategy and International Security.* Stanford: Stanford University Press.

Gorbachev, Mikhail. 1996. *Memoirs.* New York: Doubleday.

Hansell, Cristina, and Nikita Perfilyev. 2009. "Strategic Relations between the United States, Russia, and China and the Possibility of Cooperation on Disarmament." In Hansell and Potter 2009, 123–48.

Hansell, Cristina, and William C. Potter, eds. 2009. *Engaging China and Russia on Nuclear Disarmament.* James Martin Center for Nonproliferation Studies Occasional Paper no. 15. http://cns.miis.edu/opapers/op15/op15.pdf.

IISS (International Institute for Strategic Studies). 2011. *The Military Balance 2011.* London: Routledge.

Kagan, Robert. 2006. *Dangerous Nation: America's Place in the World from its Earliest Days to the Dawn of the Twentieth Century*. New York: Knopf.

Kanwal, Gurmeet. 2009. "China's Emerging Cyber War Doctrine." *Journal of Defense Studies* 3 (3): 14–22.

Kugler, Jacek, and A. F. K. Organski. 1989. "The Power Transition: A Retrospective and Prospective Evaluation." In *Handbook of War Studies*, edited by Manus I. Midlarsky, 171–94. Boston: Unwin Hyman.

Lee, Julia Joo-A. 2009. "To Fuel or Not to Fuel: China's Energy Assistance to North Korea." *Asian Security* 5 (1): 45–72.

Legro, Jeffrey W. 2000. "The Transformation of Policy Ideas." *American Journal of Political Science* 44 (3): 419–32.

Levy, Jack S. 1994. "Learning and Foreign Policy: Sweeping a Conceptual Minefield." *International Organization* 48 (2): 279–312.

Lin, Christina Y. 2010. "China, Iran and North Korea: A Triangulation of Strategic Alliance." Paper prepared for the Harry S. Truman Institute for the Advancement of Peace, the Institute for Asian and African Studies, and the Louis Frieberg Center for East Asian Studies at the Hebrew University in Jerusalem, Mount Scopus. Jerusalem, March 2. http://trumannews.huji.ac.il/upload/LinLecture.pdf.

Medeiros, Evan S. 2007. *Reluctant Restraint: The Evolution of China's Nonproliferation Policies and Practices, 1980–2004*. Stanford: Stanford University Press.

Mian, Zia, and M. V. Ramana. 2006. "Wrong Ends, Means, and Needs: Behind the U.S. Nuclear Deal with India." *Arms Control Today* 36 (1). www.armscontrol.org/act/2006_01-02/JANFEB-IndiaFeature.asp.

Müller, Harald. 2010. "Between Power and Justice: Current Problems and Perspectives of the NPT Regime." *Strategic Analysis* 34 (2): 189–201.

———. 2011. "A Nuclear Nonproliferation Test: Obama's Nuclear Policy and the 2010 NPT Review Conference." *Nonproliferation Review* 18 (1): 219–36.

Müller, Harald, and Carsten Rauch. 2011. "Managing Power Transition with a 'Concert of Powers'?" Paper presented at the Annual Convention of the International Studies Association, Montreal, March 16–19.

Müller, Harald, and Andreas Schmidt. 2009. *"Natural Friends"? Relations between the United States and India after 2001*. PRIF Report no. 87. Peace Research Institute Frankfurt, Frankfurt am Main. http://www.hsfk.de/fileadmin/downloads/prif87.pdf.

NTI (Nuclear Threat Initiative). 2011. "China Rejects Curbs on Nuclear Arsenal Expansion." Global Security Newswire, February 28. http://gsn.nti.org/gsn/nw_20110228_1719.php.

Park, John S. 2010. "Iran and China." In *The Iran Primer*, United States Institute of Peace. http://iranprimer.usip.org/sites/iranprimer.usip.org/files/Iran%20and%20China.pdf.

Rauch, Carsten. 2010. "Hushed Hope—India, the Nuclear Deal, and Nonproliferation." PRIF Working Paper 07-2010. Peace Research Institute Frankfurt, Frankfurt am Main. www.hsfk.de/fileadmin/downloads/arbeitspapier0710.pdf.

Saalman, Lora. 2009. "How Chinese Analysts View Arms Control, Disarmament, and Nuclear Deterrence after the Cold War." In Hansell and Potter 2009, 47–71.

Schroeder, Matt. 2007. "Countering the MANPADS Threat: Strategies for Success." *Arms Control Today* 37 (7). www.armscontrol.org/act/2007_09/CoverStory.

Sharma, Deepak. 2010. "Integrated Network Electronic Warfare: China's New Concept of Information Warfare." *Journal of Defense Studies* 4 (2): 36–49.

Shen, Dingli. 2006. "North Korea's Strategic Significance to China." *China Security* 4: 19–34.

Sokov, Nikolai N., Jing-dong Yuan, William C. Potter, and Cristina Hansell. 2009. "Chinese and Russian Perspectives on Achieving Nuclear Zero." In Hansell and Potter 2009, 1–23.

UNSC (United Nations Security Council). 2010. "Security Council Imposes Additional Sanctions on Iran." Department of Public Information, June 9, www.un.org/News/Press/docs/2010/sc9948.doc.htm.

US Department of Defense. 2010. *Joint Publication 1-02. Department of Defense Dictionary of Military and Associated Terms*. November 8. www.dtic.mil/doctrine/new_pubs/jp1_02.pdf.

US White House (William J. Clinton). 1994. *A National Security Strategy of Engagement and Enlargement*. Washington. http://edocs.nps.edu/govpubs/wh/1994/nss1994.pdf.

——— (George W. Bush). 2002. *National Security Strategy*. Washington. http://georgewbush-whitehouse.archives.gov/nsc/nss/2002/.

——— (Barack Obama). 2010. *National Security Strategy*. Washington. www.whitehouse.gov/sites/default/files/rss_viewer/national_security_strategy.pdf.

Walker, William. 2012. *A Perpetual Menace: Nuclear Weapons and International Order*. London: Routledge.

Weiss, Leonard. 2007. "US-India Nuclear Cooperation: Better Later than Sooner." *Nonproliferation Review* 14 (3): 429–57.

Widmaier, Wesley W., Mark Blyth, and Leonard Seabrooke. 2007. "Exogenous Shocks or Endogenous Constructions? The Meanings of Wars and Crises." *International Studies Quarterly* 51 (4): 747–59.

Woolf, Amy F. 2011. *Nonstrategic Nuclear Weapons*. CRS Report for Congress RL32572. www.fas.org/sgp/crs/nuke/RL32572.pdf.

World Bank. 2011a. "GDP Growth (Annual %)." Data. http://data.worldbank.org/indicator/NY.GDP.MKTP.KD.ZG.

———. 2011b. "Military Expenditure (% of GDP)." Data. http://data.worldbank.org/indicator/MS.MIL.XPND.GD.ZS.

Part III
Norm Entrepreneurs as Drivers of Norm Dynamics

CHAPTER SIX

Established and Rising Great Powers

The United States, Russia, China, and India

Marco Fey, Andrea Hellmann, Friederike Klinke, Franziska Plümmer, and Carsten Rauch

THEORIES OF INTERNATIONAL RELATIONS conventionally regard great powers as the most important actors in international politics. Research on norms, however, has placed little emphasis on their activities (see chapter 1). Research on great powers, in turn, has for the most part neglected the role of norms and focused mainly on material aspects. Highlighting the role of the normative fabric of the international system in this volume compels us to look at the roles great powers play as norm entrepreneurs in arms control regimes.

The theory of hegemonic stability (first articulated by Kindleberger 1973) makes the robustness of norms contingent on the productive, protective, and enforcing role of hegemonic great powers, but this theory has lost popularity with the appearance of Keohane's "After Hegemony" (1984). However, even if, as Keohane argues, a regime can be alive and well in the absence of a hegemon, great powers can still exert considerable influence on the creation, development, and decay of norms and regimes. Hegemonic stability theory, however, is of limited value because it only deals with one type of great power: those that have invested heavily in the existing order and can thus be expected to have a stake in maintaining and improving it.

As power transition theory (Organski 1958; Tammen et al. 2000) reminds us, rising powers may be less satisfied with the norms of the day that may deny them proper participation and status. Being denied the fulfillment of their ambitions, they view the existing order as unjust and try to change it by repealing existing norms and replacing them with norms that better fit their own interests and values. This notion stands in some contradiction to the proposition in norm research that middle powers have broad opportunities for norm entrepreneurship *within* an established order. Thus, some rising powers may have chosen to engage as norm entrepreneurs before they began to rise and, from this perspective, might have acquired some ownership in the existing regimes. This would lead to stabilizing rather than challenging activities.

We regard the United States and Russia as established great powers. While the United States has been the dominant power since the end of World War II, the position of Russia is somewhat delicate as it was never a global hegemon but instead was the primary challenger to the US-led international order. Both, however, played a pivotal role in the creation of the regimes under scrutiny here, given the assumption of nuclear parity. They should act valiantly in a) defending and enforcing the regimes and b) opposing norm change; something that the United States—as the permanent number one—is expected to do even more than Russia.

China and India are rising great powers. Both were great empires in the past but were subjected to repression and humiliation during the era of imperialism. They were comparatively weak when the current world order was established in the aftermath of World War II and remained on the periphery of world politics during the Cold War. From the 1980s (China) and 1990s (India) onward, both started a spectacular rise. They can thus be expected to put forward alternative norms to those existing and to justify their proposals by arguing that the present order is profoundly unjust. They might also be more hostile toward those regimes that had been established before their rise began (NPT and BWC) than toward those that have been established later (e.g., CWC, UN PoA).

THE UNITED STATES: COVERING THE WHOLE SPECTRUM OF NORM ENTREPRENEURSHIP

With the establishment of a "balance of terror" between the United States and the Soviet Union in the post–World War II era, arms control became increasingly relevant. More than any other power, the United States shaped the international order and its arms control treaties and regimes. In particular, it engaged proactively in establishing, strengthening, enforcing, and advancing the norm of WMD nonproliferation, covering the whole spectrum of entrepreneurship. The US record is ambivalent, however, because Washington has, at times, also worked toward weakening norms of disarmament and peaceful uses.

US Arms Control Politics and Policies

Depending on the respective administration, since World War II US foreign policy has oscillated between unilateralist and multilateralist approaches. Common to all is a belief in US exceptionalism and moral significance, if not superiority, that dates back to the Founding Fathers. The degree to which the United States succeeded in building a normative system based on its ideas varied according to the temperature of the Cold War but was also a function of domestic politics.

The United States rarely speaks with one voice on arms control issues. Many key players are involved, often with initially different views concerning a potential agreement. Within the administration, the White House usually leads the process. The success of negotiations often depends on the president's or his national security adviser's commitment and involvement; a lack of leadership allows the warring factions in an administration to delay and obstruct the process. The State Department traditionally views international agreements in a more positive light than the Pentagon or the Joint Chiefs of Staff, although at times the latter have played a more facilitating role than conventional wisdom would suggest. Between 1961 and 1997, the Arms Control and Disarmament Agency (ACDA) was a semi-independent yet important actor in the arms control process until it was reintegrated into the State Department in 1999. All these players often have conflicting ideas about arms control in general or the value of specific agreements. While it is thus difficult for the administrative branch to agree on a coherent position prior to or during international negotiations, it is even more difficult when it comes to winning the approval of Congress.

The legislative branch is in a strong position concerning arms control. The Senate is required to approve the international treaties that the president signs with a two-thirds majority. Congress is also responsible for general legislation and reviews the defense budget; both can have a profound impact on arms control. The ratification of treaties is often dependent on domestic politics. It is generally easier for Republican presidents to get the Senate's approval for arms control treaties. But even they need to offer many concessions, primarily to defense-minded senators. Congress can also act as a keeper of arms control: during the Reagan years, for example, Congress prevented the end of the Anti-Ballistic Missile (ABM) Treaty and urged the president to start negotiating a comprehensive test ban (Fascell 1987).

US allies also have a certain impact upon the decision-making process. The German position on the NPT and its verification mechanism during the 1960s, for example, had a major impact on the American negotiation position, as was the case with NATO's perspective on the Intermediate-Range Nuclear Forces (INF) Treaty. With regard to NPT RevCons, the United States also coordinates closely with the other nuclear weapon states (NWS). One US arms control veteran observed that these "prenegotiations" within the government and with allies typically took "more time and effort than the negotiations with the Soviets" (Bunn 1992, 6).

US Arms Control after World War II The United States, having been the world's strongest military power since 1945, played a critical—whether facilitating or blocking—role in every attempt to control, limit, or reduce all types of weapons and has initiated many of these regimes itself. The earliest attempt to put the power of the atom under international control was the 1946 Baruch Plan, which would have left the United States with a monopoly of nuclear weapons know-how. A long period of strategic build-up followed Soviet rejection of this proposal. Arms control as a third way between total disarmament and an uncontrolled, destabilizing arms race gained prominence in the late 1950s and early 1960s. The idea was to focus on small but practicable steps to ensure strategic stability (Krepon 1989, 28). Kennedy concluded the bilateral "Hot Line" agreement and the Limited Test Ban Treaty in 1963 after the Cuban missile crisis had brought the world to the brink of nuclear war. The era of détente in the late 1960s and early 1970s, as well as the years of *perestroika* and *glasnost* in the late 1980s, saw the biggest successes in arms control efforts with the NPT in 1968, the 1972 SALT (Strategic Arms Limitation Talks) Interim Agreement, ABM Treaty, and BWC, and the 1987 INF Treaty.

US Arms Control after the Cold War The "Bush 41" administration successfully seized the momentum of the benevolent environment in the early 1990s, concluded multilateral agreements (Conventional Forces in Europe, or CFE) as well as bilateral agreements (Strategic Arms Reduction Treaty, or START) and made progress with regard to negotiations on the CWC.[1] Clinton is sometimes charged with having slowed down the arms control process (Krass 1997, 3). Yet, during Clinton's presidency, the Senate ratified START II, the NPT was extended indefinitely, the Comprehensive Nuclear-Test-Ban Treaty (CTBT) opened for signature, and the CWC entered into force. Moreover, his administration implemented the Cooperative Threat Reduction (CTR) program to prevent the leakage of weapons and materials from the former Soviet nuclear complex. Clinton also supported the initiative to ban antipersonnel mines (APM) and envisaged US accession to the Ottawa Treaty by 2004. If arms control no longer held a prominent position in US foreign policy, this was to a large degree a result of the Republicans having gained control of both houses of Congress in 1994. Henceforth, the emphasis on maximum flexibility and a hostile attitude toward arms control gained strength, culminating in the rejection of CTBT ratification in 1999.

Every president since Lyndon B. Johnson (with the exception of the first Reagan administration) has agreed with the idea that arms control advances national security. The "Bush 43" years marked a clear departure. The Bush administration's contempt for multilateral instruments, in particular treaties, led to withdrawal from the ABM Treaty in 2001. Moreover, the administration abandoned the CTBT and the Ottawa Treaty; its policy was responsible for serious crises within the BWC (Sims 2003), the NPT (Johnson 2005), and the SALW PoA (Fehl 2008, 270–71). The Strategic Offensive Reductions Treaty (SORT) was as much as the Russians could obtain in terms of a binding agreement on nuclear arms control. This skeleton-like treaty reflected the administration's disdain for what it viewed as anachronistic, rigid, and slow bargaining (Ford 2008). Whereas the United States had always championed transparency, verification, predictability, and stability, the Bush administration now favored flexible, speedy, effective, informal "coalition of the willing" approaches, such as the 2002 G8 Global Partnership against the Spread of Weapons and Materials of Mass Destruction, or the 2003 Proliferation Security Initiative (PSI).

The inauguration of President Obama in 2009 marked the end of the hostile US attitude toward multilateral arms control. Obama declared working toward a world free of nuclear weapons a top priority. With subsequent initiatives, the administration demonstrated that its commitment went beyond declaratory policy. Its 2010 Nuclear Posture Review reduced the role of nuclear weapons in US national security strategy; the administration achieved New START, which entered into force in 2011; it hosted a Nuclear Security Summit in 2010 where forty-seven countries discussed strategies for securing all vulnerable nuclear materials worldwide; it revived a dormant Plutonium Disposal Agreement with Russia; it released nuclear stockpile figures for the period since 1962 and for warhead dismantlement since 1994 in an unprecedented measure of transparency; and it signaled its determination to reintroduce the CTBT to the Senate, to start talks with Russia about further nuclear reductions (including tactical weapons), and to negotiate a Fissile Material Cut-off Treaty (FMCT) in Geneva. Considering the unfavorable domestic environment of a very partisan Congress, these measures should not be dismissed; they are important steps on the road to Obama's long-term goal of global zero.

Nonproliferation versus Disarmament and Peaceful Uses

Arms control held a relatively high priority in US strategic thinking during the Cold War. Since Truman, all administrations have adhered to a universal nonproliferation policy and have worked on establishing strong norms against the spread of WMD. Although not always equally influential, the two undercurrents of denial/control on the one hand and peaceful uses/sharing of technology on the other have dominated US policy (Nye 1987, 166). Absolute denial after World War II evolved into nuclear sharing with NATO allies during the 1950s and Eisenhower's 1953 Atoms for Peace program. The spread of nuclear reactors for peaceful uses, technological progress, and above all the Chinese nuclear test of 1964, however, strengthened the position of those prioritizing nonproliferation over sharing and led to the US advocating international efforts to constrain horizontal proliferation. During the late 1960s and early 1970s, the United States was a driving force toward the NPT and the BWC.

The first American drafts for the NPT did not envisage what would eventually be known as the "grand bargain." Rather, the United States saw the balance of the treaty as lying in the renunciation of nuclear weapons by the nonnuclear weapon states (NNWS) and in the renunciation by the NWS, in turn, of the right to transfer nuclear weapons and technology to whomever they like (Holloway 2011, 154). While the United States has always committed many resources to strengthening the nonproliferation pillar of each WMD regime, it has also acknowledged that technological cooperation and exchange for peaceful uses and disarmament are legitimate concerns. Until the late 1990s, it had never tried to challenge this bargain (Joyner 2011, 37). However, the 1974 Indian nuclear explosion and the development of chemical weapons and missiles by Iraq in the early 1980s compelled Washington to establish closed exporter cartels—the Nuclear Suppliers Group (NSG) in 1975 and the Australia Group and the Missile Technology Control Regime (MTCR) in the mid-1980s—in order to prevent a "race to the bottom" regarding export policies.

Following concerns about noncompliance with Art. II of the NPT, the United States started to prioritize the nonproliferation pillar over the others at the end of the 1990s. The Bush 43 administration, which had been averse to arms control from the start, reinforced this trend with increased vigor after the terrorist attacks of 9/11 and the autumn 2001 mailings of anthrax letters. Regarding the NPT, for example, it started to deconstruct what was formerly acknowledged as unquestionable rights and obligations under Art. IV; the United States now declared the right to peaceful uses and technology exchange as strictly conditional upon the NNWS's strict adherence to their Art. II obligations as assessed by Washington (Joyner 2011, 40). Moreover, Art. IV was seen as a loophole that allowed countries to acquire nuclear weapons under the cover of peaceful energy programs. Bush even suggested in 2004 that uranium enrichment and plutonium separation capabilities be limited to states that already operate full fuel cycles and that NSG members should refuse technology and equipment sales to all other states (Bush 2004). At the same time, the administration tried to marginalize the disarmament pillar of the NPT. It did not regard Art. VI as a core provision of the regime and dismissed the "13 steps" of the 2000 RevCon final document as neither binding nor any longer relevant. Moreover, it argued that the United States was in compliance with Art. VI because its arsenal had been greatly reduced since its peak in 1967 (Ford 2007).

Some of the administration's new initiatives, such as the PSI, the Container Security Initiative (CSI), and the G8 Global Partnership, did not aim at introducing new nonproliferation norms or further developing existing ones, but rather at enforcing them through informal, quick, and effective ad hoc solutions. The imperative to find ways of dealing with WMD proliferation to, and from, nonstate actors was demonstrated by both 9/11 and the disclosure of the A. Q. Khan network. Within the BWC framework, for example, the administration made it clear that member states had to do more in terms of national implementation. It also steered the discussion about biosecurity in the direction of a laboratory-oriented approach and thus a narrow focus on the prevention of deliberate theft and misuse of dangerous pathogens (Revill and Dando 2009). This emphasis on prevention and securing materials is reflected in the administration's efforts to establish criminalizing proliferation as a new norm, leading to Security Council Resolution 1540 (van Ham and Bosch 2007, 6).

Is There a Place for Justice in US Arms Control?

The United States has usually pursued a utilitarian approach to arms control. Whereas arms control had to serve national security, some triggers for US engagement went beyond immediate security considerations. When Lyndon Johnson suggested talks about strategic limitations to the Soviets in 1967, budgetary considerations played an important role (Quester 1973, 28). Nixon found himself facing public pressure to engage in SALT negotiations and also considered arms control as part of a broader policy of détente. Reagan was urged by NATO allies to negotiate the INF Treaty and considered the talks with the Soviets as "alliance management" that helped to secure NATO countries' acceptance of US missile deployment on their territories (Hampson 1987, 78; Bunn 1992, 175–77).

Since the end of World War II, the United States has largely been in the position to shape all bilateral and multilateral agreements according to its preferences or, if this was not possible, to deny them any significance.[2] Thus, asymmetries in multilateral regimes favor the United States. Being recognized as a NWS under the NPT, it is one of only five states parties that legally possess the most powerful weapon on earth. Moreover, it is not obliged to submit its nuclear facilities to IAEA safeguards. The United States even benefits from an asymmetric complaints mechanism in the BWC, which, after all, is considered to be a nondiscriminatory regime. Since Art. VI of the convention refers complaints to the Security Council, the P5 can prevent investigations of their own programs or those of their allies (Littlewood 2005, 17). With regard to the CWC, Congress diluted the convention by enacting legislation that exempted US sites from the same verification rules that US diplomats had demanded be included in the treaty during the negotiations (Smithson 2001, 23).

The United States rarely issues an explicit justice claim. The closest it comes is the recurrent reference to the American Constitution as the highest legal authority in US statements within the context of SALW. The US demands that its domestic constitutional and policy choices, as made through a democratic system of representative government, be respected and that the Second Amendment—the right to keep and bear arms—must under no circumstances be infringed by any international agreement (see, e.g., Bolton 2001a, 2001b; Joseph 2006). This remote reference to procedural justice reflects a strong American sense of exceptionalism. While the United States does not tolerate any interference with its Constitution, it was, for example, the key norm entrepreneur with regard to S/RES/1540 with its very intrusive obligations on all states to adapt their national legislation. As one observer of US arms control put it: "Whether intended or not, the United States sometimes conveys the impression that everyone else is supposed to adhere precisely to the rules while the United

States retains full freedom of action" (Krass 1997, 187). Other countries' accusations of unjust American behavior and their justice-laden language within arms control regimes are mainly dismissed by US delegates and decision makers as strategic use of moral language to either stall or delay progress in negotiations or to improve bargaining positions. The tendency to disregard others' justice claims might to a certain degree stem from US exceptionalism. The conviction of moral superiority led officials during the Cold War, for example, to misinterpret Soviet striving for parity. The Soviets, according to this view, would not need parity for a credible second strike capability because "they know we won't attack, therefore, this build-up must be for them to get a credible first strike capability."[3]

Questions of parity and equality have stirred heated debates, also *within* the United States. The SALT I Interim Agreement codified Soviet numerical superiority in intercontinental ballistic missiles (ICBMS) and submarine-launched ballistic missile (SLBM) launchers but failed to address the US arsenal's qualitative advantage (e.g., multiple independently targetable reentry vehicles, or MIRVS, and submarines), or the numerical advantage in strategic bombers untouched (McCain 1989, 165). A number of senators, led by Democrat Henry Jackson, believed that these unequal force ceilings benefited the Soviets and, in conjunction with the ABM Treaty, might place the United States at risk. They gathered support for an amendment that obliged the administration to seek equality in all further strategic talks. This had a huge influence on the following SALT II negotiations (McCain 1989, 77–79). Reagan also made it clear from the start of his presidency that his arms control policy would be guided by the principle of equality across all fields (Rowney 1989, 70–74).

Besides equality, the United States has always put a premium on verification and compliance. It was close to an axiom that treaties, especially bilateral ones with the untrustworthy and opaque Soviets, needed to be verifiable (Haass 1987). While *adequate verification* was the standard for the first decade of strategic arms control,[4] Reagan insisted on an *effective verification* standard that would assure the detection of *every* case of Soviet cheating—regardless of its military implications (Krass 1997, 164). Concern over others' noncompliance peaked under Reagan, resulting in accusations of Soviet violation of key provisions of SALT I, SALT II, and, most significantly, the ABM Treaty. The United States also accused the Soviets of grave violations of the BWC and was, after the end of the Cold War, concerned with breaches of the NPT by Iraq, Libya, the Democratic People's Republic of Korea, and, recently, Iran. Verification and compliance disputes have often inhibited progress on arms control and have been a source of contention for opponents: if treaties are signed and not complied with, they become a security liability rather than an asset (Seignious 1987, 4).

This emphasis on equality and compliance could be interpreted as an indication that justice and fairness concerns were underlying currents of US policy (Albin 2001, 183–87). Arguments in the American arms control discourse against other countries' superiority (or even parity) do not necessarily stem from security concerns alone, but also from American self-perception that it is responsible for a stable and liberal world order: since the United States provides the public good of world security, it is entitled to freedom of action. From this perspective, parity, equality, and treaty provisions restricting a military posture that allows for all necessary policy options contradict this entitlement and are thus justice relevant indeed.

The Whole Spectrum of Entrepreneurship

Since the end of World War II, the United States has been the key actor in international arms control. The fate of virtually all treaties and agreements has depended on the American position toward them. Justice concerns impacted on the American position when US military supremacy and freedom of action were endangered by certain treaty provisions or Soviet build-ups. Utilitarian calculation, at times influenced by predominant ideologies favoring or opposing international cooperation and arms control, largely determine US policy.

The United States has used arms control either to constrain the freedom of action of others while preserving its own or to prohibit weapons of no use to its own armed forces but that could present a danger to US interests. Within this framework, the United States has operated as a proactive promoter of norms in the field of WMD nonproliferation. It has also put a lot of effort into enforcing existing regimes and has successfully worked on establishing a new norm of criminalizing the proliferation of all sorts of WMDs after 9/11. At least since the late 1990s, however, it has embarked on strengthening nonproliferation at the cost of disarmament, technological exchange, and peaceful uses. In doing so, it came close to being an active opponent of these norms. The administration and Congress also opposed new global norms in humanitarian arms control, especially with regard to APM, cluster bombs, and SALW, while at the same time remaining committed to the clearance of mines and unexploded ordnance and helping countries to dispose of small arms, light weapons, and munitions.

The Obama administration has kept alive almost all of the Bush 43 administration's initiatives and has expanded some of them. At the same time, it has returned to a policy of affirming the grand bargain of the NPT. It appears willing to undertake important steps toward nuclear disarmament. And President Obama's words may indicate that justice has become a more essential part of the equation: "As a nuclear power, as the only nuclear power to have used a nuclear weapon, the United States has a moral responsibility to act. We cannot succeed in this endeavor alone, but we can lead it, we can start it" (Obama 2009).

RUSSIA: EQUALITY FIRST

During the Cold War, the Soviet Union was one of two poles in the international system. Today's Russia inherited most of the Soviet military arsenal but has been financially incapable of maintaining it. While Russia's political and economic systems still show weaknesses, the country's energy resources account for its recent geopolitical ascendance. According to the Correlates of War Projects power index, Russia still belongs among the five most powerful states in the world (see CoW 2010).

Two identity elements that Russia inherited from the Soviet Union dominate its foreign and security policy thinking and strategies. First, Russia claims a special position in its immediate environment, the "near abroad," where it strives to be recognized as the hegemonic power. Second, Russia wants to be accepted by the United States—at least symbolically—as a world power of equal weight. In 2009 Russia defined its strategic objectives as follows: "Transformation of the Russian Federation into a world power whose activities aim at maintaining strategic stability and mutually advantageous partnerships under the conditions of a multipolar world" (Russian Federation 2009, III/21). Economic and technological backwardness and the poor condition of the armed forces, however, render the ambition to claim world power status hard to achieve, not only in comparison to the United States but also to China and India with their much larger, and still growing, populations and high economic growth rates. US military superiority further undermines the claim to be seen as equal. The modernization of Russia's nuclear arsenal and the maintenance of a large arsenal of substrategic nuclear weapons are attempts to counterbalance this at relatively moderate expense. Arms control could be an alternative way to procure an equalizer (Hansell and Perfilyev 2009).

Status Equality and Equal Security

Early Soviet thinking portrayed arms control as a "bourgeois trick" and therefore rejected it because only complete disarmament would lead to overcoming imperialism and thereby promote peace (Kokoshin 1991, 133). Several severe crises in the early 1960s, particularly the Cuban missile crisis with the concomitant specter of a nuclear war, convinced Moscow of the necessity to pursue arms control talks with the United States and thereby reduce the risk of a nuclear disaster (Kokoshin 1991, 134).

During the following decades, the Soviet Union emphasized parity and stability in its negotiations with the United States (Albin 2001, 184–85). Arms control was not only pursued for national security reasons but also to ensure the basis for both equality of status and security with the redoubtable American rival. The NPT, which saw the Soviets as a leading negotiating party and eventually a depositary power, served the same goal as it eliminated the risk of a global imbalance disfavoring the Soviet Union. In Moscow's eyes, the treaty mainly served to keep the US allies Germany and Japan nonnuclear. Throughout this period, Soviet arms control policy was conservative rather than proactive and led to the failure of attempts to create new regimes that were seen as a threat to parity—for example, mutual balance in force reductions in Europe or a chemical weapons convention (Garthoff 2001, 190–96, 230). This changed fundamentally under Gorbachev. Convinced that for domestic and security reasons, and to save humankind from a major disaster, military confrontation with the United States had to come to an end, the Soviet president took a number of initiatives (including the unilateral withdrawal of five hundred thousand soldiers from Eastern Europe) and accepted asymmetric rules for INF and the dismantlement of heavy intercontinental missiles. In addition, Gorbachev agreed to innovative and very intrusive verification measures. Indeed, before the endgame of the negotiations for the CWC, the Soviets were ready to accept far-reaching verification earlier than the United States (Evangelista 2004, 94–98). Through these years, Gorbachev had no reason to view the issue of parity with the United States as problematic: first Reagan, and later Bush 41, treated the reform-willing Soviets as equals. After the collapse of the Soviet Union, the nascent Russian Federation no longer showed the same degree of norm entrepreneurship as the late Soviet Union under Gorbachev. Moreover, with the material power base fading year by year, Russia had to accept a number of US proposals that would have been considered incompatible with equality of status and security claims in the pre-Gorbachev era, such as shrinking the substrategic nuclear arsenals or receiving US aid for the ailing Russian nuclear complex.

With Putin's rise to power, Russia returned to the arms control policies of the pre-Gorbachev Soviet Union, with a strong emphasis on equal status and equal security. Russia's national security policy reemphasized the role of nuclear weapons in order to maintain the balance of power and strategic stability (Medvedev 1999, 16; Sokov 2007, 208). Within the NPT context, Russia promoted the Additional Protocol and measures to regulate withdrawal from the NPT (Khlebnikov 1995, 7; Kislyak 1995, 10; Mostovets 2002, 1; Russian Federation 2010, 17). Russia also became a party to the CTBT in the hope that the United States would reciprocate. The only remarkable Russian act of norm entrepreneurship, however, was the Moscow Treaty (2002), which the Bush administration accepted only after strong Russian pressure. At the same time, Moscow resisted demands by nonnuclear weapon states for certain disarmament measures such as the closure of testing facilities, renouncing the development of new nuclear warheads, and reducing substrategic nuclear arsenals (Müller 2011, 221–22). It justified its reluctance by stressing the unwillingness of other NWS to emulate systematic Russian and American strategic reductions.

The question of status also dominated the Russian position on the 2010 US Nuclear Posture Review. For Moscow, the most important outcome of the review was US willingness to revive bilateral arms control and to work with Russia toward finding a solution to the difficult issue of missile defense in Europe: "Strategic stability and approximate parity with the United States in the composition and capabilities of nuclear forces are very important concepts in the domestic Russian security debate" (Podvig 2011a, 39–40). The desire to retain an elevated status vis-à-vis nonnuclear weapon states (Antonov 2004, 8) and to preserve deterrence vis-à-vis the United States played a major role.

The request to participate as an equal in NATO's missile defense in Europe is the most recent case of an attempt to maintain equal status; Russia is keen to keep its nuclear deterrent and rejects reducing its substrategic nuclear weapons in the light of US missile defense plans, NATO's conventional superiority, and China's growing military strength (Podvig 2011b, 15–20).

The orientation toward equal security also influences Russian behavior beyond nuclear issues: the refusal to accede to the Ottawa Convention not only reciprocates US and Chinese abstention but is also due to concern about securing its extensive borders with the West and China, very similar to the considerations that determine Russia's attitude toward tactical nuclear weapons (Lavrov 2011).

Economic Interests versus Arms Control

The Soviet Union was a founding member of the NSG, and Russia inherited this membership. It also acceded to the Missile Technology Control Regime (MTCR). However, its compliance with the guidelines has been contested by critics due to doubts over the effectiveness of national export controls (Crail 2010, 18–20). In addition, Russia is continuing, albeit at a reduced level and with frequent delays, its nuclear cooperation with Iran. Russia cultivates a liberal interpretation of Art. IV of the NPT. It emphasizes equality before the law and sympathizes with the developing countries' compensatory claims for non-discriminatory assistance (Kislyak 1995, 11; Titkov 1995, 6). This coincides with the interest in profitable exports since nuclear technology is one of the few modern fields in which Russia is a successful exporter. The case of Iran, which has been declared by the IAEA to have been in noncompliance with its safeguards obligations since 2002, demonstrates the priority Russia gives to civilian nuclear cooperation over proliferation concerns. Russia's criticism of Iranian policy is much less acerbic than that of Western governments. This translates into continued nuclear cooperation—including services and fuel supply for the Bushehr reactor after completion of construction—while Western nations have long since terminated any collaboration (Weiner 2011). Apart from the justice-related argument concerning equal rights, Russia justifies this policy with the need to maintain the stability of the NPT by providing assistance to NNWS in the peaceful uses of nuclear energy (Kislyak 1995).

The balance between Russian economic interest and arms control is even more tilted in the SALW field—Russia is the second largest exporter of small arms worldwide. One major stimulus for the spread of these weapons was the sales, official and non-official, of large quantities of obsolete Warsaw Treaty weapons after the end of the Cold War. However, Russia opposed any strict regulations on global conventional arms transfers. As the "birthplace" of the Khalashnikov, the most exported and used small arm, and of a strong conventional armaments industry that is one of its few high-tech export sectors, Russia has opposed strong norm building in this sector. On the one hand, Russia has been regularly submitting its annual reports (except 2004 and 2009), where it underlines its interest in strengthening the regime. In the framework of the Organization for Security and Co-operation in Europe (OSCE), it assists Uzbekistan and Armenia to make progress in implementing the PoA (Russian Federation 2002, 10). On the other hand, it does not tighten national export control regulations in order to foster PoA objectives, and there is a discrepancy between the positive tone of the reports and the growth of national arms exports, including surplus weapons (Small Arms Survey 2009, 24).

Russia strongly criticizes the lavish arms exports by the United States to states that Washington regards as allies or at least as good customers. Russia's policy instead is based on an understanding of the PoA as requiring strict equal treatment of members: "We should . . . avoid approaches which could be viewed as restrictions against any state or a group of states" (Litravin 2006). Russia insists on a categorical distinction between (prohibited) illegal and (legitimate) legal trade, based on clear definitions. The aim of this is to transform the PoA into a normative license for legal trade, whereby the decision on whom to supply remains completely under national authority, thus contradicting the objectives of the PoA initiators. Economic interests clearly serve as a limit to Russian norm entrepreneurship.

When commercial interest and arms control objectives coincide, however, Russia is capable of significant norm entrepreneurship. This applies, for example, to the tricky issue of multilateral approaches to the nuclear fuel cycle and fuel guarantees, where Russia has been pioneering two initiatives aimed at reducing the spread of national enrichment facilities. In 2007, Russia and Kazakhstan created the International Uranium Enrichment Center (IUEC), which utilizes existing enrichment capacity at the Angarsk facility in Russia. In the meantime, Ukraine and Armenia have joined the IUEC. While technology remains under Russian control, the center's member states have drawing rights on the enrichment product in proportion to their investments. In 2010, Russia concluded an agreement with the IAEA according to which Russia establishes a fuel reserve equivalent to the fuel loads for two 1,000-megawatt reactors under IAEA control; this reserve can be drawn upon by states in good standing with their safeguards agreements in the event of a supply interruption. Russia thereby wants to set a standard that can be emulated elsewhere and to mitigate the risks emerging from the rapid spread of national fuel cycle facilities (Khlopkov 2011, 6–7).

Compliance Policy and Noncompliance Problems

The security of the Russian nuclear complex, something that was of great concern in the 1990s (Potter 1993, 4–8), has been improved by domestic efforts and international help; however, problems still remain. The professional culture of the Russian nuclear community works against nuclear security (Busch and Holmes 2009). On December 16, 2011, for example, the Russian customs control at Sheremetyevo airport in Moscow stopped a piece of luggage with radioactive material bound for Tehran (Reuters 2011). Incidents like this revive doubts concerning Russia's practical implementation of export controls.

Russian institutes, funded by international financial help for unemployed nuclear scientists, have reportedly been engaged in work on Iran's internationally contested Bushehr reactor (Weiner 2011). Russian policies toward Iran and Syria show a reluctant attitude toward enforcing multilateral arms control treaties. Russia is a reluctant negotiator with regard to UN Security Council–imposed sanctions and usually works toward lessening their harshness (Orlov and Trushkin 2011).

There are also doubts about full Russian compliance with its obligations under the BWC (US DoS 2010, 23). The Soviet Union had been conducting a biological weapons program since 1926 and continued these activities after ratifying the BWC in 1975 in clear violation of its commitments. President Yeltsin admitted Soviet noncompliance in 1992 and declared the activities terminated. Concerns remained, however, even after the United Kingdom, the United States, and Russia had worked to resolve compliance concerns in the "Trilateral Process," and in 2004 the United States accused Moscow of secretly continuing its offensive biological weapons (BW) program. While Russia participated in the negotiations on a verification and compliance protocol (albeit with rather restrictive positions) it repeatedly insisted on establishing definitions of prohibited substances and related agents (Hart 2006). This, however, would have watered down the general-purpose criterion, the normative backbone of the BWC, since defining prohibited areas could allow the interpretation that all other activities are legal, and newly developed BW agents might not be covered by the prohibition (e.g., Berdennikov 1994, 6). During the negotiations, Russia also insisted that only existing provisions be used to address compliance problems (Russian Federation 1997, 2). These include a central role for the UN Security Council, and the Russian proposal can be seen as an attempt to secure this role against efforts by others to replace it with nondiscriminatory procedures that would not grant veto powers to some treaty members. Russia continued to call for the introduction of binding verification measures after the protocol negotiations failed in 2001 (e.g., Antonov 2006).

Russia has the largest stockpiles of chemical weapons worldwide, and its ratification of the CWC was delayed for political and economic reasons. Russia needs financial help to destroy all chemical weapons. Further, it called for exemptions in the convention concerning the destruction of all plants involved in the production of chemical weapons. Complying with the convention on this point would have meant the end for large parts of the Russian chemical industry and have imposed a huge financial burden on Russia (Makashov 1997). Russia has been fully committed to complete elimination of its stockpile, but the difficult socioeconomic conditions during the transition in the 1990s prevented it from focusing on chemical weapons demilitarization (Walker 2010); it will not be able to meet the ultimate CWC deadline in 2012.

In the context of the hostage crisis at the Dubrovka Theater in Moscow in 2002, Russian security forces released an unidentified aerosol incapacitant into the theater. Later, special forces stormed the theater and killed all hostage takers, but 129 hostages also died as a result of the incapacitant. Internationally, this incident was not labeled a violation of the CWC as it did not occur in armed combat, but many questions remain (Fidler 2005). There are reports that the Russian army used a similar gas in the context of another incident of hostage taking in 2005. There are also indications that Russia has continued research into incapacitants following, and building upon, the experiences gained during the Moscow incident. Taken together, this raises doubts about Russian compliance with the norms concerning the use, research, and disarmament of chemical weapons (Koplow 2006, 100–104).

Russian Norm Entrepreneurship: Equality First

The Soviet Union and Russia have shown different attitudes toward norm entrepreneurship in arms control. The Soviet Union acted conservatively, focusing mainly on ensuring norms of equality in US-initiated arms control regimes. For half a decade, in the transition from the Cold War to its end, the Soviet Union became a proactive arms control norm entrepreneur. But this only lasted while Gorbachev was in charge. For a long time after 1991 Russian politicians had no clear understanding of how to define national interests and foreign policy goals; the Russian arms control and disarmament policy was somewhat confused (Tarasov 2000, 70). It receded into passivity under Putin and mirrored positions and attitudes known from the earlier Soviet Union, perhaps with the difference of an occasionally greater acceptance of transparency and verification.

Russia's arms control policy emphasizes equality of status; this particularly implies equal security because everything else would expose Russia to pressures along its borders, a concern to which the enlargement of NATO has strongly contributed. That the material basis for claiming world power status has vanished enhances anxiety and motivates the use of justice arguments, notably in the NPT context.

The quest for status cuts two ways though. On the one hand, claims for equal security aim at curbing US superiority. On the other, Russia is reticent about demands for disarmament steps in the NPT context and also has misgivings about procedural changes regarding BWC. While in both instances these steps and changes would help to reduce the asymmetry between NWS/P5 and NNWS / non-P5, they would also diminish Russian status and security advantages. Russia thus demands equal security vis-à-vis the United States and accepts that this puts the majority of states—and certainly all NNWS—in a position of unequal security toward Russia.

Overall, Russia has an interest in, and works for, the stability and strengthening of existing norms wherever such norms move it closer to equal status and security. At the same time, status claims, the bias in favor of economic interests once they conflict with the strengthening of regime norms, and occasionally questionable compliance behavior thwart Russian norm entrepreneurship within all these fields. Indeed, instances of noncompliance might signal a degree of dissatisfaction with the norms as they stand. Status concerns and export interests can negatively impact upon Russian norm entrepreneurship and thus weaken the normative frameworks by delaying or preventing needed improvements.

CHINA: A NORM ENTREPRENEUR BETWEEN DEVELOPING COUNTRY AND NUCLEAR WEAPON STATE STATUS

Since the second half of the 1990s, the People's Republic of China has adopted a new multilateral approach in its arms control policy that oscillates between disobedience, obstruction, compliance, and cooperation. Domestically, China is undergoing a remarkable transition from a planned to a market economy and from an agrarian to an industrial state. Annual economic growth rates approaching or even exceeding 10 percent, starting in the early 1980s, changed China's international position and induced the country's leadership to consider how to shape its emergence on the global scene.

After the 1949 Communist victory, China seemed to emerge as a revisionist power, dissatisfied with the international order that isolated the "Middle Kingdom" and willing to contest rules such as nuclear nonproliferation, which it defied as discriminatory and supportive of Western imperialism. While experiences of isolation, containment, and humiliation influenced Mao Zedong to pursue a foreign policy informed by realpolitik, those generations of leadership who followed him pursued a more cooperative and international norm-oriented strategy (Feng 2009). As a result, there is increasing acceptance of international norms in China's arms control policy: China acceded to the BWC in 1984 and to the NPT in 1992, signed the CTBT in 1996,[5] ratified the CWC in 1997, and joined the NSG in 2004.

China's new multilateralism includes, but at the same time balances, motives such as cultural traditions, historical experiences, and national interests. In arms control, these motives can be in harmony with each other but also contradict each other. Their specific dimensions change depending on the respective issues in question and also change depending on the context, considerably influencing the degree to which China acts cooperatively at the international level and complies with norms. Founded on traditional Confucian and Mencian philosophy, China's current security strategy pursues the objective of a "harmonious world" and "peaceful development." As this concept views the world as generally harmonious, conflicts are rejected, but when occurring, they should be accommodated through moral, exemplary, and nonviolent persuasion (Yuan 1998, 87; Feng 2009, 172). The use of force is only considered legitimate when exercised defensively and proportionately.

Foreign policy attitudes reflect the weight of history: the forced opening by imperial powers in the nineteenth century made China shift from a "Middle Kingdom" to a semifeudal and semicolonial vassal state (Yuan 1998, 91). These experiences as well as US nuclear threats toward China during the Korean War caused a heightened appreciation of state sovereignty and an acute sense of equality and justice. Nowadays, these values are dominant parts of China's identity, leading to a dichotomy of rising self-confidence, accompanied by an increasing willingness to engage in multilateral diplomacy and institutions, and a historically founded inferiority complex leading to insistence on unconstrained sovereignty. As a consequence of those traditions, historical roots, and social experiences, national interests play an essential role in the Chinese approach to arms control. These interests predominantly include the wish to expand influence and economic growth as well as secure regional stability and resource capacities. In some cases, especially when core national interests are affected, they seem to hinder Chinese compliance and norm support.

Technically, the politics of Chinese arms control can be described as closed, concentrated, and complex. Policy is officially formulated by the Ministry of Foreign Affairs. Special responsibility is mainly assigned to the Department of Arms Control and Disarmament, founded in 1997, which is the core and nexus of related knowledge informing Chinese policy (Johnston 2008, 55) and the Department of International Organizations and Conferences, which is responsible for UN negotiations. The ministry, in turn, is supervised by the foreign policy department of the Communist Party.

Disarmament and Equal Security

Immediately after its first nuclear test in 1964, Beijing called for the complete prohibition and destruction of all nuclear weapons (China 1964). China has since repeatedly taken a position in favor of disarmament across all fields and still gives this objective higher priority than nonproliferation (e.g., Sha 1997; China 2005a).

The readiness to progress in international disarmament efforts is grounded on a distinct claim for equality, which is primarily motivated by the wish to safeguard China's status as an equal power within the international system on equal footing with the United States. "Unequal security" that would allow others to intimidate and pressure China is therefore not acceptable, particularly not in the light of the past (Foot and Walter 2011). Therefore, disarmament should be a just and reasonable process of gradual reduction toward a downward balance (e.g., China 2005a). Unilateralism as well as double or multiple standards in the regimes should be discarded (Hua 1998; Zhang 2005). The United States and Russia, possessing the largest nuclear arsenals, bear primary responsibility for nuclear disarmament (China 1999a). As long as they have not reduced their arsenals in "a verifiable and irreversible manner" (China IOSC 2009), reportedly below a thousand warheads each, China refuses to reduce its own stockpile.

Even though China supports disarmament under the terms of the NPT, it is the only NWS that is actually expanding its comparatively still small nuclear arsenal. China justifies this behavior by its right to self-defense, which, from its perspective, is jeopardized by the asymmetry in military strength between China and the United States, culminating in America's long-range, precise offensive strike options and extensive plans for missile defense (Twomey 2009). This moral dilemma between a defensive nuclear weapons posture and the improvement of its nuclear capability is openly recognized by recent Chinese white papers (Yuan 2010, 17). The principle of nuclear counterdeterrence is an argument often cited to justify China's nuclear expansion. This may also be explained, however, by Chinese anxiety about the existing international order's apparent incapacity to prevent war effectively (Yan 2011, 63–64).

China proposes that the NWS should embrace the principle "not to be the first to use nuclear weapons" (China 1999b) as long as a complete elimination of nuclear weapons is not achieved. Beijing promotes this no-first-use pledge, inter alia, via draft texts to the NPT, a bilateral declaration, and in a 2000 joint statement with the other four nuclear-weapon states.[6] No-first-use would deprive nuclear powers of an offensive, first-strike option that is conceivable only for states with large, highly sophisticated nuclear arsenals. While this posture contributes to avoiding a confrontational relationship with the United States and therefore serves China's strategic security interests, it also reflects the traditional defensive culture as well as how closely China's positions match those of the Non-Aligned Movement (NAM) (Shen 2009, 6; Feng 2009, 183).

In a 1998 white paper, the government under Jiang Zemin promoted mutual trust, mutual benefit, equality and coordination through dialogue, and the promotion of common security through cooperation as universal parts of its "new security concept." The white paper also called for guaranteeing the right of all countries to equal participation in international arms control, disarmament, and nonproliferation affairs. While promoting this normative concept in every arms control regime, China's mediation to solving the North Korean nuclear problem under the roof of the six-party talks is the first practical implementation of this diplomatic strategy (Christensen 2009).

Although its permanent membership in the UNSC strengthens China's self-confidence, Beijing continues to keep a low profile by declaring that it still sees itself as a developing country (Carlson 2006, 234). However, a readiness to engage in multilateralism with a more constructive approach is becoming more and more evident (Foot and Walter 2011). As is obvious in the six-party talks, China is even prepared to pursue regional security interests in multilateral negotiations rather than doing so unilaterally or bilaterally.

Sovereignty versus Nonproliferation

As officially stated, "in the field of arms control, disarmament, and non-proliferation, the Chinese Government always bases its policy-making on the judgment whether it serves to safeguard national sovereignty and security" (China IOSC 2006). Sovereignty and noninterference are central parts of China's historically formed identity, particularly formulated in the five principles of peaceful coexistence, promoting mutual respect for territoriality and sovereignty, noninterference in internal affairs, and equal rights for the members of the international community.

Since this approach has been incrementally changing toward the acceptance of international norms, the Chinese conception of sovereignty is undergoing a sometimes ambivalent transition as well: in the norm conflict between nonproliferation and the peaceful use of science and technology, China on the one hand claims that "non-proliferation efforts should not undermine the legitimate rights of countries, especially the developing countries" (China 2005b, 2010) and therefore sides with the NAM. Simultaneously and somehow contradictory to these claims, China also tries to strengthen nonproliferation by calling for preventing proliferation activities under the pretext of peaceful uses and supporting the role of the UN "in further consolidating international consensus and deepening international cooperation" (China IOSC 2006).

China's most significant step toward complying with international nonproliferation norms was the adoption of domestic export control laws and regulations (Medeiros 2007, 212–14). Although the 2005 white paper on arms control and disarmament states that "China values the important role of the multilateral export control mechanism in the field of non-proliferation," a gap remains between official nonproliferation policy and repeated violations of established rules and regulations (Yuan 2007). For example, China emphasizes the sovereign right of countries to choose their technological path to development and insists on the peaceful character of the transferred goods, for example, in its much criticized dealings with Pakistan or Iran. Similar to its stance regarding the North Korean crisis, China rejects economic sanctions, emphasizing principles of nonintervention in the internal affairs of other states, and seeks to settle disputes through dialogue and negotiation. While this stance clearly supports Chinese regional and strategic interests,[7] it also demonstrates China's dilemma between acting as a responsible great power and practicing solidarity with Third World states. However, what seems to be contradictory from a Western perspective owes more to different evaluations of certain situations. For example, the assistance to Pakistan in the construction of several nuclear power reactors finds justification in the exemption granted to India from the NSG embargo against non-NPT states, and the ensuing US-India deal that grants

India access to US reactor technology and fuel. Regarding Iran, Beijing, unlike many Western countries, simply sees no immediate threat in Iran's nuclear program and therefore no need for taking action such as imposing international sanctions on Iran (International Crisis Group 2010, 3).

China does not refuse arms control for SALW in general but opposes certain measures, such as export controls that violate China's understanding of state sovereignty. It insists, for example, that "[i]n the process of combating the illicit trade in SALW, the sovereignty of each State should be respected, and the right of each State to legally manufacture, possess and transfer SALW should not be infringed upon" (China 2005c). During the negotiations on the PoA, China blocked the adoption of stronger standards: it refused to accept a general norm for the protection of human rights by a ban on small arms in the preamble, which was seen as essential by many other delegations. China's refusal to also regulate state-to-state arms trade and its refusal to ratify the Firearms Protocol of 2001 underline the limits of Beijing's support for humanitarian arms control (Garcia 2006, 114).

Nonetheless, China argues for stronger supportive measures for regions in crisis where the abundance of SALW presents an actual threat (G. Wang 2006). Its growing presence in sub-Saharan Africa could even lead the Chinese government to shifting to a more forthcoming position that would protect their own nationals from falling victim to small arms and keep African pro-China sympathies.

While China is not a party to the Ottawa Convention, it announced a moratorium on the export of any mines that do not comply with the Amended Protocol II of the Convention on Certain Conventional Weapons (CCW) in 1996 and has not exported antipersonnel mines since then (ICBL 2011). China has not acceded to the Convention on Cluster Munitions "due to national defence needs" (Q. Wang 2010). It holds the view that the use or transfer of cluster munitions lies within the scope of state sovereignty. There are also commercial interests at stake because state-owned companies such as the China Northern Industry Cooperation are major producers and exporters of cluster munitions. China thus takes a largely norm-blocking position in humanitarian arms control.

In the various nonproliferation regimes, China has been notorious for its reluctance to accept verification measures. This position has been consistent throughout Chinese positions at NPT RevCons. During the 2010 conference, China opposed all efforts at increasing transparency, in particular the demand for a uniform scheme of reporting on nuclear arsenals and disarmament measures. When there was an overwhelming majority favoring this request, China eventually acquiesced and accepted the conference action plan (Müller 2011, 223).

Moreover, within the chemical weapons (CW) context, China is concerned that *challenge* inspections could infringe upon state sovereignty. Therefore, it regularly expresses its reluctance to allow access to sensitive information and has been treating challenge inspections in the CWC as an exceptional measure that is acceptable only in extremis once consultation, clarification, and cooperation on a case of suspect noncompliance have been exhausted without success.

China allegedly conducted offensive CW programs in the early years of the CWC (US DoS 2005). While this could have accounted for China's reluctance to accept stronger verification measures, more plausible reasons are the fear that other states might gain access to sensitive military information, concerns about the vulnerability of China's nuclear deterrent to a first strike by the United States, and the belief that transparency is only meant "to hurt countries that are not of equal power status" (Croddy 2002, 31).

Compensatory Justice and Nondiscriminatory Norms

While China uses equality and justice claims to defend its own position vis-à-vis the United States, it also refers to inequality, injustice, or discrimination to demonstrate its solidarity with the NAM. More than any other NWS, China, as a former victim of imperialism, supports the interests of the developing world (Gill 2009, 246). Its most significant normative project is the unconditional promise not to "use or threaten to use nuclear weapons against non-nuclear weapon States or nuclear-weapon-free zones" (Sha 1997). By also demanding unconditional security guarantees for nonnuclear weapon states China intends to mitigate the inequalities in the NPT.

The priority of cooperation with, and special assistance to, developing countries in the WMD regimes is another strand of China's pro-NAM policies. China demands, for example, broad financial and technical support in the peaceful uses of biotechnology (Q. Wang 2009). Thus, China promotes the NAM position on BWC Art. X and joins in with their concerted criticism against supposedly unjustified export controls by industrialized states. China takes the same position within the CWC context (NAM and China 2007). It sees the survival of the Convention as contingent on its nondiscriminatory implementation and an intense exchange of technologies, materials, and equipment for peaceful purposes in the field of chemistry. Existing restrictions, according to Beijing, discriminate against developing countries and thus obviate the idea of peaceful development. Hence, China supports the NAM request to adopt an action plan for realizing Art. XI (Cheng 2008).

Nevertheless, China has never formally joined the NAM. This combination of solidarity *with*, and a distanced and privileged position *toward*, the NAM can find some explanation in the traditional pre-Qin approach, assuming a hierarchical structure of power in the international system with China at its center (Sinocentrism). In that sense, the discrepancy between China's claim to be a developing country and the concurrent demand for a leadership position are not contradictory in the Chinese mind, but simply reflect two different aspects of Chinese identity (Carlson 2006, 234).

Between Developing Country and Nuclear Weapon State Status

From the Chinese point of view, "the key to international power is political power, and the key to political power is a morally informed political leadership" (Yan 2011, 12). China knows that it needs to comply better with accepted normative standards and further expand its own normative culture to become a responsible power. This is reflected in the increasing commitment to, and compliance with, multilateral norms. However, the application of these norms is weighed against persistent Chinese principles and interests.

Within multilateral arms control, China's identity oscillates between being a developing country and a nuclear weapon state. At times it acts as a norm entrepreneur, but also as a norm blocker. Influenced by tradition, history, and contemporary economic and strategic interests, China on the one hand actively promotes its own normative standards such as its "new security concept," no-first-use, security guarantees for NNWS, cooperation in peaceful use, equality, nondiscrimination, and the principles of peaceful coexistence. On the other hand, it opposes intrusive verification, harsh sanctions, strict export controls, transparency, and any other measures that could breach state sovereignty or lead to further discrimination. Both security and commercial interests explain a large share of Chinese arms control policy; yet, both factors are deeply intertwined with the sense of historical (in)justice and the claims that China asserts based on its past.

With the upcoming transfer of power in the autumn of 2012, the Chinese leadership will undergo a generational change that might also be reflected in foreign policy. In the course of technocratic professionalization and bureaucratization, it remains to be seen to what degree tradition and history remain important determinants of China's arms control policy.

INDIA: AN IMPEDED NORM ENTREPRENEUR

As a rising power India should be prone to challenge the pre-established international normative structure continuously and comprehensively. Indian idiosyncrasies, however, yield a rather ambivalent picture: Mahatma Gandhi, Nehru, and the longstanding tradition of non-alignment let India shine as a moral beacon of international politics. Indira Gandhi, Vajpayee, and the Indian nuclear bomb, on the other hand, refer to the dark side of Indian power. In the end, the idiosyncratic perspective prevails: its behavior and argumentation in the regimes under scrutiny do not qualify India as a consistent "norm challenger." Rather, New Delhi acts inconsistently across different regimes, largely due to a mixture of interest, moral, and justice-driven motivations.

India in Arms Control

Since independence, India has always regarded itself as an important international actor. Only in recent years, however, has the international community begun to recognize India as a rising great power, primarily due to its remarkable economic growth.

Moved by its colonial past but also because of the history of partition,[8] India attaches great importance to its sovereignty. This attitude strongly influences its international behavior.[9] Moreover, the central tenets of India's foreign policy are fueled by two seemingly opposing positions: on the one hand by New Delhi's dedication to the power-politics-averse principles of non-alignment, which date back to Nehru, and on the other hand by India's desire to be recognized as a great power and as a pole in a multipolar world.

This dichotomy is reflected in descriptions of India as an actor in multilateral arms control and disarmament that usually take one of two extreme positions: either India is seen as a self-serving pariah with no real interest in the aims of international arms control (Cheema 2010, 2–3), or India—largely for moral reasons—is regarded as a merely misunderstood honest champion of disarmament (Raghavan 2011, 2–3).[10]

India is neither a member of the NPT nor the CTBT and, besides North

Korea, Pakistan, and Israel, is the only non-NWS under the rules of the NPT to possess nuclear weapons (see chapter 2). On the other hand, India joined the IAEA in 1957, ratified the Limited Test Ban Treaty (LTBT) in 1963, was among the first countries calling for a CTBT, and has observed a unilaterally declared nuclear test moratorium since its 1998 weapon tests. Furthermore, India principally supports a nondiscriminatory and verifiable FMCT (India, Ministry of External Affairs 2010, 128).

In stark contrast to this rather selective engagement in the field of nuclear arms control, India has been supportive toward the other regimes dealing with weapons of mass destruction: India ratified the BWC on July 15, 1974. The CWC was signed in 1993 and ratified on September 9, 1996. This makes India one of the original signatories of the convention, a fact that India proudly reiterates in many official documents (India Ministry of External Affairs 2007, 112). India supports both regimes in general, but not in all of their aspects.[11]

India's record in humanitarian arms control is mixed. It is a member of the CCW and all subsequent protocols, and it has supported the SALW Programme of Action. On the other hand, it abstained from voting for the Arms Trade Treaty resolution in the UN and refuses to accede to the conventions on APM and cluster munitions.

Discrimination, Disarmament, and Nonproliferation

In the conflict between *nonproliferation* and *disarmament* in the context of nuclear arms control, India shows potential for real norm entrepreneurship.[12] A first misunderstanding between India and its (mainly Western) critics concerns the definition of terms.[13] Whereas it is not unusual in Western circles to distinguish sharply between arms control and disarmament (Gupta 2010, 51–52), in India both terms are seen as inseparable (M. Singh 2009, 3).[14] To pursue arms control or nonproliferation measures without concurrently aiming at meaningful disarmament is considered counterproductive: "Total elimination of nuclear weapons is the only comprehensive and effective non-proliferation measure" (Jasjit Singh 1998a, 287). India is interested in stopping and rolling back vertical proliferation.[15] Focusing only on horizontal proliferation without any disarmament component is flawed beyond redemption in Indian eyes.[16] Accordingly, India does not take part in measures that sidestep or circumvent the aim of global nuclear disarmament (Saran 2010, 10).

India itself has traditionally been proactively engaged in bringing forward global nuclear disarmament: it presented numerous proposals in the international arena toward this aim and also joined forces with other disarmament-minded actors, such as in the "Group of Eight" and the "Six-Nation, Five-Continent Peace Initiative."[17] However, it has not been very successful, even though Indian resolutions are often adopted by large majorities or even unanimously in the United Nations General Assembly.[18] Additionally, India pushes for other measures it considers suitable for bringing about nuclear disarmament, such as a no-first-use treaty, the de-alerting and de-targeting of nuclear weapons. However, India wants these measures to be embedded in a larger framework with an agreed-upon time plan and a "concrete, focused, outcome oriented approach."[19] These points are constantly and continuously made by Indian politicians, diplomats, and academics. Indian activity for nuclear disarmament is motivated not only by moral reasons, but also—even though it has become a nuclear power itself in the meantime—by the belief that a nuclear-weapon-free world would serve India's security and therefore its national interests.[20]

India proved its disarmament credentials in the context of the CWC. After initially denying it had a chemical weapons program, India confessed to the existence of a chemical arsenal in 1997 and destroyed all stocks in accordance with the rules, regulations, and timeframes—India was granted an extension of the original deadline by the Organisation for the Prohibition of Chemical Weapons (OPCW)—by 2009.

India is less active but not as destructive as its staunch criticism would suggest in the field of nuclear nonproliferation. In upholding the related norms India has—apart from its own nuclear tests (1974 and 1998)[21]—an impeccable record: it neither tried to convince the official NWS to help it with its weapons program, nor did it disseminate its knowledge or hardware once it crossed the threshold. This is all the more impressive given the approaches India rebuffed: Libya, Iraq, and Iran all sought Indian cooperation in nuclear technologies in vain (Parthasarathy 2006, 364).[22] India does, however, object to the nonproliferation enforcement system, which—in the end—lies in the hands of the UNSC and thus increases the already discriminatory nature of the global nonproliferation regime.[23]

Discrimination, Technological Exchange, and Peaceful Use

India is also engaged in and takes a firm position in the conflict between *nonproliferation* and *peaceful use*. Like many NAM states, India maintains that the original agreement has been compromised[24]: While (mainly) developing states did forgo WMD developments, the industrialized countries failed to provide the promised cooperation and free access to technologies (nuclear, biological, and chemical) in an adequate manner (Chari and Deshingkar 2002, 250–52; e.g., Sabharwal 2007). Accordingly, India works to strengthen the cooperation norm in the BWC and CWC. In the BWC, for example, India especially emphasizes the implementation of Art. X and calls continuously for a *nondiscriminatory* practice (e.g., Sood 2001). India emphasizes the destructive and norm-bending role of so-perceived *technology-denial regimes* such as the NSG and the Australia Group (e.g., Cowsik 2003), having been on the receiving end of trade restrictions (especially in the nuclear sector) for a long time. One of the primary goals of New Delhi has always been to weaken if not abolish those regimes and regain full access to technologies. It has been partly successful with the recent US-India nuclear deal (see chapter 5 in this volume).

India, however, is no opponent of export controls in general, as long as they are implemented in a nondiscriminatory manner. Thus, and in contrast to more radical actors, India emphasizes the role of both Art. III and Art. X in the BWC (e.g., India 1997).

As in other aspects (see below) India's approach to these issue areas has gradually become more pragmatic in recent years. In 2010, for example, New Delhi declared its intention to join the NSG, the MTCR, the Australia Group, and the Wassenaar Agreement. This may be related to the fact that India is increasingly becoming a technology provider, rather than merely a technology seeker.

Discrimination, Justice, and Interest

As already indicated, justice claims play an important and recurring role in the Indian argumentation. In 1968 the Indian UN ambassador cited five reasons for Indian opposition to the NPT: "It emphasized only horizontal and not vertical non-proliferation; it did not address the special status of superiority associated with nuclear weapons; it did not provide for a balance of obligations and responsibilities between the NWS and NNWS; it did not outline an approach towards nuclear disarmament; and it was discriminatory in regard to the safeguards and controls, which were imposed only on NNWS" (Sethi 2010, 250). Two of these reasons refer to the missing disarmament component (and therefore the central norm conflict), while the other three all refer to discernible justice matters. Thus, besides the fact that the Indian aim of nuclear disarmament remained unfulfilled in the NPT, the main motivation of Indian aversion—reiterated in all relevant international forums—is the discriminatory character of the regime, which points to a staunch Indian claim for (status) equality as the underlying justice principle.

This call for nondiscriminatory rules, regulations, and regimes has run through Indian statements throughout the last fifty years. As early as 1961 Nehru told the United Nations General Assembly concerning international arms control: "Those agreements cannot be merely agreements of some countries, however great. They must represent all the members of this United Nations in this great body" (Nehru 1961). During a debate in the Indian *Lōk Sabhā* his daughter Indira Gandhi reiterated this point and furthermore criticized the unequal treatment of different states (Gandhi 1968). India in turn would support nuclear disarmament as "it is only through nuclear disarmament that *discrimination* would be eliminated and *equality between nations* reestablished" (Gandhi 1968, emphasis added). More than twenty-five years later, External Affairs Minister Jaswant Singh sounds similar: "India holds that genuine and lasting non-proliferation can only be achieved through agreements that are based upon *equality* and *non-discrimination*, for only these can contribute to global peace and stability" (2000, emphasis added).

This justice-driven opposition transcends Indian domestic political party lines. Thus Prime Minister Moraji Desai, whose broad coalition of parties was able to break the dominance of the Congress Party for a short time in the late 1970s, declared to the United Nations General Assembly: "Our objection to the Treaty is because it is so *patently discriminatory*" (1978, emphasis added). The first prime minister from the Bharatiya Janata Party, who ordered the nuclear tests of 1998, likewise told the Indian parliament in the same year: "[The] balance of rights and obligations was not accepted [by the nuclear powers]" (Vajpayee 1998).

The main thrust of the moral- and justice-laden Indian critique is well captured by the notion of "nuclear apartheid" (Jaswant Singh 1998), which was coined in India.[25] However, after the nuclear tests of 1998, the Indian position has started to become gradually more pragmatic: India declared several times that it could—under certain circumstances[26]—join the CTBT. At the same time, India now seems to embrace nuclear deterrence strategies, unlike Indian politicians from Nehru to Rajiv Gandhi, who previously had demonized the deterrence system and branded it as morally unjustifiable (Bidwai and Vanaik 2000,

129). This might indicate that India's new status as de facto NWS has more influence on the Indian mindset than the ongoing rhetoric suggests.

The other WMD regimes are judged by India through the lens of (regime) justice as well. By doing so, India positively contrasts them with the NPT.[27] India praises the CWC explicitly because "it testifies to the legitimacy and validity of the global campaign—which India consistently advocated—for a universal and non-discriminatory approach to the elimination of weapons of mass destruction" (Mansingh 1997b). India's willingness to declare the existence of and destroy its chemical arsenal (see above) reinforces the credibility of Indian justice arguments within the NPT context as well: India was prepared to renounce a whole category of WMD (that it already possessed) in a regime it regards as principally "just."

In its BWC statements India also often links this regime directly or indirectly to the NP regime by maintaining that the way biological weapons have been outlawed is exemplary. India specifically praises that BWC has been "the first multilateral, non-discriminatory treaty banning an entire class of weapons of mass destruction" (India Ministry of External Affairs 2011, 122; see also Rao 2009). Sometimes the linkage is made very explicit; in these cases India claims "the Biological and Chemical Weapons Conventions provide a good example for the complete elimination of nuclear weapons" (Prasad 2006) or simply demands "[w]e need a similar effort in the area of nuclear weapons" (Prasad 2007).

In stark contrast to the nuclear field, moralistic and justice-laden arguments play no role in framing Indian positions on humanitarian arms control. Indeed, India officially recognizes the humanitarian necessity of sparing innocent civilians from the danger of these weapons (Nepram 2009, 484–85), but at the same time it maintains there is a need to strike "a balance between humanitarian and security considerations" (India Ministry of External Affairs 2011, 121). For example, India justifies not acceding to the Ottawa Convention—though principally supporting its goals—because the convention "fails to take into account the legitimate security interests of countries which necessitate the usage of landmines for defensive purposes" (India Ministry of External Affairs 2007, 113). India holds a similarly ambivalent position in the SALW context, where on the one hand it emphasizes the necessity of controlling illicit trade and preventing nonstate actors and terrorists from obtaining SALW while at the same time stressing its need to engage in legal trade with these weapons. Concerning cluster munitions India further makes the point that their use is "lawful and legitimate" (Nepram 2009, 486) as long as humanitarian international law is observed, and mainly stresses the military advantages of these weapons (Kanwal 2010, 1406). Thus, as a country that has long land borders, including borders with two difficult neighbors, perceived security interests trump the moral- and justice-laden impulse to join these regimes.

Impeded Norm Entrepreneurship

The initial expectation that India, as a rising great power, should be characterized by uniform norm-challenging behavior is not supported by evidence: Indian actions in WMD regimes differ profoundly in the nuclear realm on the one hand and the chemical and biological realms on the other hand. Justice claims and especially the disdain for discriminatory instruments of any kind may explain a large part of this variance. Indian statements clearly show that India regards the global NP regime as inherently unjust, whereas the nondiscriminatory BW and CW regimes are regarded as principally just orders, with a caveat for their cooperation norms.

The example of the NP regime shows that perceived justice problems can deter India from joining a regime, even though India shares many core norms and considers the goals of the regime as lying in its own interest. The cases of BWC and CWC show India's willingness, in principle, to contribute to multilateral arms control in "just" regimes. Yet, India's behavior in the area of humanitarian arms control shows that the *absence* of justice concerns does not guarantee Indian regime participation, especially when India feels its security interests could be disturbed.

This mixed result makes it difficult to unambiguously assign India to one specific type of norm entrepreneurship. In the nuclear realm, where it is most dissatisfied with the existing regime, it acts as norm entrepreneur, advocating disarmament continuously and proactively. At the same time, New Delhi sent ambivalent signals first by not irrevocably renouncing and by ultimately obtaining nuclear weapons, thereby compromising the credibility of the Indian position.

India's effect on international norm dynamics is therefore ambivalent. Whether ongoing Indian insistence on international compliance and the proactive proposal of its own resolutions for achieving this aim have really served disarmament, or whether Indian resistance to offer its own contribution has impeded it, is difficult to decide. It is safe to say, however, that India has not succeeded in building *momentum* for global nuclear disarmament. Rather, the Indian example could be read by other actors as a model for how to remain outside the NPT, develop nuclear weapons, and gain some sort of recognition, without being compelled to give them up. Even though—as our analysis suggests—the Indian motivation is seriously shaped by justice concerns, this does not necessarily hold true for potential imitators. In this important aspect India can thus be called an impeded norm entrepreneur at best.

CONCLUSION: IDIOSYNCRATIC NORM ENTREPRENEURSHIP

There is no uniform great power status-induced behavior in our four cases. Neither can the United States and Russia be regarded as adamant norm keepers and enforcers across all regimes and times, nor are the actions of China and India bold and defiant enough to qualify them as challengers of the entire normative system. The rising powers do indeed challenge some norms in some regimes, but they do so very selectively. In other regimes they work smoothly within and indeed try to strengthen the pre-existing framework, even if it was established before they gained their current power position.

While power status–related issues had a discernible impact on the countries' performance in the various regimes, great power status alone tells us little about the behavior of these actors in normative contexts in general and about the level of norm entrepreneurship in particular; this is just as true for rising as it is for established great powers. The impact of power status on policies is mediated by self-images, political traditions, domestic politics, and interests as defined by the ruling elites. Policies are thus quite path-dependent and idiosyncratic and defy abstract predictions based on power status alone. The belief in its exceptionalism influences US approaches toward norms and regimes; this accounts for the basic stance of retaining stability and freedom of action at the same time, a combination of objectives that at times compels the United States to work hard for maintaining established norms, while occasionally challenging them in an almost revolutionary way, as during George W. Bush's presidency. China is motivated at least to an extent by its wish to consolidate its great power status and become accepted as a *responsible* great power. This may explain the tripartite approach of engaging in multilateral efforts to keep existing norms, maintaining the freedom to interpret them in a very Chinese way, and preserving freedom of action for granting China's security vis-à-vis the United States. All in all, our findings thus corroborate Foot and Walter's surprising insight that the hegemon, rather than defending the existing normative order, displays incoherent policies of compliance and noncompliance, not out of strategic considerations but rather for domestic reasons. China "the challenger," on the other hand, demonstrates increasingly better compliance the closer it comes to posing a true challenge (Foot and Walter 2011).

Regarding the remaining two great powers, many of Russia's actions can be explained by its determination to desperately *hold onto* or *reclaim* its former status as one of the only two superpowers. The demand of both Russia and China for "equal security" vis-à-vis the United States also indicates the feeling that there is an unjustified advantage in security that compromises their desired great power status. However, the notion of equal security remains rather exclusive, as exemplified by the reluctance to accept the NNWS call for a world free of nuclear weapons, thus keeping them in a permanent situation of "unequal security." India's continued claims for nondiscrimination and equality point to its aspiration of becoming acknowledged as a member of the great powers club. So far, India is caught between being out and being in. This accounts for India's seemingly disparate policies, namely the continued calls for change, the observation of existing norms, and the refusal to acknowledge norms that may constrain national security and military power.

Justice claims are least commonly put forward by the dominant great power, the United States, and most commonly voiced by the weakest great power, India, with China and Russia falling somewhere in between. Interestingly, we find justice claims to be used both in a more tactical manner (Russia) and as a more genuine sentiment (India). One should caution, however, that, once a country's elite and population are convinced that their country is entitled (on whatever basis) to belong to the club of great powers, any action or structure perceived as discriminatory gives rise to complaints about injustice that are most probably quite authentic. Establishing precise distinctions between the various usages and levels of authenticity may not always be easy and depends on more than just the great power status of the state voicing such a complaint.

Notes

1. The forty-first president, George H. W. Bush, is referred to as "Bush 41" to distinguish his presidency from that of his son George W. Bush, or "Bush 43."

2. The Ottawa Convention, which the Clinton administration could neither control nor stop (Wurst 1997), is an exception to this generalization.

3. Interview with Morton Halperin, senior government official in the Kennedy, Johnson, Nixon, and Clinton administrations, conducted by Marco Fey, September 28, 2011, Washington.

4. The term *adequate verification* was coined in the Nixon administration and meant that the US needed to be able to detect significant violations of an agreement in time to permit an adequate reaction (Krass 1997, 164).

5. It should be noted that signing the CTBT was hotly contested, as even without ratification it imposes the duty not to act contrary to the objectives of the treaty. Some Chinese defense experts feared China's nuclear deterrent would thus remain forever technologically inferior to the US one (Johnston 2008, 106–7).

6. In a bilateral statement in 1994, China and Russia declared their mutual acceptance of this norm.

7. There is little doubt that Pakistan and Iran receive Chinese help because of their respective roles as a regional partner and as an important supplier of fossil fuel (Gill 2007, 79–82).

8. Interview with Madhu Balla, professor at the University of Delhi, conducted by Carsten Rauch, New Delhi, November 30, 2009.

9. Interview with senior official at the Ministry of External Affairs, conducted by Carsten Rauch, New Delhi, November 26, 2009; interview with Srikanth Kondapalli, professor at Jawaharlal Nehru University (JNU), conducted by Carsten Rauch, New Delhi, December 1, 2009.

10. Interview with Onkar Marwah, national security expert at the Institute of Peace and Conflict Studies (IPCS), conducted by Carsten Rauch, New Delhi, December 3, 2009.

11. India played a rather dubious role during the BWC protocol negotiations, which was overshadowed only by the even more destructive actions by the US.

12. India emphasizes the primary goal of disarmament in the other WMD regimes as well, but there is no conflict around this issue.

13. Interview with Rajiv Nayan, arms control expert at the Institute for Defence Studies and Analyses (IDSA), conducted by Carsten Rauch, New Delhi, November 25, 2009.

14. Interview with senior official at the Ministry of External Affairs, conducted by Carsten Rauch, New Delhi, December 3, 2009.

15. India believes that the NPT reverses these priorities (Sreenivasan 2010, 172).

16. Interview with senior official at the Ministry of External Affairs, conducted by Carsten Rauch, New Delhi, November 26, 2009.

17. For a detailed discussion of the initiatives see Sethi (1998) and Barnes, Ogilvie-White, and Valdés (2010).

18. E.g., the Indian resolutions "Convention on the Prohibition of the Use of Nuclear Weapons" and "Reducing Nuclear Danger," which India has been tabling annually at the UN General Assembly since 1982 and 1998, respectively.

19. Interview with senior official at the Ministry of External Affairs, conducted by Carsten Rauch, New Delhi, December 3, 2009.

20. Interview with Harinder Sekhon, senior fellow at the Observer Research Foundation (ORF), conducted by Carsten Rauch, New Delhi, November 30, 2009.

21. India emphasizes, however, that its nuclear policy did not break any signed contracts or other political commitments (Jasjit Singh 1999, 520; interview with Rajiv Nayan, arms control expert at IDSA, conducted by Carsten Rauch, New Delhi, November 25, 2009; interview with senior official at the Ministry of External Affairs, conducted by Carsten Rauch, New Delhi, December 3, 2009). This is a debatable claim, as it is disputed whether the test of 1974 can truly be regarded as a *peaceful nuclear explosion*. See Perkovich (1999).

22. India on the one hand refuses to sign the CTBT and criticizes it for its lack of disarmament perspective and its discriminatory character (Gupta 2010, 57; Sethi 2000, 1820), but on the other hand India maintains its unilaterally declared nuclear test moratorium of 1998.

23. India is thus the only great power under scrutiny here that is not routinely included in this system.

24. Interview with A. Vinod Kumar, arms control expert at IDSA, conducted by Carsten Rauch, New Delhi, November 25, 2009.

25. In similar fashion a former high-ranking Indian diplomat described the nuclear order as a kind of "colonial situation" and an "emotional thing." Interview conducted by Carsten Rauch, New Delhi, December 4, 2009.

26. E.g., ratifications by the US, China, and Pakistan, a certification of the credibility of the existing arsenal, and verification that India's "nuclear complex is capable of subcritical testing and simulation-based improvisations" (Kumar 2009).

27. Indian diplomats repeatedly discuss India's position concerning nuclear disarmament even at BWC or CWC meetings, underlining the centrality of nuclear issues for India. E.g., Mansingh 1997a; Ghose 1996.

References

Albin, Cecilia. 2001. *Justice and Fairness in International Negotiation*. Cambridge: Cambridge University Press.

Antonov, Anatoly. Russian Federation. 2004. Statement to the PrepCom for the 2005 NPT RevCon. NPT/CONF.2005/PC.III/SR.3. New York, August 3.

———. 2006. Statement to the 6th BWC RevCon. Geneva, November 20.

Barnes, Natasha, Tanya Ogilvie-White, and Rodrigo Álvarez Valdés. 2010. "The NPT Holdouts—Universality as an Elusive Goal." *Nonproliferation Review* 17 (1): 95–113.

Berdennikov, Grigori. Russian Federation. 1994. Statement to the BWC Special Conference. BWC/SPCONF/SR.3. Geneva, September 20.

Bidwai, Praful, and Achin Vanaik. 2000. *New Nukes: India, Pakistan and Global Nuclear Disarmament*. Oxford: Signal Books.

Bolton, John R. 2001a. Plenary Address to the UN Conference on the Illicit Trade in Small Arms and Light Weapons, New York, July 9.

———. 2001b. Press Conference at UN Headquarters, New York, July 9.

Bunn, George. 1992. *Arms Control by Committee: Managing Negotiations with the Russians*. Stanford: Stanford University Press.

Busch, Nathan E., and James R. Holmes. 2009. "Russia's Nuclear Security Culture." In Busch and Joyner 2009, 325–42.

Busch, Nathan E., and Daniel H. Joyner, eds. 2009. *Combating Weapons of Mass Destruction: The Future of International Nonproliferation Policy*. Athens: University of Georgia Press.

Bush, George W. 2004. "Remarks on Weapons of Mass Destruction Proliferation." Remarks at the National Defense University, February 11.

Carlson, Allen. 2006. "More Than Just Saying No: China's Evolving Approach to Sovereignty and Intervention since Tiananmen." In *New Directions in the Study of China's Foreign Policy*, edited by Alastair I. Johnston and Robert S. Ross, 217–41. Stanford: Stanford University Press.

Carnesale, Albert, and Richard N. Haass, eds. 1987. *Superpower Arms Control: Setting the Record Straight*. Cambridge: Ballinger.

Chari, P. R., and Giri Deshingkar. 2002. "India: Straddling East and West." In *Biological Warfare and Disarmament: New Problems/New Perspectives*, edited by Susan Wright, 239–61. Lanham: Rowan and Littlefield.

Cheema, Zafar Iqbal. 2010. *Indian Nuclear Deterrence: Its Evolution, Development, and Implications for South Asian Security*. Karachi: Oxford University Press.

Cheng, Jingye. China. 2008. Statement to the 2nd CWC RevCon, The Hague, April 8.

China. 1964. "The Atomic Bomb. Statement of the Government of the People's Republic of China." *People's Daily*, October 16.

———. 1999a. "Implementations of the Provisions of NPT Relating to Non-proliferation of Nuclear Weapons, Nuclear Disarmament and Security Assurances." Working paper. NPT/CONF.2000/PC.III/15. New York, May 13.

———. 1999b. "Proposed Elements to Be Included in Chairman's Working Paper." NPT/CONF.2000/PC.III/37. New York, May 19.

———. 2005a. "Nuclear Disarmament and Reduction of the Danger of Nuclear War." Working paper. NPT/CONF.2005/WP.2*. New York, April 26.

———. 2005b. "Peaceful Uses of Nuclear Energy." Working paper. NPT/CONF.2005/WP.6. New York, April 26.

———. 2005c. "Report on the Implementation of the UN Programme of Action to Prevent, Combat and Eradicate the Illicit Trade in Small Arms and Light Weapons in All Its Aspects." New York. June 23.

———. 2010. "Peaceful Uses of Nuclear Energy." Working paper. NPT/CONF.2010/WP.65. New York, May 6.

China IOSC (Information Office of the State Council of the People's Republic of China). 2006. "China's Endeavours for Arms Control, Disarmament and Non-Proliferation." Beijing, September 1.

———. 2009. "China's National Defense in 2008." Beijing, January 20.

Christensen, Thomas J. 2009. "Shaping the Choices of a Rising China: Recent Lessons for the Obama Administration." *Washington Quarterly* 32 (3): 39–104.

CoW (Correlates of War). 2010. "National Material Capabilities (v4.0)." June 30. www.correlatesofwar.org/COW2%20Data/Capabilities/nmc4.htm.

Cowsik, Shyamala B. India. 2003. Statement to the 1st CWC RevCon, The Hague, April 29.

Crail, Peter. 2010. *Assessing Progress on Nuclear Nonproliferation and Disarmament.* 2009–2010 Report Card, Arms Control Association.

Croddy, Eric. 2002. "China's Role in the Chemical and Biological Disarmament Regimes." *Nonproliferation Review* 9 (1): 16–47.

Desai, Moraji. 1978. "Quest for Peace." Statement to the Special Session of the UNGA, New York, June 9.

Evangelista, Matthew. 2004. "Turning Points in Arms Control." In *Ending the Cold War: Interpretations, Causation, and the Study of International Relations*, edited by Richard Herrmann and Richard Ned Lebow, 83–106. Gordonsville: Palgrave Macmillan.

Fascell, Dante B. 1987. "Congress and Arms Control." *Foreign Affairs* 65 (4): 730–49.

Fehl, Caroline. 2008. "Living with a Reluctant Hegemon: The Transatlantic Conflict over Multilateral Arms Control." *European Journal of International Relations* 14 (2): 259–87.

Feng, Huiyun. 2009. "A Dragon on Defense: Explaining China's Strategic Culture." In *Strategic Culture and Weapons Of Mass Destruction*, edited by Jeannie L. Johnson, Kerry M. Kartchner, and Jeffrey A. Larsen, 171–87. New York: Palgrave Macmillan.

Fidler, David P. 2005. "The Meaning of Moscow: "Non-lethal" Weapons and International Law in the Early 21st Century." *International Review of the Red Cross* 87 (859): 525–52.

Foot, Rosemary, and Andrew Walter. 2011. *China, the United States, and Global Order.* Cambridge: Cambridge University Press.

Ford, Christopher A. 2007. "Debating Disarmament: Interpreting Article VI of the Treaty on the Non-Proliferation of Nuclear Weapons." *Nonproliferation Review* 14 (3): 401–28.

———. 2008. "A New Paradigm: Shattering Obsolete Thinking on Arms Control and Nonproliferation." *Arms Control Today* 38 (9): 12–19.

Gandhi, Indira. 1968. "Non-Proliferation Treaty." Lōk Sabhā Debate on Foreign Affairs, New Delhi, April 5.

Garcia, Denise. 2006. *Small Arms and Security: New Emerging International Norms*. London: Routledge.

Garthoff, Raymond. 2001. *Journey through the Cold War: A Memoir of Containment and Coexistence*. Washington: Brookings Institution Press.

Ghose, Arundhati. India. 1996. Statement to the 4th RevCon of State Parties to the BWC, Geneva, November 26.

Gill, Bates. 2007. *Rising Star: China's New Security Diplomacy*. Washington: Brookings Institution Press.

———. 2009. "China's Changing Approach to Nonproliferation." In Busch and Joyner 2009, 245–63.

Gupta, Arvind. 2010. "Nuclear Disarmament and Arms Control." In *India and Global Nuclear Disarmament*, edited by V. R. Raghavan, 44–61. New Delhi: Macmillan India.

Haass, Richard N. 1987. "Verification and Compliance." In Carnesale and Haass 1987, 303–28.

Hampson, Fen O. 1987. "SALT I Interim Agreement and ABM Treaty." In Carnesale and Haass 1987, 65–103.

Hansell, Christina, and Nikita Perfilyev. 2009. "Together towards Nuclear Zero." *Nonproliferation Review* 16 (3): 435–61.

Hart, John. 2006. "The Soviet Biological Weapons Program." In *Deadly Cultures: Biological Weapons since 1945*, edited by Mark Wheelis, Lajos Rósza, and Malcolm Dando, 132–56. Cambridge: Harvard University Press.

Holloway, David. 2011. "The United States and the NPT 'Double Bargain.'" In *Nuclear Proliferation and International Order: Challenges to the Non-Proliferation Treaty*, edited by Olav Njølstad, 151–66. New York: Routledge.

Hua, Liming. China. 1998. Statement to the 3rd Session of the CWC CSP, The Hague, November 16.

ICBL (International Campaign to Ban Landmines). 2011. *Landmine and Cluster Munition Monitor*. Country Profile: China. www.the-monitor.org/custom/index.php/region_profiles/print_profile/243.

India. 1997. "Measures to Strengthen Implementation of Article X of the BTWC." Working paper. BWC/AD HOC GROUP/WP.131. Geneva, March 10.

India Ministry of External Affairs. 2007. *Annual Report, 2006–2007*. http://www.mea.gov.in.

———. 2010. *Annual Report, 2009–2010*. http://www.mea.gov.in.

———. 2011. *Annual Report, 2010–2011*. http://www.mea.gov.in.

International Crisis Group. 2010. "The Iran Nuclear Issue: The View from Beijing." Asia Briefing no. 100, Beijing/Brussels.

Johnson, Rebecca. 2005. "All Talk, No Action." *Bulletin of the Atomic Scientists* 61 (4): 19–20.

Johnston, Alastair Iain. 2008. *Social States: China in International Institutions, 1980–2000*. Princeton: Princeton University Press.

Joseph, Robert G. US. 2006. Remarks at UN Review Conference on the Illicit Trade in Small Arms and Light Weapons, June 27.

Joyner, Daniel. 2011. *Interpreting the Nuclear Non-Proliferation Treaty*. Oxford: Oxford University Press.

Kanwal, Gurmeet. 2010. "Ban on Anti-personnel Landmines: An Update." *Strategic Analysis* 34 (2): 1405–8.

Keohane, Robert O. 1984. *After Hegemony: Cooperation and Discord in the World Political Economy*. Princeton: Princeton University Press.

Khlebnikov, Nikolai. Russian Federation. 1995. Statement to the 1995 NPT RevCon. NPT/CONF.1995/MC.II/SR.1. New York, April 24.

Khlopkov, Anton. 2011. "Practical Implementation: The Russian Experience." In *Multilateralization of the Nuclear Fuel Cycle: The First Practical Steps*, edited by Yuri Yudin, 5–44. New York: United Nations.

Kindleberger, Charles Poor. 1973. *The World in Depression, 1929–1939*. Berkeley: University of California Press.

Kislyak, Sergey. Russian Federation. 1995. Statement to the PrepCom for the 1995 NPT RevCon. NPT/CONF.1995/PC.IV/SR.3. New York, February 17.

Kokoshin, Andrei. 1991. "Arms Control: A View from Moscow." *Daedalus* 120 (1): 133–43.

Koplow, David. 2006. *Non-lethal weapons: The Law and Policy of Revolutionary Technologies for the Military and Law Enforcement*. Cambridge: Cambridge University Press.

Krass, Allan S. 1997. *The United States and Arms Control: The Challenge of Leadership*. Westport: Praeger.

Krepon, Michael. 1989. "Has Arms Control Worked?" *Bulletin of the Atomic Scientists* 6 (4): 27–28.

Kumar, A. Vinod. 2009. "India and the CTBT: The Debate in New Delhi." *Bulletin of the Atomic Scientists*, November 4. www.thebulletin.org/print/web-edition/features/india-and-the-ctbt-the-debate-new-delhi.

Lavrov, Sergej. Russian Federation. 2011. Statement to the CD, Geneva, March 1.

Litravin, Petr. Russian Federation. 2006. Statement to the Conference to Review Progress Made in Implementation of PoA, New York, June 27.

Littlewood, Jez. 2005. *The Biological Weapons Convention: A Failed Revolution*. Aldershot: Ashgate.

Makashov, Albert. 1997. "Our Chemical Weapons May Be Kept for Another Forty Years, and They Do Not Disturb Anyone." Interview by Masha Katsva. *Yaderny Kontrol Digest*, Spring, 21–22.

Mansingh, Lalit. India. 1997a. Statement to the 1st Session of the CWC CSP, The Hague, May 8.

———. 1997b. Statement to the 2nd Session of the CWC CSP, The Hague, December 2.

McCain, Morris. 1989. *Understanding Arms Control: The Options*. New York: Norton.

Medeiros, Evan S. 2007. *Reluctant Restraint: The Evolution of China's Nonproliferation Policies and Practices, 1980–2004*. Stanford: Stanford University Press.

Medvedev, Vladimir. 1999. "Russia's Nuclear Deterrence: A Look into the Next Decade." *Yaderny Kontrol*, no. 10, 16–21.

Mostovets, Alexander. Russian Federation. 2002. Statement to the PrepCom for the 2005 NPT RevCon. NPT/CONF.2005/PC.I/SR.3. New York, June 6.

Müller, Harald. 2011. "A Nuclear Nonproliferation Test: Obama's Nuclear Policy and the 2010 NPT Review Conference." *Nonproliferation Review* 18 (1): 219–36.

NAM (Non-Aligned Movement) and China. 2007. "Indicative Elements of a Plan of Action on the Full Implementation of Article XI." Working paper by the States Parties to the CWC that are members of the NAM, and China. C-12/NAT.1. November 6.

Nehru, Jawaharlal. 1961. "The Problems of Disarmament." Speech at UNGA, New York, November 10.

Nepram, Binalakshm. 2009. "India and the Convention on Cluster Munitions." *Strategic Analysis* 33 (4): 483–87.

Nye, Joseph S. 1987. "The Superpowers and the Non-Proliferation Treaty." In Carnesale and Haass 1987, 165–90.

Obama, Barack. 2009. "Remarks at Hradcany Square." Prague, April 5.

Organski, A. F. K. 1958. *World Politics*. New York: Knopf.

Orlov, Vladimir, and Ivan Trushkin. 2011. "The Iranian Nuclear Program: Dilemmas Facing Russia." *Security Index: A Russian Journal on International Security* 17 (2): 27–37.

Parthasarathy, Gopalaswami. 2006. "Nuclear Disarmament, Nuclear Proliferation and WMD Proliferation: An Indian Perspective." In *Arms Control after Iraq: Normative and Operational Challenges*, edited by Waheguru Sidhu, Pal Singh, and Ramesh Thakur, 353–66. Tokyo: United Nations University Press.

Perkovich, George. 1999. *India's Nuclear Bomb: The Impact on Global Proliferation*. Berkeley: University of California Press.

Podvig, Pavel. 2011a. "Instrumental Influences: Russia and the 2010 Nuclear Posture Review." *Nonproliferation Review* 18 (1): 39–50.

———. 2011b. "Russia's Nuclear Forces: Between Disarmament and Modernization." *Proliferation Papers* 37 (Spring).

Potter, William C. 1993. "Nuclear Exports from the Former Soviet Union: What's New, What's True?" *Arms Control Today*, January/February: 3–10.

Prasad, Jayant. India. 2006. Statement to the 6th BWC RevCon, Geneva, November 20.

———. 2007. Statement to the BWC Meeting of Experts, Geneva, August 20–24.

Quester, George H. 1973. *The Politics of Nuclear Proliferation*. Baltimore: Johns Hopkins University Press.

Raghavan, V. R. 2011. Introduction to *Nuclear Disarmament: India-EU Perspectives*, edited by V. R. Raghavan, 1–5. New Delhi: VIJ Books India.

Rao, Hamid Ali. India. 2009. Statement to the Meeting of State Parties to the BWC, Geneva, December 7.

Reuters. 2011. "Russia Seizes Iran-Bound Radioactive Material." Reuters, December 16.

Revill, James, and Malcolm Dando. 2009. "The Rise of Biosecurity in International Arms Control." In *Biosecurity. Origins, Transformations and Practices*, edited by Brian Rappert and Chandré Gould, 41–59. Basingstoke: Palgrave Macmillan.

Rowney, Edward L. 1989. "Principles and Initiatives in United States Arms Control Policy." In *Multilateral Aspects of the Disarmament Debate*, edited by United Nations, 70–75. New York: Taylor & Francis.

Russian Federation. 1997. "Basic Principles and Procedures for Consideration of Requests Relating to Alleged Violations of the BTWC." Working paper. BWC/AD HOC GROUP/WP.181. Geneva, July 22.

———. 2002. PoA National Implementation Report. www.poa-iss.org/CASACountryProfile/PoANationalReports/2002@163@2002-National-Report-Russia%28en%29.pdf.

———. 2009. Russia's National Security Strategy to 2020. www.scrf.gov.ru/documents/99.html.

———. 2010. National Report on the Implementation of the NPT by the Russian Federation for the 2010 NPT RevCon. NPT/CONF.2010/28. New York, May 3.

Sabharwal, Neelam D. India. 2007. Statement to the 12th Session of the CWC CSP, November 5–9.

Saran, Shyam. 2010. "Nuclear Zero—The Shining City on the Hill." In *India and Global Nuclear Disarmament*, edited by V. R. Raghavan, 6–11. New Delhi: Macmillan India.

Seignious, George M. 1987. "Introduction: The Recent History of American-Soviet Arms Control Negotiations." In *Arms Control and Nuclear Weapons: U.S. Policies and the National Interest*, edited by W. G. Nichols and Milton Boykin, 1–6. New York: Greenwood.

Sethi, Manpreet. 1998. "The Struggle for Nuclear Disarmament." In Jasjit Singh 1998b, 75–95.

———. 2000. "Indian Signature on the CTBT: What's the Hurry?" *Strategic Analysis* 23 (10): 1819–21.

———. 2010. "NPT RevCon 2010: An Opportunity to Refocus Priorities." *Strategic Analysis* 34 (2): 246–54.

Sha, Zukang. China. 1997. Statement to the PrepCom for the 2000 NPT RevCon. NPT/CONF.2000/PC.I/SR.2. New York, August 19.

Shen, Dingli. 2009. "Toward a Nuclear Weapons Free World: A Chinese Perspective." Lowy Institute for International Peace, Sydney. www.cas.fudan.edu.cn/picture/1783.pdf.

Sims, Nicholas A. 2003. "Biological Disarmament Diplomacy in the Doldrums: Reflections after the BWC Fifth Review Conference." *Disarmament Diplomacy* 70: 11–18.

Singh, Jasjit. 1998a. "Nuclear Diplomacy." In Jasjit Singh 1998b, 286–305.

———, ed. 1998b. *Nuclear India*. New Delhi: Knowledge World.

———. 1999. "India's Nuclear Policy: The Year After." *Strategic Analysis* 23 (4): 509–30.

Singh, Jaswant. 1998. "Against Nuclear Apartheid." *Foreign Affairs* 77 (5): 41–52.

———. India. 2000. Statement to Parliament on the NPT Review Conference, New Delhi, May 9. www.acronym.org.uk/dd/dd46/46india.htm.

Singh, Manmohan. 2009. "Inaugural Address." In *Towards a Nuclear Weapon Free World*, edited by Manpreet Sethi, 1–3. New Delhi: KW.

Small Arms Survey. 2009. *Shadows of War: A Project of the Graduate Institute of International Studies Geneva*. Oxford: Oxford University Press.

Smithson, Amy E. 2001. "U.S. Implementation of the CWC." In *The Chemical Weapons Convention: Implementation Challenges and Solutions*, edited by Jonathan B. Tucker, 23–29. Monterey: Monterey Institute of International Studies.

Sokov, Nikolai. 2007. "The Origins of and Prospects for Russian Nuclear Doctrine." *Nonproliferation Review* 14 (2): 207–26.

Sood, Rakesh. India. 2001. Statement to the 5th BWC RevCon, Geneva, November 20.

Sreenivasan, T. P. 2010. "Bringing India's Dream to Fruition." *Washington Quarterly* 33 (2): 169–79.

Tammen, Ronald L., Jacek Kugler, Douglas Lemke, Allan C. Stamm III, Mark Abdollahian, Carole Alsharabati, Brian Efrid, and A. F. K. Organski. 2000. *Power Transitions: Strategies for the 21st Century*. New York: Seven Bridges Press.

Tarasov, Alexander. 2000. "Arms Control in Russia Today." *Comparative Strategy* 19 (1): 69–77.

Titkov, Alexei. Russian Federation. 1995. Statement to the 1995 NPT RevCon. NPT/CONF.1995/MC.III/SR.1. New York, April 28.

Twomey, Christopher P. 2009. "Chinese-U.S. Strategic Affairs: Dangerous Dynamism." *Arms Control Today* 39 (1): 17–20.

US DoS (US Department of State). 2005. *Adherence to and Compliance with Arms Control, Nonproliferation, and Disarmament Agreements and Commitments*. Washington: US Department of State, August. www.state.gov/t/avc/rls/rpt/51977.htm.

———. 2010. *Adherence to and Compliance with Arms Control, Nonproliferation, and Disarmament Agreements and Commitments*. Washington: US Department of State, July. www.state.gov/t/avc/rls/rpt/170924.htm.

Vajpayee, Atal Behari. 1998. Suo Moto Statement in the Indian Parliament, New Delhi, May 27.

van Ham, Peter, and Olivia Bosch. 2007. "Global Non-Proliferation and Counter-Terrorism: The Role of Resolution 1540 and Its Implications." In *Global Non-Proliferation and Counter-Terrorism: The Impact of UNSCR 1540*, edited by Olivia Bosch and Peter van Ham, 3–23. The Hague: Clingendael Institute; London: Chatham House; Washington: Brookings Institution Press.

Walker, Paul. 2010. "Abolishing Chemical Weapons: Progress, Challenges, and Opportunities." *Arms Control Today* 40 (9): 22–30.

Wang, Guanya. China. 2006. Statement to the UN Conference to Review Progress Made in the Implementation of the PoA, Geneva, June 26.

Wang, Qun. China. 2009. Statement to the BWC MSP, Geneva, December 7.

———. 2010. Statement, 10th MSP to the MBT, Geneva, November 29.

Weiner, Sharon. 2011. "Retooling Efforts to Stop the Proliferation of WMD Expertise." *Arms Control Today* 41 (10): 14–20.

Wurst, Jim. 1997. "Closing In on a Landmine Ban: The Ottawa Process and U.S. Interests." *Arms Control Today* 27 (4): 14–18.

Yan, Xuetong. 2011. *Ancient Chinese Thought, Modern Chinese Power*. Princeton: Princeton University Press.

Yuan, Jing-dong. 1998. "Culture Matters: Chinese Approaches to Arms Control and Disarmament." *Contemporary Security Policy* 19 (1): 85–128.

———. China. 2007. China's Proliferation and the Impact of Trade Policy on Defense Industries in the United States and China. Testimony before the U.S.-China Economic and Security Commission, July 12, 2007.

———. 2010. *Chinese Perceptions of the Utility of Nuclear Weapons: Prospects and Potential Problems in Disarmament*. Institut Français des Relations Internationales. Proliferation Papers, no. 34 (Spring).

Zhang, Yan. China. 2005. Statement to the 2005 NPT RevCon, New York, May 03.

CHAPTER SEVEN

Good International Citizens

Canada, Germany, and Sweden

Una Becker-Jakob, Gregor Hofmann,

Harald Müller, Carmen Wunderlich

THE PHRASE *GOOD INTERNATIONAL CITIZENSHIP* was coined by former Australian foreign minister Gareth Evans in the late 1980s (Hanson 1999, 1). It denotes states that conduct an ethically motivated foreign policy that blends realist with idealist prescriptions and places internationalism and the "common good" ahead of the pursuit of narrow material interests (e.g., Linklater 2007, 63). In Evans's understanding, such a foreign policy would be inextricably linked with activism and leadership in international affairs (Hanson 1999, 1, 7–9). While formulated as a doctrine for Australian foreign policy, the term was later adopted by academics who applied it to other actors (e.g., Wheeler and Dunne 1998; Dunne 2008) or linked it with discussions of international order in various strands of political and International Relations theory, most prominently the English School, but also realism, democratic peace, and, in one critical view, cosmopolitanism, as well as traditional internationalism (e.g., Linklater 1992, 2007; Hanson 1999; Lawler 2005; Linklater and Suganami 2006; Dunne 2008).

It invites connections with social constructivism. First, the association with actors who consider themselves to be and act as "local agents of a world common good" (Bull 1984, 223; see Lawler 2005, 433) corresponds to constructivist ideas of agency in international relations. Second, the deliberate construction and subsequent conceptualization of a distinct foreign policy profile ties in with role theory (e.g., Harnisch, Frank, and Maull 2011) and research on identity (e.g., Katzenstein 1996), as its discussion in connection with the concept of civilian power shows (Lawler 2005, 432).

Ethically motivated good international citizenship does not exclude the pursuit of national interests, because "[t]here may be occasions when security concerns are uppermost and considerations of order are privileged over the value of justice. [. . .] What is *not* permitted is for narrow conceptions of self-interest to prevail over a particular moral commitment when the latter has acquired a high degree of legitimacy" (Dunne 2008, 16, original emphasis).

Altruistic ethical orientations and self-interest might amalgamate at times, as the pursuit of common goods—for example, a stable international order or international law—might also serve national interests (Hanson 2012, 72). This is certainly true for middle powers and small states to which good international citizenship has been frequently ascribed (Dunne 2008, 15).

While theorists focusing on good international citizenship have reflected critically on the cosmopolitan notion of universal values (Lawler 2005; Linklater 2007), the concept itself has a normative bias first because it implies that the values pursued are beneficial to a broader population, if not universally, and second because the definition of the "common good" is somewhat arbitrary. Indeed, operationalization shows that it is grounded in Western (democratic) political practice and thought, because sources of good international citizenship are said to include a strong liberal or social-democratic tradition (Linklater 2007, 65; Dunne 2008, 15), an internationalist orientation in the classical sense (Lawler 2005), and possibly a deliberate departure from past foreign policy practice or historical baggage (Wheeler and Dunne 1998).

Tim Dunne has derived policy orientations from the English School theorizing that he considers compatible with good international citizens' foreign policy (2008, 23–26); from these, we deduce expectations of arms control and disarmament behavior on the part of good international citizens (table 7.1).

Arms control and disarmament combine rationalist and idealist motives (see introduction). Pertinent efforts are usually carried out through established international structures and are based on existing international (humanitarian) law. This policy field should thus present itself as a natural candidate for good international citizen activism, since war avoidance and prevention of the spread and use of inhumane weapons are probably among the least contested "common goods" (disagreement over appropriate strategies notwithstanding), are tantamount to a moral imperative, and serve the security interests of middle powers (for the latter see Hanson 1999). Considering that according to Evans good international citizenship entails international leadership (Hanson 1999, 7–9), and taking into account the expectations deduced above, we can expect good international citizens to act as prototype norm entrepreneurs in arms control and disarmament (see chapter 1).

Table 7.1. Principles of "solidarist" and "pluralist" interpretations of international society compatible with good international citizenship and expectations for arms control and disarmament behavior by good international citizens deduced from them

Principles Compatible with Good International Citizenship	Expectations Deduced for Arms Control and Disarmament
Sovereignty as "conditional and multi-faceted," taking into account the relevance of actors other than states, while accepting that established principles of sovereignty may remain valid for others	Preference for arms control and disarmament to be conducted multilaterally and inclusively, not unilaterally and/or coercively; willingness to cooperate with actors other than states
Acceptance of "restraints on war" and on the means of warfare	Support for arms control and disarmament; work for effective regimes
Preference for "preserving an equilibrium of power," assumption of "great power responsibility"	Efforts to integrate great powers into existing or emerging regimes
Diplomacy as culturally sensitive "mediation" and "multilateralized" endeavor in which the interests of all those affected are taken into account	Bridge-building roles in negotiations and regimes
"Institutional adaptation" and "reform" to take into account "legitimate interests" of actors while also working to overcome structural inequalities	Work toward more equitable, just regimes

The principles in the left-hand column are taken from Dunne 2008, 23–26.

Being strongly internationalist, with an explicit normative orientation in their foreign policy, and with strong liberal and social-democratic political cultures, Canada and Sweden can be considered good international citizens par excellence (Dunne 2008, 13). While Germany is usually classified as a "civilian power" (e.g., Katzenstein 1997), and although the nature of Germany's good international citizenship might differ slightly from Canada's and Sweden's, it fits into this category, too, given its foreign policy posture of the last decades (Lawler 2005, 443–44). All three have an exceptional record as supporters of cooperative multilateral arms control and disarmament.

CANADA: LEADERSHIP IN RETREAT

Canada has consistently supported international arms control and disarmament since the 1950s and made crucial political and technological contributions to all negotiations that were initiated in the late 1980s (Legault and Fortmann 1992; Fortmann, Hogg, and Jobin 2006, 238–52). Particular efforts were invested in the area of verification: Canada maintained its expertise from the 1950s onward and institutionalized it in the Verification Research Programme (VERPROG), a research unit housed within the Department of Foreign Affairs and International Trade Canada (DFAIT) from 1982 to 1998 and tasked with providing technical expertise and input to negotiations.[1] This was one important factor in Canada's ability to act as norm entrepreneur in so many areas. Another was the post of ambassador for disarmament (1984–94), the holder of which was based in Ottawa, took the lead in the negotiations, and was responsible for domestic outreach, thereby fostering domestic support. Canadian activism was highly visible in the 1980s and 1990s but has receded since 2006 when the Conservative Stephen Harper became prime minister.

Canada defines itself as a middle power. Two strands of thought in foreign policymaking have often converged in similar policy prescriptions but have at times led to tensions and inconsistencies. On one hand, there is a tradition of "liberal internationalism" that dates back to the 1940s and 1950s and is associated with former Liberal foreign minister and prime minister Lester Pearson but was also adopted by Conservative governments (Nossal 1997, 154–59). It emphasizes normative issues in foreign affairs (Waisová 2011), disapproves of the notion of foreign policy as a mere means for advancing material national interests (Munton and Keating 2001, 531), and has been expressed in strong Canadian support for the UN system, human rights, and international law. It has been argued that this support used to be matched by practical and material contributions until the early to mid-1990s but has since receded to a declaratory level (Waisová 2011, 56). These changes notwithstanding, into the 2000s Canadian foreign policy continued to be informed by a self-image of being an honest broker, a benign middle power, and a good international citizen. On the other hand, the commitment to international security institutions has been considered of prime interest to a country such as Canada, which would not be able to guarantee its security independently (Gellman 1988/89) (or, arguably, has not been willing to spend the necessary resources). During the Cold War, these ideas largely converged, resulting in active support for international institutions including arms control and disarmament. In the 1990s, most prominently under Foreign Minister Lloyd Axworthy (1996–2000), human security became a Canadian foreign policy paradigm that informed most areas and policy positions (Michaud 2007, 344), including a focus on humanitarian arms control (e.g., the banning of antipersonnel mines). Nevertheless, Canada continued to play its role as a strong norm promoter and keeper in traditional arms control fields.

One long-standing cause of tension in Canadian foreign policy thinking and policymaking concerns the relationship with the United States (Waisová 2011, 56): it is Canada's most important ally and trading partner, its closest friend, and, in terms of Canadian identity, the country's principal alter ego and counterpart. Thus, foreign policy entails efforts to distinguish Canada from the United States while maintaining close relations. Depending on the political views and preferences of the prime minister, and on how compatible US foreign policy was perceived to be with Canada's, there was at times a continentalist focus on US-Canadian relations at the cost of internationalism (Roussel and Robichaud 2004, 169). Moreover, Canada's NATO membership has sometimes posed a dilemma for Canada by requiring it to either compromise on its foreign policy principles or risk confrontations with its allies (Waisová 2011, 57).

Under Conservative prime minister Harper, Canadian foreign policy has shifted away from the policy of a liberal internationalist and good international citizen toward a more realist and neoconservative inspired policy of national interest and national strength. With some delay due to the persistence of a pro–arms control bureaucratic culture within DFAIT, this has negatively affected Canada's policy in the regimes. While Ottawa has not withdrawn its support in principle, the degree of proactivism and norm entrepreneurship has declined.

Disarmament

The best-known case of Canadian norm entrepreneurship was in the field of antipersonnel mines. Canada was not among the initiators of the norm against these weapons but joined the small group of supporters late in the CCW Review Conference in 1996 (Cadham 2008, 296). Ottawa then took the lead in the international campaign to ban these weapons, and in an unprecedented move the Canadian foreign ministry under Lloyd Axworthy launched a "fast-track" negotiation process for a mine ban convention outside the established negotiation forums that resulted in the Ottawa Convention in 1997 (Lawson et al. 1998). Canada pushed for a strong treaty but was willing to make concessions to gain US support (Cadham 2008, 301), and upon ratification it declared an "additional understanding" related to cooperation with nontreaty members that was criticized as weakening the treaty (ICBL 1999). This slight ambivalence notwithstanding, Canada's positions were informed by a strong normative orientation in favor of the abolition of these inhumane weapons and by moral concerns, as documented in a 1997 UNGA verbatim record: "The humanitarian crisis caused by anti-personnel mines did not end with the meeting in Ottawa, however. . . . [A]nti-personnel mines already in the ground have a devastating humanitarian impact and a profound and lasting social and economic cost. These landmines must be cleared, and those injured by them must be assisted" (UNGA 1997, 4).

On cluster munitions, a field comparable to antipersonnel mines, Canada took a more hesitant position (CMC 2009b). It was not part of the core group that pushed for a comprehensive ban but joined other "like-minded" US allies who worried that a new norm "which, for political reasons, would probably be difficult for them to resist joining, would create legal and operational headaches in terms of interoperability with major allies not party to the treaty," in particular the United States (Borrie 2008, 41). Canada supported strong provisions on victim assistance and international cooperation and promoted the convention after its conclusion (CMC 2010), but it was "among the toughest" negotiators with regard to interoperability (Borrie 2008, 49). This stance was criticized by civil society (CMC 2009b; Waisová 2011, 57) and led to a domestic controversy that blocked Canadian ratification (CMC 2011).

In the area of weapons of mass destruction (WMD), Canada has strongly supported the abolition of chemical and biological weapons and, though less energetically, nuclear weapons since the 1960s. Canadian diplomats made constructive proposals for the negotiations for the Biological Weapons Convention (BWC) and the Chemical Weapons Convention (CWC) (Legault and Fortmann 1992, 292–313; Stock 1995, 26). Having been the first country to voluntarily renounce a nuclear weapon (NW) capability left Canada with an identity as a NNWS and a strong commitment to nuclear disarmament (Becker, Müller, and Wisotzki 2008, 843). In the negotiations for the NPT, Canada mediated between non-aligned states and the NWS, persuading the former to lower their disarmament demands while pushing the latter to make concessions (Epstein 1985, 180, quoted in Findlay 2008, 203). In an effort to prevent the negotiations from collapsing, it helped formulate Art. VI. In the ensuing norm conflict, Canada supported nuclear disarmament as a long-term goal (e.g., McPhail 1980c, 92; McDougall 1999). Its alliance with the United States and its NATO membership have restrained its activity (Roche 2000/2001), but did not render it silent: Canada did not join the New Agenda Coalition (NAC) even though it shared their ideas; it was, however, the first NATO member to vote for the annual NAC UN resolution in 2002 (Becker, Müller, and Wisotzki 2008, 841). Moreover, Ottawa (unsuccessfully) proposed a change in NATO's nuclear doctrine in 1998 against the preferences of its closest allies. Since the 1960s Canada has called for a Comprehensive Nuclear-Test-Ban Treaty (CTBT) and a Fissile Material Cut-off Treaty (FMCT) as crucial steps toward nuclear disarmament (e.g., MacEachen 1975, 56; McPhail 1980c, 92; Westdal 2000). It contributed actively to the conclusion of the CTBT in 1996 (Legault and Fortmann 1992, 340–74; Johnson 2009, 106, 182), and a Canadian diplomat (Shannon 1995) worked out the first FMCT negotiation mandate (which, however, never found consensus in the Conference on Disarmament, or CD).

Nonproliferation, Export Controls, and Cooperation

In the late 1990s, Foreign Minister Axworthy and his staff identified small arms and light weapons (SALW) as the next important humanitarian arms control initiative after the Ottawa Treaty. Canada was one of the initiators of the process that led to the adoption of the UN Programme of Action on Small Arms and Light Weapons (PoA) in 2001 (Parsons and Epps 2008, 1) and maintained a high level of activity in some issue areas. Nonetheless, it lagged behind in others, in particular regarding marking and tracing. Moreover, developments in Canada's domestic gun control policy may compromise some of its previous commitments (Parsons and Epps 2008).

Canada has promoted strong nonproliferation measures in all WMD control areas while at the same time showing empathy for the concerns of developing countries and regularly acknowledging the importance of international cooperation as provided for in the treaties (see, e.g., MacEachen 1975, 55, 58; McPhail 1980c, 92; Jacoby 1990, 5; Moher 1996; Westdal 2001; BWC 2001, 3–5; Hays 2005, 3). It has supported strong measures for biological and chemical export controls and the continued existence of the Australia Group (Littlewood 2005, 155). It has also been involved in all efforts to establish a strong nonproliferation norm since the 1960s and played an important role in the NPT negotiations in which it "sought a balance of rights and responsibilities between nuclear-weapon and non-nuclear-weapon States" (Legault and Fortmann 1992, 260, 262). This remained a theme in Canada's NPT policy, such as when Canada supported demands to put civilian nuclear facilities in NWS under IAEA safeguards in order to "mitigate the discriminatory aspect in the present operation of the safeguard system" (Hamel 1975, 246; see also Mason 1990, 4). However, this "discriminatory aspect" did not prevent Canada from participating fully in the NPT and IAEA safeguards: it was one of the first countries to conclude the required safeguards agreement with the IAEA and continued to support the safeguards system in various ways (Hamel 1975, 245; Mason 1990, 4). India's abuse of Canadian technology for a nuclear test in 1974 led Canada to adopt a stringent nuclear export policy (Findlay 2008, 207). In the intra–Western Group conflict over export controls, Canada was among the nonproliferation supporters and as early as 1980 supported comprehensive safeguards as a condition for nuclear transfers (McPhail 1980b, 293), a condition on which Canada, as the first country, had already based its nuclear deals since 1976 (Findlay 2008, 208). Being a large nuclear exporter, Ottawa has always promoted the peaceful use of nuclear energy, while maintaining its nonproliferation stance (e.g., Jacoby 1990, 3; Wright 2005). Canada was a founding member of the Nuclear Suppliers Group (NSG) and the Vienna-based "Group of Ten" that has promoted strong nonproliferation measures since 1980 (Findlay 2008, 209). However, by re-establishing nuclear trade relations with India (e.g., CBC News 2009), Canada has recently abandoned one previously essential principle—namely, conducting nuclear trade with NPT members only (Legault and Fortmann 1992, 273–74).

Verification, Compliance, and Transparency

Verification, compliance, and transparency have been core areas of Canadian activism: Canada provided extensive technical expertise and crucial impetus in the negotiations, inter alia, for the CTBT (Johnson 2009, 303n17), the BWC Compliance Protocol, and the CWC (Legault and Fortmann 1992, 309–13). In the latter case, Canada made numerous efforts to contribute to the establishment of a strong and effective verification system (e.g., Canada 1982; Canada and Norway 1987), such as through a proposal to group relevant chemicals in three lists according to the risk they pose (Stock 1995, 19–20), the organization of trial inspections (24) and training courses for future inspectors before and after the CWC was concluded (e.g., Wall 2006; Kenyon and Feakes 2007, 108), and strong and constructive input made by the Canadian chemical industry.[2] Canada continued to support an effective inspection system and a "more equitable distribution of inspections" (Wall 2008; see also Hays 2005) in certain chemical facilities, even though the latter meant an increased burden for Western countries, thus placing regime effectiveness before its own immediate interests.

In the BWC, Canada was an early supporter of the Swedish initiative to strengthen the compliance system in 1980–82 (Sims 1988, 173–74), maintaining that existing measures did not allow for equal access for all states and should be complemented by a nondiscriminatory mechanism (McPhail 1980a, 4–5). Once BWC members were on track to strengthen the treaty's compliance measures, Ottawa made numerous contributions to the technical debates about verification in 1992–93 and to the protocol negotiations (e.g., Canada 1992, 1995, 1996, 1997, 2001). A Canadian proposal in 1991 to reframe "verification" (as in checking and possibly discovering other states' [non]compliance) as "compliance" (as in demonstrating one's own compliance) was intended to make the issue more acceptable to the United States; this approach was maintained during the negotiations and after their failure in 2001 (Canada DEAIT 1991, 21; Canada 2006; Canada and Switzerland 2011). Ottawa has also contributed to the introduction of and consistently supported confidence-building measures in the BWC regime (e.g., Canada 1986, 19–20; 1991, 38–42; 2011).

In the Ottawa Process, Canada was willing to accept weak compliance procedures for the sake of the treaty's rapid conclusion, as it considered verification "neither achievable nor necessary" for antipersonnel mines (Moher 1997a, 8).

Regime Strengthening

Not only did Canada play crucial roles in the various treaty negotiations, but it was also committed to supporting, strengthening, or maintaining the respective regimes, including through its own implementation. It was a significant player in shaping the mine ban regime and maintained its high level of financial and technical support for mine action for at least a decade, thus contributing to the regime's effectiveness (e.g., ICBL 2000, 2002, 2004). National implementation and implementation assistance were also important elements of Canada's CWC policy after 1993 (Kenyon and Feakes 2007, 211, 216). In the BWC regime Canada proposed an "Accountability Framework" in 2006 as a point of reference for strengthening it in the absence of a legally binding protocol (Sims 2009, 94–99; Canada 2006), and as a member of the JACKSSNZ group it continued to work toward the same objective.[3] In the NPT, which Canada supported strongly "notwithstanding its discriminatory features" (MacEachen 1975, 55), it made various proposals aimed at strengthening the treaty, including a proposal for annual meetings and the concept of "permanence with accountability" (e.g., Westdal 1995; Moher 1997b; Wright 2005), and helped secure outcomes for at least two

RevCons. At the first RevCon in 1975 it played a crucial role in preparing the first consensual final declaration (Legault and Fortmann 1992, 277), and in 1995 it undertook initiatives (in part together with South Africa) that enabled the indefinite extension of the NPT (Johnson 1995).

From Good Citizen to Realpolitik?

For several decades, Canada was an important player in establishing, maintaining, and strengthening arms control and disarmament regimes. Strategies in Ottawa's policy included working with like-minded countries to enhance the effectiveness of its efforts, contributing technical expertise, working at all available levels (including the treaty regimes, the UN, regional organizations, and through bilateral contacts), and trying to broker middle-ground consensus between hard-line positions. In most of the regimes under scrutiny here, Canada's roles can be described as norm initiator, promoter, and keeper. Canada's state identity as a benign middle power and good international citizen, combined with a value-driven foreign policy culture (Michaud 2007) and supported by a conducive security perception, represented the enabling framework for this commitment: normative concerns inspired activism in all areas; a sense of moral obligation prevailed in humanitarian arms control, whereas justice considerations appeared in the WMD regimes, and the security interests as framed by the benign middle power pointed in the same direction for a long time. Institutional arrangements, such as VERPROG, the post of disarmament ambassador and rotational practice in Ottawa, and the commitment of key personalities added favorable conditions. Occasional inconsistencies originated from Canada's relationship with the United States and its membership in NATO, as both have sometimes inhibited Canada's actions or have led Ottawa to adopt weaker positions than its arms control and disarmament preferences would otherwise have demanded.

Before 2006, changes in government did not alter policy in this field fundamentally, but Prime Minister Stephen Harper's election has led to a gradual but significant shift. In many instances, this has meant a decrease in Canada's level of activity, but not a fundamental departure from previous positions. In the case of cluster munitions, however, Canada gave interoperability and alliance solidarity priority over the goal of establishing the strongest possible prohibition norm. It remains to be seen to what extent Harper's Conservative ideology will be able to replace the previous foreign policy tradition that enjoyed broad support in Canadian public opinion (Munton and Keating 2001), or whether at some point it will be considered an aberration in an otherwise impressive record of norm entrepreneurship.

GERMANY: FROM LAGGARD TO ENTREPRENEUR

West Germany was a reluctant arms control actor until the late 1960s. Until then, the government had given priority to the rehabilitation of the country; this included rearmament and opposition to international recognition of the communist regime in East Berlin. After 1969, West Germany committed to arms control and disarmament, signed and ratified the NPT and the BWC,[4] and led the way in conventional arms control and confidence building in Europe. After unification, Germany engaged in norm entrepreneurship across the full spectrum of arms control and disarmament, with a focus on disarmament, transparency, and export controls. Multilateral arms control is today a mainstay of German security policy for three reasons.

First, war experiences have inculcated doubts in the people about the utility and an aversion to the bloody consequences of military action. This has not changed after the grudging assent to the occasional necessity of humanitarian intervention. The notion of "civilian power" is deeply rooted in German political culture (Maull 1990; Katzenstein 1997). For most Germans, the Cold War's end has marginalized defense policy and armament (Arora 2006).

Second, after 1945 integration into NATO and the EU was chosen as the alternative to a policy of dominating Europe. Consequently, Germany's security and prosperity thrived at an unprecedented level. After the 1969 shift to détente, good neighborliness and multilateralism were extended eastward; Germany became the staunchest supporter of the Conference on Security and Co-operation in Europe (CSCE) process and multilateral arms control to overcome the East-West impasse (Berger 1998; Duffield 1999) and gave up any nuclear or military ambitions during the transition to *Ostpolitik*. Acceptance of inequality, sealed by membership in the NPT, was not easy for conservatives, but within a generation it became part of German identity (Müller 2003).

Third, the German constitution decentralizes power. The role of parliament, federalism, the strong position of the Constitutional Court, and rules governing proportional election set limits to the power of the executive and force all parties to collaborate. This leads to continuity: the most important principles of German arms control policy were in place by 1969. The 1986 Annual

Report on Disarmament stated: "Arms control today is more than ever a key issue for the future development in Europe and the whole world" (German Federal Government 1987, 10), an orientation echoed in the 2010 report: "It is of central political importance to continue the efforts in all areas of arms control, disarmament and non-proliferation" (German Federal Government 2011, 7–8).

Germany provides for its security through NATO and the EU, which implies recognizing the interests of key allies. Allied NWS impose loyalty limits on German disarmament activism. Yet both organizations, albeit to a greater degree the EU, offer platforms for promoting its arms control and disarmament preferences. Armament is unpopular, as reflected in a military budget that is only about 75 percent of the French and British budgets, even though Germany's GNP surpasses that of its European peers by up to 50 percent (Noetzel and Schreer 2008; SIPRI 2011a). Because the domestic market has shrunk, Germany's arms industry has been looking abroad, but unpopular transfers, tarnishing Germany's "civilian power" image, regularly lead to uproar.

Germany is a multilaterally oriented "civilian power" preferring cooperative, peaceful conflict solution and preventive policies. Arms control and disarmament are essential parts of this concept, having both an instrumental (security) and a moral (peace, avoidance of human suffering) value (Berger 1998). NATO and the EU, and bilateral relations with France and the United States, are important but not determining parameters for German policies.

Peaceful Uses of Dual-Use Technologies and Export Controls

From 1968 on, West Germany feared that its nuclear industry—then the cutting edge of technological-industrial development—might be placed at a disadvantage compared with the NWS. Creating a level playing field was seen as part of the "inalienable right" noted in Art. IV of the NPT, which, for Germany, extended to the unimpeded exchange of nuclear technology as long as IAEA safeguards covered exported items (Moersch 1975). As stated in an NPT conference statement, "the long-term success of the non-proliferation policy must depend on the elimination of any discrimination against non-nuclear weapon states" (von Dohnanyi 1980).

These demands were embedded in a philosophy that gave all pillars of the NPT equal weight so that peaceful uses would not be hindered: "The commitments embodied in the Treaty, more particularly non-proliferation, peaceful use of nuclear energy, supplemented by appropriate safeguards, and the pledge to disarm, formed a cohesive whole which, in the interests of all signatories, should not be altered" (Möllemann 1985).

In the first RevCon, Germany based this claim on egalitarian solidarity with the developing countries: "Participation by all nations on equal terms in technological development and in the opportunity to use nuclear energy" (Möllemann 1985). Consequently, Germany opposed nuclear export restrictions, defended its 1974 plans to supply a full fuel cycle to Brazil, and proved a reticent member of the NSG until the late 1980s. Today, Germany still points out the right to enjoy the peaceful uses of nuclear energy, but with decreasing fervor (Fischer 2005). Germany's stance on exports changed for several reasons. Export scandals led to a revamping of German export control policy. When national unification was achieved, the need to act as a responsible international "force for the good" grew strong, given the concern of neighbors about a more powerful Germany. Finally, Germans lost their enthusiasm for nuclear technology, viewing it increasingly as a liability. At the 1990 NPT RevCon, Germany declared its intention of applying a condition of full-scope safeguards to all nuclear exports and to extend export controls to dual-use goods and technology (Genscher 1990). The Iranian case persuaded Germany to make Art. IV rights conditional upon proven compliance with all NPT obligations (Fischer 2005). Berlin also made an innovative proposal to establish a multilateral enrichment facility under IAEA supervision to dissuade states from national fuel cycle activities (Meier 2006; Hoyer 2010).

In the BWC, Germany proposed that all member states, not only those owning relevant biological agents, install export controls that could be modeled on the export licensing system of the Australia Group (German Federal Government 2011, 45–46). Emphasis on the importance of export controls also guides German promotion of an instrument on marking and tracing to curb the illegal trade in SALW, which Germany pursued as a new initiative together with like-minded states (Pleuger 2003). In addition, Germany tried to integrate the norms of the EU Code of Conduct on Arms Exports (Council of the EU 1998) into the UN PoA but failed due to US resistance. It tried the same in the OSCE, only to be rebuffed anew by the United States. The German objectives are defined as follows: "We consider strict export criteria and transparency in arms transfers as legitimate and essential standards that can and should be met by all exporters of weapons on whatever continent. We share the call for 'No more arms for atrocities'" (Pleuger 2003).

Disarmament

Though covered by the US nuclear umbrella, Germany claimed the right to call for disarmament as the only state that had already legally renounced all WMD in the 1954 Protocol to the Brussels Treaty (Möllemann 1985), thus reminding the NWS repeatedly of their Art. VI undertakings (Moersch 1975; Wegener 1984b, 1985; Kinkel 1995; Hoyer 2010). Until the end of the Cold War, the objective was a balance of forces at minimum level; complete nuclear disarmament was beyond the horizon (von Dohnanyi 1980; Wegener 1985; Möllemann 1985).

The "German record argument" reappeared at the 1986 BWC RevCon (von Stülpnagel 1986) and in the CWC negotiations that were concluded under German chairmanship in 1992 (Stock 1995; Ruth 1982; Wegener 1983, 1984c; Genscher 1988). At the latter, a claim for all states to escape the CW threat (Wegener 1984a) was combined with rejection of the inhumane nature of these weapons (von Stülpnagel 1988a).[5] The special responsibility of major CW holders was emphasized (similar to arguments in the NPT; Moersch 1975; Genscher 1988; von Stülpnagel 1988a). After the CWC entered into force, Germany invested approximately €350 million in assistance to Russian efforts to dismantle chemical weapons (CW) (German Federal Foreign Office 2011). This contrasts with the refusal to help disarm Russian weapons plutonium. There were proposals in the 1990s to fabricate MOX (mixed oxide) reactor fuel from Russian plutonium using an idle fuel fabrication facility in Hanau, Germany, or to transfer this factory to Russia. The first option foundered on opposition from both the Greens and the Social Democrats (Schaper 1996); the second failed in 2001 because the German federal government did not grant an export credit to ensure the deal.

In the Ottawa Process, Germany was an early member of the core group and worked closely with the NGOs pushing for the convention (Long and Hindle 1998, 253). During the negotiations on banning cluster munitions, by contrast, it favored a weak norm in defense of air force positions (CMC 2009a, 78–82). Germany preferred an additional CCW Protocol to a new treaty and supported an initiative "to address the humanitarian concerns posed by cluster munitions" (Austria et al. 2006). It advocated a compromise between humanitarian concerns and military necessities with a three-step approach (Germany 2007), proposed the exclusion of cluster munitions meeting certain technical criteria from the prohibition, demanded a long transition period, and, like Canada, successfully lobbied for provisions in Article 21 that allow military cooperation with states not party to the convention—a major concern for NATO (CMC 2009a, 81).

Germany emphasized nuclear disarmament more strongly after 1990, including a plea for binding negative security guarantees for NNWS (Genscher 1990). Foreign Minister Klaus Kinkel's 1993 "Non-Proliferation Initiative" contained, inter alia, the indefinite extension of the NPT, a CTBT (a long-standing German goal; von Dohnanyi 1980; Wegener 1984b, 1985), and an FMCT plus an international plutonium regime (German Federal Foreign Office 1993, point 8). In 1995, Kinkel emphasized disarmament at the NPT Review and Extension Conference: "In recent years, the nuclear disarmament obligation in Art. VI had been fulfilled to an extent no one could have imagined. That process must be vigorously continued; the five nuclear Powers must fulfil that obligation since it had been the very reason for the accession to the Treaty of the great majority of the community of nations" (Kinkel 1995).

During the following RevCons, Germany increasingly focused on substrategic nuclear weapons, some of which are still deployed in Germany under US control. In the run-up to the 2000 NPT RevCon, Germany helped persuade its European partners to insert the demand for the reduction and eventual elimination of those weapons in the EU Common Position; this language made it into the RevCon's final document. Germany now also connected nuclear disarmament with nonproliferation compliance.

In 2009, the Liberals succeeded in inserting removal of substrategic weapons and termination of the nuclear role of the German Air Force into the new Liberal/Conservative government's program for its four-year term (CDU/CSU/FDP 2009). The new policy was sealed by a parliamentary resolution of March 26, 2010, supported by all parties except the former communists (German Bundestag 2010). The goal of "global zero" was integrated into the Foreign Ministry's diplomacy, again with a focus on substrategic weapons (German Federal Government 2010, 4; see also Hoyer 2010).

NATO solidarity prevented unilateral moves on this issue (Weiland 2010), but Germany succeeded in inserting it in the EU Common Position for the 2010 NPT RevCon. The German delegation led a group of ten European countries that pressed for the inclusion of language on substrategic nuclear weapons in the final declaration, against strong Russian opposition and without support from NATO's NWS. The final document indeed called for the inclusion of "all nuclear weapons regardless of their type or their location" (NPT 2010, 21) in the disarmament process.

Transparency and Verification

Across the regimes Germany has promoted transparency and verification to make the regimes effective; it regards strengthening of mutual confidence and possibilities for detecting norm breaches as essential and transparency and verification as the best instruments.

Creating equal burdens for the industries of all parties played a central role in the NPT. When Germany signed the treaty, it demanded that all civilian nuclear industries should be subjected to inspections to mitigate the asymmetry of parties' rights and duties (German Federal Government 1969; see also Moersch 1975). That the NPT prescribed no verification in NWS was seen as an unfair disadvantage for those who had acquiesced to military nuclear inequality. In the 1990s, German attitudes began to change: now it argued for *strengthening* NPT verification (Kinkel 1995) but still insisted that some of this should apply to NWS. In the late 1980s this position superseded defensive attempts to protect the German nuclear industry from "too much" intrusion. Germany worked as the constructive partner of the United States on reform of the IAEA verification system in the early 1990s; the Additional Protocol is thus very much the product of these two allies and the IAEA (Hartmann 1999; Ischinger 2000). After 1995, Germany promoted universalization of the Additional Protocol and requested strict enforcement, eventually through the UN Security Council (Fischer 2005). This orientation was mirrored in German proposals for a procedure to respond to withdrawal from the NPT that were introduced in the preparatory process for the 2005 RevCon (Germany 2004) and later became common EU policy (European Union 2007). In a similar way, Germany wanted a future CTBT to be effectively verifiable (Wegener 1984b; Ischinger 2000). The boldest transparency proposal was contained in Foreign Minister Kinkel's 1993 initiative that called for a "nuclear arms register" as a disarmament-supporting measure; predictably, the minister was reprimanded by the three Western NWS (Müller and Frank 1997).

Germany engaged intensively in developing CWC verification (Stock 1995). Experiences from the nuclear regime shaped its approach to avoiding undue burdens for industry. Consequently, the government involved the German chemical industry, inter alia, by including its representatives as delegation members. Companies and their associations cooperated constructively (von Stülpnagel 1988a, 1988b). Later, it called for the timely adaptation of the system to technological changes. In addition to the insistence on nondiscrimination, the strength of a norm bolstered by efficient verification was prominent in Germany's arguments (e.g., Genscher 1982; Ruth 1982; Elbe 1983; Wegener 1984a; von Stülpnagel 1987, 1988c). In particular, Germany proposed using challenge inspections not just in noncompliance crises but in a regular way, in order to build confidence (Steinmeier 2007).

Nondiscrimination and effectiveness also characterized the German approach to the BWC regime (Wegener 1982; Elbe 1983; Hartmann 1999; Brasack 2005; Gröning 2006; Germany 2006; Hoffmann 2009). Germany was one of the leading EU nations in the negotiations for the compliance protocol, although here again it kept industry interests in mind (Littlewood 2005) and, after the protocol's failure, played a crucial role in the establishment of the first intersessional process (Brasack 2005). In cooperation with Norway, Switzerland, and the Geneva Forum, Germany undertook an initiative in 2010–11 to review and revise the confidence-building measures to make them more effective transparency tools.

In the Ottawa Process, Germany set up a meeting on verification in 1997 to introduce some measures in the treaty's implementation process (Long and Hindle 1998, 250). Even in the negotiations on the SALW PoA, transparency and confidence were key elements of the German position (Pleuger 2003), and Germany later took the initiative in attempting to integrate SALW into the UN Conventional Arms Register.

Between "Civilian Power" and "Trading State"?

With the beginning of détente policy in the late 1960s, Germany emerged as a norm entrepreneur with mixed motives: to the extent that it aimed at stabilization of East-West military relations, cooperative policy was used to pursue *security*. The promotion of strict export controls starting in the late 1980s also served to enhance security by foregoing a race to the bottom among exporters. At the same time, the German government wanted to *avoid competitive disadvantages* after Germany had strengthened national export controls. The goal of regime effectiveness and the normative principle of *equality among sovereign states* dominated German norm entrepreneurship across the regimes. Germany pressed for disarmament obligations among actors possessing weapons destined for elimination, at times risking quarrels with allies, while not pushing too far in the nuclear and chemical weapons fields. Transparency was considered a means for promoting equality as it placed obligations on weapons possessors and at the same time served the *effectiveness* of the regimes. The extension of the Additional Protocol to the NWS was another example of Germany's equality orientation: the justice motive amalgamated with status considerations and concerns about competitive disadvantages.

Commitment to the SALW PoA and promotion of the Mine Ban Treaty (MBT) demonstrated the goal of reducing human suffering, even though these measures might constrain Germany's related exports. Moral orientation influenced Germany's activities both here and regarding CW. In the last few years, however, this commitment might have weakened, considering that Germany is the third largest exporter of small arms today (Small Arms Survey 2011, 11).

Occasionally, Germany undertook demonstrative national action such as the 1990 declaration on full-scope safeguards. More frequently, however, Germany worked through the EU (e.g., on substrategic nuclear weapons) or with like-minded countries (Ottawa Convention, BWC). Much effort is devoted to persuading reluctant allies and to mediating between hard-line positions, while Germany tries to avoid tougher instruments such as pressure or shaming and blaming.

SWEDEN: CHAMPION OF DISARMAMENT IN DECLINE

Ever since Olof Palme coined the phrase *active internationalism* in the 1970s, Sweden has gained a reputation as a "force for good in the world" (Dahl 2002, 140) pursuing a foreign policy based on multilateralism, cooperative security, international solidarity and equality, the protection and promotion of international law, and good international citizenship.

Sweden's political culture reflects Social Democratic standards and Protestant roots, leading Swedish diplomats to strive for social justice and solidarity with the underprivileged (Bergman 2007, 84). Non-alignment has shaped the country's identity and allowed Sweden to act as a mediator between the two superpowers, to enhance its international reputation, and to win trust (Bjereld, Johansson, and Molin 2008). Non-alignment and active internationalism also served Sweden's interest in gaining international influence and contributing to cooperative security. Sweden's role as a (self-appointed) "moral superpower" (Nilsson 1991) or "global conscience" (Bjereld, Johansson, and Molin 2008) is manifested in its arms control and disarmament policy.[6]

Swedish commitment to multilateral arms control dates back to the 1960s: in light of the superpower arms race, Sweden temporarily pursued both a "nuclear option policy" and active engagement in arms control negotiations (Prawitz 1995, 12). During the NPT negotiations, Sweden played a crucial role (van Dassen 1998, 21). Consequently, its plans to acquire a nuclear capability were abandoned on ratification of the NPT in 1970 (Jonter 2001; Rublee 2009, 169–84), although Art. VI fell short of Stockholm's expectations (Myrdal 1977, 171–77); now a nuclear weapons program was deemed detrimental to national security (e.g., Bodstrom 1985; Eliasson 1995). Since then, "it became a national interest for Sweden [. . .] to contribute to the success of the treaty and the regime it defines" (Prawitz 1995, 27), and Sweden turned into "a nonproliferation and disarmament powerhouse" (Bergenäs 2010), advocating the elimination of all WMD, and humanitarian arms control. Swedish norm entrepreneurship centers around two issues: disarmament and effective verification. However, Swedish proactivism is clouded by the country's record as one of the world's largest arms exporters: part of the moral high ground has been paved with hard-nosed security and economic interests. Disarmament activism flourished between 1962 and 1994, when a well-staffed "disarmament delegation" chaired by a high-ranking political appointee supervised negotiation efforts and advised the government.[7] The downgrading of the post coincided with devaluation of the subject matter under Prime Minister Carl Bildt in the early 1990s.[8] Although Sweden excelled with some initiatives thereafter, the importance attributed to disarmament has been diminishing.

With the beginning of the twenty-first century, Sweden's foreign policy has undergone a transformation consistent with changed external conditions—the country has moved away from traditional approaches to peace and international security (Bjereld, Johansson, and Molin 2008). The new security doctrine has replaced non-alignment with the option of participating in EU military operations. Creating and maintaining a "European identity" (Agius 2006, 143) has become a priority that is reflected in the country's arms control profile. While predictions of declining activism due to Sweden's EU accession turned out to be premature, since the center-right government took office in 2006 nuclear arms control and disarmament have become lower priorities than under Social Democrat leadership. Whereas in the past Sweden acted as an advocate for the non-aligned states, joining in their call for the elimination of nuclear weapons and a balanced interpretation of NPT norms, nowadays Sweden focuses on preventing WMD proliferation jointly with its EU partners, and current government policies are criticized as overly passive (e.g., Sweden's silence on the United States–India nuclear deal or reduced governmental funding for the Blix Commission (Bergenäs 2010).[9] Disarmament idealism has given way to pragmatism.

Disarmament

Sweden's commitment to disarmament is related to its status as a non-aligned country and has been motivated by security *and* moral considerations. Non-alignment and international activism provided a security strategy (Bjereld, Johansson, and Molin 2008, 344) for maintaining Sweden's sovereignty and independence and for furthering international peace understood as common security (van Dassen 1998, 26). The combination of a security policy oriented toward neutrality and a progressive, internationalist foreign policy characterized postwar Swedish policy, labeled by Kent Zetterberg "real-politik in the immediate vicinity, idealism globally" (quoted in Hallenberg 2000, 20).

For over thirty years, Sweden has promoted nuclear disarmament. Sweden focused on issues where it could bring to bear its status as a neutral state and its nuclear weapons expertise. The technical knowledge obtained through its NW research provided Sweden with leverage for developing high-profile disarmament activities within the UN.

The NPT has been the cornerstone of Swedish disarmament policy; much effort has been expended on its universalization (e.g., Sweden, Denmark, et al. 1985, 1990). Sweden attaches particular importance to the full implementation of Art. VI (disarmament), thus joining forces with the NAM: "Sweden has repeatedly stressed that the concept of the systematic and progressive efforts by the nuclear-weapon States must be given a concrete content. The steps must be identified and fully translated into concrete action. It is indeed important that these commitments be fully observed in nuclear doctrines and translated into deeds, if confidence in the NPT process is to be maintained" (Sweden 1998).

Due to its neutral status and its technical expertise, Sweden took over the role of "spokesperson" within the NPT group of non-aligned states and of "honest broker" (Garris 1973, 201) between them and the NWS, insisting on the original "bargain" of the NPT.[10] Sweden also supported the NAM complaint that the NWS have not fulfilled their commitments and that this is a direct cause of proliferation: "The NPT is based on balanced commitments. The majority of states have agreed to forego the nuclear option in return for negotiations in good faith, chiefly among the five nuclear-weapon states, towards nuclear disarmament. Our common goal is a nuclear-weapon-free world. This is the foundation of the global non-proliferation regime. The absence of negotiations on disarmament would risk eroding the NPT regime" (Lindh 2000).

Until today Sweden has insisted on the balanced character of the NPT and the importance of implementing Art. VI. This motivated its membership in the New Agenda Coalition (NAC), an initiative established in 1998. After the NPT was extended indefinitely in 1995, the NAC persuaded the NWS at the 2000 RevCon to agree to an action plan for gradual nuclear disarmament. Sweden is one of the few EU states persistently calling for the disarmament of tactical nuclear weapons on European soil (van Dassen and Wetter 2006, 257; e.g., Lindh 2000; Freivalds 2005).

According to the Swedish view, complete nuclear disarmament is to be approached through multilateral efforts to strengthen the nonproliferation regime with a verifiable CTBT, FMCT, and other measures intended to increase transparency and efficiency like negative security assurances or nuclear-weapon-free zones. As early as 1960, Sweden proposed initiatives such as establishing a "non-atom club" (Undén Proposal; e.g., Brodin 1965), a nuclear-weapon-free corridor in Central Europe, or efforts within the Six-Nation Initiative (also Five-Continent Peace Initiative) toward a nuclear freeze on testing, production, and deployment of nuclear weapons (e.g., NPT 1985). Even before signing the NPT Sweden called for a CTBT, presenting various draft texts at the CD (Mallin 1994). In 1994, a Swedish draft opened the treaty negotiations.

Sweden also called for banning biological and chemical weapons early on, played an active role in the negotiations, drawing on its national technical expertise, and contributed to the conclusion of the BWC and CWC. The Swedish Defense Research Establishment (FOA; now the Swedish Defence Research Agency, FOI) and the Stockholm International Peace Research Institute (SIPRI) supported Swedish diplomatic efforts to achieve a complete CW ban and a verification regime for the BWC.

In 2003, the Swedish government established the Weapons of Mass Destruction Commission chaired by Hans Blix to provide new impetus for global disarmament and nonproliferation. In the same year, Foreign Minister Anna Lindh initiated the EU WMD Strategy and reiterated demands for the EU to play a proactive role in nuclear disarmament.

Strengthening Verification for Enhanced Regime Efficiency

Sweden advocates verification across all arms control fields. During the 1970s, Alva Myrdal, then cabinet minister for disarmament, tirelessly promoted the creation of "an international verification agency [that] should encompass all aspects of disarmament control and monitoring, in whatever field an agreement was envisaged, [to] be set up immediately to accelerate work on disarmament agreements" (Myrdal 1977, 306). However, Sweden had no success with this proposal and finally fell back on the idea of a standing consultative mechanism treaty by treaty (Sims 2009, 132).

Much of Sweden's efforts drew on FOA's expertise offering support for risk assessment, detection, sampling, analysis, medical countermeasures, and decontamination on issues relating to nuclear, biological, and chemical weapons (Roffey 2002). Technological knowledge helped Sweden take an active part in the CWC negotiations, where it advocated a strong verification mechanism (e.g., for early efforts, Sweden 1972; Hjelm-Wallén 1997). Later, Sweden provided the OPCW with a Chemical Support Team that can be requested by CWC parties in case of CW use or chemical releases (Roffey 2002).

From the outset, Sweden advocated a comprehensive ban on biological weapons but criticized the lack of verification arrangements in the treaty as weak, and for this reason it delayed signing the BWC until 1975 (Roffey 2002). Unhappy about the procedures for dealing with supposed noncompliance via the UN Security Council, in 1982 the country tabled a proposal to amend the BWC (UNGA 1982; Sims 1988, 168–98), in order to establish "a more flexible, more objective, less discriminatory pattern of verification" (Myrdal 1977, 275) to deal with compliance issues (see also BWC 1980; Lidgard 1980). Its "historical discontent with the BWC's provisions" (Littlewood 2005, 55) was also emphasized by the promotion of politically binding confidence-building measures. Thus, Sweden took the role as one of the "committed *reformists* who not only acted as the conscience of the Convention but also provided the impetus for further development" (Littlewood 2005, 190, original emphasis).

Sweden also took the lead in developing an international system for seismic detection of nuclear testing ("detection club") as part of a campaign for a CTBT (Sweden 1965). The country initiated the establishment in 1976 of an Ad Hoc Group of Scientific Experts to work out plans for a seismic verification system (Sweden 1976) and has called for far-reaching verification arrangements ever since (Ramaker et al. 2003, 11–12).

Sweden's extra-budgetary financial, technical, and personnel contributions to the IAEA aimed at increased efficiency and transparency of the agency's safeguards (van Dassen and Wetter 2006, 256–57). Sweden suggested extending the safeguard system to peaceful nuclear activities of the NWS to allow for full transparency and to improve the possibilities for detecting noncompliance with the NPT (Hyltenius 1989, 20; see also Ugglas 1993): "Placing the nuclear industries of the nuclear-weapon and non-nuclear weapon States on an equal footing, would certainly help to promote international co-operation in the peaceful uses of nuclear energy" (Bodstrom 1985, 30).

Since the 1980s, Sweden has been a member of the "Vienna Group of Ten" (G11 since 1991)—like-minded Western countries calling for strengthening nuclear nonproliferation measures, the safeguard system, and export controls and advocating the multilateral control of the fuel cycle (Sweden, Australia, et al. 1995, 2000). Throughout NPT RevCons, Sweden encouraged all states to accede to the Comprehensive Safeguard Agreement and—after 1997—the Additional Protocol.

Swedish Arms Exports Policies: Ethically Compromising?

Compared to its exemplary commitment to WMD disarmament, Sweden has a mixed record in humanitarian arms control as moral considerations come into conflict with national interests. To underwrite "armed neutrality," Sweden built a huge arms industry with increasing arms exports—nowadays, the country is one of the world's largest arms exporters (SIPRI 2011b). Once meant to guarantee national defense and sovereignty (but also to gain prestige and competitiveness), arms exports today aim at ensuring "the participation of Sweden in strategically important cooperations" (Manga 2010, 3) in order to grant interoperational efficiency (Sweden 2011). Since the mid-1990s, Swedish arms exports have been increasing. Although Sweden applies strict trade restrictions and outstanding transparency in arms exports,[11] revelations like the 1986 bribe scandal between India and the Swedish company Bofors AB or Swedish antitank weapons ending up in the hands of Colombian FARC (Revolutionary Armed Forces of Columbia) guerillas compromise the record of Sweden's good international citizenship.

On a rhetorical level, however, Sweden attaches much importance to controlling the trade in and use of SALW (Marsh 2006, 237). In the light of the humanitarian suffering caused by cluster bombs in the 1970s in the Indochina wars, Sweden advocated the improvement of humanitarian law focusing on "incendiaries, anti-personnel cluster weapons and a series of other munitions" (Prokosch 1994, 183). When the CCW entered into force in 1980, it failed to live up to Swedish expectations. However, the Oslo Process leading to the prohibition of cluster ammunition illustrates the dilemma of being a "moral conscience" and having to rely on a huge arms industry simultaneously. While Sweden was actively engaged in the Oslo Process (Borrie 2009, 83), it tried to exempt the Swedish Bombkapsel 90 (BK 90) cluster munition from the ban, claiming it was "a type of cluster weapon with high reliability levels and does not leave behind unexploded submunitions that risk harming innocent civilians" (Mikael Oldenberg, cited in CMC 2009c). While Sweden signed the CCM in 2008 and dropped its demand for exemption of the BK 90, military and economic considerations still delayed ratification.

Sweden was one of the first countries to demand a global ban on mines in 1994 and presented—unsuccessfully—the first draft of a complete ban on antipersonnel mines at the CCW's 1994 review conference. The Swedish government finally decided to implement a unilateral moratorium and completed the destruction of national stockpiles in 2002. Surprisingly, Sweden was involved in the Ottawa Process only to a limited degree and was not part of the core group that initiated the negotiations for the MBT (Human Rights Watch 1999, 655–57).

Activism Torn between Idealism and Interests

Sweden has shown a long-standing commitment to disarmament and nonproliferation, and its diplomats and politicians have made noteworthy contributions to achieving these goals. Among the factors contributing to Swedish norm entrepreneurship, national technical and scientific expertise has created a soft power capability exceeding the country's material resources. Knowledge provided the basis for Swedish proposals in various treaty negotiations (e.g., the CTBT, NPT, and BWC) and earned authority and respect for Sweden among its partners (e.g., G10/11, NAC, NAM). It also afforded Sweden the opportunity to act as a trusted interlocutor with the developing states, to which it provided technical and knowledge assistance. While the Swedish government (up to the 1990s) provided a well-staffed disarmament infrastructure, activism was attributable to the commitment of people such as Olof Palme, Alva Myrdal, Inga Thorsson, Hans Blix, and Rolf Ekéus.

However, recently Swedish norm entrepreneurship seems to have been in a (temporary?) state of decline. Since the center-right government took office in 2006, advocacy of nuclear disarmament has paled in comparison with nonproliferation efforts. Humanitarian arms control, in addition, has to be reconciled with interests tied to arms exports. Hence, Swedish norm entrepreneurship was essential in contributing to the development of the regimes on biological, chemical, and nuclear weapons, while Sweden's commitment to humanitarian arms control does not go beyond mere support.

Sweden's norm entrepreneurship has left a deep impression on its national identity, interwoven with a Social Democratic legacy and reflecting Swedish core values: solidarity, equality, the protection and promotion of international law, consensus, and democracy. Positions in various arms control forums feature both a pragmatic, security-based, and principled approach. Sweden's commitment to peaceful conflict solution and the protection of small countries based on international law equally motivate its active commitment to WMD disarmament and nonproliferation, as do normative considerations related to the inhumane consequences of such weapons. Most arguments include a normative undertone, even where hard security interests usually prevail. The persistent call for nuclear disarmament, the request to subject the NWS to IAEA verification, and the proposal to develop an unbiased BWC compliance procedure show a distinct justice orientation, while emphasis on verification aims at the common good of regime efficiency. A "missionary instinct"[12] together with a commitment to "notions of justice"[13] and the legacy of neutral status led Sweden to strive for the elimination of weapons that are seen as cruel and an obstacle to human development.

CONCLUSION: "GOOD INTERNATIONAL CITIZENS" WITH MINOR FLAWS

Conforming to expectations, all three countries—Canada, Germany, and Sweden—showed norm entrepreneurial behavior in most arms control and disarmament fields. They focused on similar themes: verification, transparency, export controls as a nonproliferation tool, balancing disarmament and nonproliferation obligations, and humanitarian arms control. While Canada and Sweden based many of their contributions on significant technical expertise, in particular in verification, Germany used its considerable political capital to promote its goals. All three employed similar strategies such as working with like-minded countries (Ottawa core group, G10 or NAC), providing technical input (e.g., for the CTBT, CWC or BWC protocol negotiations), offering support to the various regimes (as in providing training, making financial contributions, offering assistance to others), and "leading by example" through comprehensive national implementation of and compliance with all obligations.

Moreover, all three have, in different areas, initiated singular actions aimed at establishing new norms (antipersonnel mines, SALW) or strengthening existing ones (BWC, nuclear disarmament).

None of the three countries confined their activism (or "leadership," as Gareth Evans calls it; Hanson 1999, 7) to single areas, but all displayed some form of norm entrepreneurship in most fields, cluster munitions being the conspicuous exception. Canada and Sweden maintained their activism over decades but have shown a decline in recent years. In both countries, this coincides with phases in which good international citizenship has taken a back seat as a foreign policy principle in favor of other overarching principles. Germany displayed the reverse trend: while its commitment was average until 1990, it has shown an upward trend in terms of engagement ever since. In Germany's case, good international citizenship stemmed from historical circumstances that have become all the more salient.

Norm entrepreneurial activities of all three countries can be classified as norm initiation (APM, nuclear nonproliferation), norm promotion, and norm keeping (in all negotiations and existing regimes except cluster munitions). With one exception, all three have refrained from a norm-enforcing role (Germany has been one of the chief negotiators to end Iran's ambiguous nuclear program; however, it pursued a more "civilian-minded" course than its Western partners). Moreover, all three refrain from confrontational strategies such as shaming and blaming, which are typical strategies of classical norm entrepreneurs (see chapter 1). Arguably, such strategies would not be compatible with elements of good international citizenship: the self-image as bridge builder that Canada and Sweden in particular have cultivated for decades; and the foreign policy culture of (political and military) restraint Germany has chosen. The activities were mostly aimed at strengthening or maintaining norms within established normative orders, the only exception being antipersonnel mines; here the driver for the pursuit of an alternative agenda, namely a complete ban negotiated outside established forums and procedures, was moral concern about the devastating humanitarian catastrophe caused by these weapons.

Normative issues and a concern with regime effectiveness appear as major drivers of all three countries' active commitment. This includes the moral imperative to rid the world of inhumane weapons, to prevent their use and spread (and to achieve both objectives through multilateral institutions and in keeping with international law), and to help those most affected by such weapons. Moral reasoning was most visible in humanitarian arms control. Justice concerns surfaced most in the earlier phases of the NPT and BWC regimes (and to some extent in the CWC) and centered on fair distribution of rights and obligations, equal burden sharing, and equal opportunities for addressing compliance concerns. The unequal distribution of duties under the original IAEA safeguards system provoked different reactions. While Germany initially tried to minimize verification burdens for its own industry, Canada, induced inter alia by the 1974 Indian experience, promoted strict safeguard measures from the beginning while trying to broaden their application. Germany pursued the same objectives after 1990. With regard to technological exchange and development, another norm conflict common to all WMD regimes, our sample countries do not employ much justice-related rhetoric even though they are sympathetic to the concerns of developing countries and sensitive to the relevance of justice-based conflict to the viability of the respective regimes.

All three countries have at times subordinated parochial industry interests to the "common good" of effective arms control and disarmament (e.g., Canada in the case of nuclear exports, Germany and Sweden in the case of anti-personnel mines) or have tried to reconcile both (as in the case of the CWC). Sometimes, however, national interests have prevented more active engagement, as in the case of Germany's export control policy prior to 1991, Canada's nuclear disarmament policy, and Sweden's role in conventional arms control and disarmament, when they clashed with idealist orientations though still not prevailing over them.

For the two alliance members, Canada and Germany, competing role images impacted on policy when good international citizenship was at odds with expectations directed at "good allies" (Becker, Müller, and Wisotzki 2008, 849)—for instance, in the case of nuclear disarmament (for Canada) or cluster munitions (for both). Genuine security concerns could rarely be identified as challenges to norm entrepreneurship. Rather, more often than not, their status as (self-defined) middle powers and the associated interest in a stable international security environment served as an additional driver *for* norm entrepreneurship.

Notes

1. See DFAIT (2012); interviews with current and former government officials.

2. Interviews with government officials and industry representatives by Una Becker-Jakob.

3. The JACKSNNZ group consists of Japan, Australia, Canada, South Korea, Switzerland, Norway, and New Zealand.

4. The late (1983) ratification was due to an Allied-German controversy over the treaty's applicability to West Berlin that took several years to be resolved (German Bundestag 1982, 13, 16–20).

5. "To speak for those who have suffered from chemical weapons use, it is no exaggeration to say that the Conference on Disarmament has to meet its responsibility to mankind" (von Stülpnagel 1990).

6. All English translations are by Carmen Wunderlich.

7. Email exchange with Jan Prawitz, researcher at the Swedish Institute of International Affairs, October 24, 2007.

8. Disarmament ambassador Alva Myrdal held the rank of cabinet minister in 1966, Inga Thorsson (1972–82) served as under-secretary of state for disarmament affairs, while Maj-Britt Theorin (1983–91) was only appointed ambassador for disarmament affairs. After 1994, the delegation ceased to meet.

9. Interviews with Swedish politicians and experts, September 2010; email exchange with Laila Naraghi, Olof Palme International Center, August 10, 2010.

10. The group of non-aligned states (G-21) within the CD is not to be confused with the NAM, though membership overlaps. With its accession to the EU in 1995, Sweden left the G-21.

11. Sweden set a precedent in 1985 by providing public information on its arms exports and helped to diffuse the norm of transparency within the SALW field (e.g., Garcia 2006, 153).

12. Email exchange with Alyson Bailes, former director of the Stockholm International Peace Research Institute (SIPRI), October 2, 2007.

13. Email exchange with Lars van Dassen, November 6, 2007.

References

Agius, Christine. 2006. *The Social Construction of Swedish Neutrality: Challenges to Swedish Identity and Sovereignty*. Manchester: Manchester University Press.

Arora, Chaya. 2006. *Germany's Civilian Power Diplomacy: NATO Expansion and the Art of Communicative Action*. Basingstoke: Palgrave Macmillan.

Austria, Holy See, Ireland, Mexico, New Zealand, and Sweden. 2006. "Proposal for a Mandate to Negotiate a Legally-Binding Instrument That Addresses the Humanitarian Concerns Posed by Cluster Munitions." Working paper. CCW/CONF.III/WP.1. Geneva, October 25.

Bailes, Alyson J. K., Gunilla Herolf, and Bengt Sundelius, eds. 2006. *The Nordic Countries and the European Security and Defence Policy*. Oxford: Oxford University Press.

Becker, Una, Harald Müller, and Simone Wisotzki. 2008. "Democracy and Nuclear Arms Control—Destiny or Ambiguity?" *Security Studies* 17 (4): 810–54.

Bergenäs, Johan. 2010. "The Rise of a White Knight State: Sweden's Nonproliferation and Disarmament History." NTI Articles, February 10. www.nti.org/analysis/articles/swedens-nonproliferation-history.

Berger, Thomas. U. 1998. *Cultures of Antimilitarism: National Security in Germany and Japan*. Baltimore: Johns Hopkins University Press.

Bergman, Annika. 2007. "Co-constitution of Domestic and International Welfare Obligations: The Case of Sweden's Social Democratically Inspired Internationalism." *Cooperation and Conflict* 41 (1): 73–99.

Bjereld, Ulf, Alf W. Johansson, and Karl Molin. 2008. *Från igelkott till världssamvete? En bok om Sverige under kalla kriget*. Stockholm: Santérus Förlag.

Bodstrom. 1985. Statement to the 3rd NPT RevCon. NPT/CONF.III/SR.2. Geneva, August 28.

Borrie, John. 2008. "How the Cluster Munition Ban Was Won: Oslo Treaty Negotiations Conclude in Dublin." *Disarmament Diplomacy*, no. 88, 40–53.

———. 2009. *Unacceptable Harm: A History of How the Treaty to Ban Cluster Munitions Was Won*. Geneva: United Nations, UNIDIR (United Nations Institute for Disarmament Research).

Brasack, Bernhard. Germany. 2005. Statement to the BWC Meeting of States Parties, Geneva, December 5.

Brodin, Katarina. 1965. "The Undén Proposal." *Cooperation and Conflict* 1 (4): 18–29.

Bull, Hedley. 1984. *Justice in International Relations: The 1983 Hagey Lectures*. Waterloo: University of Waterloo. Reproduced in *Hedley Bull on International Society*, edited by Kai Alderson and Andrew Hurrell, 206–45. Basingstoke: Macmillan, 2000.

BWC (Biological Weapons Convention). 1980. "Background Paper Relating to the Convention on the Prohibition of the Development, Production and Stockpiling of Bacteriological (Biological) and Toxin Weapons and on Their Destruction." BWC/CONF.I/4. Geneva, February 20.

———. 2001. "Background Document on Compliance by States Parties with all Their Obligations under the BWC." BWC/CONF.V/3/Add.6. Geneva, November 28.

Cadham, John. 2008. "Negotiating the Convention on Anti-personnel Landmines." In *Canada's International Policies: Agendas, Alternatives, and Politics*, edited by Brian W. Tomlin, Norman Hillmer, and Fen Osler Hampson, 293–304. Oxford: Oxford University Press.

Cameron, Maxwell A., Robert J. Lawson, and Brian W. Tomlin, eds. 1998. *To Walk without Fear: The Global Movement to Ban Landmines*. Oxford: Oxford University Press.

Canada. 1982. "A Proposed Verification Organization for a Chemical Weapons Convention." Working paper. CD/313. Geneva, August 16.

———. 1986. Proposal by Canada et al. on Art. V of the BWC. BWC/CONF.II/9. Geneva, September 22.

———. 1991. Declaration of National Biological Defence Research and Development Programme. BWC/CONF.III/17. Geneva, September 2–13.

———. 1992. "Airborne Remote Sensing: Illustrative Costs." Working paper. BWC/CONF.III/VEREX/WP.63. Geneva, November 25.

———. 1995. "The Role of Trial Inspections in Informing Arms Control Negotiations and Implementation, with Particular Emphasis on the BTWC." Working paper. BWC/AD HOC GROUP/WP.1. Geneva, January 4.

———. 1996. "Concerns about Abuse of Challenge Inspection." Working paper. BWC/AD HOC GROUP/WP.59. Geneva, July 15.

———. 1997. "Canadian Views on Non-Challenge Visits." Working paper. BWC/AD HOC GROUP/WP.193. Geneva, July 28.

———. 2001. "Article III, Section F." Working paper. BWC/AD HOC GROUP/WP.433. Geneva, February 26.

———. 2006. "Accountability Framework." Working paper. BWC/CONF.VI/WP.1. Geneva, October 20.

———. 2011. "Strengthening the Existing Confidence-Building Measure Submission and Review Process." Working paper. BWC/CONF.VII/WP.25. Geneva, November 29.

Canada DEAIT (Department of External Affairs and International Trade). 1991. "Disarmament Bulletin No. 17, Fall 1991." Ottawa: Department of External Affairs and International Trade.

Canada and Norway. 1987. "General Procedures for Verification of Alleged Use of Chemical Weapons." Working paper. CD/766. Geneva, July 1.

Canada and Switzerland. 2001. "National Implementation of the BTWC: Compliance Assessment." BWC RevCon 2011. www.unog.ch/80256EDD006B8954/%28httpAssets%29/ADE0A27F0649DA49C125795D00595CEB/$file/BWC+7RC+Canada+&+Swiss+WP.pdf.

CBC News. 2009. "Canada, India Conclude Nuclear Trade Talks." CBC News, November 28. http://www.cbc.ca/news/canada/story/2009/11/28/canada-india-nuclear.html.

CDU/CSU/FDP (Christian Democratic Union/Christian Social Union/Free Democratic Party). 2009. *Growth. Education. Unity. The Coalition Agreement between the CDU, CSU and FDP. 17th Legislative Term*. Berlin.

CMC (Cluster Munition Coalition). 2009a. *Banning Cluster Munitions: Government Policy and Practice*. www.the-monitor.org/cm/2009/banning_cluster_munitions_2009.pdf.

———. 2009b. *Cluster Munition Monitor 2009*. Country Report: Canada. www.the-monitor.org/index.php/publications/display?act=submit&pqs_year=2009&pqs_type=cm&pqs_report=canada&pqs_section=.

———. 2009c. *Cluster Munition Monitor 2009*. Country Report: Sweden. www.the

-monitor.org/index.php/publications/display?act=submit&pqs_year=2009&pqs_type=cm&pqs_report=sweden&pqs_section=.

———. 2010. *Cluster Munition Monitor 2010*. Country Report: Canada. www.the-monitor.org/index.php/cp/display/region_profiles/theme/119.

———. 2011. *Cluster Munition Monitor 2011*. Country Report: Canada. www.the-monitor.org/index.php/cp/display/region_profiles/theme/866.

Council of the EU. 1998. *EU Code of Conduct on Arms Exports*. http://ec.europa.eu/external_relations/cfsp/sanctions/codeofconduct.pdf.

Dahl, Ann-Sofie. 2002. "Activist Sweden: The Last Defender of Non-Alignment." In *Activism and (Non)alignment: The Relationship between Foreign Policy and Security Doctrine*, edited by Ann-Sofie Dahl and Norman Hillmer, 139–50. Stockholm: Utrikespolitiska Institutet.

DFAIT (Foreign Affairs and International Trade Canada). 2012. "International Security Research and Outreach Programme (ISROP)." www.international.gc.ca/arms-armes/isrop-prisi/index.aspx?view=d.

Duffield, John S. 1999. "Political Culture and State Behavior: Why Germany Confounds Neorealism." *International Organization* 53 (4): 765–803.

Dunne, Tim. 2008. "Good Citizen Europe." *International Affairs* 84 (1): 13–28.

Elbe, Frank. Germany. 1983. Statement to the UNGA 1st Committee. A/C.1/38/PV.33. New York, November 17.

Eliasson, Jan. Sweden. 1995. Statement to the 5th NPT RevCon. NPT/CONF.1995/SR.7. New York, April 20.

Epstein, William. 1985. "Canada." In *Nonproliferation: The Why and the Wherefore*, edited by Jozef Goldblat. London: Taylor & Francis.

European Union. 2007. "Withdrawal from the Treaty on the Non-proliferation of Nuclear Weapons: European Union Common Approach." Working paper. NPT/CONF.2010/PC.I/WP.25. Vienna, May 10.

Findlay, Trevor. 2008. "Canada and the Nuclear Club." In *Canada among Nations 2007*, edited by Jean Daudelin and Daniel Schwanen, 198–224. Montreal: McGill-Queen's University Press.

Fischer, Joschka. Germany. 2005. Statement to the 7th NPT RevCon. New York, May 2.

Fortmann, Michel, William Hogg, and Catherine Jobin. 2006. "Le Canada et le contrôle des armements durant les années 1990." In *Mémoire de guerre et construction de la paix*, edited by Serge Jaumin and ôric Remacle, 235–54. Brussels: Peter Lang.

Freivalds, Laila. Sweden. 2005. Statement to the 7th NPT RevCon. New York, May 3.

Garcia, Denise. 2006. *Small Arms and Security: New Emerging International Norms*. London: Routledge.

Garris, Jerome. 1973. "Sweden's Debate on the Proliferation of Nuclear Weapons." *Cooperation and Conflict* 8 (4): 189–208.

Gellman, Peter. 1988/89. "Lester B. Pearson, Collective Security, and the World Order Tradition of Canadian Foreign Policy." *International Journal* 44 (1): 68–101.

Genscher, Hans-Dietrich. Germany. 1982. Statement to the CD. CD/PV.190. Geneva, February 2.

———. Germany. 1988. Statement to the CD. CD/PV.437. Geneva, February 4.

———. Germany. 1990. Statement to the 4th NPT RevCon. NPT/CONF.IV/SR.4. New York, November 16.

German Bundestag. 1982. Drucksache 9/1951. Official Record 9/1951. December 8. http://dipbt.bundestag.de/dip21/btd/09/019/0901951.pdf.

———. 2010. Drucksache 17/1159. Official Record 17/1159. March 24. http://dipbt.bundestag.de/dip21/btd/17/011/1701159.pdf.

German Federal Foreign Office. 1993. Deutsche 10-Punkte-Erklärung zur Nichtverbreitungspolitik. Bonn, December 15.

———. 2011. "Global Partnership." www.auswaertiges-amt.de/EN/Aussenpolitik/Friedenspolitik/Abruestung_/GlobalePartnerschaft_node.html.

German Federal Government. 1969. "Erklärung der Bundesregierung aus Anlaß der Unterzeichnung des Vertrages am 28 November 1969." In *Bonn und die Bombe: Deutsche Atomwaffenpolitik von Adenauer bis Brandt*, edited by Matthias Küntzel, 326–28. New York: Campus, 1992.

———. 1987. Jahresabrüstungsbericht 1986. Official Record 10/5762. Bonn: German Bundestag.

———. 2010. Jahresabrüstungsbericht 2009. Official Record 17/445. Berlin: German Bundestag.

———. 2011. Jahresabrüstungsbericht 2010.Official Record 17/4620. Berlin: German Bundestag.

Germany. 1984. "Proposal on 'Prohibition of Transfers' and 'Permitted Transfers' in a Future CW Agreement." Working paper. CD/439. New York, February 24.

———. 2004. "Strengthening the NPT against Withdrawal and Non-compliance: Suggestions for the Establishment of Procedures and Mechanisms." Working paper. NPT/CONF.2005/PC.III/WP.15. New York, April 29.

———. 2006. "Assessment of National Implementation of the Biological and Toxin Weapons Convention (BWC)." Working paper submitted on behalf of the European Union. BWC/CONF.VI/WP.3. Geneva, October 20.

———. 2007. "Draft CCW Protocol on Cluster Munitions." Working paper. CCW/GGE/2007/WP.1 and Corr.1. Geneva, May 1.

Gröning, Friedrich. Germany. 2006. Statement to the 6th BWC RevCon. Geneva, November 20.

Hallenberg, Jan. 2000. "Swedish Foreign and Security Policy." In *Sweden and the European Union Evaluated*, edited by Lee Milles, 19–32. London: Continuum.

Hamel, P. E. Canada. 1975. Statement to the 2nd NPT RevCon. NPT/CONF/C.II/SR.3. Geneva, May 13.

Hanson, Marianne. 1999. "Australia and Nuclear Arms Control as 'Good International Citizenship.'" Working paper 1999/2000. Canberra: Australian National University.

———. 2012. "Advocating the Elimination of Nuclear Weapons: The Role of Key Individual and Coalition States." In *Slaying the Nuclear Dragon: Disarmament Dynamics in the Twenty-First Century*, edited by Tanya Ogilvie-White and David Santoro, 56–84. Athens: University of Georgia Press.

Harnisch, Sebastian, Cornelia Frank, and Hanns W. Maull, eds. 2011. *Role Theory in International Relations*. London: Routledge.

Hartmann, Rüdiger. Germany. 1999. Statement to the CD. CD/PV.821. Geneva, March 25.

Hays, Daniel. Canada. 2005. Statement to the 10th Session of the CWC CSP. The Hague, November 7.

Hjelm-Wallén. Lena. Sweden. 1997. Statement to the 1st Session of the CWC CSP. The Hague, May 6.

Hoffmann, Hellmut. Germany. 2009. Statement to the BWC Meeting of States Parties. Geneva, December 7.

Hoyer, Werner. Germany. 2010. Statement to the 8th NPT RevCon. New York, May 4.

Human Rights Watch. 1999. *Landmine Monitor Report: Toward a Mine-Free World. International Campaign to Ban Land Mines*. New York: Human Rights Watch.

Hyltenius, Carl-Magnus. 1989. *Sverige i det internationella nedrustnigsarbetet*. Stockholm: Utrikesdepartementet.

ICBL (International Campaign to Ban Landmines). 1999. *Landmine Monitor 1999*. Country Report: Canada. www.the-monitor.org/index.php/publications/display?act=submit&pqs_year=1999&pqs_type=lm&pqs_report=canada&pqs_section=.

———. 2000. *Landmine Monitor 2000*. Country Report: Canada. www.the-monitor.org/index.php/publications/display?act=submit&pqs_year=2000&pqs_type=lm&pqs_report=canada&pqs_section=.

———. 2002. *Landmine Monitor 2002*. Country Report: Canada. www.the-monitor.org/index.php/publications/display?act=submit&pqs_year=2002&pqs_type=lm&pqs_report=canada&pqs_section=.

———. 2004. *Landmine Monitor 2004*. Country Report: Canada. www.the-monitor.org/index.php/publications/display?act=submit&pqs_year=2004&pqs_type=lm&pqs_report=canada&pqs_section=.

Ischinger, Wolfgang. Germany. 2000. Statement to the 6th NPT RevCon. New York, April 24.

Jacoby, G. Canada. 1990. Statement to the 4th NPT RevCon. NPT/CONF.IV/MC.III/SR.2. Geneva, August 28.

Johnson, Rebecca. 1995. *Indefinite Extension of the Non-Proliferation Treaty: Risks and*

Reckonings. A Report of the 1995 NPT Review and Extension Conference, New York, 17 April to 12 May 1995. Acronym Report no. 7. www.acronym.org.uk/acrorep/acro7.htm.

———. 2009. *Unfinished Business: The Negotiation of the CTBT and the End of Nuclear Testing*. New York: United Nations, UNIDIR (United Nations Institute for Disarmament Research).

Jonter, Thomas. 2001. *Sweden and the Bomb: The Swedish Plans to Acquire Nuclear Weapons, 1945–1972*. SKI Report 01:33. Stockholm: Swedish Nuclear Power Inspectorate.

Katzenstein, Peter J., ed. 1996. *The Culture of National Security: Norms and Identity in World Politics*. New York: Columbia University Press.

———. 1997. *Tamed Power: Germany in Europe*. Ithaca: Cornell University Press.

Kenyon, Ian, and Daniel Feakes, eds. 2007. *The Creation of the Organisation for the Prohibition of Chemical Weapons: A Case Study in the Birth of an Intergovernmental Organisation*. The Hague: T. M. C. Asser Press.

Kinkel, Klaus. Germany. 1995. Statement to the 5th NPT RevCon. NPT/CONF.1995/SR.2. New York, April 20.

Lawler, Peter. 2005. "The Good State: In Praise of 'Classical' Internationalism." *Review of International Studies* 31 (3): 427–49.

Lawson, Robert J., Mark Gwozdecky, Jill Sinclair, and Ralph Lysyshyn. 1998. "The Ottawa Process and the International Movement to Ban Anti-personnel Mines." In Cameron, Lawson, and Tomlin 1998, 160–84.

Legault, Albert, and Michael Fortmann. 1992. *Diplomacy of Hope: Canada and Disarmament, 1945–1988*. Montreal: McGill-Queen's University Press.

Lidgard, Curt. Sweden. 1980. Statement to the 1st BWC RevCon. BWC/CONF.I/C/SR.3. Geneva, March 12.

Lindh, Anna. Sweden. 2000. Statement to the 6th NPT RevCon. NPT/CONF.2000/SR.3. New York, April 25.

Linklater, Andrew. 1992. "What Is a Good International Citizen?" In *Ethics and Foreign Policy*, edited by Paul Keal, 21–43. Canberra: Allen & Unwin.

———. 2007. *Critical Theory and World Politics: Citizenship, Sovereignty and Humanity*. London: Routledge.

Linklater, Andrew, and Hidemi Suganami. 2006. *The English School of International Relations: A Contemporary Assessment*. Cambridge: Cambridge University Press.

Littlewood, Jez. 2005. *The Biological Weapons Convention: A Failed Revolution*. Aldershot: Ashgate.

Long, David, and Laird Hindle. 1998. "Europe and the Ottawa Process." In Cameron, Lawson, and Tomlin 1998, 248–68.

MacEachen, Allan. Canada. 1975. Statement to the 1st NPT RevCon. NPT/CONF/SR.5. Geneva, May 7.

Mallin, Maurice A. 1994. "The June, 1993 Swedish Draft Comprehensive Nuclear Test-Ban Treaty: Implications and Issues for Negotiations." CNSN occasional paper. McLean: Science Applications International.

Manga, Edda. 2010. "Swedish Arms Export: From National Interest to Global Utopia." *New Routes* 15 (3): 3–6.

Marsh, Nicholas. 2006. "The Nordic Countries and Conventional Arms Control: The Case of Small Arms and Light Weapons." In Bailes, Herolf, and Sundelius 2006, 234–51.

Mason, Peggy. Canada. 1990. Statement to the 4th NPT RevCon. Geneva, August 24.

Maull, Hans W. 1990. "Germany and Japan: The New Civilian Powers." *Foreign Affairs* 69 (5): 91–106.

McDougall, Robert. Canada. 1999. Statement to the 3rd PrepCom for the 6th NPT RevCon. New York, May 12.

McPhail, Donald. Canada. 1980a. Statement to the 1st BWC RevCon. BWC/CONF.I/C/SR.3. Geneva, March 12.

———. Canada. 1980b. Statement to Main Committee II of the 2nd NPT RevCon. NPT/CONF.II/C.II/SR.7. New York, August 26.

———. Canada. 1980c. Statement to the 2nd NPT RevCon. NPT/CONF.II/SR.8. Geneva, August 15.

Meier, Oliver. 2006. "The Growing Nuclear Fuel-Cycle Debate." *Arms Control Today* 36 (November). www.armscontrol.org/act/2006_11/NAFuel.

Michaud, Nelson. 2007. "Values and Canadian Foreign Policy-making: Inspiration or Hindrance?" In *Readings in Canadian Foreign Policy: Classic Debates and New Ideas*, edited by Duane Bratt and Christopher J. Kukucha, 341–56. Oxford: Oxford University Press.

Moersch, Karl. Germany. 1975. Statement to the 1st NPT RevCon. NPT/CONF/SR.3. Geneva, May 6.

Moher, Mark. Canada. 1996. Statement to the 4th BWC RevCon. Geneva, November 26.

———. Canada. 1997a. Statement to the CD. CD/PV.754. Geneva, February 6.

———. Canada. 1997b. Statement to the PrepCom for the 6th NPT RevCon. New York, April 8.

Möllemann, Jürgen. Germany. 1985. Statement to the 3rd NPT RevCon. NPT/CONF.III/SR.4. Geneva, August 29.

Müller, Harald. 2003. "Germany and WMD Proliferation." *Nonproliferation Review* 10 (2): 1–20.

Müller, Harald, and Katja Frank. 1997. "A Nuclear Weapons Register: Concepts, Issues and Opportunities." In *Developing Arms Transparency: The Future of the UN Register*, edited by Malcolm Chalmers, Mitsuro Donowaki, and Owen Green, 233–55. Bradford: University of Bradford.

Munton, Don, and Tom Keating. 2001. "Internationalism and the Canadian Public." *Canadian Journal of Political Science* 34 (3): 517–49.

Myrdal, Alva. 1977. *The Game of Disarmament: How the United States and Russia Run the Arms Race*. Manchester: Manchester University Press.

Nilsson, Ann-Sofie. 1991. *Den moraliska stormakten: En studie av socialdemokratins internationella aktivism*. Stockholm: Timbro.

Noetzel, Timo, and Benjamin Schreer. 2008. "All the Way? The Evolution of German Military Power." *International Affairs* 84 (2): 211–21.

Nossal, Kim Richard. 1997. *The Politics of Canadian Foreign Policy*. Scarborough: Prentice-Hall Canada.

NPT (Nuclear Non-Proliferation Treaty). 1985. "Basic Facts within the Framework of the United Nations in Connection with the Implementation of Articles I and II of the NPT." NPT/CONF.III/3. Geneva, September 17.

———. 2010. Eighth NPT RevCon. Final Document. NPT/CONF.2010/50 (Vol. 1). New York, June 18.

Parsons, Adam, and Kenneth Epps. 2008. *Review of the Progress in Canadian Implementation of the UN Programme of Action on Small Arms*. Ottawa: Project Ploughshares.

Pleuger, Gunter. Germany. 2003. Statement to the 1st Biennial Meeting of States to Consider the Implementation of the PoA. New York, July 2003.

Prawitz, Jan. 1995. *From Nuclear-Option to Non-Nuclear Promotion: The Sweden Case*. Research Report no. 20. Stockholm: Swedish Institute of International Affairs.

Prokosch, Eric. 1994. "Arguments for Restricting Cluster Weapons: Humanitarian Protection versus 'Military Necessity.'" Special issue, *International Review of the Red Cross* 34 (299): 194–216.

Ramaker, Jaap, Peter D. Marshall, Robert Geil, and Jennifer Mackby. 2003. *The Final Test: A History of the Negotiations for a Comprehensive Test Ban Treaty*. Vienna: Preparatory Commission for the CTBTO.

Roche, Douglas. 2000/2001. "Stuck in the Middle? Canada's Record and Role in Promoting Disarmament." *Disarmament Diplomacy* 2000/2001 (53): 8–12.

Roffey, Roger. 2002. "Threats from Chemical and Biological Weapons: A Swedish View." Paper presented at the Conference Exploring Functional Security: National Responses and Prospects for Nordic and European Collaboration, at the Swedish Institute of International Affairs, Stockholm, October 24–25.

Roussel, Stéphane, and Claude Robichaud. 2004. "L'État post-moderne par excellence? Internationalisme et promotion de l'identité internationale du Canada." *Études internationales* 35 (1): 149–70.

Rublee, Maria Rost. 2009. *Nonproliferation Norms: Why States Choose Nuclear Restraint*. Athens: University of Georgia Press.

Ruth, Friedrich. Germany. 1982. Statement to the CD. CD/PV.166. Geneva, March 25.

Schaper, Annette. 1996. "Using Existing European MOX Fabrication Plants for the Disposal of Plutonium from Dismantled Warheads." In *Selected Papers from Global '95 Conference "Evaluation of Emerging Nuclear Fuel Cycle Systems" Concerning Plutonium*, edited by W. G. Sutcliffe, 197–209. UCRL-ID-124105. Livermore: Lawrence Livermore National Laboratory.

Shannon, Gerald E. 1995. Report of Ambassador Gerald E. Shannon of Canada on Consultations on the Most Appropriate Arrangement to Negotiate a Treaty Banning the Production of Fissile Material for Nuclear Weapons or Other Nuclear Explosive Devices. CD/1299. Geneva, March 24.

Sims, Nicholas. 1988. *The Diplomacy of Biological Disarmament: Vicissitudes of a Treaty in Force, 1975–85*. New York: St. Martin's Press.

———. 2009. *The Future of Biological Disarmament: Strengthening the Treaty Ban on Weapons*. London: Routledge.

SIPRI (Stockholm Peace Research Institute). 2011a. "The SIPRI Military Expenditure Database 2011." http://milexdata.sipri.org.

———. 2011b. "SIPRI Arms Transfers Database." www.sipri.org/databases/armstransfers.

Small Arms Survey. 2011. *Small Arms Survey 2011: States of Security*. Cambridge: Cambridge University Press.

Steinmeier, Frank-Walter. 2007. "Opening Speech for the Conference Marking the 10-Year Anniversary of the Chemical Weapons Convention." Berlin, April 25. www.auswaertiges-amt.de/DE/Infoservice/Presse/Reden/2007/070425-CWUE.html.

Stock, Thomas. 1995. *History of the Negotiations on the CWC—Short Overview*. SIPRI-Saskatchewan-Frankfurt Research Group on Implementation of the Chemical Weapons Convention. Paper no. 13.

Sweden. 1965. "Memorandum on International Cooperation for the Detection of Underground Explosions." ENDC/154. Geneva, September 2.

———. 1972. Statement to the CD. CCD/PV.555. Geneva, April 11.

———. 1976. "Working Paper on Co-operative International Measures to Monitor a CTB." CCD/482. Geneva, March 26.

———. 1998. Statement to the PrepCom for the 2000 NPT RevCon. Geneva, April 30. *Disarmament Diplomacy* 1998 (26). www.acronym.org.uk/dd/dd26/26doc.htm.

Sweden. 2011. "Strategic Export Control in 2010: Military Equipment and Dual-Use Products." Government Communication 2010/11:114. Stockholm, March 10. www.isp.se/documents/_English/Publications/GC/GC_1011_eng.pdf.

Sweden, Australia, Austria, Canada, Denmark, Finland, Hungary, Ireland, the Netherlands, New Zealand, and Norway. 1995. "Article III—Safeguards." Working paper. NPT/CONF.1995/MC.II/WP.2. New York, April 21.

Sweden, Australia, Austria, Canada, Denmark, Hungary, Ireland, the Netherlands, New Zealand, and Norway. 2000. "Export Controls." Working paper. NPT/CONF.2000/MC.II/WP.4 New York.

Sweden, Denmark, Finland, Iceland, and Norway. 1985. "Letter Dated 15 July 1985 from the Permanent Representatives of Denmark, Finland, Iceland, Norway and Sweden Addressed to the Provisional Secretary General of the Third Review Conference." Letter. NPT/CONF.III/16. New York, July 15.

———. 1990. "Letter Dated 10 July 1985 from the Permanent Representatives of Denmark, Finland, Iceland, Norway and Sweden Addressed to the Provisional Secretary General of the Third Review Conference." Letter. NPT/CONF.IV/18. New York, July 17.

Ugglas, Margaretha. Sweden. 1993. Statement to the CD. CS/PV.641, Geneva, February 4.

UNGA (United Nations General Assembly). 1982. "UN General Assembly Resolution 37/98 C: Chemical and Bacteriological (Biological) Weapons." A/RES/37/98. New York, December 13.

———. 1997. Official Records 52nd Session, 75th Plenary Meeting, December 17, 1997. UN Doc. A/52/PV.75. www.undemocracy.com/A-52-PV.75.pdf.

van Dassen, Lars. 1998. *Sweden and the Making of Nuclear Non-proliferation: From Indecision to Assertiveness.* SKI Report 98:16. Stockholm: Swedish Nuclear Power Inspectorate.

van Dassen, Lars, and Anna Wetter. 2006. "Nordic Nuclear Non-proliferation Policies: Different Traditions and Common Objectives." In Bailes, Herolf, and Sundelius, 252–66.

von Dohnanyi, Klaus. Germany. 1980. Statement to the 2nd NPT RevCon. NPT/CONF.II/SR.4. New York, August 13.

von Stülpnagel, Paul-Joachim. Germany. 1986. Statement to the 2nd BWC RevCon. BWC/CONF.II/SR.3. Geneva, September 9.

———. Germany. 1987. Statement to the CD. CD/PV.389. Geneva, February 17.

———. Germany. 1988a. Statement to the CD. CD/PV.458. Geneva, April 19.

———. Germany. 1988b. Statement to the CD. CD/PV.474. Geneva, August 16.

———. Germany. 1988c. Statement to the CD. CD/PV.481. Geneva, September 13.

———. Germany. 1990. Statement to the CD. CD/PV.554. Geneva, April 24.

Waisová, Šárka. 2011. "Canada: A Humane Internationalist in the Shadow of a Larger Neighbour." In *Ethics in Foreign Policy: Postmodern States as the Entrepreneurs of Kantian Ethics*, edited by Šárka Waisová and Lasislav Cabada, 35–60. Frankfurt am Main: Peter Lang.

Wall, Jim. Canada. 2006. Statement to the 11th Session of the CWC CSP. The Hague, December 5.

Wall, Jim. Canada. 2008. Statement to the 13th Session of the CWC CSP. The Hague, December 2.

Wegener, Henning. Germany. 1982. Statement to the CD. CD/PV.151. Geneva, February 4.

———. Germany. 1983. Statement to the CD. CD/PV.197. Geneva, February 24.

———. Germany. 1984a. Statement to the CD. CD/PV.245. Geneva, February 28.

———. Germany. 1984b. Statement to the CD. CD/PV.254. Geneva, March 29.

———. Germany. 1984c. Statement to the CD. CD/PV.256. Geneva, April 5.

———. Germany. 1985. Statement to the CD. CD/PV.289. Geneva, February 5.

Weiland, Severin. 2010. "Union sieht Westerwelles Abrüstungskurs skeptisch." *SPIEGEL Online*, March 5. www.spiegel.de/politik/ausland/0,1518,681493,00.html.

Westdal, Christopher. Canada. 1995. Statement to the 5th NPT RevCon. NPT/CONF.1995/PV.17. New York, May 11.

———. Canada. 2000. Statement to Main Committee I of the 6th NPT RevCon. New York, May 2.

———. Canada. 2001. Statement to the 5th BWC RevCon. Geneva, November 19.

Wheeler, Nicholas J., and Tim Dunne. 1998. "Good International Citizenship: A Third Way for British Foreign Policy." *International Affairs* 74 (4): 847–70.

Wright, Jim. Canada. 2005. Statement to the 7th NPT RevCon. New York, May 2.

CHAPTER EIGHT

Non-aligned Reformers and Revolutionaries

Egypt, South Africa, Iran, and North Korea

Carmen Wunderlich, Andrea Hellmann, Daniel Müller, Judith Reuter, and Hans-Joachim Schmidt

THE CONCEPT OF NORM ENTREPRENEURSHIP has so far remained restricted to analyzing actors engaged in the promotion of supposedly "good" norms and working toward reproducing or incrementally reforming the prevalent normative order with a view to enhance its quality and efficiency (see chapter 1)—their attitude may thus be described as affirmative. Yet, as "agents of social change" (Björkdahl 2002, 45), norm entrepreneurs often take an oppositional stance to, express dissent from, and advocate a more or less radical modification of the existing normative structure. Depending on the purpose of the intended change, oppositional norm entrepreneurship may take various forms.

First, change may aim at *reform* of the existing order within the boundaries of existing rules and structures. This incremental approach may result in small shifts in emphasis and interpretation of norms. Second, norm entrepreneurship oriented toward *renovation* may aim at a return to the "original" normative order as perceived from an actor's perspective. Third, *revolutionary* norm entrepreneurs may aim at an upheaval in the system and the establishment of a new order in line with their normative preferences. Revolutionary states refuse to play by the rules of the system. As members of the international community, they are subject to constant efforts at resocialization into what they perceive to be "an unequal, oppressive, and immoral structure of international authority, devised by the established powers in their own interests" (Armstrong 1993, 1, 3).

This chapter looks at non-aligned countries that often take an oppositional stance toward the prevalent power structure and follow a normative policy that differs strongly from their Western counterparts. With the foundation of the Non-Aligned Movement (NAM) in 1961, developing countries joined forces to work toward achieving their goals.[1] NAM states not only play a crucial role in the success or failure of arms control negotiations due to their sheer number, but in addition they may be relevant norm entrepreneurs due to their desire for a modification of the international norm fabric.

It is thus imperative to inquire into the potential of those states that perceive themselves as a counterpart to the industrialized world to be norm entrepreneurs. Despite being a heterogeneous group, NAM countries are united in their goal of promoting the interests of the developing world and seeking compensation for centuries of marginalization and exploitation. Motivated by the historical experience of colonialism, they advocated the realization of principles such as anti-imperialism, national sovereignty, and noninterference, resulting in a policy of strict non-alignment during the Cold War. They demanded equal participation in international decision-making processes, strengthening of multilateralism, peaceful resolution of conflicts, development objectives, and "general and complete disarmament."[2] Even after the end of the Cold War, the goals of NAM countries did not lose their relevance (Braveboy-Wagner 2009, 24)—some changes in mode of action and reorientation of principles notwithstanding (Potter and Mukhatzhanova 2012, 12).

Membership within the organization is defined by their common experience and by "prior acceptance of broad but globally significant basic norms that guide the group's actions in specific spheres" (Braveboy-Wagner 2009, 24).[3] For the realization of these goals, "they have had to establish channels for the *promotion of alternative norms* and strategies" (Braveboy-Wagner 2009, 13; emphasis added).

NAM countries pursued arms control actively within the UNGA and the CD, calling for nondiscriminatory measures to curb the illicit spread of WMD with a strong focus on nuclear weapons. In light of the great powers' reluctance to carry out (nuclear) disarmament, NAM countries focused on measures to enhance the security of NNWS: the establishment of nuclear-weapon-free zones (NWFZS) or weapons of mass destruction free zones (WMDFZS), negative security assurances, and repeated calls on the NWS to fulfill their disarmament obligation (see, e.g., Muni 1988; Strydom 2007, 11; Potter and Mukhatzhanova 2012). Another NAM priority "has . . . been to ensure that NNWS that have foregone the right to develop nuclear weapons are adequately compensated for their sacrifice via the provision of nuclear technology for peaceful purposes" (Ogilvie-White 2007, 461), accompanied by concern about the West's tacit approval of Israel's nuclear opacity.

From the large NAM group we have selected four countries for closer scrutiny. We have chosen the supposed *norm reformers* Egypt and South Africa and the supposed *norm revolutionaries* Iran and North Korea.[4]

Egypt and South Africa are both NAM "heavyweights" with leadership roles and have proven able to generate broad support for their positions among fellow developing countries. At the same time, both countries exhibit peculiarities in arms control policy: South Africa stands out due to the unique voluntary rollback of its weapons of mass destruction programs; Egypt, although facing a nuclear-armed adversary, has never taken serious steps to develop the same capabilities.

Opposition against and dissent over the existing normative order is often decried as "norm hostility." This opprobrium hits especially "pariah" states such as the Islamic Republic of Iran and the Democratic People's Republic of Korea (DPRK). Within the NAM, both states take extreme positions, often rejecting accommodation as well as challenging the existing normative order. This has led the international community, particularly the United States, to consign both states to the "axis of evil" as "rogue states." Becoming the defining adversary in the US security narrative during the 1990s (Homolar 2010, 18), rogue states have been characterized as dictatorships and autocracies whose behavior is unpredictable and undeterrable and who therefore pose a "threat to the entire community of democratic nations and its fundamental principles" (Senn 2009, 14). Rogue states are depicted as outsiders that reject the central rules of the existing normative order (see, e.g., Lake 1994; Klare 1995; Henriksen 2001; Caprioli and Trumbore 2005). Breaking norms is regarded as their foremost attribute. The indicators identified in the scholarly literature on rogue states converge around the violation of four basic norms: human rights violations, the support of terrorism, the pursuit of WMD, and territorial aggression (Nincic 2005, 15). Some authors assume these states to be "*anomic*, unsavory, and troublesome places" (Rotberg 2007, 8; emphasis added).

It might thus appear to be an oxymoron to discuss the norm entrepreneurial potential of countries that are depicted as part of the "axis of evil" and the "worst of the worst" (Rotberg 2007). But it may be worthwhile to challenge the mainstream and to look for empirical proof or disproof of the thought-experiment that behind their rejectionist attitude a serious effort to establish alternative norms might be found.[5]

EGYPT: AN ARMS CONTROL CHAMPION TORN IN CONFLICT

Egypt, the self-confident Arab "leader," longtime opponent of nuclear-armed Israel, and central actor in the Middle East, has never seriously attempted to establish nuclear-military parity. When faced with internal power struggles or financial and organizational problems, Egypt "never made the kind of national commitment that would have made the bomb reality" (Walsh 2001, 172). Instead, it became a proponent of nuclear arms control. It participated in the negotiations on the NPT (Shaker 1980), was one of the first signatories, and ratified it in 1981. It struggles for the NPT's universalization, the creation of a Middle East NWFZ or WMDFZ, and promotes nuclear disarmament, negative security assurances (NSA), and the right to the peaceful uses of nuclear energy. Yet Egypt is predicating cooperation in biological and chemical arms control on progress in the nuclear issue. The BWC was signed but not ratified, the CWC supported but not signed. Egypt's claims for sovereignty rights set limits on humanitarian arms control. It is a member of neither the Convention on Cluster Munitions (CCM) nor the Mine Ban Treaty (MBT). Egypt can thus be described as pursuing three types of policies in arms control: promoting nuclear, abstaining from chemical and biological, and resisting measures supporting humanitarian arms control.

National security is interwoven with regional security. Egypt, a front state in the Middle East conflict, has always claimed a *regional leadership* position and is sensitive to shifts in the regional power and security structure. The hot conflict and the cold peace with Israel have been both a pivotal condition and a core objective of Egypt's arms control policy, but the ambitions of other regional powers, especially of Iran since the late 1980s, exert a strong influence as well (IISS 2008).

A second feature of Egypt's arms control policy is its ambition of *multilateral leadership* as a matter of identity rather than interest (Landau 2006), within and beyond the Arab League (AL) and on a global level within the NAM (Boutros-Ghali 1982, 785). During the 1970s, Egypt made a turn toward the West, particularly the United States (Heikal 1978, 726), opted for diplomatic handling of the conflict with Israel, and became a close ally of the United States, Israel's protector and nowadays the strongest (nuclear) superpower. Although this temporarily cost Egypt its AL membership, the new attitude to Israel was eventually accepted by most Arab states. Egypt's reentry into the AL and a renewed leadership position ensued (Boutros-Ghali 1982). This constellation engenders frequently contradictory consequences for Egypt's foreign and security policy, which has always been centralized in the hands of the current political leader (Heikal 1978, 714). Moreover, its long-standing profile in international arms control has become a part of Egypt's self-perception and a guideline for "appropriate" behavior and normative commitment.

Peace, Equal Security, and Leadership at the Regional Level

Egypt's arms control policy is closely connected to the region's nuclear asymmetry and broader security situation. Taking into account its difficulties in establishing a nuclear program (see Walsh 2001), nuclear arms control was seen as the best way to counter Israel's military superiority (Rublee 2009, 115). As the verbatim record of the 639th meeting of the Conference on Disarmament states: "Egypt was amongst the original signatories of the Treaty . . . because of her . . . fervent hope that by taking this high road other States, in and beyond . . . [the] region . . . , would be encouraged to do the same" (Moussa 1993). Cairo hoped that Israel would follow its lead (Bahgat 2007, 6), or at least that the international community, especially the United States, would build up pressure (Rublee 2009, 114). When Egypt's signing of the NPT did not have the desired effect, it ratified the treaty nonetheless and began the quest for the treaty's universality and the creation of a NWFZ or WMDFZ. After this approach proved unsuccessful, Cairo used the occasion when in 1995 the NPT was at stake. Its indefinite extension, strongly desired by the United States, was rejected by many states (especially by the NAM) as a perpetuation of the nuclear imbalance. Egypt succeeded in making Israel's nuclear status and progress toward a NWFZ in the Middle East a decisive contingency for agreement on the treaty's extension: "anxiety concerning the situation in the Middle East was among the main reasons why Egypt was not in favor of a decision for indefinite extension" (Zahran 1995). In the run-up to the 1995 conference, Egypt pressed the members of the AL to link their consent to an indefinite extension on Israel's accession to the NPT (Landau 2006, 136–37) and insisted on this position in negotiations with the United States (Dhanapala 2005, 56). Egyptian diplomacy proved successful in uniting a significant number of Arab and NAM states behind this position (see Johnson 1995; Dhanapala 2010, 8). A resolution on the Middle East calling for negotiations on a NWFZ (Dhanapala 2010, 20) became part of the "package deal"—Egypt had made the Middle East issue a "fourth pillar" (Acheson and Spies 2008, 1) of the NPT bargain and played a significant role in convincing all remaining Arab states to accede to the NPT before the 2000 RevCon. Its engagement for regional arms control and disarmament measures has always been a quest for "the total equality of the States of the region . . . with regard to their level of security" (Elaraby 1994). The creation of a NWFZ or WMDFZ is meant to "guarantee balanced security in the Middle East" (Elaraby 1994). But considering the "lack of implementation by the depositary States of their commitment to the special resolution on the Middle East" (Abdelaziz 2006), Egypt felt betrayed (Lewis and Potter 2011), inequalities in security were perpetuated, and the burden of obligations was unjustly distributed. If a NWFZ could not be realized, Egypt feared that "the indefinite extension would be based on imposing additional commitments on the Arab States while exempting Israel from any commitments at all" (Abdelaziz 2008).

The effect of double standards, imbalances, and noncompliance became visible at the 2005 RevCon where Egypt—tit for tat—blocked new nonproliferation measures (see Johnson 2010). That Egypt staunchly defended the Middle East Resolution in 2005 and 2010 was also due to the fact that it felt obliged to the Arab states after convincing them to accede to the NPT and to agree to the treaty's indefinite extension in return for the Middle East Resolution (Johnson 2005; Misher 2009). In 2010 Egypt effectively combined its roles as chair of both NAM and the New Agenda Coalition (NAC) to compel the international community, especially the United States, to accept far-reaching concessions (see Johnson 2010; Müller 2011). The RevCon's final document confirmed the resolution of 1995, urged Israel to accede to the NPT, scheduled a conference for 2012 to negotiate a WMDFZ, and called for the appointment of a facilitator responsible for preparing the 2012 conference and implementing its outcome.

Egypt's commitment to regional security via promotion of arms control measures is conducive to consolidating its leadership ambitions within the AL and as the region's representative. For Egypt, the risk of regional WMD proliferation poses what is probably a greater threat than Israel's old "opaque" nuclear arsenal (Feldman 1997, 125–26). Cairo does not want Iran to gain nuclear weapons. Already in 1993 then President Mubarak feared that "if Iran succeeds in acquiring the bomb, it will be a great danger for the world" (cited in Einhorn 2004, 63). A WMDFZ "should be based on the guarantee that no state in the region—including Iran—will seek to acquire nuclear weapons" (Abdelaziz 2006). The threat of proliferation is a matter of (in)security, but hindering the proliferation of nuclear weapons also helps in keeping regional competitors at bay (Misher 2009).

The conflict in the Middle East and Israel's nuclear program affect all areas of Egypt's arms control policy. Egypt endorses central norms of the BWC and the CWC: "The prohibition of the development, production, and stockpiling of bacteriological and toxin weapons is a position which . . . [Egypt] remains committed to, not only due to . . . [its] recognition of the unacceptable consequences related to this type of weapon from both the humanitarian and moral perspective, but also because of . . . [its] relentless diplomatic efforts to achieve the total elimination of all weapons of mass destruction both globally and regionally" (Shoukry 2006). Nonetheless, it did not join the CWC and refrained from ratifying the BWC. Egypt's accession to the BWC and CWC are contingent upon Israel's accession to the NPT (e.g., Fahmy 2011): "Egypt has repeatedly stressed that it is ready, able, and willing to ratify the Chemical Weapons Convention and the Biological Weapons Convention in a package that must include Israel's ratification of the NPT" (Abdelaziz 1998b). It has even been urging other states to follow this linkage policy: "The rationale is clear: security cannot be divided among various types of weapons of mass destruction, on the one hand, and between weapons of mass destruction and conventional weapons, on the other" (Abdelaziz 1998a). Consequently Egypt has been continuously active for a WMDFZ since 1990, stressing "the necessity to prohibit WMD in the Middle East without exception, whether nuclear, chemical, or biological weapons" (Shoukry 2006). This once again reveals a desire to be given equal treatment and equal security; to tolerate Israel's "ambiguous nuclear capabilities and policies to protect its security while all Arab countries should forgo their security concerns and ratify the CWC and the BWC" (Shoukry 2006) is a notion that is unthinkable to Egypt.

Toward Global Nuclear Disarmament and Equality of Rights and Obligations

Egypt's commitment to nuclear disarmament has been shaped by concerns about "the imbalance of obligations and responsibilities . . . between the nuclear-weapon and non-nuclear-weapon States" (El Shafei 1980) and the denial of "equal security as a sovereign right of each state" (Badawi 1986). The nuclear imbalance, a discriminatory treaty, a lack of legally binding security assurances, and noncompliance with disarmament obligations are considered grave injustices. Egypt was concerned that indefinitely extending the NPT would be seen by the NWS as "an absolute right to maintain that status for as long as any of them sees fit, while the other States which have voluntarily rejected the nuclear option are left without any effective and legally binding protection in the event of aggression" (Zahran 1995). When the NWS, especially the United States under the Bush administration, ignored or even denied their disarmament obligations, Egypt saw its fears confirmed. Its strong commitment to leveling these inequalities by means of nuclear disarmament has afforded Egypt a prominent political position within NAM. The importance Egypt attaches to nuclear disarmament led to its cofounding the NAC in 1998 and assuming an active role in that group ever since (Abdelaziz 1998a). Egypt never lowered its normative commitment, although a stocktaking of forty years of political activism yields an only marginally successful balance. All this is a strong indication that its commitment is fairly robust despite political shocks. The crucial factor might be Egypt's pride in its still impressive diplomatic record (Boutros-Ghali 1982, 785).

Equal Right to Peaceful Cooperation and Sovereignty

The 1974 initiative for a NWFZ in the Middle East and the ratification of the NPT in 1981 were also part of the struggle for cooperation in the peaceful use of nuclear energy in the face of an energy crisis (Walsh 2001, 176–80). Sadat's *infitah* ("Open Door") policy after the Yom-Kippur war turned Egypt away from costly and militarily disastrous nationalism and pan-Arabism toward the United States and the West (Solingen 2007, 239; Walsh 2010, 28–30). Although interest in starting a civil nuclear program fizzled out due to bad economics and the discovery of gas reserves in the mid-1980s and has only recently been revived (IISS 2008), the defense of all NPT members' sovereign right to cooperation in the peaceful uses of nuclear energy has remained a morally charged issue for Egypt.

In the face of what was seen as "attempts of some parties to impose false conditions and unjustified restrictions or to raise false pretexts to prevent non-nuclear-weapon NPT Member States from acquiring the materials and technology required to develop their peaceful nuclear programmes" (Abdelaziz 2009) during the Bush administration, the perception of an imbalance of rights and obligations within the regime grew stronger. In 2005 and 2010 Egypt defended Iran's entitlement to pursue its national fuel cycle policies, even though these present a security nightmare to Cairo and could enable Iran to contest Egypt's regional position. That Egypt is vehemently advocating a right that it has not used for decades and that might run counter to core security interests demonstrates its strong perception of injustice: because Egypt sees the NNWS as being deprived of the rights to the disarmament of nuclear weapons and NSAS, it defends their remaining rightful "claims."

Egypt hesitates to accede to any humanitarian arms control treaty, although it recognizes the devastating effects of these weapons (ICBL 2011a). Concerned about potential threats to territorial sovereignty and the "inalienable right to self-defense" (ICBL 2011e, 4), Cairo warns against "unfair denials" (ATT 2010) and strict regulation of SALW that "could result in extensive hurdles to civil industry and contradict with [sic] industrial and developmental aims of many developing states" (ICBL 2011e, 2) and the "right of States to produce and export arms" (El Shafei 1980). The Oslo Process on cluster ammunition and the MBT are criticized for bypassing the UN (e.g., ICBL 2011a, 2011c) and, in the case of the MBT, for its "unbalanced nature" (ICBL 2011b) and the fact that mine producers should be held accountable. The quest for sovereign rights, noninterference, and strengthening UN processes are classic NAM positions founded on the principle of sovereign equality and therefore a justice issue. What is at stake is nothing less than for Egypt to be respected in its autonomy and to be treated as a diplomatic partner of equal value. But Egypt, as in the area of SALW, follows hard interests as well: it produces, sells, and stockpiles cluster munitions and sees mines as necessary to secure its borders (e.g., ICBL 2011b).

Norm Entrepreneurship under Complicated Circumstances

Egypt's WMD policy moves in a narrow channel between a complex set of needs and partially contradictory "appropriatenesses." At the regional level, it must bring its demand for leadership in the AL and its ambition to be valued by the United States as a regional partner on a par with Israel into accordance with its role as conflict mediator. In global terms, Egypt adopts policies that meet its ambition to be seen and treated as the major power in its region, a NAM leader, and proactive diplomatic "heavyweight." Notions of injustice, especially violations of "sovereign equality" in matters of security, rights, obligations, and opportunities, have rendered Egypt's position intransigent at times and have provoked it to engage in policies that clash with norms and even work against its security interests and aspirations for regional leadership. The proud Arab power reacts sensitively when it does not feel treated as an equal partner—especially at the regional level.

Egypt's dedication to the NPT's universality and the creation of a regional NWFZ or WMDFZ, in which it always addresses Israel (but in fact is also directing its statements at other regional actors), serves its security interests and regional leadership ambitions. This commitment is also compatible with its demand for NAM leadership, which is underlined by Egypt's quest for cooperation in the peaceful uses of nuclear energy, nuclear disarmament, sovereign equality, and noninterference. Followed in a moderate form, these policies are also suitable for maintaining the country's position within the NAC. To achieve the greatest political support and impact, Egypt skillfully combines its roles in the AL, NAM, and the NAC. Framing its political goals as matters of justice, equality, and developmental needs, or as being in the best (security) interest of all states, renders its concerns coherent with existing norms and compatible with the political context.

In terms of regime evolution, Egypt has to be given credit (originally together with Iran) for introducing into the regime's agenda the concept of a Middle East NWFZ/WMDFZ as an accepted goal. The commitment to the NPT's universality serves the same purpose. That it makes its accession to the BWC and CWC dependent on progress on Israel's status is—at least—troublesome due to Egypt's scope of influence in the region. But even such linkage conflicts could result in a strengthening of the regimes: in its commitment to a WMDFZ, Egypt consciously constructed for itself a "rhetorical entrapment" case that will inevitably lead to its legally renouncing BW and CW if such a zone were to ever be established.

SOUTH AFRICA: AN ALMOST PERFECT *NAM* REFORMER WITH A STRONG MORAL VOICE

During apartheid, South Africa was an international pariah. The perceived threat of a "total onslaught" orchestrated by the Soviet Union, Cuba, the front states, and the African National Congress (ANC) was reinforced by international isolation and induced the government in the late 1970s to order the production of six nuclear warheads and the initiation of a BWC program named "Project Coast" (Purkitt, Burgess, and Liberman 2002, 188).

After the Cold War, "total onslaught" fears disappeared. President de Klerk, in office since 1989, wanted to break the isolation through far-reaching reforms

(Long and Grillot 2000, 28). He pursued improved diplomatic and economic relations, notably with the West, hoping for prosperity as a result. Internally, the stepwise elimination of apartheid and the achievement of democratization were put on the agenda. Nuclear disarmament was seen as the ticket back into the world (Liberman 2001, 84). The process was completed around 1991 and was followed by the dismantling of "Project Coast," though in a more bumpy way (Purkitt and Burgess 2005, 129).

This change shifted South Africa's status from "pariah" to "paragon" and a respected international actor (Geldenhuys 2006, 93). The new foreign policy corresponded to the ideals of the ANC, elected to government in 1994: a more humane world for all people, peace, and prosperity. Under President Mandela, South Africa committed to democracy, multilateralism, peaceful conflict resolution, the promotion of human rights, and humanitarian law (van Wyk 2004, 116).

Improved relations with the West enabled Pretoria to serve as a bridge builder between North and South (van Wyk 2004, 128). Although it generally managed this role well, South Africa could not escape tensions between the roles of bridge builder and the NAM leader. At times, some NAM states accused it of pursuing its own economic interests at the expense of its peers (van Wyk 2004, 114). President Mbeki, elected in 1998, reacted by embracing the concept of "African Renaissance," which focused on the interests of developing, particularly African, countries (Landsberg and Monyae 2006, 133).

After reintegration into many international organizations, South Africa emerged as a rising middle power with substantial influence within multilateral forums. It took a leading position in the African Union (AU) and the NAM in promoting the interests of developing countries, such as economic growth, poverty reduction, and social justice (see Mandela 1998; Landsberg and Monyae 2006, 133).

South Africa became a champion of disarmament and arms control concerning all WMD, a policy that "forms an integral part of [the] subsequent South African government's commitment to democracy, human rights, sustainable development, social justice and environmental protection" (du Preez and Maettig 2010, 315) and was later extended to humanitarian arms control (Geldenhuys 2006, 103). In addition to moral motivations, this policy is designed to serve as a valuable instrument for enhancing peace and security (e.g., Priscilla 2003; Goosen 2004). To get closer to that aim, at least in Africa, Pretoria played, due to its expertise, an important role in the conclusion of the 1995 Pelindaba Treaty for an African nuclear-weapon-free zone (see Beri 1998; Adeniji 2002, 61).

Arms control policy is a matter for the executive (Jordaan 2010, 83). In coordination with the president, the Department of International Relations is the lead agency. It inherited from the apartheid era a well-trained and organized diplomatic corps that quickly developed concepts for disarmament policy in various areas.

South Africa sees itself as "a symbol of democracy" (van Wyk 2004, 115), "a moral voice" of the international community. But moral ambition and national interests are not always in harmony, as arms sales to countries with a doubtful human rights record indicate. While over time the moral authority and the image of "paragon" have diminished, South Africa is still capable of "a policy of moral multilateralism and global norm entrepreneurship" (Vickers 2002, 81). Key features are the mediating position between industrial and developing countries, the insistence on balanced treatment of treaty obligations, and a humanitarian motivation.

South Africa as Bridge Builder

Due to its unique role in nuclear disarmament, South Africa possesses high moral authority; in addition, its membership in the Nuclear Suppliers Group (NSG) since 1995 as the first NAM country facilitates mediating between NWS and developing NNWS (Shelton 2000, 123; du Preez and Maettig 2010, 316), though not without experiencing role conflicts from time to time.

After South Africa acceded to the NPT in 1991 as an NNWS "because it felt that its security would be guaranteed by the Treaty's provisions" (Nzo 1995), it coined, together with Canada, the victorious formula *perpetuity with accountability*, which enabled the RevCon 1995 to extend the treaty indefinitely without a vote (Ogilvie-White 1999, 322). The "invention" of an enhanced review process that would work according to agreed standards ("Principles and Objectives"), including working toward disarmament, supplied a balanced "give and take" around which the contrasting positions could converge. South Africa promoted this formula, calling on the NWS to follow its example of nuclear disarmament. South Africa's proposals aimed at eliminating the inherent inequality in the treaty in the long term, the main concern of the skeptics concerning indefinite extension (Dhanapala 2005).

Some NAM states, although not wrecking the extension decision, were dissatisfied with the result, which deprived them of their only "bargaining chip." They feared the end of disarmament, since the "Principles" were not legally binding and did not contain a timeframe (Landsberg and Masiza 1996, 25). Hence, they accused South Africa of having betrayed them for economic advantages as a reward for siding with the West (Taylor 2006, 176). Pretoria was also criticized for supporting mainstream Western thinking by opposing NAM proposals for a time-bound framework for eliminating nuclear weapons during the following NPT PrepComs (Rauf 1998, 128).

South Africa found itself in a similar situation during negotiations on the CTBT. Again, the country was reprimanded for leaning too much toward the West because it did not insist sufficiently on the linkage between a CTBT and an explicit undertaking of the NWS to move toward nuclear weapons abolition (Beri 1998).

Despite this criticism, the country worked successfully to build bridges between NWS and NNWS in the ensuing years—that is, at NPT RevCons and in the CD where it promoted, inter alia, a Fissile Material Cut-off Treaty (FMCT) (Shelton 2000, 126). Its leading role in the NAC from 1998 onward involved Pretoria in developing new proposals for the disarmament agenda, having a positive effect on the successful 2000 RevCon (see Ogilvie-White 1999, 324; Simpson 2001).

The mediating role became increasingly difficult when the disarmament process stagnated and the George W. Bush administration rejected in 2005 the disarmament undertakings of the 2000 RevCon. The hope of eliminating inequality faded away: "All non-nuclear-weapon States, including South Africa, believe that maintaining this indefinite discriminatory approach is incompatible with our common objective of a world free of nuclear weapons, and indeed also with the obligations contained in the NPT" (Minty 2007).

South Africa's rejection of policies that would even enlarge the asymmetry in the NPT led it to oppose constraints on national fuel cycle policies, to insist on remaining at liberty to use highly enriched uranium for research purposes, and to defend Iran's right to use nuclear energy (Boureston and Lacey 2007). This brought Pretoria into conflict with American preferences. In fact, South Africa takes a middle position regarding Iran: it refuses an outright condemnation of Iran, but at the same time, it calls on Tehran to comply fully with its undertakings (Pahad 2006).

During the Obama presidency thus far, South Africa has reduced its anti-NWS rhetoric because it hopes for progress in disarmament (see, e.g., Gumbi 2009). During the 2010 RevCon its delegation resumed traditional bridge-building activities and contributed to the adoption of the Action Plan.

Having ratified the CWC in 1995, South Africa has worked since 2009 on solving the dispute about how to handle the time limit for disarmament, because some states were unable to meet the deadline (see, e.g., South Africa 2009b, 2010b, 2011a, 2011b, 2011c). Anxious to ensure the treaty's viability, Pretoria seeks a middle position in the dispute: not meeting the deadline is not to be taken as undermining the integrity and credibility of the convention—the position of some NAM states—or even as a breach of the convention (Iran), but care should be taken lest the convention be undermined by sloppy implementation, and that the possessors of CW take seriously their obligation to disarm expeditiously.

In the BWC regime too, South Africa frequently seeks middle ground positions between the NAM insistence on strengthened technological cooperation and efforts to strengthen the security elements and implementation of the BWC.

Finally, South Africa assumed a bridge-building role in the Ottawa process. After it had unsuccessfully tried to achieve a norm for the elimination of land mines in the CCW (to which it had acceded in 1995), it joined the ranks of "like-minded states," drawing most of its African friends toward supporting the Ottawa process (Grobbelaar 2003, 187).

Justice Concerns: Fighting for a Balance in Treaty Obligations

In all WMD regimes, Pretoria presses for the implementation of disarmament obligations, nonproliferation, and cooperation in the civilian uses of the respective technologies in a balanced manner (see, e.g., Goosen 2004; Mabhongo 2008).

In the NPT, South Africa has been a consistent promoter of politically binding disarmament steps, from the 1995 "Principles and Objectives" through the 2000 "13 Steps for Disarmament" to the 2010 "Action Plan." Pointing to the "legal and moral obligation" (Goosen 2003) of NWS to rid the world of nuclear weapons, South Africa has consistently called for nuclear disarmament and for legally binding negative security assurances (e.g., Minty 2005). Its pro-disarmament involvement in the CWC has already been discussed. Based on past WMD activities, South Africa provided expertise to support practical disarmament steps, such as in Iraq in 2003.

At the same time, South Africa takes nonproliferation seriously. This is why it joined the Zangger Committee, the NSG, and the Missile Technology Control Regime. While not a member of the Australia Group, it adapted its export control lists based on the AG's model and does not call for the group's abolition as many NAM states do. Its comprehensive agreement with the EU contains a "WMD clause" with far-reaching export control and nonproliferation provisions.

South Africa places considerable emphasis on verification: it has concluded an Additional Protocol with the IAEA and calls on others to emulate its example (e.g., Minty 2000, 2005, 2010). South Africa was one of the most active negotiators on a BWC compliance protocol, submitting a series of working papers based on the country's expertise. After negotiations failed, South Africa continued to call for efforts to strengthen verification and compliance in the BWC (e.g., South Africa 2001, 2005, 2006). Pretoria regards CWC verification as the "key element" of the convention and differs from NAM by not insisting on the "hierarchy of risk" and not opposing challenge inspections in general, but with due attention to cost (e.g., Priscilla 2003; Molaba 2005).

When the Bush administration backed new nonproliferation measures but refused to implement agreed disarmament steps (such as the CTBT), South Africa became increasingly frustrated about the perpetuation of the NPT's inherent injustice: "The problems of imbalance and selective emphasis on preferred aspects of the NPT have been exacerbated in the recent past by the sole emphasis that is being placed on non-proliferation" (Goosen 2004). It demanded "to address these issues in a balanced way" (Goosen 2004). Likewise, in the CWC, South Africa insists on "equal emphasis and attention" to disarmament and nonproliferation (Selebi 1995).

The call for a balance led to skepticism about proposals to multilateralize the fuel cycle that were discussed in an IAEA expert group with South African participation in 2004–5. Pretoria points to the "inalienable right" to the peaceful uses of nuclear energy and rejects "unwarranted restrictions" that would enlarge asymmetries of rights and duties in the NPT and undermine its legitimacy: "The imposition of additional restrictive measures on some NPT States Parties while allowing others to have access to these capabilities only serves to exacerbate existing inequalities that are already inherent in the NPT and undermines one of the central bargains that are contained in the Treaty" (Minty 2005).

The emphasis on equality of undertakings and implementation among states parties (e.g., Minty 2007) extends to the BWC and CWC as well (e.g., Priscilla 2003; Molaba 2005; South Africa 2009a, 2010a). Focusing on this balance has taken on more prominence in South African policies, with demands like this now permanent features of South African statements in the NPT context: "The

Treaty must be implemented in all its aspects without favour or prejudice" (Minty 2010).

In the CWC South Africa is calling increasingly for "non-discriminatory implementation of all provisions of the Convention" (South Africa 2011b), and in the BWC South Africa insists that the regime can best be strengthened by equal implementation of all provisions (e.g., South Africa 2010a).

The same balanced approach has been pursued in humanitarian arms control. South Africa completed the destruction of its own antipersonnel mine (APM) arsenal in 1997 and promoted the strict observation of the disarmament deadline in the MBT, which it ratified in 1998 (e.g., South Africa 2003). As a proactivist promoter of the SALW POA, South Africa destroyed excess stocks of arms and assisted neighbors in implementing the norm. South Africa has also committed to the prohibition of cluster munitions, after initial opposition due to their perceived military utility. It signed the CCM in 2008 and submitted a plan for dismantling its own cluster munition stocks in 2011 (ICBL 2004b).

Stopping the spread of conventional weapons is an important South African objective; thus, Pretoria played a prominent role in installing the MBT Implementation Support Unit in 2001, and it works hard to ensure universal membership in the MBT and effective implementation in Africa (e.g., ICBL 2004b). South Africa has an exemplary arms export law that is complemented regionally by the Protocol on the Control of Firearms of the Southern African Development Community (SADC) (Lamb, 2009). Pretoria is convinced that a stronger global norm, an Arms Trade Treaty (ATT), is needed in order to stop the illegal trade in SALW, with the caveat that it must not compromise the right of self-defense (Dye 2009).

At the same time, Pretoria engages in practical cooperation in all humanitarian arms control regimes by helping other states in national implementation, dismantling of weapons, and victim assistance; South Africa's own experience is useful in these activities, which point to another strong motive in Pretoria's policy: humanitarianism.

Mandela's Legacy: Promotion of Humanitarianism

Former president Nelson Mandela promoted "new humanitarianism," which emerged in the 1990s as a norm for protecting civilians in violent conflicts. He led the national NGO network South African Campaign to Ban Landmines (SACBL). In his tradition, South African arms control policy is guided by humanitarian ideas such as saving human life, ending the "indiscriminate devastation upon innocent civilian populations" (Goosen 1998), and responsibility to future generations (e.g., Nzo 1997). After Mandela's retirement, humanitarianism continued to influence Pretoria's arms control policy. Alluding to the new CCM, in 2009 the South African delegate noted at the MBT RevCon: "The international community now has two instruments of international humanitarian law that seek to eliminate the unnecessary suffering caused by these inhumane weapons to innocent civilian populations" (Nel 2009).

Humanitarian objectives extended to improving life quality through economic growth and fighting diseases in developing countries. Cooperation programs for the exchange of knowledge and technology for nuclear, biological, and chemical (NBC) civilian uses (e.g., the IAEA Technical Cooperation Programme or the OPCW Program for Africa) are, from a South African perspective, meant to "adequately address the needs of the under-developed areas of the world" (Minty 2007, see also Mkhize 2007). This call for fulfilling the needs of the poor—that is, justice based on need—has been strengthened recently in connection with the concept of the "African Renaissance." This approach is guiding the South African request for cooperation in victim assistance, demining, and the removal of cluster munitions remnants for which poor states often have no resources (e.g., South Africa 2003, 2011a). The commitment has consistently grown (e.g., the "mine action assistance programme," which supports the reintegration of victims of mines).

However, there are some inconsistencies in realizing humanitarianism due to economic interests. The strict export legislation has not prevented arms transfers to human rights violators such as Sudan or into conflict-ridden countries such as Ruanda or Pakistan (Lamb 2009). Nevertheless, humanitarian motives are still influential, now combined with the attempt to serve the interests of developing countries.

From Pariah to Paragon

After its singular path to nuclear disarmament, South Africa emerged as a norm entrepreneur, partly for security reasons, partly because of development and humanitarian motives related to preferences of President Nelson Mandela.

In accordance with its own history of colonial repression and an unjust regime, South Africa places emphasis on justice. The demand for effective nuclear disarmament and peaceful cooperation and a balanced implementation of duties under the NPT, but also the BWC and CWC, have become increasingly obvious. Unlike other NAM states that give priority to disarmament and cooperation at the cost of nonproliferation, South Africa places equal emphasis on nonproliferation measures.

Its support of humanitarian arms control is based on concern for civilians, victims, and the weak, as well as on the development needs of poor countries, with an emphasis on Africa. While the "balance" policy refers to an understanding of justice as equality and equal rights, the humanitarian justice motive promotes justice based on the needs of the disadvantaged.

Bridge building afforded South Africa a twofold influence in the industrialized and the developing worlds. It played this role occasionally in the NAC or among the like-minded states in the Ottawa process. Its own experience in armament and disarmament supplied expertise that helped in obtaining a distinct disarmament profile. South Africa most often uses the strategy of framing an issue in moral and justice terms to convince other states of its positions.

South Africa is a norm reformer that has been trying to move the regimes in a balanced and just direction and to eliminate inequalities that mirror Western superiority associated with colonial repression. Its principles for regime reform are balanced: it emphasizes nonproliferation as much as disarmament and cooperation; at times this leads to tensions with other NAM actors. Occasional doubtful arms exports, serving the interests of the powerful arms industry, mar its record to a certain degree but do not generally compromise South Africa's reformist norm entrepreneurship.

IRAN: (SELF-APPOINTED) GUARDIAN OF JUSTICE AND EQUITY FOR HUMANKIND

The Islamic Republic of Iran (IRI)—part of what the United States has coined the "axis of evil"—is not known for its efforts to curb the spread of WMD but makes headlines for its supposed support of terrorism, its continued human rights violations, and its alleged striving to achieve a nuclear weapons capability in breach of international norms. Yet a closer look at its normative orientations reveals that at times Iran pursues norm-promoting activities that bear substantial resemblance to those of "good international citizens," although with quite different strategies and means.

Iran is a unique country in many respects—as an ancient culture it has a history full of cultural and scientific achievements, has suffered two centuries of Western imperialism without ever formally losing its sovereignty, is located in a strategic position, and possesses huge reserves of oil: the Shiite theocracy has the status of an important regional power.[6] The defining characteristic for Iran's policy course has been the Islamic Revolution in 1979, which aimed at undoing the historical experience of humiliation and subordination. Since then, Iran has pursued a revisionist foreign policy aiming at "the formation of an Islamic world society" (Firooz-Abadi 2012, 52) by reforming the unjust and illegitimate status quo as perceived by Iran. Iranian political culture is shaped by doctrinaire Shia Islam with its "emphasis on suffering and martyrdom" (Mukhatzhanova 2010, 59) and the revolutionary values of independence, equality, and status.

Despite a fragmented political system, these values remained consensual throughout Iran's postrevolutionary history. A phase of radicalization during the war with Iraq (1980–86) was followed by a pragmatist attempt at reintegration into the world (economic) system and political reforms leading toward liberalization. With Mahmud Ahmadinejad assuming power in 2005, however, Iran embarked on a collision course; the country experienced a conservative rollback and repression of massive public dissent, pressed ahead with its nuclear program, and kept on refusing to play by rules imposed by the United Nations Security Council (UNSC) and the IAEA (Senn 2009, 87–90; Müller 2010).

Like the overall political system, Iran's arms control policies are characterized by "parallel institutions, the bifurcation of the government between elected and appointed officials, the informal networks" (Thaler et al. 2010, 113) and factional controversies. The Supreme Leader is the ultimate (decision-making) authority, combining the position of head of state, commander in chief, and Iran's highest cleric, with control of the Islamic Revolutionary Guard Corps. The latter is entrusted with the operation of and custody over possibly deployed WMD as well as dual-use products. The next level of the decision-making elite is filled by the president and the head of the Expediency Council, while the Ministry of Defense and the Ministry for Foreign Affairs are entrusted with the more technical aspects of arms control policy (Cordesman, Burke, and Seitz 2009, 18).

Iran's credibility regarding its commitment to arms control is severely hampered by the dubious maneuvering regarding its nuclear policy. The story of Iran's nuclear program (e.g., Jones 1998; Chubin 2006; Squassoni 2009; Mukhatzhanova 2010) began in the 1950s under Shah Mohammad Reza Pahlavi, growing more ambitious over the course of the 1970s when suspicion regarding the pursuit of a nuclear weapons option arose for the first time (Cordesman and Rhodan 2006, 166–67). The program was terminated after the revolution, only to be revived in the situation of complete isolation in the war against Iraq and after Iraq's massive CW use. In 2002 an Iranian opposition group revealed the existence of clandestine fuel cycle activities. In May 2003, President Mohammad Khatami offered to enter into negotiations over the nuclear program and to shift Iran's position on the Middle East peace process. Rapprochement with the West, however, was blocked by the Bush administration's rejection of the Iranian offer in the hope of regime change instead (Bertram 2008, 31; Takeyh 2009, 217–19). Ever since Mahmud Ahmadinejad took over the presidency, Iran has maneuvered to push the program forward in defiance of the UNSC and the IAEA.

However, Iranian officials have consistently denied any intention of weaponization and insist on the program's peaceful nature, emphasizing that nuclear weapons are in contravention of (Shia) Islam (e.g., Khoshroo 2003; Alikhani 2012, 11).[7]

Iran's nuclear policy is based on a complex mixture of motives (e.g., Chubin 2006; Mukhatzhanova 2010). Security concerns fueled by perceived threats rooted in its past experience of external interference and vulnerability as well as the hostility with Israel and the United States are complemented by Iran's striving for greater regional and international status. Technological evolution is seen as a means of elevating Iran's prestige and thus a matter of national pride (Ehteshami 2008, 28). International requests to keep Iran's nuclear program in check are framed "as a continuation of unjust (Western) behavior and as a strategy of preventing Iran from legitimate modernization steps," resuming the long history of external oppression and a new form of imperialism to exclude Iran from "the right to be a member of the international 'club' of developed, nuclear nations" (Senn 2009, 96).

Iran claims to have terminated its comprehensive CW program, launched during the Iran-Iraq War in response to Iraqi use of chemical agents, in 1988 (Cordesman and Kleiber 2007, 158). Although Tehran signed the CWC in 1993 (ratification in 1997), committing itself to destroying its CW arsenal by 2012, ambiguities remain about Iran's capabilities. While Iranian officials claimed all stockpiles were destroyed prior to the CWC's entry into force (see, e.g., Khoshroo 2003), the United States accused Iran of having used CW against Iraq in 1988 (in breach of the Geneva Protocol to which Iran is party without reservations) and having retained CW assets (US DoS 2005, 2010). Even though Iran joined the BWC in 1973, the United States suspect it of maintaining clandestine BW capacities as well (US DoS 2005, 2010).

Iran does not support the regimes on APM and cluster ammunition, arguing that both weapon types are needed for frontier protection (e.g., ICBL 2011d). Iran is a member of the SALW PoA, but rejects a legally binding ATT.

Avenger of the Dispossessed

Today's Iranian political culture is mainly based on a political stream of Shia Islam, striving for justice and a discourse of independence that is accompanied by anti-imperialistic or anti-US undertones (Moshirzadeh 2007; Holliday 2011; Ehteshami and Molavi 2012a, 1). The search for justice is rooted in Shia political philosophy; Iran "sees itself as commissioned to expand justice throughout the world and establish a just international order and system" (Firooz-Abadi 2012, 53) by reforming the international system fundamentally in line with the principle of equality and freedom from domination and suppression. Iranians "reflect an extreme sensitivity to any appearance of dependence, dictation, or domination by others as well as a desire to be taken seriously, treated without discrimination, and accorded the status that Iran's importance in the world merits" (Chubin 2006, 19). Iran's quest for international status fits its self-depiction as an "Islamic vanguard state" (Senn 2009, 91), as a role model for all Muslim nations. The struggle between a pure inner core and the corrupt external sphere serves as leitmotif and is epitomized in the demonization of the United States as the "Great Satan" (Beeman 2005). Culturally averse to compromise (on Iranian negotiating culture see Jones 2012, 203), Iran promotes a discourse of resistance, the delegitimization of the "unjust and discriminatory nature of the existing system," and the "formation of an anti-hegemonic coalition" (Firooz-Abadi 2012, 54, 48).

It seeks alliances particularly with fellow NAM countries. The goal of "revolutionary opposition" is to gain independence from external forces and interference, "to force the United States to recognize Iran's right to be treated as an equal member of the international community" (Beeman 2005, 190), and to guarantee equity to the underprivileged developing countries. Its self-perception as "avenger of the dispossessed" serves as a constant theme in and a driving force for Iranian arms control policies, which focus on security assurances, the application of equal rights, reciprocity, and nondiscriminatory procedures.

Assistance and Protection against the Use or Threat of Use of WMD

Iran's emphasis on security assurances might be due to the legacy of the Iran-Iraq War, when Iran fell victim to massive CW use by Iraq, but also arises out of general security considerations. Although Iraq violated the stipulations of the 1925 Geneva Protocol, the reactions of the international community were lukewarm, causing Iran to conclude that international rules could not be relied upon and "that international instruments and guarantees are only useful if you are a friend of the great powers" (Jones 1998, 41). Whereas the immediate reaction was to launch BWC retaliation capabilities, ever since Iran has called for legally binding security assurances within the NPT and places a very strong emphasis on assistance and protection measures in the framework of the BWC and CWC (e.g., Sajjadi 2011).

No CWC meeting passes without a reference to Iran being a victim of CW use and the historical injustice of the international community's inadequate response as is illustrated by the following statement: "The commitment of the Islamic Republic of Iran to the Chemical Weapons Convention goes far beyond a mere legal undertaking. It stems from a very bitter experience in our recent history" (Ziaran 2008). Consequently, Iran takes an active role in the OPCW and places strong emphasis on Art. X of the CWC on measures for assistance and protection against CW (e.g., Alborzi 1998; Khoshroo 2003). A 2003 Iranian proposal to set up an international support network for the victims of CW was adopted by the sixteenth Conference of the States Parties (CSP) in 2011 (CSP 2011).

Having been a victim of CW use also influenced Iran's position within the BWC. Iran repeatedly asked the signatories of the Geneva Protocol to withdraw their reservations (e.g., Soltanieh 2001; Moaiyeri 2006). In this spirit, Iran in 1996 (and again in 2006) proposed adding an explicit ban on BW use to the title and Art. 1 of the BWC (Iran 1996, 2006). Although uncontroversial in substance, the proposal failed because member states feared that an amendment might cause the BWC to disintegrate (Sims 2009, 142–45).

In the NPT, Iran has consistently advocated legally binding and unconditional security assurances. At the 2010 RevCon, Tehran proposed to "establish an Ad-Hoc Committee to work on a draft of a legally binding instrument on the illegality of nuclear weapons and providing unconditional security assurances by the five nuclear-weapon States" (Iran 2010). Security assurances are also insisted upon by Iran as part of the negotiation package regarding Iran's nuclear program.[8]

Equal Access and the Right to Technological Cooperation

Together with most NAM states, Iran emphasizes the balance of obligations in the treaty regimes. However, in line with its insistence on the right to peaceful cooperation, Iran has repeatedly interpreted the BWC as consisting of "three pillars, disarmament, material and technological transfer, and peaceful cooperation" and attaches particular importance to the cooperation norm within the CWC (e.g., Nasseri 1996; Sajjadi 2011, Dehghani 2009).

Iran insists upon its "inalienable right" to the peaceful uses of dual-use technology and regards unhampered technological cooperation as an "important promoter of the country's modernization" (Senn 2009, 93). Consequently, Tehran insists upon its legitimate right as an NPT member state to maintain a self-sufficient nuclear program and mastery of the full fuel cycle without restrictions.

Together with other "NAM hard-liners" (Sims 2009, 67), Iran complains that peaceful cooperation as guaranteed by the treaty regimes "had proved to be a mirage" (Nasseri 1994).[9] The NSG and the Australia Group are criticized for being discriminatory instruments of the West aimed at preventing economic and technological progress of developing countries: "Application of any ad-hoc and arbitrary restrictions to exchange of technology, material and equipment for peaceful purposes between the CWC States Parties runs counter to the spirit and letter of the Convention and is, therefore, unlawful and tries to create a scientific and technological apartheid" (Mottaki 2006b). Thus, Iran demands that supplier groups outside treaty regimes be abolished (see, e.g., Akhondzadeh 2010).[10]

Concerns about unhampered economic development and national sovereignty also cause Iran to reject a legally binding ATT while participating in the PoA (which covers the illicit arms trade only) (see, e.g., Mottaki 2006a).

Toward Reciprocity of Obligations and Nondiscriminatory Procedures

Iran instantiates its self-assumed role as "standard bearer of a just government" (Sadjadpour 2009, 10) particularly in its critique of the unbalanced, discriminatory structures of the treaty regimes and the double standards applied within them. Tehran often expresses a "sense of victimization" and "sentiment of unfair treatment" (Gohari 2012, 209). Justice is invoked not only to justify Iran's current nuclear policy; promoting central and universal justice is also seen as a moral responsibility.

Notions of justice abound in Iranian speeches at the NPT RevCons. Foremost, there is the justice-based critique of the treaty's discriminatory nature, of the "imbalance in the pillars of the NPT" (Jalili 2010) and the systematic usage of "double standards" by the NWS regarding the treatment of states not members to the NPT. Iran has repeatedly accused the United States (and the wider international community) of following a double standard in the interpretation of core NPT norms: "During the last several decades some have tried to redefine the international non-proliferation and disarmament treaties to their own liking. They represent themselves as the voice of the international community and guardians of these norms. Likewise, they perceive themselves above the international law and ignore their own obligations" (Mottaki 2006b).

The reciprocity of mutual obligations is particularly called for regarding the broken disarmament obligation of the NWS. Iran emphasizes the original bargain underlying the treaty and has consistently urged the NWS to honor their commitments, often embarking on shaming and blaming. At the first NPT RevCon in 1975 (thus during the times of the shah), the Iranian delegate complained that "the inability or unwillingness of the superpowers to reduce the deterrents which ensured their preponderance made it difficult for near-nuclear countries to sign the Treaty" (Fartash 1975). In 1998 an Iranian delegate bemoaned that "those who hypocritically preach that others should comply are themselves guilty of serious non-compliance in the context of article I, II, IV and VI of the NPT and the agreements reached at the 2000 NPT Review Conference. That has given rise to the pervasive concern that some nuclear-weapon States have no genuine will to accomplish the disarmament part of the NPT bargain" (Al Habib 1998).

In accord with NAM demands, Iran calls for the total elimination of nuclear weapons and the implementation of agreements reached at the NPT RevCons in 1995 and 2000, particularly the realization of the "Thirteen Steps" for disarmament. In accordance with the NAM position, Iran advocates the idea of a time-bound framework for nuclear disarmament and repeatedly expressed support for a Nuclear Weapons Convention (NWC). It has repeatedly called for an ad hoc committee on nuclear disarmament to be established within the CD (see, e.g., Velayati 1995; Ahmadinejad 2010b). Though often concurring in substance with NAM, there are, however, differences regarding rhetoric and strategies: Iran often assumes the role of a hardliner within the movement, making ample use of destructive strategies and disruptive actions (see also Potter and Mukhatzhanova 2012, 15, 34).

Recently, Iran tried to counter the efforts by President Obama on "Global Zero." Parallel to the Washington Nuclear Security Summit, Iran hosted the Tehran International Conference on Disarmament and Non-Proliferation in April 2010. Though Ahmadinejad's main objective might have been to prevent another round of sanctions (Rajiv 2010), the meeting can also be interpreted as an indicator of Iranian norm entrepreneurship. It not only served "principally as a platform for Iranian attacks on US nuclear policy" (Butters 2010), but it also served to emphasize Iran's efforts to achieve complete nuclear disarmament and to insist on the right to the peaceful use of nuclear energy. Calling itself a "forerunner in the global campaign against nuclear armaments,"[11] Tehran requested that all future nuclear disarmament negotiations be convened by NNWS like Iran. It called for a "comprehensive, non-discriminatory, and legally binding Convention on the total ban on development, production, transfer, stockpiling, use or threat to use such weapons, in order to achieve a world free from nuclear weapons."[12] A follow-up conference was held in June 2011, smaller in scale, but according to participating experts more substantial than the previous one.[13] The discussion focused on the establishment of a NWFZ in the Middle East (Bagheri 2011; Salehi 2011) and the scheduled related conference in 2012. Together with Egypt, Iran was the first country to put forward such a proposal in 1974 (A/RES/3263). This issue is closely intertwined with Iran's insistence on Israel's unconditional adherence to the NPT and the call for the universalization of the treaty regime.

Furthermore, the burden sharing within the NPT is regarded as unjust: strong obligations were placed on the NNWS in order to verify compliance, but no such provisions apply to the "haves," although they have not been living up to their treaty commitments. Feeling deprived of its legitimate right to peaceful uses of dual-use technology, Iran accuses the West of illegitimately favoring non-NPT members such as India or Israel: "While the Zionist regime has stockpiled more than 200 nuclear warheads . . . , it is still under absolute support of the United States and their allies and it receives required assistance for further development of nuclear weapons" (Ahmadinejad 2010b).

Equal treatment also drives Iran's position regarding the target date for the destruction of CW capabilities. Iran called the fact that Russia and the United States will not meet the deadline until the end of 2012 "a clear and serious case of non-compliance" (Ziaran 2008). Tehran's intransigence on that issue caused a stalemate during recent meetings of the CWC (Meier 2009).

Iran's justice-driven policy concerns procedural rules as well. Based on an attitude directed against any form of hegemonic domination, Iran strives to abolish procedural inequalities such as decision-making authority by supplier groups (e.g., Iran 1996) and the overrepresentation of industrialized countries within the UNSC, the CWC Executive Council (e.g., Sajjadi 2009), or the IAEA Board of Governors (e.g., Ahmadinejad 2010a).

Maneuvering between Norm Revolution and Renovation

Iran can be characterized as an actor committed to a strong cause (the right to the peaceful use of nuclear energy and the plea for a nuclear-weapons-free world) based on perceived grievances (imbalances and double standards) within the existing normative framework. Iran—labeled a "rogue state" due to consistent violations of international norms—partly advocates norms typical for ideal type norm entrepreneurs such as Canada or Sweden or embraces the norm-advocating activities of its NAM peers.

Iran's arms control and disarmament priorities have been "consistent and enduring" (Jones 1998, 50): nuclear disarmament, legally binding security guarantees and protection against potential WMD attacks, equal access to technology, equal burden sharing, and nondiscriminatory procedures. Occasionally, Tehran also introduced or supported the establishment of new norms (a NWFZ in the Middle East, a nuclear weapons convention). To a large extent, Iran's activism is due to the long-standing expertise and a well-staffed and skilled bureaucratic and diplomatic apparatus that also accounts for Iran's influential position within the NAM (Ogilvie-White 2012, 261; Potter and Mukhatzhanova 2012, 31).

Iran's approach to arms control is influenced by its perceived role as avenger of the dispossessed, intertwined with the values of independence, equality, and status. Though part of Iran's positioning may follow a strategic rationale and be motivated by reasons of security and a striving for status and regional leadership, some elements of "ideational commitment" (see chapter 1) typically attributed to norm entrepreneurs can be identified. It is most of all the recourse to a "discourse of justice" (Moshirzadeh 2007, 533–35) that can be perceived as an illustration of Tehran's ideational commitment. The thrust of Iran's entrepreneurial activities is the leveling of formal and informal privileges of great powers, nuclear weapon and industrialized states, and the US superpower in particular.

Within the multilateral arms control regimes to which it is party it works closely with, and regards itself as leader of, the NAM, although the presidency of Ahmadinejad has created distrust in leading NAM countries. Iran's position within NAM is not uncontested; frictions abound, such as during the 2010 NPT RevCon, when Iran attempted to overthrow the compromise that finally led to the adoption of the final document, but it was reined in by the NAM leadership (see Johnson 2010; Müller 2010). Iran also aims to win nongovernmental actors over to its cause: for example, by approaching them during RevCons and inviting them to participate at the 2010 and 2011 nuclear summits in Tehran.[14]

Though Iran shares positions on a declaratory level with other nonnuclear weapon and developing states, its rhetoric and strategies differ. Tehran often follows a confrontational strategy and strives to undermine—or alter—regimes that it regards as unjust and partisan. While agitating for adherence to regime norms on the one hand, Iran vows to work toward a reversal of the system with the objective of establishing an alternative order, based on the "right" interpretation of the old one. In order to advocate their positions, Iranian delegates often use disruptive strategies such as repeated interventions or procedural filibuster that may result in delaying deliberations and even risk failure of negotiations.

However, most Iranian norm activities mainly proceed within the established regimes—revolutionary rhetoric notwithstanding. Iran works actively within established arms control regimes, such as the OPCW, occasionally contributing to their evolution. Simultaneously, its resentment of the unfair and discriminatory nature of the regimes leads the country to block progress. Insisting on what Tehran believes to be the original, right interpretation of regime norms often results in fighting against regime evolution.

Departing from a reformist approach through its more radical, uncompromising attitude, Iran appears to be a fundamentalist norm renovator that strives for a return of the current normative order to its supposedly pure and true origins.

NORTH KOREA: OPPOSITIONAL NORMS AND NONCOMPLIANCE AS A TOOL OF NORM ENTREPRENEURSHIP?

Like Iran, the DPRK is often labeled a "rogue state" or "state of concern." Its authoritarian rule, closed society, and suppression of freedom of speech leave no space for open domestic discourse about norms. Usually, statements on norms and justice claims are uttered or at least influenced by the state leadership. Interviews with decision makers are either not possible or may not be authentic or truthful. The leadership of the country tries to establish an aura of mystery and ambivalence about its security policy, in order to increase unpredictability and thereby enhance deterrence. All this makes research on policies, objectives, let alone motives, more difficult than it is with other actors. Decision making on security is in the hands of a small group of people, the party, army, and core intelligence leadership; the leader himself is the ultimate decision maker. Ministries and their bureaucracies are mere decision takers.[15]

North Korea is a very poor country with low regional and global influence.[16] Its economy is not integrated into the global economy and is neither competitive nor capable of supplying goods for the basic needs of the population. This is a consequence of its outdated Stalinist communist regime and its "military first (*son'gun*)" policy that provides the armed forces with the bulk of available resources. North Korea has one of the largest conventional armies in the world as it is confronted by a vastly superior coalition led by the United States. The unbearable costs to modernize the conventional forces are one reason why the DPRK wants to acquire a nuclear deterrent. In addition, the North Korean leadership uses military brinkmanship to press its neighbors and the United States for additional assistance to compensate for the deficiencies of its economic system.

In the early years of the DPRK, then leader Kim Il Sung promoted a national ideology (*Juche*) for the country's development that was proclaimed to represent a particularly enlightened, North Korean version of Marxism-Leninism and focused mainly on economic autarchy, a statist economy, strong military capabilities, and strict, dictatorial hierarchical rule (French 2005). While the system proved a failure, Kim's dynastic successors continued to proclaim the self-image of exceptionality. As a failed economy, under the pressure of a vastly successful South Korean market democracy and confronted with the powerful coalition of South Korea with the United States and, indirectly, Japan, preserving the current regime *and* territorial integrity coincide as the dominant political goals of North Korean leadership. Welfare or at least fulfilling the basic needs of the people takes a back seat. Armament and arms control strategy must be understood in this light.

Two moderately successful tests of nuclear devices in 2006 and 2009 have documented the determination of the leadership to obtain nuclear weapons.

The start of the nuclear weapons program may date back to the 1960s, when Pyongyang acquired its first research reactor from the Soviet Union (H. Park 2006, 38). Reportedly, North Korea also owns a sizable CW arsenal (Bermudez 2001, 226, 230). There is rumor, but no hard evidence, for BW activities (ICG 2009, 10–13). While the DPRK acceded to the NPT in 1985 and withdrew from it in 2003, it became party to the BWC in 1987 and the 1925 Geneva Protocol in 1989, each time together with South Korea. It has not joined the CWC but keeps its later accession open. With regard to the BWC, the DPRK has not participated in confidence-building measures and maintains almost no profile. North Korea neither participates in the regimes on humanitarian arms control nor does it make any statements regarding these issues. Thus, only nuclear arms control is discussed here.

Disarmament and Security: Noncompliance as a Fairness Issue

The DPRK was pressured into the NPT by the Soviet Union in 1985. It delayed the conclusion of the obligatory safeguard agreement with the IAEA, and by doing so stalled on-site inspections, until 1992. When the first inspections found indications of clandestine plutonium diversion activities, North Korea, after a major crisis, negotiated an Agreed Framework with the United States that obliged the DPRK to give up its nuclear weapons program in return for security assurances, help for its civilian nuclear energy program, and energy assistance (Wit, Poneman, and Gallucci 2004, 295–330).

Profound dissatisfaction in the North Korean leadership was fueled by the reported targeting of North Korea in the framework of the 1997 Presidential Directive 60, the delayed implementation of the Agreed Framework, and finally by the confrontational approach of the George W. Bush administration—which placed the DPRK on the "axis of evil" (Senn 2009, 63). This provided enough motivation for the North Koreans to initiate a secret uranium enrichment program in the late 1990s with the help of the Khan network. With the US termination of the Agreed Framework in the fall of 2002 after the DPRK admitted the existence of its uranium enrichment program (Harrison 2005, 99–110; Bolton 2007, 99–117), Pyongyang resumed reprocessing plutonium and began nuclear weaponization. In 2005 it ended the secrecy about its plutonium program and about its ambition to become a nuclear power. After the crisis over the disputed uranium enrichment program in the fall of 2002, North Korea withdrew from the NPT in the winter of 2002–3. In response, China initiated the six-party talks in 2003, the first multilateral approach in East Asia, to defuse the crisis and, if successful, to tackle additional security issues. But relations between Washington and the North Korean leadership never reached a level that would dissuade Pyongyang from its path of noncompliance. Its two tests changed the character of the six-party talks from preventive diplomacy into an institution for promoting nuclear disarmament on the peninsula. After the discontinuation and partial disarmament of the plutonium program in 2007 and 2008, the talks broke down in 2009, followed by the second North Korean test. Serious efforts to get negotiations back on track have had no final success at the time of writing.

The history of North Korean noncompliance with its undertakings under the NPT shows a close relationship between security, reciprocity, disarmament, and noncompliance. This relationship is illustrated by the discussion of the NPT norms. Not surprisingly, the basic objective of North Korea's accession to the NPT was to increase its own security. In 1990 at the fourth NPT RevCon it declared that it had acceded to the NPT "by the intention to avert the danger of nuclear war and promote nuclear disarmament, and in particular, by the pressing need to remove the grave nuclear threat" (DPRK 1990a). The North Korean leadership saw the most important means for this purpose in the disarmament norm of Art. VI. All other norms of the NPT were subordinated. Therefore, just a few months after its accession, it asked for the establishment of a NWFZ on the Korean Peninsula in order to remove US tactical nuclear weapons from South Korea (DPRK 1986, 1987, 1989). In this context, it supported the inclusion of two new norms based on earlier proposals of NAM and the Soviet Union: in 1990 it demanded the prohibition of all nuclear weapons on foreign territory, and in 1991 it asked for the inclusion of nuclear weapons in the new UN Register of Conventional Arms when they were transferred and deployed in foreign countries, a suggestion that was supported by Egypt and other Arab states with regard to Israel's nuclear capability (Tcheul 1990; Kim 1990). Later on, the Intermediate-Range Nuclear Forces (INF) Treaty and the unilateral presidential nuclear initiative (PNI) to withdraw all US nuclear weapons from South Korea in 1991–92 were welcomed by the DPRK as steps in the right direction (Kim 1990). The same held true for South Korean acceptance of the NWFZ on the Korean Peninsula after the announcement of PNI.[17] The withdrawal of US nuclear weapons contributed to the conclusion of the safeguards agreement in 1992 and the Joint (North-South) Declaration on the Denuclearization of the Korean Peninsula.

North Korea labels the NPT "an unequal and discriminatory Treaty that has accepted the legitimate right to the possession and use of nuclear weapons by nuclear weapon states but imposed unreasonable non-proliferation obligations on the non-nuclear weapon states" (Pak 1994).

North Korea bemoans that debates on disarmament are not impartial, objective, or substantive and do not address the real threat. Pyongyang claims that it is necessary "to discuss sincerely and frankly the issues of peace and security and justice and impunity" (Jon 2003). However, from the North Korean perspective, the implementation and application of the NPT is the most inequitable (e.g., Choe 2009). North Korea does not demand the strengthening of the disarmament norm or of negative security assurances because of security interests alone. Of equal importance appears to be its goal of changing the imbalance in this regime in favor of the NNWS. By doing so it intended to reduce the NPT's discriminatory structure: "unconditional and legally binding security assurance for the non-nuclear weapon States is a prerequisite to a balanced and symmetric implementation of the Treaty provisions" (DPRK 1990b). First, the NWS should comply with their commitments, and then the NNWS should follow through with their obligations.

The DPRK tried to strengthen the disarmament norm by supporting other measures and negotiations: it welcomed the CTBT and the planned negotiations on a FMCT, and later it supported the demand for a nuclear weapon convention (see, e.g., DPRK 1995). It demanded a binding timetable for the abolition of nuclear weapons, a favorite NAM demand. After leaving the NPT and starting its own nuclear weapons program, Pyongyang has not questioned the disarmament norm in principle (Korean Central News Agency 2006). It was even President Kim Il Sung's last instruction and ultimate goal to denuclearize the peninsula. However, North Korea added the condition that it will comply with this norm only when the United States and all other NWS end their hostile policies.

This demonstrates the importance North Korea attaches to negative security assurances by the NWS. Together with other NNWS, it demanded a legally binding unconditional security commitment from the NWS not to threaten or attack them with nuclear weapons under any circumstances (a request that, so far, only China's nuclear doctrine fulfills) (see, e.g., So 2011). However, North Korea and other NNWS were never successful in getting such a legally binding commitment from all NWS. This may have contributed to the DPRK's final withdrawal from the NPT in 2003. Pyongyang justified its withdrawal with the argument of a growing nuclear threat by the United States one year after the "axis of evil" speech and soon after the attack on Iraq. Its own breach of the rules has thus been justified by the need to reciprocate against alleged US violations of its duties to the DPRK as a NNWS: violating the nonproliferation norm as an act of fairness! Even as a miniature nuclear power, it believes that security assurances are vital for the security of the NNWS (e.g., So 2011). However, Pyongyang has not offered such assurances now that it has declared itself to be a nuclear weapon state.

Bargaining for Recognition: The United States as "Significant Other"

A part of North Korean policy is clearly caused by security interests, the politics of domestic rule preservation, and the attempt to keep a bargaining chip for assistance by repeatedly making compromises while retaining sufficient elements of the nuclear program (Snyder 1999, 154). At the same time, a strong motivation lies in the North Korean leadership's desire to receive recognition by the United States as a worthy and formally equal interlocutor and a respected partner in a regional order (see also Hayes 2007, 135).

North Korean demands are primarily addressed to the United States. They call for major bilateral concessions, inter alia, a peace treaty between the United States and the DPRK that would establish peaceful relations, independent of the ups and downs in the North-South Korean relationship. Repeated private invitations to prominent US actors betray a desire for a communication channel to the superpower that would help establish an eye-to-eye relationship. Vice versa, the DPRK's hostile reactions to perceived anti-DPRK shifts in US policy indicate a feeling of betrayal and disappointment that may go beyond a purely rational assertion of material interests as is indicated by an analysis of North Korean statements uttered at various arms control forums (see, e.g., Choe 2009; Pak 1994; Ho 2008).

The negotiation tactic that North Korea employs in dealing with the United States—such as upping the ante—might be seen as an instrument for pursuing the same objective. After the United States unilaterally withdrew their tactical nuclear weapons from South Korea, North Korea demanded the renunciation of US nuclear extended deterrence. In this way, the leadership manages to attract continued attention from the desired partner. Ostentatious noncompliance moves may serve the same objective. North Korea's harsh rejection of UN sanctions as unlawful (Choe 2009) means more than a cheap move to defend and maintain its noncompliance activities. These sanctions, imposed on the initiative of the United States, are seen as a particular type of hostile US move. In spite of its withdrawal from the NPT, the DPRK still keeps open the possibility of returning to the regime. However, such a move will be considered only after the "cessation of hostile acts" (Choe 2007) against the DPRK.

Nonproliferation, Peaceful Uses, and Commercial Interests

Pyongyang was not interested in strengthening the nonproliferation norm without any quid pro quo. Rather, it always maintained the inseparability of the most important nuclear disarmament norm and nonproliferation. From its point of view, proliferation is always a consequence of the existence of nuclear weapons. Therefore, it emphasizes vertical over horizontal proliferation. This causal proposition (not part of the NPT norm system) was often used to justify linkages between the fulfillment of the safeguards agreement/verification obligations and the disarmament norm. It is extended by North Korea to the nonproliferation obligation not to contribute to nuclear weapons programs or unsafeguarded nuclear facilities in NNWS. It appears that North Korea assumes it is at liberty to violate Art. III.2 of the NPT, which proscribes nuclear exports and assistance without IAEA safeguards, at least on the exported items unless, in Pyongyang's view, the disarmament obligation of the NWS has been implemented. North Korea's present relationship to the nonproliferation norm is ambivalent. On the one hand, it has defied the international community by transfers of its nuclear know-how and materials to countries like Iran and Syria. On the other hand, it has declared that it "will always sincerely implement its international commitment . . . of nuclear non-proliferation as a responsible nuclear weapons state" (Pollack 2009, 269). Declaration and reality display an obvious gap.

In spite of its civil nuclear program and the often expressed eagerness to expand it, the DPRK has rarely referred to Art. IV of the NPT. Pyongyang insists, however, on cooperation and assistance promised in bilateral and regional agreements. It has strongly criticized delay in the construction of the 2000 MW light water reactors promised in the Agreed Framework and insisted on the right to receive civil nuclear energy in the Joint Statement of September 19, 2005.[18] Furthermore, it refuses every move to use the nonproliferation norm as an instrument for denying the right of access to peaceful nuclear energy (e.g., Choe 2009). North Korea always argues that it is its sovereign right to have a civil peaceful nuclear program and that no other state or institution should constrain it.

On-site verification as in the NPT system or in a future regional arrangement for a NWFZ is highly problematic for North Korea's leadership. Because the structure of the North Korean government is based on authoritarian rule and a closed society, transparency and verification hold the potential to threaten both the stability of its political system and military deterrence. Consequently, the request to apply these standards makes the leadership feel insecure. Therefore, North Korea tries to weaken verification demands and conditions their acceptance on reciprocal concessions. Granting limited transparency is skillfully employed as a means for obtaining such concessions: sometimes the regime invites former US officials and experts to inform the world about the present status of its nuclear program or new developments in order to attract international attention and enhance its threat posture (Hecker 2010). In doing this it signals that additional international assistance is needed if the international community wants to constrain these new threats.

An "Autistic" Approach toward Norms

North Korea criticizes the asymmetric and discriminatory character of the NPT regime and calls for changes in regime practices in order to create a more balanced treaty. On a declaratory level, it supports measures that would enhance nuclear disarmament, such as the CTBT, the FMCT, or a nuclear weapons convention for NWS and NNWS. In the past, North Korea supported establishing new norms (no nuclear weapons on foreign territories, transparency about their transfer) in order to enhance disarmament and a nuclear-weapon-free Korean peninsula. The most original "entrepreneurial" stance is the making of Art. III.2 obligations—not to contribute to NNWS's pursuit of nuclear weapons programs—conditional upon the implementation of Art. VI and security assurances. North Korea has selectively promoted some norms that relate to reducing discrimination through daring disarmament measures, negative security assurances, and reciprocity between disarmament and nonproliferation. This normative agenda corresponds to, and in its last part even transcends, time-honored NAM demands. Its objectives reflect in parallel the antidiscrimination and sovereignty claims of a former colony under pressure by a great power and the unfettered effort of a ruthless autocracy to keep its rule. Embedding them in an agenda for pursuing equality and the right to recognition is not all that different from Iran's posture. Noncompliance is a tool North Korea sees as completely legitimate to pursue its objectives; unlike Iran, it admits its norm-breaching activities. Even after its withdrawal from the NPT and after its announcement that it had become a nuclear power, North Korea did not change this approach in principle and is still arguing along its previous lines, although with greater difficulties. This demonstrates that the leadership has a certain interest in being credible in its reformist approach.

Nevertheless, the status of norm entrepreneurship is doubtful for three reasons. First, while North Korea has picked a set of norm proposals that resonate with long-standing NAM aspirations, most of the time it has pronounced them as national positions without a lasting effort to attract allies and shape coalitions to collectively promote these norms. There was no approach to nongovernmental actors critical of NWS that populate the scene of the nonproliferation regime. North Korea's pronouncements on its preferred norms have assumed a quasi-autistic character.

Second, the DPRK denies discussing its responsibility for the violation of the NWFZ on the Korean Peninsula. Disputes about its own noncompliance were never discussed or, if so, were either labeled as a "US political fabrication" or framed in a way aimed at creating a positive picture of the DPRK (e.g., Ri 2005). The compatibility of North Korea's calls for nuclear disarmament and security assurances with its own nuclear armament and occasional threats against non-nuclear South Korea is never considered or justified. These obvious contradictions within a morally founded position are alien to the concept of norm entrepreneurship that calls for a certain degree of coherence and an aura of credibility.

Third, the majority of North Korea's noncompliance, nuclear armament, military provocations on the peninsula, and demands for reformist norms appear to be addressed to the United States.[19] They try to pass off responsibility for the overall nuclear situation to the United States and intend to force the United States to recognize North Korea as a partner as it is (H. Park 2006, 42). If we assume that this is the pivotal objective of Pyongyang's political moves, then promoting norms is purely instrumental for altering a bilateral relationship. This implies that North Korea would happily drop the proposed norms once Washington conceded the desired recognition—with the concomitant improvements in national and regime security for the North Korean leadership; the disinterest in the Art. IV debate while North Korea was struggling for nuclear assistance at home supports this proposition.

This narrow concern is not what we understand as norm entrepreneurship, which aims at broader goals and would not surrender preferred norms in exchange for political concessions. While North Korea's appearance when it speaks norm language is that of an oppositional reformer, the analysis does not justify ascribing the label *norm entrepreneur* to the actors in Pyongyang.

CONCLUSION: OPPOSITIONAL NORM ENTREPRENEURSHIP BETWEEN REFORM, RENOVATION, AND TACTICAL MANEUVERING

The NAM states analyzed here all embarked on some kind of norm entrepreneurial behavior with regard to arms control norms, ranging from what might be labeled classic norm entrepreneurship to a more oppositional stance aimed at a more or less radical change of the existing normative structure. Most surprisingly in view of it often being labeled a presumed anomic rogue state, even Iran showed a considerable degree of norm entrepreneurship.

The different attitude to established arms control norms is reflected in the countries' stances on the overarching norm conflict concerning the balance of treaty obligations transcending all the arms control fields analyzed, in terms of both the weighting as well as the strategies employed: South Africa advocates a balance of rights and obligations and pays due attention to disarmament, peaceful cooperation, and nonproliferation on a rhetorical *and* practical level by making use of classical norm entrepreneurial tools. In principle, Egypt's arms control policy is motivated by the claim for equal security, leading the country to emphasize a balanced approach. Yet, if it feels betrayed—the tacit approval of Israel's nuclear capacity being a sore spot—Egyptian leaders act as uncompromising bargainers risking nonproliferation in order to gain leverage. Feeling betrayed by the NWS and rejecting Western hegemony, Iran from time to time transcends reformist opposition and adopts a confrontational, even obstructive posture. The right to the peaceful uses of dual-use technology and the disarmament obligation inherent in the treaty regimes are accorded priority over nonproliferation by Tehran. Since its withdrawal from the NPT, North Korea stands outside any arms control regimes (with the exception of the BWC). Like Iran, Pyongyang harshly criticizes the unjust nature of arms control institutions but does not appear as a norm entrepreneur working for their modification—nonproliferation is used as a quid pro quo only if North Korea deems it appropriate.

In line with their common NAM legacy, all states have focused on similar themes, such as the right to the peaceful uses of nuclear and dual-use technology and the requirement of technological cooperation, negative security assurances, and (nuclear) disarmament. Access to technology is regarded as an "inalienable right" and a means of approaching the industrialized world's economic development. While all four countries frame the issue in justice language, Iran also stresses the need for technological modernization as a matter of status and what it regards as an entitlement to a sovereign right in return for having abandoned weapons capacities.

With the exception of South Africa, the countries examined in this chapter stress the priority of nuclear disarmament while regarding nonproliferation as of secondary importance. While North Korean emphasis on the disarmament norm seems to be mostly security driven, Iranian and Egyptian delegates tend to frame the issue as a justice concern: with great vigor they complain that the NWS are required to honor their commitments and that they should refrain from applying a double standard. A reference to Israel's nuclear opacity and the demand to establish a NWFZ or WMDFZ in the Middle East as well as emphasis on universalization accompany these claims.

A major driver for the norms promoted by the NAM countries analyzed appears to be a concern for justice. Alienated by what the developing countries regard as discriminatory, unbalanced structures of oppression regarding agenda setting and decision making, they strongly advocate being treated as equal partners. Having abandoned WMD capacities, they feel entitled to participate in technological cooperation. But as Egypt's linkage policy shows, there is also concern about unequal treatment involving the tacit acceptance of Israel's nuclear capabilities and the application of double standards when it comes to technology transfer.

At the same time, the four countries are driven by security considerations. Being located in dangerous regional contexts and—for Iran and North Korea—being confronted with superior US military power translate into an insistence on security assurances and the effort to establish WMDFZ/NWFZ. This also explains why three of the countries analyzed show reluctance or keep a low profile in humanitarian arms control. Here, national interest prevails over justice and humanitarian considerations. South Africa, despite some doubtful export activities, is the shining exception.

The two norm reformers South Africa and Egypt applied classic norm entrepreneurial tools: they joined forces with like-minded countries and NGOs and framed issues in moral and justice terms to convince other states of their positions. Both Egypt and South Africa made ample use of their NAC and NAM membership to gain support for their positions and took on the role of a bridge builder within the organizations (Egypt) or between the developing NNWS and the industrialized NWS (South Africa). Both states worked toward reaching consensual solutions. They also embarked upon blaming, although less acrimoniously than Iran. That this at times led to role conflicts is also attributable to the controversial Iranian nuclear program, which put severe strain on the coherence of the NAM. Though often concurring in substance, Iran frequently acted as a hardliner within the NAM and pursued destructive strategies and took disruptive action. Its shaming and blaming strategies are primarily directed against the United States and have to be looked at in the light of the mutual demonization referred to above. North Korea also engages in this kind of rhetorical denunciation, albeit not with the aim of promoting norms but foremost to press the United States into recognizing Pyongyang as equal.

Although all four states are united in their dissent from the existing normative structure, they engage in different kinds of oppositional norm entrepreneurship. For South Africa and Egypt, this leads to a policy of reforming the prevalent arms control regimes characterized by consensus seeking, constructive solutions, and bridge-building efforts between the developing and nuclear weapon states. For these two, rhetoric and actual commitment to arms control norms seem to be congruent. The regional focus of Egyptian policy and the stronger impact of national security interests on its policy lead to more selective support for arms control norms and occasionally a more confrontational strategy.

Iran, in contrast, appears to be torn between leading the existing normative order back to what is seen as the original, correct interpretation of norms and an upheaval of existing structures, for which purpose it refuses to play by the rules of the system: it abandons and undermines negotiations with fellow NAM states, risks failure of conferences and negotiations, and chooses confrontational strategies such as procedural filibusters, repetitive interventions, and often confrontational statements. North Korea embarks on such a course as well but omits the coherent and consistent active commitment to norms, ignoring classic norm entrepreneurial tactics. It is far less active in global-multilateral settings than in regional and bilateral ones. North Korean dissent does not translate into active norm entrepreneurship but leads to more tactical maneuvering resulting in an isolationist policy course. Iran seems to be reluctant to completely forsake the diplomatic track—notwithstanding harsh rhetoric and saber rattling, it can be anticipated that Iran will eventually return to the negotiation table and try to change the normative structure from within.

Notes

1. For a historical overview on the NAM see, for instance, Jackson (1983) or Morphet (2004). We considered addressing NAM as an organizational actor in chapter 9 but decided against doing so because of the new study by Potter and Mukhatzhanova (2012).

2. For further information see the official NAM website at www.nam.gov.za.

3. For an overview on policy-making structures within NAM see Potter and Mukhatzhanova (2012, chapter 1).

4. For both types we could have chosen other actors as well. As at some point decisions need to be made, we opted for Egypt, South Africa, and Iran due to their influential role within the movement. North Korea is included due to its rejectionist attitude toward the international (arms control) order. Although recently Brazil has engaged in some interesting norm-promoting activities in the nuclear field, we did not select it for in-depth case analysis due to several reasons. While Brazil actively engages in NAM deliberations, it has only observer status within the movement and thus does not qualify as a designated NAM reformer. We could as well have considered Brazil as a "good international citizen" (see chapter 7) but decided against this because Brazil's proactive arms control record remains basically restricted to the nuclear field, and its NAC-fellows such as Canada or Sweden look back to a much older and broader track record on arms control proactivism.

5. It goes without saying that this hypothesis does not mean an endorsement of any norms the two states might pursue.

6. For the history of Iran see, e.g., Takeyh (2009) and Axworthy (2010).

7. In 2003 Ayatollah Ali Khamenei reportedly issued a fatwa prohibiting the development and use of weapons of mass destruction; see, e.g., Eisenstadt and Khalaji (2011).

8. For a history of proposals on the Iranian nuclear program see www.armscontrol.org/factsheets/Iran_Nuclear_Proposals.

9. For similar statements in the context of the NPT, CWC, and PoA see, e.g., Afra (1990); Akhondzadeh (2010); Mottaki (2006a).

10. For similar argumentation on the NPT/IAEA see, e.g., Kharrazi (2000).

11. See press release by the Iranian Foreign Ministry, "Spokesman Terms Iran 'Forerunner of Campaign against N. Armaments,'" October 4. http://english.farsnews.com/newstext.php?nn=8901161047.

12. Conclusion of Tehran Conference on Disarmament and Non-Proliferation. April 17–18, 2010. http://cms.mfa.gov.ir/cms/cms/Tehranicd/en/ConcusionofDiscussion.

13. Confidential email conversation with a participating scholar, July 20, 2011.

14. Background conversation with several civil society actors and NGO representatives, Vienna, April 2012.

15. For a detailed analysis of foreign and security policy decision making see K. Park (2010).

16. North Korea's GNP is estimated at 40 billion USD in 2009 and ranks 98th, and its per capita income ranks 192nd in the world. See www.cia.gov/library/publications/the-world-factbook/geos/kn.html.

17. Joint Declaration on the Denuclearization of the Korean Peninsula, 1992, www.fas.org/news/dprk/1992/920219-D4129.htm.

18. Joint Statement of the Fourth Round of the Six-Party Talks, Beijing, September 19, 2005, www.acronym.org.uk/docs/0509/doc04.htm.

19. North Korea's provocative policy may also be a result of the increasing dependency from China and thus a signal of disassociation toward its northern neighbor.

References

Abdelaziz, Maged A. Egypt. 1998a. Statement to the UNGA 1st Committee. A/C.1/53/PV.5. New York, October 14.

———. 1998b. Statement to the UNGA 1st Committee. A/C.1/53/PV.11. New York, October 20.

———. 2006. Statement to the UNGA 1st Committee. A/C.1/61/PV.4. New York, October 4.

———. 2008. Statement to the UNGA 1st Committee. A/C.1/63/PV.4. New York, October 8.

———. 2009. Statement to the UNGA. A/64/PV.33. New York, November 2.

Acheson, Ray, and Michael Spies. 2008. "Looking Ahead: Recommendations for the Rest of the 2010 Review Cycle." *Reaching Critical Will, News in Review*, no. 9 (May 12). http://www.reachingcriticalwill.org/disarmament-fora/npt/2008/nir/1964-12-may-2008-final-edition.

Adeniji, Oluyemi. 2002. The Treaty of Pelindaba on the African Nuclear-Weapon-Free Zone, Geneva, UNIDIR (United Nations Institute for Disarmament Research).

Afra, Naimi. Iran. 1990. Statement to the 1990 NPT Revcon. NPT/CONF.IV/SR.8. New York, December 11.

Ahmadinejad, Mahmoud. Iran. 2010a. Speech to the 1st International Conference on Disarmament and Non-Proliferation. Tehran, April 17. www.president.ir/en/print.php?ArtID=21266.

———. 2010b. Statement to the 2010 NPT RevCon. New York, May 03.

Akhondzadeh, Mohammad Mahdi. Iran. 2010. Statement to the 15th Session of the CWC CSP. C-15/NAT.15. The Hague, November 29.

Alborzi, Mohammad. Iran. 1998. Statement to the 3rd Session of the CWC CSP. Geneva, November 20.

Al Habib, Eshagh. 1998. Statement at the 7th Meeting of the UNGA's First Committee. A/C.1/63/PV.7. New York, October 13.

Alikhani, Ali Akbar. 2012. "Iran's Religious Fundaments and Principles in Interaction with the International System." In Ehteshami and Molavi 2012b, 33–42. London: Routledge.

Armstrong, David. 1993. *Revolution and World Order: The Revolutionary State in International Society*. Oxford: Clarendon Press.

ATT (Arms Trade Treaty legal blog). 2010. "Day 4 of the PrepCom." July 15. http://armstradetreaty.blogspot.de/2010/07/day-4-of-prepcom.html.

Axworthy, Michael. 2010. *History of Iran: Empire of the Mind*. New York: Basic Books.

Badawi, Ibrahim. Egypt. 1986. Statement to the UNGA 1st Committee. A/C.1/41/PV.4. New York, October 14.

Bagheri, Ali. Iran. 2011. Deputy Secretary of the Supreme Council of National Security of the Islamic Republic of Iran. www.ipis.ir/pdf/disarmament-conference/dr.bagheri-eng.pdf. Concluding remarks of the Second Tehran International Conference on Disarmament and Nonproliferation.

Bahgat, Gawdat. 2007. "The Proliferation of Weapons of Mass Destruction: Egypt." *Arab Studies Quarterly* 29 (2): 1–15.

Beeman, William O. 2005. *The "Great Satan" vs. the "Mad Mullahs": How the United States and Iran Demonize Each Other*. Chicago: University of Chicago Press.

Beri, Ruchita. 1998. "South Africa's Nuclear Policy." *Strategic Analysis: A Monthly Journal of the IDSA* 22 (77): 975–92.

Bermudez, Joseph S. 2001. *The Armed Forces of North Korea*. New York: Taurus.

Bertram, Christoph. 2008. *Rethinking Iran: From Confrontation to Cooperation*. Western European Union Institute for Security Studies, Chaillot Paper no. 110.

Björkdahl, Annika. 2002. *From Idea to Norm: Promoting Conflict Prevention*. Lund: Lund University Press.

Bolton, John R. 2007. *Surrender Is Not an Option: Defending America at the United Nations and Abroad*. New York: Simon & Schuster.

Boureston, Jack, and Jennifer Lacey. 2007. "Shoring Up a Crucial Bridge: South Africa's Pressing Nuclear Choices." *Arms Control Today* 37 (1). www.armscontrol.org/act/2007_01-02/BourestonLacey.

Boutros-Ghali, Boutros. 1982. "The Foreign Policy of Egypt in the Post-Sadat Era." *Foreign Affairs* 60 (4): 769–88.

Braveboy-Wagner, Jaqueline Anne. 2009. *Institutions of the Global South*. New York: Routledge.

Busch, Nathan, and Daniel H. Joyner, eds. 2009. *Combating Weapons of Mass Destruction: The Future of International Nonproliferation Policy*. Athens: University of Georgia Press.

Butters, Andrew Lee. 2010. "Ahmadinejad's Answer to Obama's Nuclear Summit." *Time World*, April 19. www.time.com/time/printout/0,8816,1982962,00.html.

Caprioli, Mary, and Peter F. Trumbore. 2005. "Rhetoric versus Reality: Rogue States in Interstate Conflict." *Journal of Conflict Resolution* 49 (5): 770–91.

Choe Il Yong. DPRK (Democratic People's Republic of Korea). 2007. Statement to the UNGA 1st Committee. A/C.1/62/PV.23. New York, October 31.

———. 2009. Statement to the UNGA 1st Committee. A/C.1/64/PV.19. New York, October 27.

Chubin, Shahram. 2006. *Iran's Nuclear Ambitions*. Washington: Carnegie Endowment for International Peace.

Cordesman, Anthony H., Arleigh A. Burke, and Adam C. Seitz. 2009. *Iranian Weapons of Mass Destruction: Doctrine, Policy and Command*. Washington: CSIS Press.

Cordesman, Anthony H., and Martin Kleiber. 2007. *Iran's Military Forces and Warfighting Capabilities: The Threat in the Northern Gulf*. Washington: CSIS Press.

Cordesman, Anthony H., and Al Rodhan. 2006. *Iran's Weapons of Mass Destruction: The Real and Potential Threat*. Washington: Center for Strategic and International Studies.

CSP (Conference of State Parties). 2011. "Decision: The Establishment of the International Support Network for Victims of Chemical Weapons and the Establishment of a Voluntary Trust Fund for This Purpose." C-16/DEC.13. December 2.

Dehghani, Gholamhossein. Iran. 2009. Statement to the 14th Session of the CWC CSP. C-14/NAT.9. The Hague, December 01.

Dhanapala, Jayantha. 2005. Multilateral Diplomacy and the NPT: An Insider's Account. With Randy Rydell. Geneva: United Nations, UNIDIR.

———. 2010. "Planning for the 2010 NPT Review Conference: A Practitioner's Overview." *Pugwash Issue Brief* 6 (1): 1–31. www.pugwash.org/publication/pb/NPT Review6-1.pdf.

DPRK. 1986. Statement of the Government of the Democratic People's Republic of Korea. S/18191. New York, June 30.

———. 1987. Statement dated 13 July 1987 by the Ministry of Foreign Affairs of the DPRK. S/18981. New York, July 15.

———. 1989. Statement dated 9 November 1989 by the Ministry of Foreign Affairs of the Democratic People's Republic of Korea. S/20964. New York, November 13.

———. 1990a. Proposal by the DPRK Concerning the Safeguards Agreement and an Agreement to Assure the DPRK against the Use or Threat of Use of Nuclear Weapons. NPT/CONF.IV/33. New York, August 31.

———. 1990b. Suggested Elements to Be Included in the Final Declaration. NPT/CONF.IV/MC.I/WP. New York, August 30.

———. 1995. Extension of the Treaty on the Non-proliferation of Nuclear Weapons. Joint draft. NPT/CONF.1995/L.3. New York, May 5.

du Preez, Jean, and Thomas Maettig. 2010. "From Pariah to Nuclear Poster Boy: How Plausible is a Reversal." In *Forecasting Nuclear Proliferation in the 21st Century*. Vol. II, *A Comparative Perspective*, edited by William C. Potter and Gaukhar Mukhatzhanova, 302–34. Stanford: Stanford University Press.

Dye, Dominique. 2009. *Africa and an Arms Trade Treaty*. ISS Paper no. 191. Pretoria: ISS.

Ehteshami, Anoushiravan. 2008. "Iran's Nuclear Program as an International Concern." *Orient: German Journal for Politics, Economics and Culture of the Middle East* 1: 28–36.

Ehteshami, Anoushiravan, and Reza Molavi, eds. 2012a. Introduction to Ehteshami and Molavi 2012b, 1–2.

———, eds. 2012b. *Iran and the International System*. London: Routledge.

Einhorn, Robert J. 2004. "Egypt: Frustrated but Still on a Non-nuclear Course." In *The Nuclear Tipping Point: Why States Reconsider Their Nuclear Choices*, edited by Kurt M. Campbell, Robert J. Einhorn, and Mitchell B. Reiss, 43–82. Washington: Brookings Institution Press.

Eisenstadt, Michael, and Mehdi Khalaji. 2011. *Nuclear Fatwa: Religion and Politics in Iran's Proliferation Strategy*. Policy Focus no. 115. September 21. Washington: Washington Institute for Near East Policy.

Elaraby, Nabil. Egypt. 1994. Statement to the UNGA 1st Committee. A/C.1/49/PV.14. New York, November 7.

El Shafei, Omran. Egypt. 1980. Statement to the 1980 NPT RevCon. NPT/CONF.II/SR.12. New York, August 19.

Fahmy, Nabil. 2011. "Salvaging the 2012 Conference." *Arms Control Today* 41 (7). www.armscontrol.org/2011_09/Salvaging_the_2012_Conference.

Fartash, Manouchehr. Iran. 1975. Statement to the 1975 NPT RevCon. NPT/CONF/SR.4. Geneva, 7 May.

Feldman, Shai. 1997. *Nuclear Weapons and Arms Control in the Middle East*. Cambridge: MIT Press.

Firooz-Abadi, Dehghani. 2012. "The Islamic Republic of Iran and the Ideal International System." In Ehteshami and Molavi 2012b, 43–58.

French, Paul. 2005. *North Korea: The Paranoid Peninsula: A Modern History*. London: Zed Books.

Geldenhuys, Deon. 2006. "South Africa's Role as International Norm Entrepreneur." In *In Full Flight: South African Foreign Policy after Apartheid*, edited by Walter Carlsnaes and Philip Nel, 93–107. Midrand: Institute for Global Dialogue.

Gohari, Nadir. 2012. "Concluding Thoughts." In Ehteshami and Molavi 2012b, 207–11. London: Routledge.

Goosen, Peter. South Africa. 1998. Statement to the CD. CD/PV.800. Geneva, July 30.

———. 2003. Statement to the PrepCom for the 2005 NPT RevCon. Geneva, May 01.

———. 2004. Statement to the PrepCom for the 2005 NPT RevCon. New York, April 26.

Grobbelaar, Neuma. 2003. "South Africa and Anti-personnel Mines: Setting and International Precedent." *South African Yearbook of International Affairs 2002/03*: 187–96. Johannesburg: South African Institute of International Affairs.

Gumbi, Leslie. South Africa. 2009. Statement to the PrepCom for the 2010 NPT RevCon. New York, May 04.

Harrison, Selig S. 2005. "Did North Korea Cheat?" *Foreign Affairs* 84 (1): 99–110.

Hayes, Peter. 2007. "North Korean Proliferation and the End of US Nuclear Hegemony." In *Nuclear Proliferation and International Security*, edited by Morten Bremer Mæerli and Sverre Lodgaard, 118–36. London: Routledge.

Hecker, Siegfried S. 2010. *A Return Trip to North Korea's Yongbyon Nuclear Complex*. CISAC Report, November 20. http://iis-db.stanford.edu/pubs/23035/HeckerYongbyon.pdf.

Heikal, Mohamed Hassanein. 1978. "Egyptian Foreign Policy." *Foreign Affairs* 56 (4): 714–27.

Henriksen, Thomas H. 2001. "The Rise and Decline of Rogue States." *Journal of International Affairs* 54 (2): 349–71.

Holliday, Shabnam J. 2011. *Defining Iran: Politics of Resistance*. Farnham: Asghate.

Homolar, Alexandra. 2010. "Rebels without a Conscience: The Evolution of the Rogue State Narrative in US Security Policy." *European Journal of International Relations* 17 (1): 1–23.

Ho Sin Son. DPRK. 2008. Statement to the UNGA 1st Committee. A/C.1/63/PV.7. New York, October 13.

ICBL (International Campaign to Ban Landmines). 2004a. *Landmine Monitor 1999*. Country Report: South Africa. www.the-monitor.org/index.php/publications/display?url=lm/2004/south_africa.html.

———. 2004b. "South Africa. Mine Ban Policy." www.the-monitor.org/custom/index.php/region_profiles/print_profile/371.

———. 2011a. "Egypt: Cluster Munition Ban Policy." February 18. www.the-monitor.org/index.php/cp/display/region_profiles/theme/734.

———. 2011b. "Egypt: Mine Ban Policy." October 27. www.the-monitor.org/custom/index.php/region_profiles/print_theme/315.

———. 2011c. "Egypt: Mine Ban Policy." October 31. www.the-monitor.org/index.php/cp/display/region_profiles/theme/947.

———. 2011d. "Iran: Mine Ban Policy." October 21. www.the-monitor.org/custom/index.php/region_profiles/print_profile/289.

———. 2011e. "A Thematic Overview." *Arms Trade Treaty Monitor* 1 (2). www.reachingcriticalwill.org/legal/att/monitor/ATTMonitor1.2.pdf.

ICG (International Crisis Group). 2009. *North Korea's Chemical and Biological Weapon Programs*. Asia Report no. 167. Seoul/Brussels: ICG.

IISS (International Institute for Strategic Studies). 2008. *Nuclear Programmes in the Middle East: In The Shadow of Iran*. London: Hastings.

Iran. 1996. "A Proposal." Working paper. BWC/CONF.IV/COW/WP.2. Geneva, November 28.

———. 2006. "Prohibition of Use of Biological Weapons." Working paper. BWC/CONF.VI/WP.25. Geneva, November 23.

———. 2010. "Working Paper Submitted by the Islamic Republic of Iran on the Issue of Negative Security Assurances." Working paper. NPT/CONF.2010/WP.50. New York, May 03.

Jackson, Richard L. 1983. *The Non-Aligned Movement, the UN, and the Superpowers*. New York: Praeger.

Jalili, Saeed. Iran. 2010. Statement to the International Conference on Nuclear Disarmament and Non-Proliferation, Tehran, April 17. http://cms.mfa.gov.ir/cms/cms/Tehranicd/en/Generaldebate/Specialguest.html. (Available at http://www.voltairenet.org/article165011.html.)

Johnson, Rebecca. 1995. *Indefinite Extension of the Non-Proliferation Treaty: Risks and Reckonings*. Acronym Report no. 7. www.acronym.org.uk/acrorep/acro7.htm.

———. 2005. "Politics and Protection: Why the 2005 NPT Review Conference Failed." *Disarmament Diplomacy*, no. 80 (November 1). www.acronym.org.uk/dd/dd80/80npt.htm.

———. 2010. "Assessing the 2010 NPT Review Conference." *Bulletin of the Atomic Scientists* 66 (4): 1–10.

Jon Yong-Ryong. DPRK. 2003. Statement to the UNGA 1st Committee. A/C.1/58/PV.23. New York, November 06.

Jones, Peter. 1998. "Iran's Threat Perceptions and Arms Control Policies." *Nonproliferation Review* 1998 (Fall): 39–55.

———. 2012. "Learning to Live with a Nuclear Iran." *Nonproliferation Review* 19 (2): 197–217.

Jordaan, Eduard. 2010. "Fall from Grace: South Africa and the Changing International Order." *Politics* 30 (1): 82–90.

Kharrazi, Kamal. Iran. 2000. Statement to the 6th NPT RevCon. NPT/CONF.2000/SR.4. New York, April 25.

Khoshroo, Ali G. Iran. 2003. Statement to the PrepCom for the 2005 RevCon of the State Parties to the NPT. NPT/CONF.2005/PC.II/SR.4. Geneva, April 29.

Kim Chang Guk. DPRK. 1990. Statement to the UNGA 1st Committee. A/C.1/46/PV.20. New York, October 20.

Klare, Michael. 1995. *Rogue States and Nuclear Outlaws: America's Search for a New Foreign Policy*. New York: Hill and Wang.

Korean Central News Agency. 2006. DPRK Foreign Ministry Clarifies Stand on New Measure to Bolster War Deterrent." *Korean News KCNA*, October 3. www.kcna.co.jp/item/2006/200610/news10/04.htm#1.

Lake, Anthony. 1994. "Confronting Backlash States." *Foreign Affairs* 73 (2): 45–55.

Lamb, Guy. 2009. *The Enigma of South Africa's Arms Trade*. Pretoria: ISS.

Landau, Emily B. 2006. *Arms Control in the Middle East: Cooperative Security Dialogue and Regional Constraints*. Brighton: Sussex Academic Press.

Landsberg, Chris, and Zondi Masiza. 1996. "Fission for Compliments? South Africa and the 1995 Extension of Nuclear Nonproliferation." *Policy: Issues and Actors* 9 (3).

Landsberg, Chris, and David Monyae. 2006. "South Africa's Foreign Policy: Carving a Global Niche." *South African Journal of International Affairs* 13 (2): 131–45.

Lewis, Patricia, and William C. Potter. 2011. "The Long Journey Towards a WMD-Free Middle East." *Arms Control Today* 41 (7). www.armscontrol.org/2011_09/The_Long_Journey_Toward_A_WMD-Free_Middle_East.

Li Hyong Chol. DPRK. 1998. Statement to the UNGA 1st Committee. A/C.1/53/PV.7. New York, October 16.

Liberman, Peter. 2001. "The Rise and Fall of the South African Bomb." *International Security* 26 (2): 45–86.

Long, William J., and Suzette R. Grillot. 2000. "Ideas, Beliefs, and Nuclear Policies: The Cases of South Africa and Ukraine." *Nonproliferation Review* 7 (1): 24–40.

Mabhongo, Xolisa. 2008. Statement to the 2nd CWC RevCon. Den Haag, April 8.

Mandela, Nelson. South Africa. 1998. Speech to the UNGA. New York, September 21.

Meier, Oliver. 2009. "States Approve OPCW Budget, Not Report." *Arms Control Today* 39 (1): 28.

Minty, Abdul S. South Africa. 2000. Statement to the 2000 NPT RevCon. NPT/CONF.2000/SR.2. New York, April 24.

———. 2005. Statement to the 2005 NPT RevCon. NPT/CONF.2000/PC.2/II. New York, May 3.

———. 2007. Statement to the PrepCom for the 2010 NPT RevCon. Vienna, May 1.

———. 2010. Statement to the 2010 NPT RevCon. New York, May 5.

Misher, Kimberly. 2009. *Egyptian Nuclear Leadership: Time to Realign?* Carnegie Policy Outlook. Carnegie Endowment for International Peace. http://carnegieendowment.org/files/egypt_nuclear_leadership.pdf.

Mkhize, Hlengiwe B. South Africa. 2007. Statement to the 12th Session of the CWC CSP. The Hague, November 6.

Moaiyeri, Ali Reza. Iran. 2006. Statement to the 6th BWC RevCon. Geneva, January 20.

Molaba, Talent, South Africa. 2005. Statement to the 10th Session of the CWC CSP. The Hague, November 7.

Morphet, Sally. 2004. "Multilateralism and the Non-Aligned Movement: What Is the Global South Doing and Where Is It Going?" *Global Governance* 10: 517–37.

Moshirzadeh, Homeira. 2007. "Discursive Foundations of Iran's Nuclear Policy." *Security Dialogue* 38 (4): 521–43.

Mottaki, Manouchehr. Iran. 2006a. Statement before the UN Conference to Review Progress Made in the Implementation of the PoA. New York, June 28.

———. 2006b. Statement to the 11th Session of the CWC CSP. The Hague, December 6.

Moussa, Amre. Egypt. 1993. Statement to the CD. CD/PV.639. Geneva, January 28.

Mukhatzhanova, Gaukhar. 2010. "Pride and Prejudice: Understanding Iran's Nuclear Program." In *Forecasting Nuclear Proliferation in the 21st Century*, vol. 2: *A Comparative Perspective*, edited by William C. Potter and Gaukhar Mukhatzhanova, 42–75. Stanford: Stanford University Press.

Müller, Harald. 2010. "The 2010 NPT Review Conference: Some Breathing Space Gained, but No Breakthrough." *International Spectator* 45 (3): 5–18.

———. 2011. "A Nuclear Nonproliferation Test: Obama's Nuclear Policy and the 2010 NPT Review Conference." *Nonproliferation Review* 18 (1): 219–36.

Muni, S. D. 1988. "Third World Arms Control: Role of the Non-Aligned Movement." In *Arms Transfer Limitations and Third World Security*, edited by Thomas Ohlson, 198–211. New York: Oxford University Press.

Nasseri, Sirous. Iran. 1994. Statement to the BWC Special Conference. BWC/SPCONF/S.3. Geneva, September 26.

———. 1996. Statement to the 4th RevCon of the BWC. Geneva, November 26.

———. 1997. Statement to the 1st Session of the CWC CSP. The Hague, May 8.

Nel, Andries. South Africa. 2009. Statement at the 2nd MBT RevCon. Cartagena, December 4.

Nincic, Miroslav. 2005. *Renegade Regimes: Confronting Deviant Behavior in World Politics*. New York: Columbia University Press.

Nzo, Alfred. South Africa. 1995. Statement to the 1995 NPT RevCon. NPT/CONF.1995/SR.4. New York, May 19.

———. 1997. Statement to the 1st Session of the CWC. The Hague, May 7. CD/PV.800.

Ogilvie-White, Tanya. 1999. "SA's Non-proliferation and Disarmament: The Importance of the Middle Ground." *South African Yearbook of International Affairs 1999/2000, 321–26*. Johannesburg: South African Institute of International Affairs.

———. 2007. "International Responses to Iranian Nuclear Defiance: The Non-Aligned Movement and the Issue of Non-compliance." *European Journal of International Law* 18 (3): 453–76.

———. 2012. "The Defiant States. North Korea and Iran." In *Slaying the Nuclear Dragon: Disarmament Dynamics in the Twenty-First Century*, edited by Tanya Ogilvie-White and David Santoro, 249–78. Athens: University of Georgia Press.

Pahad, Aziz. 2006. "A Balance of Rights and Obligation." *Umrabulo* 26. www.anc.org.za/show.php?id=2847.

Pak Gil Yon. DPRK. 1994. Statement to the UNGA 1st Committee. A/C.1/49/PV.8, New York, October 21.

Park, Han S. 2006. "The Rationales Behind North Korean Foreign Policy." In *North*

Korea Policy: Japan and the Great Powers, edited by Linus Hagström, and Marie Söderberg, Marie, 38–52. London: Routledge.

Park, Ki Tae. 2010. "Analyzing North Korea's Decision-Making Process on its Nuclear Weapons Programs with the Rational Choice and Cognitive Choice Models." PhD. diss. Pardee RAND Graduate School. Santa Monica. June 2010.

Pollack, Jonathan D. 2009. "North Korea's Nuclear Weapons Program to 2015." In Busch and Joyner 2009, 263–80.

Potter, William, and Gaukhar Mukhatzhanova. 2012. *Nuclear Politics and the Non-Aligned Movement: Principles vs. Pragmatism*. London: Routledge.

Priscilla, Jana, South Africa. 2003. Statement to the 1st Special Session of the CWC. The Hague, April 28.

Purkitt, Helen E., and Stephen F. Burgess. 2005. *South Africa's Weapons of Mass Destruction*. Bloomington: Indiana University Press.

Purkitt, Helen E., Stephen F. Burgess, and Peter Liberman. 2002. "Correspondence: South Africa's Nuclear Decisions." *International Security* 27 (1): 186–94.

Rajiv, Samuel C. 2010. "Iran and the NPT RevCon 2010." IDSA Comment. May 4.

Rauf, Tariq. 1998. "The April 1998 NPT PrepCom." *Nonproliferation Review* 5 (2): 121–31.

Ri Jang Gon. DPRK. 2005. Statement to the UNGA 1st Committee. A/C.1/60/PV.14, New York, October 18.

———. 2007. Statement to the UNGA 1st Committee. A/C.1/62/PV.23, New York, October 31.

Rotberg, Robert I. 2007. "Repressive, Aggressive, and Rogue Nation-States: How Odious, How Dangerous?" In *Worst of the Worst: Dealing with Repressive and Rogue Nations*, edited by Robert I. Rotberg, 1–39. Washington: Brookings Institution Press.

Rublee, Maria Rost. 2009. *Nonproliferation Norms: Why States Choose Nuclear Restraint*. Athens: University of Georgia Press.

Sadjadpour, Karim. 2009. *Reading Khamenei: The World View of Iran's Most Powerful Leader*. Washington: Carnegie Endowment for International Peace. PDF e-book.

Sajjadi, Reza. Iran. 2011. Statement to the 7th BWC RevCon. December 7.

Salehi, Ali Aliakbar. Iran. 2011. Statement to the International Conference on Disarmament and Non-Proliferation. Tehran, April 17. www.ipis.ir/pdf/disarmament-conference/dr.salehi-eng.pdf.

Selebi, Jackie. South Africa. 1995. Statement to the CD. CD/PV.719. Geneva, September 21.

Senn, Martin. 2009. *Wolves in the Woods: The Rogue State Concept from a Constructivist Perspective*. Baden-Baden: Nomos.

Shaker, Mohamed. 1980. *The Nuclear Non-Proliferation Treaty: Origin and Implementation, 1959–1979*. Geneva: Oceana.

Shelton, Garth. 2000. "South Africa and the Nuclear NPT: A New Agenda for Disarmament." In *South African Yearbook of International Affairs* 2000/01, 123–30. Johannesburg: South African Institute of International Affairs.

Shoukry, Sameh. Egypt. 2006. Statement to the 6th BWC RevCon. New York, November 20–December 8.

Simpson, John. 2001. "The 2000 NPT Review Conference." In *SIPRI Yearbook 2001: Armaments, Disarmament and International Security*, 487–502. Oxford: Oxford University Press.

Sims, Nicholas A. 2009. *The Future of Biological Disarmament: Strengthening the Treaty Ban on Weapons*. London: Routledge.

Sin Son Ho. DPRK. 2008. Statement to the UNGA 1st Committee. A/C.1/63/PV.7. New York, October 13.

Snyder, Scott. 1999. *Negotiating on the Edge: North Korean Negotiating Behavior*. Washington: US Institute for Peace.

So Se Pyong. DPRK. 2011. Statement to the UN and Other International Organizations at the Conference on Disarmament. Geneva, March 10. http://www.unog.ch/80256EDD006B8954/%28httpAssets%29/B87ADCBD699F3308C125784F00498236/$file/1215DPRK.pdf.

Solingen, Etel. 2007. *Nuclear Logics: Contrasting Paths in East Asia and the Middle East.* Princeton: Princeton University Press.

Soltanieh, Ali-Asghar. Iran. 2001. Statement to the 5th BWC RevCon. November 19.

South Africa. 1998. "Security Assurances: A South African Perspective." Working paper. NPT/CONF.2000/PC.II/2. Geneva, May 27.

———. 2001. Strengthening Confidence-Building Measures. Working paper. BWC/CONF.V/COW/WP.1. Geneva, November 16.

———. 2003. Statement, MBT 5th MSP. Bangkok, September 16.

———. 2005. "Codes" in the Context of the BWC. Working paper. BWC/MSP/2005/MX/WP.25. Geneva, June 20.

———. 2006. Confidence Building Measures. Working paper. BWC/CONF.VI/WP.21. Geneva, November 20.

———. 2009a. Statement to the BWC MSP. Geneva, December 7.

———. 2009b. Statement to the OPCW Executive Council. EC-58/NAT.9. The Hague, October 13.

———. 2010a. Statement to the BWC MSP. Geneva, December 6.

———. 2010b. Statement to the OPCW Executive Council. EC-60/NAT.4. The Hague, April 20.

———. 2011a. Statement, CCM 2nd MSP. Beirut, September 13–16.

———. 2011b. Statement to the OPCW Executive Council. EC-63/NAT.10. The Hague, January 15.

———. 2011c. Statement to the OPCW Executive Council. EC-61/NAT.7. The Hague, June 29.

Squassoni, Sharon. 2009. "The Iranian Nuclear Program." In Busch and Joyner 2009, 281–301.

Strydom, Hennie. 2007. "The Non-Aligned Movement and the Reform of International Relations." In *Max Planck Yearbook of United Nations Law*, vol. 2, edited by Armin von Bogdandy and Rüdiger Wolfrum, 1–46. Leiden: Martinus Nijhoff.

Takeyh, Ray. 2009. *Guardians of the Revolution: Iran and the World in the Age of the Ayatollahs*. Oxford: Oxford University Press.

Taylor, Ian. 2006. "South Africa and the Nuclear Non-Proliferation Treaty." In *The New Multilateralism in South African Diplomacy*, edited by Donna Lee, 159–204. Basingstoke: Palgrave.

Tcheul Ri. DPRK. 1990. Statement to the 1990 NPT RevCon. NPT/CONF.IV/SR.6. New York, November 30.

Thaler, David E., Alireza Nader, Shahram Chubin, Jerrold D. Green, Charlotte Lynch, and Frederic Wehrey. 2010. *Mullahs, Guards, and Bonyads: An Exploration of Iranian Leadership Dynamics*. Santa Monica: RAND Corporation.

US DoS (Department of State). 2005. *Adherence to and Compliance with Arms Control, Nonproliferation, and Disarmament Agreements and Commitments*. Washington: US Department of State, August. www.state.gov/t/avc/rls/rpt/51977.htm.

———. 2010. *Adherence to and Compliance with Arms Control, Nonproliferation, and Disarmament Agreements and Commitments*. Washington: US Department of State, July. www.state.gov/t/avc/rls/rpt/170924.htm.

van Wyk, J. K. 2004. "South Africa's Post-Apartheid Foreign Policy: A Constructivist Analysis." *Politeia* 23 (3): 103–36.

Velayati, Ali Akbar. 1995. Statement to the 1995 NPT RevCon. NPT/CONF.1995/SR.8. New York, April 21.

Vickers, Brendan. 2002. "Pulpit Morality or Penny-Pinching Diplomacy? The Discursive Debate on Mandela's Foreign Policy." *Politeia* 21 (2): 80–100.

Walsh, James Joseph. 2001. "Bombs Unbuilt: Power, Ideas, and Institutions in International Politics." PhD diss., Massachusetts Institute of Technology. PDF e-book.

——— (Jim). 2010. "Will Egypt Seek Nuclear Weapons? An Assessment of Motivations, Constraints, Consequences, and Policy Options." In *Forecasting Nuclear Proliferation in the 21st Century*, vol. 2: *A Comparative Perspective*, edited by William C. Potter and Gaukhar Mukhatzhanova, 13–41. Stanford: Stanford University Press.

Wit, Joel S., Daniel B. Poneman, and Robert L. Gallucci. 2004. *Going Critical: The First North Korean Nuclear Crisis*. Washington: Brookings Institution Press.

Zahran, Mohamed Mounir. Egypt. 1995. Statement to the CD. CD/PV.707. Geneva, June 8.

Ziaran, Bozorghmehr. Iran. 2008. Statement to the 2nd CWC RevCon. April 7–18.

CHAPTER NINE

Beyond the State

Nongovernmental Organizations, the European Union, and the United Nations

Harald Müller, Alexis Below, and Simone Wisotzki

NO STUDY OF NORM ENTREPRENEURS would be complete without considering the role of nonstate actors who have acquired a reputation as serious players in International Relations (Keck and Sikkink 1998; Björkdahl 2002, 45–51). The growth of transnational civil society, as well as international institutions above the state level, and its international impact has been one of the characteristics of the era of globalization. The term denotes, for our field, international governmental organizations (IGOs) and nongovernmental organizations (NGOs) (Simmons and Martin 2001). Whereas the influence of NGOs and individuals for the evolution of norms has been acknowledged for a wide range of fields, the role of IGOs so far remains underexposed. This chapter pays due attention to the norm entrepreneurial activities of both types of nonstate actors.

While the security sector is definitely the hardest to penetrate for civilian actors lacking state power and the sources of state legitimacy, NGOs have still emerged as influential actors in arms control. Especially at times of stagnation or of suddenly emerging opportunities, they have jumped in and pushed reluctant governments to tackle issues of over-armament or of atrocious types of weapons.

More than a hundred years ago the first NGOs campaigned for disarmament. After World War II, their activities became more focused on *nuclear* disarmament. The global peace movement protested in cycles against the nuclear arms race. Experts established the Pugwash movement in the mid-1950s, and other networks of scientists such as the Federation of Atomic Scientists searched for ways out of the nuclear stalemate (Rotblat 1982, 1995; Knopf 2012, 191). With the end of the Cold War, the issue of a nuclear-weapon-free world gained new prominence (Fisher 1999). At the same time, movements and the commitment to humanitarian, conventional arms control gained unprecedented momentum. In this chapter, we focus on both nuclear arms control and humanitarian arms control because these areas are where the strengths and limits of NGOs are most evident.

IGOs are also credited with growing importance as globalization forces nation-states to pursue national objectives by international cooperation. However, IGOs can do only what member states permit. The assumption that they have the ability to draft an independent agenda is, however, the prerequisite for conceptualizing IGOs as norm entrepreneurs: they must be capable of devising a normative vision and acting strategically over time to turn this vision into reality.

In the second section, we assess the role of NGOs—the archetype norm entrepreneurship—on norm evolution within the fields of WMD and humanitarian arms control. In the third section, we scrutinize the record of norm entrepreneurship of two quite different international entities, the EU and the United Nations.

NONGOVERNMENTAL ORGANIZATIONS AS NORM ENTREPRENEURS

According to Jeffrey Knopf, NGOs are usually defined by what they are not, governments or international organizations. Some definitions stress that NGOs work beyond pure self-interest and that they are motivated by shared moral convictions. Others point to the nonviolent character of NGOs in order to distinguish them from other nonstate actors such as guerilla movements. This chapter follows the definition by Knopf, who includes interest groups and social movements but explicitly excludes profit-seeking business associations (Knopf 2012, 171–75).

The relevance of NGOs in arms control has increased in the last two decades due to a shift of concern away from traditional national security to human security (Atwood 2002, 6). With the International Campaign to Ban Landmines (ICBL), the first transnational action network (TAN) successfully lobbied for a ban on an entire weapon category (Carpenter 2011). The ICBL managed to speak with one voice and served as a model for other TANs such as the Cluster

Munitions Coalition (CMC). In humanitarian arms control, NGOs and their transnational action networks have become successful norm entrepreneurs in the different stages of norm dynamics. Regarding WMD, their role has been far more limited.

Jeffrey Knopf (2012) distinguishes four types of NGOs according to their orientation (elite/grassroots) and policy focus (consulting/neutrality): advocacy groups, think tanks, social movements, and education groups. Beyond these characteristics, NGOs differ regarding their form of organization, membership, and aims. Expert NGOs, such as the Acronym Consortium, the Programme for Promoting Nuclear Non-Proliferation (PPNN), the Monterey Institute of International Studies (MIIS), or the Verification Research, Training and Information Centre (VERTIC), aim at providing information to diplomats and contributing knowledge to arms control negotiations. Other NGOs, such as Greenpeace or the British Campaign for Nuclear Disarmament (CND), focus on mobilizing and campaigning for the abolition of nuclear weapons. While Greenpeace is hierarchically organized, CND was established through strong democratic procedures, including its broad-based membership (Johnson 2000, 52). Thus, there is considerable variety in the structures of NGOs that strive toward the same objectives.

Humanitarian arms control campaigns developed professional skills for organizing themselves as transnational action networks. The International Campaign to Ban Landmines (ICBL) was founded in 1992 as a coalition of NGOs with a common goal: as humanitarian aid organizations, they were interested in curbing the effects of the unlimited and indiscriminate use of antipersonnel mines in intrastate conflicts and in taking preventive action against the misuse of mines.[1] In 1996—at the peak of the campaign—the ICBL had more than six hundred members from forty countries with diverse backgrounds (Price 1998, 620). The International Action Network on Small Arms (IANSA) also began in 1999 as a group composed of a few NGOs and grew rapidly over the years. Some of IANSA's members had already participated in the MBT campaign, where they had gained some knowledge and experience in lobbying for arms control. The CMC is the most recent transnational network. Launched in 2003 and consisting of three hundred members from more than eighty states, it was set up by founding members of the ICBL: Human Rights Watch and the ICBL itself. Such "hub organizations" seem to be a key to success in vetting advocacy agendas and gaining influence on norm generation processes (Carpenter 2011).

This chapter highlights the diversity of norm-promoting activities ranging from agenda setting to implementing normative provisions.

Issue Framing and Agenda Setting: Two Success Stories

Strategies of framing an issue and seeking change in discursive practices are among the most prominent strategies of norm entrepreneurs when they identify a problem in need of a solution (Benford and Snow 2000; Payne 2001; Björkdahl 2002). NGOs have a threefold advantage when it comes to framing and setting agendas. First, NGOs might be professional and self-interested organizations (Martens 2005), but they usually follow a moral agenda of which their membership and their leaders are deeply convinced. They are bound neither by the straitjacket of supposed "national interests" nor by the narrow protocols of diplomatic practice. That appeals to the general public and helps to build bridges over national boundaries. Second, and for the same reason, NGOs can "think outside the box," leaving the trodden paths, and can seize new issues. Third, they are capable of mass communication through scandalizing actions (Greenpeace), through mobilizing membership and followers, and, in more recent times, through skillful use of the Internet.

Examples of successful framing strategies include the NGO engagement for nuclear arms control, dating back to the nuclear test ban initiative of the 1950s. Following the "Bravo" test at the Bikini atoll and the later fifty-metric-ton test by the Soviet Union over Novaja Semlja, a global mass movement consisting of grassroots organizations and peace activists supported by organizations such as Pugwash emerged in support of banning nuclear testing. The focus was less on classical arms control and disarmament than on the threat posed to health and the environment by these surface tests. The NGOs and peace activists succeeded in getting the item onto the agenda of the two superpowers, prompting them to enact a test moratorium and to resume negotiations on a test ban that resulted in the 1963 Limited Test Ban Treaty (LTBT) (Wittner 1998; Knopf 2012, 177).

The activities of NGO groups did not stop once the issue had been successfully framed. As the global antinuclear mass movement waned, NGOs such as Greenpeace continued to push for a complete test ban by attracting public attention. The violent sabotage of the Greenpeace ship *Rainbow Warrior* in Auckland harbor by French intelligence agents gained tragic prominence in 1985 when Greenpeace protested against French nuclear testing on Muroroa. Moreover, Greenpeace unsuccessfully lobbied for a Comprehensive Nuclear-Test-Ban Treaty (CTBT) at the third and fourth Nuclear Non-Proliferation Treaty (NPT) RevCon. At the beginning of the 1990s, Greenpeace changed its campaigning strategy: it abstained from targeting nuclear weapons and instead relied on environmental arguments tied to growing public concern. This changed the discursive practice and resulted in a French moratorium on testing. When France resumed testing in 1996, the global public outcry forced it to limit the test series and furthered the aim of a zero-yield CTBT (Johnson 2000, 60–67; 2009).

The test ban issue also illustrates another NGO strategy: led by Parliamentarians for Global Action (PGA) in the mid-1980s, various NGOs successfully approached the non-aligned countries by making use of PGA's contacts to governments. Mexican insistence on endorsing a CTBT (supported by the omnipresent PGA representative in Geneva), however, failed due to US and UK objections. The PGA nevertheless succeeded in persuading the Non-Aligned Movement (NAM) to call for an amendment conference to the LTBT, which could have—theoretically—turned that treaty into a CTBT. Predictably, the effort failed, but the issue was back on the agenda, leading in an astonishingly brief time first to a moratorium on testing and then to negotiations on a comprehensive ban (Schrag 1992).

During the Reagan years, the combined power of the US freeze campaign and the European peace protest mass movement forced a reluctant US administration to return to the negotiating table (Knopf 2012, 178). The Intermediate-Range Nuclear Forces (INF) Treaty, the result of these negotiations, heeded the European movement's demand for the removal of all intermediate nuclear arms and opened the "golden" five years culminating in the Chemical Weapons Convention (CWC) and Strategic Arms Reduction Treaty (START) II during which arms control propelled the process leading to the end of the Cold War and was in turn pushed forward by the political progress that this process enabled (Risse-Kappen 1988).

NGOs also participated in the global debate about the future of nuclear weapons. Nongovernmental initiatives, such as the World Court Project or the 1995 Canberra Commission, helped to frame global discourse toward more interest in "global zero" after the end of the Cold War.[2] The World Court Project persuaded UNGA to pass a resolution in December 1994 to ask the International Court of Justice (ICJ) for an advisory opinion on the legality of nuclear use. While the ICJ's decision in July 1996 presented a careful compromise, it stressed the obligation of the NWS to carry out nuclear disarmament. NGOs relied on this document to make their point at the NPT extension conference (Fisher 1999, 41).

With the end of the Cold War, the NGO community did not manage to speak with a single voice, but the expert NGOs in particular, based in the

United States and in Europe, proposed multiple ideas on how to achieve a nuclear-weapons-free world (Fisher 1999, 36). The community of nuclear experts was composed of policy research institutions, senior retired military commanders, and former civilian defense officials who worked on strategies of nuclear arms control and disarmament. They were challenged by the "abolitionists" who lobbied for uncompromising disarmament efforts (Atwood 2002, 8). The 1995 NPT Review and Extension Conference served as a window of opportunity to allow the diverse NGOs to coalesce around the aim of nuclear disarmament: the social action network Abolition 2000 became active in advocating this goal (Abolition 2000 2012). While NGOs relied on arguments stressing the immorality of nuclear weapons, they differed in their convictions about how to reach "global zero." At the 1995 RevCon, expert NGOs supported Western states' pursuit of indefinite extension because they feared that the threat of future proliferation was too menacing to allow the NPT to expire (Knopf 2012, 173). Grassroots activists, in contrast, were afraid to lose the decisive tool for holding the NWS accountable for the pursuit of disarmament; this position corresponded to the attitude of key NAM governments.

In 1997, a group of NGOs published a model Nuclear Weapons Convention (NWC).[3] A decade later, the newly established International Campaign to Abolish Nuclear Weapons (ICAN) worked on the revision of this model. They gained the support of Costa Rica and Malaysia, which submitted together the document to the UN as a basis for further discussion (Hawkins 2010, 40). After the NAM had tried, in vain, to place the item in the final declaration of the 2000 and 2005 NPT RevCons, their alliance with NGOs helped to persuade UN secretary-general Ban Ki-moon to make the convention part of his five-point plan for nuclear disarmament in 2008. This commitment, in turn, enabled like-minded states at the 2010 NPT RevCon to insert a reference to this proposal, without endorsement, into the "action plan," the consensus part of the final document (Müller 2010b).

Despite serious setbacks, the loose global NGO network renewed its efforts to lobby for "global zero." In December 2008, a group of more than a hundred prominent personalities launched a new organization called Global Zero (Knopf 2012, 182). NGOs in the field of nuclear arms control generally sought to establish close links with like-minded governments or the UN. In 2009, the UN Department of Public Information organized an NGO meeting, "For Peace and Development: Disarm now!" where 1,200 NGOs gathered in Mexico to discuss future strategies for NGO activities concerning nuclear disarmament.

When measured in terms of successful norm entrepreneurship, the ICBL and the CMC have been the most influential networks in terms of framing and agenda setting. Both campaigns challenged the discourse on the military utility of the weapons category by introducing new arguments connected to existing belief systems.

The idea of a ban on landmines was developed as early as 1975 by the International Committee of the Red Cross (ICRC), but it was countered by governments pointing to the defensive use of these weapons (ICRC 1975). With the end of the Cold War, the conditions under which NGOs lobbied for a ban improved. The ICBL and the ICRC relied strongly on arguments about the humanitarian tragedy caused by landmines. Contrary to the ICRC, the ICBL had to prove its trustworthiness by providing reliable information. With NGOs such as the Vietnam Veterans, Medico International, and Human Rights Watch, victims of landmine violence and humanitarian aid organizations provided first-hand information on a global humanitarian crisis. Their arguments were based on existing ethical standards such as the proportionality of war within the framework of international humanitarian law, and described the indiscriminate effects and the socioeconomic consequences of the misuse of the weapons and the suffering of the civilian population (HRW 1993). Framing the issue as a matter of (in)justice helped to gain public attention worldwide. The agenda setting was successful, because the NGO campaign managed to "graft" the new ban norm onto prior sets of norms, such as the earlier bans on chemical and biological weapons, as well as on existing norms of international humanitarian law (Price 1998). The ensuing public resonance induced governments to support the cause and led others to change positions later on. This process led to stigmatization of the weapons and became the starting point for the norm-building process (Borrie et al. 2009, 20).

IANSA members argued that the use of small arms in wars and postwar situations violated human rights and individual security and undermined developmental goals. Still, their framing efforts were inhibited by the fact that small arms and light weapons (SALW) could not be banned, as states perceived them as legitimate weapons for police and military forces. The legitimacy of their framing efforts was additionally contested by the "firearms community," led by the influential American National Rifle Association (NRA), which opposed any global civilian gun control (Atwood 2002, 8).[4] IANSA drew on injustice frames, such as the human rights abuses and the human suffering caused by illicit proliferation of SALW (Small Arms Survey 2002, 155; IANSA 2001). They publicly denounced the responsibility of those parties—mostly Western democracies—who produced weapons and exported them to the Third World. IANSA reminded states of their responsibilities for people's security by providing facts and figures, but also by giving the issue a "human face." The network presented eyewitnesses from zones of conflict, such as physicians from Uganda, who vividly described the humanitarian catastrophe to the diplomats. The aim of the NGOs was to ensure an emotional impact on the diplomats involved in the negotiations (Price 1998, 622).

As these success stories illustrate, effective issue framing and agenda setting hinge on persuading and mobilizing public opinion. Framing the issues in moral terms, particularly concerning the injustice of the indiscriminate use of weapons against civilians, provided an important means for mobilizing public opinion in the home countries of the NGOs and for reaching out to governments. Effective lobbying and media campaigns helped to raise public attention and put governments under effective pressure to adhere to the ban (Atwood 2002, 11).

Accessing Negotiations and Influencing Outcomes

"NGOs have long played a vital galvanizing role in this area, mobilizing public opinion and motivating political leaders to act with determination to promote disarmament": with this statement, UN secretary-general Kofi Annan sought to encourage the Advisory Board on Disarmament Matters in 2003 to explore ways of involving civil society in advancing disarmament issues (Annan 2003). Following this advice, the board changed the traditional session with representatives of the NGO community in New York and Geneva from a ritual of courtesy to a serious input into its own work, asking for statements on the specific items that were on its agenda at the time.[5] While recent years clearly witnessed increased NGO involvement in arms control processes at the UN level, their influence on norm-building efforts differs according to the various issue areas.

Compared with other policy fields, such as human rights or the environment, multilateral arms control clearly lags behind when it comes to NGO participation in relevant institutions, such as the UN or the CD (Carroll 2002, 15).

The ICBL was very successful in forming a strategic partnership with the mounting coalition of like-minded states. For both sides, this form of "new diplomacy" was advantageous: while the ICBL gained direct access to the negotiation process of the MBT, the like-minded states sought democratic legitimacy for their action through NGO participation (Cooper 2002; Rutherford, Brem, and Matthew 2003). The Canadian minister of foreign affairs, Lloyd Axworthy, summarized the role of the transnational social network as follows: "Clearly, one can no longer relegate NGOs to simple advisory or advocacy roles in this process. They are now part of the way decisions have to be made. They have been the voice saying that governments belong to the people, and must respond to the people's hopes, demands and ideals" (Axworthy 1997, 67). NGOs were granted access to the general debates as well as to the subcommittees that sought compromises on the more contested norms. The ICBL also contested US attempts to weaken the treaty by seeking exemptions. With their campaign of "no exceptions, no reservations, no loopholes," they relied on strategies of public naming and shaming to counter the US attempts during the final negotiations in Oslo (ICBL 1997, 1).

Whereas the global campaign was mostly based on actions with a strong public relations effect—particularly at the national level—the members of the steering committee also became negotiation experts and put forward their own proposals and draft treaties in the course of the negotiations. The NGOs tried to place the focus of the negotiations on questions of fair distribution and, in particular, on the special needs of the landmine-infested states and their civilian populations. In the case of the Ottawa Convention, they succeeded in convincing the states to commit themselves to including the funding of victim rehabilitation programs as a norm in the convention. With the support of Norway, the ICBL and the ICRC successfully lobbied for the inclusion of Art. 6 on international assistance and victim rehabilitation. IANSA drafted, inter alia, its own version of the Action Programme on Small Arms, expressing the ideas of the transnational network. IANSA members organized regular meetings of experts with diplomatic representatives, for example, in Geneva, in order to reach an agreement on the range of the Action Programme on Small Arms. With the diplomatic backing of the United States, the World Forum of Sports and Shooting Societies effectively prevented any norms on restricting civilian gun ownership when the UN Programme of Action on Small Arms and Light Weapons (PoA) was negotiated in 2001 and also at the successive review conference in 2006 (Batchelor 2002, 38). Nevertheless, NGO access to PoA conferences has improved since 2001. In general, NGOs attend all plenary states meetings. IANSA has become a credible knowledge broker recognized by UN member states. While negotiations are often held in informal consultations between states, IANSA members have established close links with like-minded governments that provide them with relevant information.

NGO access to WMD arms control negotiations has been subject to more restrictions. Access is reasonably granted as long as negotiations are conducted in the CD. NGOs are well represented in Geneva and have good contacts with delegates. Numerous seminars organized by NGOs, by delegations, or by the UN Institute for Disarmament Research (UNIDIR) offer opportunities to convey ideas during preparation or in the course of negotiations. Once negotiations are completed, or when the CD is idle, as for more than a decade now, these communication channels close or are of little use.

Access constraints existed in the NPT, as they did in CWC and BWC negotiations. NGOs have been allowed to attend NPT RevCons as observers since 1975, but since the 1997 PrepCom one plenary session has been set aside for NGO presentations (Knopf 2012, 187). According to rule 43 of the NPT RevCon's Rules of Procedure, plenary meetings or meetings of the main committees must be held in public. NGOs are free to offer seminars and briefings during the conferences at UN premises and make frequent use of this possibility. Rule 42 further specifies that meetings of other organs of the conference must be held in private. Most sessions are held in cluster working groups and are therefore closed to NGOs. Crucial deliberations on contested issues frequently take place outside the formal structure of the conference—for example, in the missions of state delegations to which NGOs do not have access. Some states have circumvented such restrictions by including expert NGO representatives in their national delegations (Regehr 2003, 10).

At the 1995 NPT Review and Extension Conference, NGOs prodded the NWS to intensify nuclear disarmament. In all, sixty-five NGOs at the UN had drafted the Abolition Statement calling for a treaty to eliminate nuclear weapons by the year 2000. At the end of the 1995 Conference, six hundred NGOs worldwide had signed the "Abolition 2000" petition, but in the meantime over two thousand organizations have joined the call for abolition and are promoting the nuclear weapons convention (Ware 2007, 8; Abolition 2000 2012). Among supporters of indefinite extension, PPNN was an influential player helping to craft a compromise; the idea—which was ultimately successful—of having an enhanced review process with a standard for measuring progress and implementation was formed in a discussion involving a handful of people on the fringe of a PPNN briefing seminar for future members of delegations to the coming conference. In addition, PPNN members worked in various delegations of all the groups represented in the 1995 conference; one of the directors was in the Secretariat, and a long-standing member happened to be the president of the conference (Dhanapala 2005). Particularly in the case of the long-standing WMD regimes, expert NGOs have become a kind of institutional memory for new delegates (Knopf 2012, 184).

In the case of the BWC, the NGO community is small and highly specialized (Dando 2010). Because there is "little of the traditional, grass roots NGO advocacy, ever since 1995 a dedicated group of expert NGOs has accompanied the Ad Hoc Group's deliberations (AHG) on a verification protocol (Rissanen 2002, 33; see also Feakes 2003). For more than six years experts from the University of Bradford and the Federation of American Scientists have actively participated in deliberations on the protocol through analyses of various aspects of the emerging document. Access to the negotiations was limited to plenary meetings, which in practice implied that NGOs could only listen to the opening and closing remarks while in-depth negotiations went on behind closed doors (Rissanen 2002, 34).[6]

Assisting Implementation

NGOs and their networks have pursued significant activities in implementing norms and have thus occasionally taken over the state's function in zones of limited governance. This applies particularly to humanitarian arms control, where NGOs such as the Mine Advisory Group clear landmine-infested territories, or NGOs such as Safer Rwanda regularly organize community awareness and weapon collection programs in order to create safer neighborhoods (Safer Rwanda 2011). In the case of SALW, regional and subregional approaches to combating the illicit trafficking of these weapons have proven highly important for adjusting to the region-specific causes and problems of seemingly unlimited proliferation of SALW. NGOs in the regions of Africa, Latin America, Asia, and the Caribbean help implement the UN PoA by taking practical measures such as raising public awareness and education (Batchelor 2002, 37).

The ICBL has also become a crucial agent for ensuring compliance to the MBT. When negotiating the treaty, states explicitly avoided a rigid verification scheme and instead opted for regular state meetings and state reports on progress in implementation. This soft mechanism of compliance is complemented by the annual Landmine Monitor published by the ICBL, which provides information from civil society to the member states. The Landmine Monitor offers a comprehensive picture of the stages of progress in implementing the MBT and sometimes also serves as an additional source of information for putting states' reports in perspective (Carroll 2002, 22). In the case of the UN PoA, the Geneva-based think tank Small Arms Survey, British-based NGOs such as Saferworld, and the IANSA regularly assess progress in the implementation of the program in their publications (IANSA 2005; Parker 2011). WMD arms control, by contrast, has not yet become a field conducive to NGO implementation activities. The BWC intersessional process, however, opens up more and more opportunities for such activity.

Agenda Setters, Global Conscience, and Negotiation Partner

NGO engagement in arms control and disarmament has been vast, intense, and at least partly successful. In particular, transnational action networks on humanitarian arms control have become crucial agents in mobilizing the global public, raising concern about the human tragedy caused by the indiscriminate use of weapons, and gaining access to relevant negotiations. The broad-based nature of their constituencies has added to their success because the ICBL, IANSA, and also the CMC can rely on a broad membership from the North and the South combining scientific expertise with grassroots campaigning skills. Despite their heterogeneous membership, the TANs rely on centralized organization and have become increasingly professional over the years. The ICBL presented the diplomatic community with a nearly solid front for an MBT (Atwood 2002, 8). In contrast, NGOs working on WMD are less centrally organized and often disagree about strategy, as the example of Global Zero indicates. Nevertheless, NGOs and global peace movements have occasionally been influential in pressuring states to take normative action on nuclear arms control and nuclear testing in particular.

The strategies NGOs pursue in order to influence the normative order and shape advocacy agendas are as diverse as the heterogeneity of their membership. Framing efforts have been an important tool of NGOs for changing discursive practice in order to attract public and state attention. In humanitarian arms control, TANs have frequently made use of injustice frames, such as pointing to human suffering and human rights abuses and relying on other need-based arguments. In the case of antipersonnel mines and cluster munitions, especially, NGOs had to counter arguments about the military utility of these weapons by demonstrating the humanitarian agony. The "abolitionist" movement has also relied on moral arguments to neutralize the logic of deterrence employed by the NWS. NGOs succeeded in making nuclear disarmament a topic of sustained public interest and helped to raise the issue of "global zero." NGOs helped to strengthen the norm against proliferation, but they also strengthened the focus on the linkage between nonproliferation and disarmament (Fisher 1999, 58).

When NGOs attempt to influence the normative agenda, access to negotiations has become a core strategy of their campaign efforts. Quite frequently NGO networks first had to overcome states' opposition in order to be perceived as a credible knowledge broker. The strategic partnership with like-minded states has often been advantageous for both sides: while NGOs gained access to negotiations, states could point to the legitimacy of their efforts by relying on the support of civil society. For NGOs this form of "new diplomacy" might occasionally involve the risk of losing critical distance and granting states democratic legitimacy for a contested policy. Nevertheless, the TANs in humanitarian arms control frequently rely on multiple strategies: they seek strategic partnership with like-minded states and also organize global public protest campaigns either at the international level or within their domestic constituencies.

INTERNATIONAL GOVERNMENTAL ORGANIZATIONS

International governmental organizations (IGOs) are credited with growing importance as globalization forces nation-states to pursue national objectives through international cooperation. However, IGOs can do only what member states concede. The assumption that they are able to draft an independent agenda is, however, the prerequisite for conceptualizing IGOs as norm entrepreneurs: they must be capable of devising a normative vision and acting strategically over a period of time to turn this vision into reality.

We want to examine the assumption that agency and norm entrepreneurship by IGOs is possible: attributes enabling them to develop the quality of norm entrepreneurship should be, first, an institutional setting that designates specific bodies of the organization that are to become active in creating and promoting norms. Second, organizations with a specific mandate to work in the realm of arms control, disarmament, and nonproliferation should be better capable of acting as norm entrepreneurs in this area. Third, there should be institutional tools available for norm entrepreneurship. Fourth, the more homogeneous an IGO is in terms of the value orientation of its members, the more it should be capable of norm entrepreneurship.

We study two cases of IGOs at different ends of the spectrum for these variables. Through its decision-making council and, in the meantime, through the European External Action Service and its head, the virtual European "foreign minister," the EU possesses agency-capable institutions. By contrast, the question of the degree to which the UN Security Council (UNSC), the General Assembly (UNGA), and the UN secretary-general (UNSG) possess this quality is an open one. Since 2003 the EU has had a mandate, even detailed strategies, in foreign and security policy and in nonproliferation and disarmament. The prescriptions in the UN Charter are of a more general nature; it was never the ambition of its membership to conduct a joint foreign and security policy. The EU has developed instruments—Common Strategies, Common Positions, and Joint Actions—that oblige member states to engage in activities of varying scope and thus can serve as forms of norm entrepreneurship (Otto, Patterson, and Bohle 2010). The UN is confined to resolutions, binding ones by the Security Council and nonbinding ones by the General Assembly. Furthermore, all EU members are liberal democracies sharing a long history, while the UN is the most diverse and heterogeneous organization in the world. We should thus expect much stronger norm entrepreneurship by the EU than by the UN, if at all.

The European Union as a "Civilian Power": The Ideal Norm Entrepreneur?

Given the material, diplomatic, institutional, financial, and technical resources of both the member states and the European Commission (EC), the EU seems well equipped to have a lasting impact on policy outcomes in arms control. The self-perception and identity of the EU lends itself to the task of spreading norms of transparency and stability and promoting an international order based on trust, cooperation, and peaceful conflict resolution (Diez 2005, 613). This assumption derives from the principles inherent in the EU's *acquis communautaire*: sustainable peace, freedom, democracy, human rights, rule of law, equality, social solidarity, sustainable development, and good governance (Manners 2008). Since the adoption of the Maastricht Treaty in 1992 and the formation of a Common Foreign and Security Policy (CFSP) as a third pillar of European integration, the EU has become increasingly involved as a collective actor in global arms control. Common positions and decisions of the EU in this area are determined by the foreign ministers of the member states in the monthly Foreign Affairs Council, which is served by three working groups on nonproliferation (CONOP), arms control, and disarmament in the UN (CODUN), and conventional arms exports (COARM).

The European Security Strategy of 2003 (ESS) regards the proliferation of WMD to be "potentially the greatest threat to [EU] security" and refers to the positive impact of international treaties and export control arrangements (Council of the EU 2003c). It sets out two strategic objectives: building security in Europe's neighborhood and promoting an international order based on "effective multilateralism." The main tenets of the ESS conform well to the concept of a "civilian power," which is understood as being committed to multilateralism, peaceful conflict resolution, constraining the use of military force, promotion of the rule of law, and institutionalization of world politics (Maull 2010). The ESS has been spelled out in terms of nonproliferation in the 2003 WMD strategy. Also in 2003, the EU High Representative appointed his personal representative for WMD nonproliferation to help implement the WMD strategy and report on its progress at six-month intervals (Anthony 2009). This section focuses on the EU's activities within the nuclear nonproliferation regime and takes a brief look at EU behavior in other fields of global multilateral arms control.

The European Union and the Nuclear Nonproliferation Regime The EURATOM Treaty of 1957 established a verification and inspection regime for the civilian nuclear fuel cycle. Installations and commodities in the military domain and related to national security, however, were exempted from the treaty. While there had been some competition and duplication of verification measures in the past (Lindroos 1997, 331–32), the relationship between the IAEA and European Atomic Energy Community (EURATOM) has improved in terms of cooperation and a "constructive spirit" (Kobia 2008, 43).[7]

Broader activities of the EU in the nuclear nonproliferation regime date back to 1981 when the members of the European Community set up a working group on nonproliferation, initially working in secrecy because of French and British reservations. The group worked out the first European contribution to an NPT Review Conference (RevCon) in 1990, the European Council's "Dublin Declaration" (Müller and van Dassen 1997). By 2011, all EU member states had signed and ratified the main nuclear nonproliferation treaties and arrangements, including the NPT and the CTBT. The obligations created by these treaties and arrangements have shaped the activities of the EU, while differences with respect to nuclear weapons have persisted. France and the UK are recognized as nuclear powers under the NPT, and twenty-one EU states are members of NATO, whose strategic concept rests on nuclear deterrence. While France is a staunch defender of nuclear weapons, Ireland, Sweden, and Austria are committed abolitionists; there are proponents of arms control and disarmament (Germany, Netherlands) in the middle. Strong believers in nuclear energy, (France, Slovakia) are pitted against resolute opponents (Austria, Germany), all shaping EU policy output.

Despite its internal differences, the EU has established itself as an important actor at multilateral forums such as the NPT RevCons. Prior to adopting the ESS the EU had played a crucial role in securing the indefinite extension of the NPT in 1995. The diplomatic campaign conducted in the run-up to the conference was guided by a Joint Action, adopted in 1994, that called for the indefinite and unconditional extension of the NPT (European Council 1994). It led to a series of declarations by the presidency on behalf of the EU made at every major diplomatic encounter before the conference. The sum of European demarches and declarations is credited with increasing participation and building consensus at the conference (Grand 2000, 16). During the 2000 NPT RevCon, the EU helped to shape the final document, which contained new and specific disarmament commitments by the NWS. A Common Position had again been adopted before the conference (Council of the EU 2000), which was implemented both through national actions and collective actions in the form of statements delivered by the presidency (Portugal) (Anthony 2001, 603). At times, EU members caucused on the conference floor in order to achieve common negotiating positions. At the conference, the EU was represented in two key groups, the group of NWS and the New Agenda Coalition.

Agreeing on a Common Position in the run-up to the 2005 NPT RevCon was difficult because of NWS reneging on their 2000 disarmament commitments, but nevertheless possible (Council of the EU 2005a). The EU's performance, however, was mixed at best. Despite some successes, the internal divisions of the EU mirrored the differences on the global stage (Müller 2005). At the 2010 NPT RevCon, Baroness Ashton spoke for the first time in the General Debate as the new High Representative for Foreign Affairs and Security Policy, and the EU submitted an impressive number of working papers;[8] it was assigned a specific task in the final document of the RevCon, namely to help prepare a conference of the regional parties in the Middle East to explore ways and means of fostering a nuclear-weapons-free zone (NPT 2010). Nonetheless, the EU appeared less dynamic and weak as an actor, with France pursuing its interests as a nuclear weapons state, while other EU members remained passive (Müller 2010b, 11–13).

With regard to norm conflicts in the regime, its positions place the EU under some tension with the NAM. EU statements made at NPT conferences since 1990 have stressed the need for a "balanced" approach between the three pillars of the NPT and made numerous references to both Arts. IV (right to peaceful use of nuclear energy) and VI (nuclear disarmament). While supporting civilian nuclear technology development through contributions to the IAEA Technical Cooperation Fund and a new nuclear fuel bank, however, the EU has advocated universal adoption of the IAEA Safeguards Agreement and its Additional Protocol, multilateral fuel cycle arrangements, and measures to curb the illicit trade in fissile material, making withdrawal from the NPT more difficult and preventing nuclear terrorism since 9/11—all steps that stand in conflict with preferences held by a majority of NAM members.

In the disarmament field, the EU has succeeded in putting substrategic nuclear weapons on the agenda, first in 2000, when related language from the EU's Common Position made it into the final document, and again in 2010, when a request for including these weapons in the arms reductions process was indirectly recognized in the final document ("nuclear weapons of all types and locations"). The EU succeeded in this endeavor even though member states pursued the issue with different degrees of enthusiasm (Simpson 2001; Müller 2010b).

Justice concerns are almost nonexistent in the EU's common approach, which focuses on enhancing regime efficiency, norm compliance, and enforcement. EU interventions at NPT conferences since 1990 have regularly condemned violations of nonproliferation norms by specific actors. North Korea has repeatedly been the target of calls for the country's full compliance with UNSC and IAEA resolutions and a return to the NPT, from which the country withdrew in 2003. Similar demands from Iran have been made at the RevCons since 2004. In Iran's case, Germany, France, and the UK, together with the EU High Representative, Javier Solana, are credited with having prevented an escalation of the dispute over North Korea's nuclear activities, successfully facilitating mediation talks that included the United States, China, and Russia (Sauer 2008; Tocha 2009). Apart from condemning India's and Pakistan's 1998 nuclear tests, references to these two nonparties and to Israel have never been as pointed and forceful as in the cases above, reflecting a consensus to only selectively engage proliferation offenders. These findings reflect overriding economic and political interests that dissuade EU member states from engaging those states more forcefully.

Individual members dissatisfied with EU compromises on disarmament have, by contrast, pursued national justice claims through stronger demands for disarmament measures in other groupings in parallel with their EU engagement, notably Ireland and Sweden in the New Agenda Coalition in 2000 and 2010.

Norm Entrepreneurship through Agreements and Material Support The EU's "weapons of mass destruction clause" (WMD clause), modeled after the highly effective human rights clause (Grip 2009, 3–4), was adopted in November 2003 as part of implementing the EU's WMD Strategy. It is designed to mainstream nonproliferation goals into the EU's wider relations with non-EU states ("third countries") (Council of the EU 2003b). The clause constitutes an "essential element" that must be included in all third-party "mixed" agreements[9] and represents a declaratory commitment by partners to nonproliferation policies that they have already signed (Council of the EU 2003b). It also includes additional commitments for a partner to take steps to ratify or implement all other relevant international instruments and to establish effective national export controls. These two further elements might be considered essential "on a case by case basis."

The EU has concluded agreements with almost a hundred countries (as of December 2010) that include a WMD clause "compatible with the spirit and the content of the WMD standard clause" (Council of the EU 2010c, 47).[10] However, there are few criteria for evaluating whether a third party has followed the nonproliferation standards agreed upon (Grip 2009). While not a party to the NPT, India has refused to include a WMD clause during negotiations for a free trade agreement with the EU (Grip 2009, 10). Nonetheless, the WMD clause functions as an important tool of the EU's entrepreneurial activity.

Finally, the EU has provided financial support for international nuclear arms control institutions and programs. For example, there have been five Joint Actions since 2003 that set out budgetary and voluntary measures to support the IAEA; the EU was also the first donor to the IAEA Nuclear Security Fund established in November 2008 with up to €25 million (Council of the EU 2004a, 2008a, 2008b). The EU has financed Cooperative Threat Reduction programs and regional disarmament assistance in Russia (spending about €28.5 million in 1999–2007) (Council of the EU 2007b) and committed about €800 million in the framework of the G8 Global Partnership.[11] Finally, the "Instrument for

Stability" of the European Commission is scheduled to spend about €317 million on preventing the proliferation of WMD in 2007–2011 (Bril 2009).[12] The EU also released Common Positions with pledges for supporting confidence-building measures after the Indian and Pakistani nuclear tests in 1998 (Council of the EU 1998) and contributed to the Korean Peninsula Energy Development Organization (KEDO) in its early days both financially and through the supply of equipment.[13]

The European Union in Other Multilateral Arms Control Regimes All EU states are parties to the BWC. The EU's WMD strategy emphasizes the threat posed by biological weapons (BW) (Council of the EU 2006b, 2008c) and the importance of the BWC, in particular increased transparency (see Council of the EU 2003a, 2003b). Since 1996, the EU has developed an integrated approach to BW control at multilateral forums (Nixdorff and Zanders 2006): while the Common Position for the 4th RevCon of BWC in 1996 still referred to "Member States" seeking progress on verification measures (Council of the EU 1996), the EU presidency's opening statement to the 5th RevCon (2001) included the first public reference to the EU as a single actor in the field of BW control (EU 2001). The EU made a substantial contribution toward creating the 2003–5 intersessional process after the failure of the 2001 Review (Zanders 2006). The Common Position for the 6th RevCon in 2006 stated that the EU's objective is to further strengthen the BWC and work toward more effective compliance mechanisms (Council of the EU 2006a). The EU submitted eight working papers and twelve proposals, making it one of the most active actors at the conference (Pearson 2006).

The same year, the EU adopted an Action Plan that aimed at reactivating confidence-building measures (CBMS) and outlined EU assistance for promoting the universality of the BWC and supporting implementation of the treaty by signatory states (Council of the EU 2006b). According to EU progress reports, many states new to the BWC—such as Montenegro, Kazakhstan, Trinidad and Tobago, and Gabon—have benefited from EU training and assistance, which have also taken place in the Middle East and East Asia (Council of the EU 2008d, 9).[14] A new Joint Action to support biosafety measures of up to €2 million was adopted in 2008, as well as further universalization measures worth up to €1.4 million.[15]

All EU members have signed and ratified the CWC. The Union's WMD strategy calls for universalization of the CWC, and the EU has provided significant financial and technical support through several Joint Actions to the OPCW. The first Joint Action was adopted in 2004 and provided €1.8 million for programs dealing with universal adherence to the CWC, national implementation measures, and international cooperation in chemical activities (Council of the EU 2004b); this was renewed with a portfolio of about €1.7 million in 2005 (Council of the EU 2005b). The Council Joint Action in March 2007 committed €1.7 million for a period of eighteen months in support of the OPCW, which was updated by a Council decision in July 2009 to strengthen the multilateral disarmament, nonproliferation, and cooperation measures of the OPCW with €2.1 million (Council of the EU 2009a). At the fourteenth Session of the Conference of the States Parties to the CWC, the OPCW director-general expressed his appreciation of the EU's "active and visible role in supporting the OPCW" and stated that the support has been "absolutely essential in enabling the Secretariat to offer increased assistance to other Member States" (OPCW 2009). The EU claims that since the adoption of the first Joint Action in 2004, a total of 21 countries have signed and ratified the CWC, bringing the number of CWC members up to 188 (Council of the EU 2010b). In tandem with similar measures in the nuclear realm, there have also been disarmament assistance programs designed to support the destruction of Russian chemical weapons stockpiles.[16]

There was no Common Position adopted for the 2003 1st CWC RevCon, although Greece stressed on behalf of the EU the need for effective challenge inspections (EU 2003). There was a Common Position approved for the 2nd CWC RevCon in 2008, which mostly mirrored previous commitments to enhance the verification regime, destroy chemical weapons stockpiles, and aim for universality of the treaty (Council of the EU 2007a). At the conference, a statement was read by the Slovenian presidency on behalf of the EU, but it is not clear how the EU shaped the outcome of the conference itself (EU 2008).

The EU has been a major force in creating and strengthening the SALW PoA (Krause 2002; Wisotzki 2008). EU member states focused their attention at a very early stage on the problem of illicit trafficking of small arms and light weapons. They soon became one of the crucial norm entrepreneurs seeking the PoA. Already in 1997 the EU member states developed the Program on Illicit Trafficking of Conventional Arms. This was intended to strengthen national export control legislation and to encourage cooperation with third-party states. In 1998, the EU member states approved the EU Code of Conduct on Arms Exports. Controlling the legal arms trade became one of the core aims of the EU during the PoA negotiations in 2001. Since then, the EU has sought rigorously to implement the PoA norms and provisions. It acted as a key player in drafting a new instrument on the marking and tracing of SALW in 2005 as well as in regulating brokerage by nonstate actors through a new norm (Wisotzki 2009, 19).

All EU members participate in the various international export control regimes. The EU has established a Community-wide dual-use export control regime (in 1992) with elaborated guidelines, a peer review process, the safeguards function of the EU Commission, and an EU Community Customs Code that harmonizes member states' customs practices. This structure enables the EU to take a unitary position in deliberations on the revision of guidelines in meetings of the export control regimes. As mentioned above, export controls are part of the WMD clause that the EU requests its partners to accept in "mixed agreements" (Wetter 2009; Anthony 2009, 210–13).

The European Union as a Norm Entrepreneur The EU has played a strong initiating, promotional, and supportive role in all regimes analyzed here. It has often served as a "laboratory of consensus" (Grand 2000, 48) on divisive issues in view of the variety of member positions, thus presenting proposals that can be more acceptable than a national document. The Union has functioned as a *norm keeper* working toward the internalization of nonproliferation norms (e.g., through the inclusion of a WMD clause in agreements with third states) and as a (selective) *norm enforcer* in dealing with norm violators (Iran, North Korea). The EU has also strengthened international arms control architecture through practical support: since 2003, it has adopted more than twenty Joint Actions in support of arms control, including many measures that provided financial and technical assistance to international organizations and third countries. This is another type of *norm promoting*: it strengthens the physical fabric of the nonproliferation regime.

Nevertheless, the EU has potential to improve. Divisions between NWS and NNWS (and among NNWS) continue to prevent a more unified and forceful stance in the nonproliferation regime and contribute to giving priority to effectiveness over justice concerns. The EU has failed to adopt a common stance on the US-India nuclear deal, and the insertion of a WMD clause appears to have been abandoned in trade negotiations with India. This criticism notwithstanding, the EU has had an important function as an innovator and enforcer in the field of nuclear nonproliferation.

The United Nations: A Norm Entrepreneur?

The initial words of the UN Charter, "We, the people," suggest the existence of a strategy-capable political will; in reality, the UN is an institution with the widest possible heterogeneity, including deadly enemies. Mustering a unitary will to pursue an objective over time seems impossible. Even if we assume such a collective will, the UN's capacity to *act* depends on its member states taking decisions and providing personnel and funding to implement them and to strengthen the organization's capabilities. Thus, we can think of the UN as being simply the sum of its frequently quarreling members and acting within the small room for maneuvering granted by them. Alternatively, we can conceive of the UN as an *actor* consisting of its staff and bureaucratic procedures (Barnett and Finnemore 1999, 707; Archer 2001, 65–110).

The UN's mandate in disarmament and arms control is restrictively formulated in the Charter. The organ with the strongest formal authority—the Security Council (UNSC)—showed no interest in working toward an arms regulation plan after the early abortive effort to ban nuclear weapons. Nevertheless, the UN—that is, its various organs dealing with different aspects of arms control and disarmament—has evolved as an important site in this issue area. But have these organs proved ready and capable of acting as norm entrepreneurs by using their potential for norm development, promotion, and enforcement purposefully and systematically?

The United Nations Security Council The Charter gives the UNSC three tasks for developing norms in the field of arms control and disarmament: creating norms, facilitating their implementation, and enforcing compliance. The first two tasks arise from Art. 26, which calls on the UNSC to work out plans for "the establishment of a system for the regulation of armaments," and Art. 47, which entrusts the Military Staff Committee with supporting the UNSC through its military expertise. The enforcement role is implied by the UNSC's general authority to ensure peace and security (see chapters 5 and 6). The Charter possesses various instruments for implementing this mission. The UNSC can issue a statement through its president, as in 1992 when it declared the proliferation of weapons of mass destruction in all its aspects to be a threat to international peace and security. It can adopt a resolution that is binding on all UN members, and it not only can adopt resolutions under Chapter VII of the Charter that are binding but can also impose sanctions even as far as military action against noncompliant members in order to ensure compliance with established norms.

The gap between the language of the Charter and the practices of member states has remained large. For nuclear disarmament it is a constraining factor that the five permanent members with their veto power possess nuclear weapons. This status compromises their interest in a nuclear-weapons-free world (Regehr 2009). Throughout the Cold War, the UNSC's disarmament activities were impeded by the antagonism of the veto powers, the United States and the Soviet Union. For both, armament was an instrument needed to engage in their rivalry. Disarmament rhetoric was more for winning uncommitted states (notably those emerging from decolonialization) over to their own camp than a serious attempt to establish comprehensive disarmament norms (Bourantonis 1993). There were occasional arms embargos against outlawed states (Southern Rhodesia, South Africa), but little more.

Change came with the end of the Cold War. After the 1991 Gulf War the Security Council mandated the dismantling of Iraq's WMD and missile programs and created a new institutional instrument, the UN Special Commission on Iraq (UNSCOM), replaced in 2002 by the UN Monitoring, Verification, and Inspection Commission (UNMOVIC), both endowed with intrusive rights in regard to the target state. In parallel, the UNSC mandated sanctions with a view to preventing the reconstitution of Iraq's WMD programs; UNSCOM (and, for the nuclear sector, the IAEA) was tasked with supervising this embargo (Findlay 2006). The UNSC thus created an incipient norm for what deviant UN members must endure to once again be in good standing. Whether this norm will endure depends on its application to additional cases, something that the Security Council—despite opportunities regarding North Korea and Iran—has not yet done.

Nevertheless, the UNSC has been concerned with compliance and enforcement activities in several cases, because it is the ultimate guarantor of the integrity of the regimes covering weapons of mass destruction in cases of serious noncompliance. This role is written into the BWC and the CWC and is in the IAEA Statute: when non-NWS parties to the NPT are in serious noncompliance with their safeguards agreements with the IAEA, then the IAEA Board of Governments reports the case to the UNSC. The Security Council's related performance was limited. It took note of the North Korean case and referred it first to bilateral negotiations between the United States and the DPRK and, after the Framework Agreement of 1994 between these two parties had broken down, to the six-party talks that have been held intermittently since 2003. When North Korea shocked the international community by carrying out nuclear tests in 2006 and 2009, the UNSC imposed only limited sanctions; China was not willing to turn away from its difficult ally completely. In the case of Iran, the UNSC mandated sanctions and upgraded them step by step as Iran defied its requests to stop uranium enrichment and cooperate fully with the IAEA. Even these sanctions were designed to not be too painful; China and Russia did not want to burn bridges with Tehran and pleaded to keep open the doors to cooperative relationships. The UNSC's ability to act suffered regularly from its members' political differences and diverging geopolitical and economic interests (Müller 2010a, 40–41).

However, the UNSC worked as a norm creator in one important case: Resolution 1540 (April 2004) obliged all member states to take measures to prevent nonstate actors from gaining access to materials, equipment, and technologies useful for obtaining WMD. Implicitly, the same measures, which contained export controls, were also effective in curbing proliferation of WMD by state actors. It was only the second time (after measures to curb the financing of terrorism) that the UNSC established global legislation, imposing duties on the members not just in an ad hoc and case-specific mode, but in a lasting way. There were concerns about this role on the grounds of its lacking procedural justice and of illegal violation of the sovereign rights of UN member states (Joyner 2008), but S/RES/1540 was adopted anyway. In addition, the UNSC established a supervisory committee to enhance compliance, an expert unit to assist this committee and the UNSC, and a mechanism for revisiting the resolution periodically. The UNSC followed up S/RES/1540 with subsequent resolutions 1673 (2006) and 1810 (2008), which specified or extended the stipulations of the original resolution (Craft 2004).

The UNSC thus did more than just agenda setting or one-off ad hoc regulation. It proved its capacity to act as a unitary actor (despite the misgivings of some nonpermanent members), and it acted strategically and sustainably: it showed, in this case, key attributes of a successful norm entrepreneur. While the United States initiated the new norm, the final product was the work of the Security Council as a whole. The conditions enabling this success are rare in the UNSC: unity through a common threat,[17] a sense of urgency, and relatively smooth arrival at a solution—because all P5 had already adopted measures embodied in S/RES/1540 on a national basis or as members of export control regimes such as the Nuclear Suppliers Group or the Australia Group. Thus, for the foreseeable future, the UNSC will probably be a norm entrepreneur only under extraordinary circumstances.

The United Nations General Assembly The UNGA harbors even more diversity than the Security Council but can act through majority decisions. In addition, the Assembly's powers are limited: it can only make recommendations to the UNSC and member states on matters of disarmament, as mentioned in Art. 11 of the Charter. The UNGA works through two subinstitutions, the Disarmament Commission (DC) and the First Committee (Boulden, Thakur, and Weiss 2009b, 7–8). The DC is a deliberative body that works for several weeks during each UNGA session and takes up two items per session period. Political disagreements between member states have prevented the DC from working effectively as an agenda setter, not to speak of norm entrepreneurship. Norm creation was "outsourced" by the UNGA in the late 1950s to an independent body that started as the Ten Nations Committee on Disarmament and, after numerous metamorphoses, ended as the current Conference on Disarmament (CD) (Piasecki and Gati 1993, 754–57, 763–64).[18]

The First Committee covers the whole spectrum of arms control and disarmament issues, whether it is the international arms trade, the prevention of an arms race in outer space, or nuclear disarmament; it deliberates and prepares resolutions, which are then voted upon by the UNGA Plenary. Since many resolutions are adopted each year anew without any substantive changes, a superficial observer might conclude that the First Committee is engaged in a circular ritual, repeating the same utterances endlessly and that it is just another paper tiger. But this assessment would be wrong. The fact that many resolutions are repetitive reflects an unfinished agenda and the frustration felt by the nonaligned states, for whom UN resolutions are an instrument for criticizing the lack of progress in disarmament and the reliance of leading industrialized states on armed superiority for both their national security and collective defense, as well as their preponderance in world affairs.

Despite or maybe even due to this repetitiveness, the UNGA has provided a forum for agenda setting and at rare times seems to have worked as a norm entrepreneur. Repetition keeps items on the agenda and may, over time, encourage and enable more concrete norm building, as in the case of small arms, where the UNGA persisted with the subject until it was possible to move to the action program (see chapter 3).

The UNGA's most powerful tools were its special sessions on disarmament

(SSOD). SSOD I in 1978 established, on the basis of an expert report, guiding principles for establishing nuclear-weapons-free zones (including the rules that it must be freely agreed to by the members of the respective region and honored by the NWS by giving legally binding security guarantees to zone members). The principles subsequently functioned as a template in all negotiations on nuclear-weapons-free zones in Africa, Southeast Asia, and Central Asia, thus demonstrating their normative character. Overall, the work program adopted by SSOD I has framed the debates and initiatives in the UNGA First Committee and also in the CD ever since. Disagreements among the membership prevented later SSODs from reaching the same level of effectiveness (Piasecki and Gati 1993).

In regular sessions, the UNGA has adopted a resolution on nonproliferation (in 1961) that formed the basis for later negotiations on the NPT. After having called for a Comprehensive Nuclear-Test-Ban Treaty for decades, the General Assembly rescued, in 1996, the CTBT draft from a stalemated CD, adopted it, and opened it up for signature (Johnson 2009, 137–43). It has deliberated on (in 2001) and eventually established (in 2002) the UN Register on Conventional Arms, which involves the export and import of seven categories of major conventional weapon systems, one of the few global transparency measures on arms (Chalmers et al. 1994; Boothby 2002, 20–21). From 1973 on, the UNGA pushed for a ban on certain, particularly inhumane, conventional weapons; this work resulted in the Inhumane Weapons Convention, adopted by a special UN conference convoked by the UNGA in 1981, with its ensuing protocols (Piasecki and Gati 1993, 759; Boothby 2002, 23–24). It also initiated the small arms program, perhaps the most momentous disarmament measure ever, as these weapons have killed the majority of victims of armed conflict and criminal violence in the last fifty years (Kytömäki and Yankey-Wayne 2003). It has also kept alive the notion of complete nuclear disarmament, throughout all the ups and downs during and after the Cold War, in spite of the preferences of the NWS.

Despite these merits, we hesitate to ascribe norm entrepreneur status to the UNGA. It is more appropriate to define it as a forum and an arena where norm entrepreneurs can pursue their own projects. The term *forum* designates an environment in which issues can be deliberated and where agreements are reached by persuading and convincing partners. The term *arena* means an antagonistic institution where states fight to win over supporters for their own point of view. The UNGA has worked at times in either way (Peterson 2009, 55).

The nuclear-weapons-free zone project, for example, was pushed by Egypt and some African members. The 1961 nonproliferation resolution was at the initiative of Ireland and its formidable foreign minister, Frank Aiken. The CTBT was inserted into the 1996 UNGA by Australia on behalf of a group of pro-CTBT states. The small arms issue was pursued by a coalition of NGOs and like-minded states committed to the concept of human security. And nuclear disarmament was stubbornly kept alive by the leaders of the NAM and, after 1998, the New Agenda Coalition.

The emergence of the norm of nonproliferation and disarmament education presents an interesting case. It was introduced by a nongovernmental expert member into the UNSG's Advisory Board on Disarmament Matters, a deliberative body composed of about twenty governmental and nongovernmental experts from all world regions. Dr. William Potter proposed a UN study on the issue, and the Advisory Board was invited by the UNSG to develop that into a draft recommendation to the UNGA. After several sessions, the board came up with a consensus final draft. The Mexican member then decided to recommend to his government turning the board's text into a draft resolution; Mexico brought the resolution to the UNGA as a national initiative. The UNGA adopted the draft in 2000 (UN 2000, 187, 322–23). An expert group was installed that reported back to the UNGA in 2002 (UN 2002, 239–47). This report stimulated a number of implementation activities by the UN Secretariat and by member states.[19] In 2010, the NPT RevCon recommended such activities to all parties to the NPT.

In all cases, thus, entrepreneurship was with units *below* UNGA level, whether individual states, state groups, or NGOs. The UNGA was indispensable in giving the efforts of these actors legitimacy and amplification (Peterson 2009, 67), but it was not an entrepreneur in itself. It thus works largely as a forum, an arena, a norm keeper, and, at times, a norm factory, which entrepreneurs use to achieve their objectives. That this is possible is remarkable: the UNGA reflects all the justice disputes between the NAM and the others that we know from the regimes. But at times, if not always, these disputes can be turned into productive compromises.

The Secretariat and the Secretary-General The embodiment of the organization in a single person, the UNSG, supported by an expert secretariat, seems to provide the best conditions for norm entrepreneurship. However, the secretariat of an IGO is meant to act as agent of its principals, the member states, and not to have a policy of its own (Traub 2007). Yet, it is generally accepted that strong organization leaders, supported by a capable staff and bureaucratic procedures, can assume actor qualities. Art. 99 of the Charter provides a legal underpinning: the UNSG is entitled to bring all issues to the attention of the UNSC that he or she deems essential for international peace and security. Under the doctrine of "implied powers," this is a far-reaching mandate for agency (Johnstone 2007, 131).

Specialized disarmament staff supports the UNSG. Initially limited to the nuclear sector, today the unit covers the full spectrum of disarmament; from a few people it has grown to its present size of about fifty. The name of the unit and how it is organized has changed over time: group, center, department, and, presently, office, headed by an undersecretary-general. Thus, the UNSG, if interested in disarmament, can rely on professional administrative and advisory support (Rydell 2009, 75–90).

Secretaries-general have filled their role in different ways, depending on their personal commitment to disarmament. All have emphasized the importance of the issue for humankind. Few, however, went beyond admonishing, requesting some action, or emphasizing issues (frequently the need for nuclear disarmament) to embark on a specific course with some perseverance. The demands of the day or different priorities have prevented secretaries-general from acting in a more entrepreneurial way.

Surprisingly, Boutros Boutros-Ghali came closest to norm entrepreneurship, even though he was reputed to have low interest in disarmament. He integrated disarmament into peace building in his 1995 "Supplement to an Agenda for Peace" by coining the term *micro disarmament* and elaborating on the destabilizing effects of small arms and light weapons in conflict-prone environments (Boutros-Ghali 1995); NGOs and like-minded states had identified the collection and dismantlement of former combatants' weapons as an essential condition for lasting peace and human development. Subsequently, disarmament became part of "DDR" (disarmament, demobilization, and reintegration), which is now UN routine in postconflict peace-building missions. Importing this element into peace-building practice is a consequential normative development, and Boutros-Ghali has promoted this achievement. His initiative also had an impact on the process that produced the Ottawa Convention and on the installation of the UN Action Programme on small arms and light weapons (see chapter 3) (Rydell 2009, 95–96; Boothby 2002, 30–35).

In comparison to Boutros-Ghali as an unexpected norm entrepreneur for disarmament, Kofi Annan was rather passive. This is astonishing: Annan was no doubt committed to the cause, as proven by his public speeches, which notably addressed nuclear disarmament and nonproliferation (Rydell 2009, 96–97). However, Annan missed the opportunity to emphasize arms control and disarmament in his strongest effort as a norm entrepreneur, the 2005 UN reform. Annan had appointed a High Level Panel to provide arguments for persuading the membership of the need for wide-ranging reforms. He then tasked his Advisory Board on Disarmament Matters with providing input to the panel's work: the board delivered on time (UN 2004), but the panel's secretariat largely ignored this advice; the panel's report included only a meager disarmament section. In Annan's ensuing report, "In Larger Freedom" (Annan 2005), the topic appeared only as a side issue. Perhaps the panel, as well as the UNSG, had other priorities (Responsibility to Protect, Security Council Reform) and wanted to avoid another controversial issue for the debate. Eventually, the antidisarmament juggernaut of the Bush administration blocked the inclusion of even the tiniest traces of the disarmament issue in the 2005 UNGA summit resolution (Boulden, Thakur, and Weiss 2009b, 3).

Current secretary-general Ban Ki-moon entered office with the reputation of not being very interested in disarmament. But then he introduced a plan for nuclear disarmament, including the contested proposal for a nuclear weapons convention (Ban 2009). This initiative gave supporters of such a convention, notably the NAM, their first opportunity ever to insert it into the final document of the 2010 NPT RevCon, not as a proposal endorsed by the conference but as a quotation from the UNSG. It is now part of an agreed NPT document—that is, it incorporates language that can be referred to in future proceedings. While the outcome of this process cannot be predicted, this could be the beginning of a norm creation process.

In summary, the UNSG has the potential for disarmament norm entrepreneurship due to the office's visibility, legitimate authority, and bureaucratic backup, but officeholders have utilized this potential only rarely and selectively, probably because of anticipated resistance and diverging priorities.

The United Nations: A Vital Institution but Weak Norm Entrepreneur In evaluating the roles of the three UN bodies, one can cautiously ascribe "weak entrepreneurship" potential to the UN. It is weak because it applies to some but not all of the bodies discussed (mostly to the UNSC and the UNSG), whose entrepreneurship attributes cover only some steps in the process of entrepreneurship (UNGA), with potential only rarely tapped into (UNSC, UNSG), while most of the time the bodies instead act as a forum, an arena, a factory, or a facilitator for the entrepreneurship projects of others. Even so, the UN is an indispensable institution for norm dynamics. Altogether, the main function of the UN is as a "funnel for processing arms control and disarmament proposals" (Boulden, Thakur, and Weiss 2009b, 22).

CONCLUSION: DECISIVE NONSTATE NORM ENTREPRENEURSHIP

NGOs have become efficient and professional actors across the spectrum of multilateral arms control, where their influence naturally varies depending on opportunities, the success of campaigning, and their ability to form coalitions with like-minded states and actors in international organizations. NGO norm entrepreneurship does not focus on agenda setting and norm generation processes alone. Their activism at the implementation stage has evolved considerably over the last decade. This is especially applicable to humanitarian arms control: numerous NGOs provide modes of governance in areas of weak statehood where they run mine clearance campaigns, attempt to raise public awareness, or organize weapon collection programs. Moreover, TANs such as the ICBL provide soft skills of verification and thus assume important roles in implementing the ban on antipersonnel mines. Overall, transnational action networks and NGOs have become credible and decisive entrepreneurs within the norm dynamics of arms control and disarmament.

As for NGOs, the question whether IGOs, despite the fact they "rent" their power from member states, can act as norm entrepreneurs can be answered in the affirmative. Yes, they can. However, differing organizational structures and mandates and the homogeneity or heterogeneity of their membership decide to what degree they can realize this potential. The EU's activities show that the explicit mission to develop a CFSP, the instruments created for this purpose, and the decision-making and representative structures all help with norm entrepreneurship that is visible in nuclear policy and even more so in other arms control fields, as briefly illustrated in this chapter. Nuclear policy is the hard case: heterogeneity (NWS versus NNWS, NATO members versus neutral parties, proponents of and those opposed to nuclear energy) presents the strongest impediments, and yet norm entrepreneurship remains visible and, occasionally, effective.

The UN has a less clear mandate and less sophisticated instruments. While the institutional structure includes bodies with an entrepreneurial potential

(UNSC and UNSG), in reality the vaster heterogeneity of UNSC membership, persistent conflicts of interest, and enduring rivalries among the P5, as well as regional conflicts and divergences between developing and developed countries, make norm entrepreneurship more difficult for the bodies best suited for it, and almost impossible for the UNGA. Their functions as arena and forum for normative discourse, in agenda keeping, and as an occasional norm factory are nevertheless an important aspect of norm dynamics. That entrepreneurship occurs, at times, is quite impressive evidence of the strength of contemporary multilateralism, bearing out the power inherent in this mode of deliberation and decision making on norms, all skeptical protestations notwithstanding.

The visibility of nonstate actors in the realm of multilateral arms control is probably a sign of hope. They are not wedded to parochial and national interests or as easily susceptible as national governments to the siren songs of powerful bureaucracies and industrial lobbying. The limitation of their resources might thus be balanced, to a degree, by their freedom of action and their greater inclination to give aspects of the common good their due. They find allies in the world of states, namely "good citizens" and non-aligned reformers. In humanitarian arms control the impact of these coalitions was impressive. Perhaps that augurs well for making future inroads into the more arcane and state-dominated realms of WMD arms control.

Notes

1. Founding members of the ICBL were Handicap International (France), Human Rights Watch (United States), Medico International (Germany), Mines Advisory Group (Great Britain), Physicians for Human Rights (United States), and Vietnam Veterans of America Foundation (United States); see Rutherford (2009, 133).

2. Members of the World Court Project were the International Peace Bureau, International Physicians for the Prevention of Nuclear War, and the International Associations of Lawyers Against Nuclear Arms.

3. The model convention was written by a consortium of international experts and thinkers convened by the International Association of Lawyers against Nuclear Arms (IALANA), the International Network of Engineers and Scientists against Proliferation (INESAP) and International Physicians for the Prevention of Nuclear War (IPPNW).

4. The NRA's success in hindering a ban on SALW illustrates that NGO engagement may also hinder norm evolution; see Bob (2012).

5. Conversation with Harald Müller, who was a member of the Advisory Board on Disarmament Matters from 1999 to 2005.

6. When in 2001 the verification protocol experienced staunch opposition from the United States and finally failed, the NGOs succeeded in attracting public and media attention.

7. Art. 70 of the 1977 EURATOM-IAEA Safeguard Agreement (INFCIRC/193) grants the IAEA the right to verify the effectiveness of EURATOM safeguards.

8. The working papers were based on the Common Position (Council of the EU 2010a); for a list of various working papers submitted by the European Union, see UN (2010).

9. These are agreements between the EU and a third country that include a combination of economic and political elements.

10. For a complete list of agreements, see Council of the EU (2009b, 2010b).

11. For an overview of the EU's G8 Global Partnership contributions, see Council of the EU (2007c).

12. Regulation (EC) No. 1717/2006 of the European Parliament and of the Council of November 15, 2006, establishing an Instrument for Stability.

13. KEDO was created in 1994 to finance the provision of two 1000-megawatt light water reactors to be built in North Korea and meeting the cost of providing the country with oil that can be used to generate electricity to compensate for energy lost through its commitment to canceling two large nuclear reactors as part of the 1994 US–North Korea Agreed Framework (Anthony 2001, 606).

14. See also other WMD progress reports since 2006 (Council of the EU 2012).

15. The WHO is the implementing organization (see Council of the EU 2008d).

16. See measures under the CTR and G8 Partnership (see Council of the EU 2007b, 2007c).

17. The crucial condition here was complete agreement between the five permanent members, all of which had experienced terrorist threats and acts during the last decade, and all of which were thus keen to prevent, as far as possible, the specter of a terrorist attack munitioned by weapons of mass destruction.

18. The CD is not directly subordinated to the UN and is therefore not analyzed in this chapter.

19. Reports on these activities can be found in the UN Disarmament Yearbooks, starting with the year 2003.

References

Abolition 2000. 2012. "About." Abolition 2000: Global Network to Eliminate Nuclear Weapons. www.abolition2000.org/?page_id=2.

Annan, Kofi. 2003. "Secretary-General Warns of 'Disturbing' Erosion in International Norms: On Weapons of Mass Destruction, in Remarks to Disarmament Board."

Press release. New York, February 6. http://www.un.org/News/Press/docs/2003/sgsm8598.doc.htm.

———. 2005. "In Larger Freedom: Towards Development, Security and Human Rights for All." Report of the Secretary-General for Decision by the Heads of State and Government in September 2005. www.un.org/largerfreedom.

Anthony, Ian. 2001. "European Union Approaches to Arms Control, Non-proliferation and Disarmament." In *SIPRI Yearbook 2001: Armaments, Disarmament and International Security*, 599–614. Oxford: Oxford University Press.

———. 2009. "The Role of the European Union in WMD Nonproliferation." In *Combating Weapons of Mass Destruction*, edited by Nathan E. Busch and Daniel H. Joyner, 197–221. Athens: University of Georgia Press.

Archer, Clive. 2001. *International Organizations*. London: Routledge.

Atwood, David C. 2002. "NGOs and Disarmament: Views From the Coal Face." *Disarmament Forum* 2002 (1): 5–14.

Axworthy, Lloyd. 1997. "Notes for an Address by the Honourable Lloyd Axworthy, Minister of Foreign Affairs, to the Oslo NGO Forum on Banning Anti-personnel Landmines." Statement, Oslo, September 10.

Ban, Ki-moon. 2009. "A Five-Point Plan to Rid World of Nuclear Bombs." *Gulf Times* (Qatar), August 3.

Barnett, Michael N., and Martha Finnemore. 1999. "The Politics, Power, and Pathologies of International Organizations." *International Organization* 53 (4): 699–732.

Batchelor, Peter. 2002. "NGO Perspectives: NGOs and the Small Arms Issue." *Disarmament Forum* 2002 (1): 37–40.

Benford, Robert D., and David A. Snow. 2000. "Framing Processes and Social Movements: An Overview and Assessment." Annual Review of Sociology 26: 611–39.

Björkdahl, Annika. 2002. *From Idea to Norm: Promoting Conflict Prevention*. Lund: Lund University.

Bob, Clifford. 2012. *The Global Right Wing and the Clash of World Politics*. Cambridge: Cambridge University Press.

Boothby, Derek. 2002. "The United Nations and Disarmament." International Relations Studies and the United Nations Occasional Papers no. 1. www.acuns.org/membersubm/disarmamen/theunitedn.

Borrie, John, Maya Brehm, Silvia Cattaneo, and David Atwood. 2009. "Learn, Adapt, Succeed: Potential Lessons from the Ottawa and Oslo Processes for Other Disarmament and Arms Control Challenges." *Disarmament Forum* 2009 (1–2): 19–25.

Boulden, Jane, Ramesh Thakur, and Thomas G. Weiss, eds. 2009a. *The United Nations and Nuclear Orders*. Tokyo: United Nations University Press.

———. 2009b. "The United Nations and Nuclear Orders: Context, Foundations, Actors, Tools, and Future Prospects." In Boulden, Thakur, and Weiss 2009a, 1–27.

Bourantonis, Dimitris. 1993. *The United Nations and the Quest for Nuclear Disarmament*. Aldershot: Dartmouth.

Boutros-Ghali, Boutros. 1995. *An Agenda for Peace 1995*. New York: United Nations.

Bril, Louis-Victor. 2009. "The Stability Instrument: The Longer-Term Component." Presentation at the International Workshop on Improving Cooperation under Article X for Disease Surveillance, Detection, Diagnosis and Containment, Brussels, November 11–12.

Carpenter, R. Charli. 2011. "Vetting the Advocacy Agenda: Network Centrality and the Paradox of Weapons Norms." *International Organization* 65 (1): 69–102.

Carroll, Simon. 2002. "NGO Access to Multilateral Fora: Does Disarmament Lag Behind?" *Disarmament Forum* 2002 (1): 15–26.

Chalmers, Malcolm, Owen Greene, Edward Laurance, and Herbert Wulf, eds. 1994. *Developing the UN Register of Conventional Arms*. London: Westview Press.

Chesterman, Simon, ed. 2007. *Secretary or General? The UN Secretary-General in World Politics*. Cambridge: Cambridge University Press.

Cooper, Andrew F. 2002. "Like-Minded Nations, NGOs, and the Changing Pattern of Diplomacy within the UN System: An Introductory Perspective." In *Enhancing Global Governance: Towards a New Diplomacy?*, edited by Andrew F. Cooper, John English, and Ramesh Thakur, 1–18. Tokyo: United Nations University Press.

Council of the EU. 1996. "Common Position of 25 June 1996 Defined by the Council on the Basis of Article 5.2 of the Treaty on European Union, Relating to Preparation for the Fourth Review Conference of the Convention on the Prohibition of the Development, Production and Stockpiling of Bacteriological (Biological) and Toxin Weapons and on Their Destruction (BTWC) (96/408/CFSP)." *Official Journal of the European Communities* 39 (168): 3.

———. 1998. "Common Position of 26 October 1998 Defined by the Council on the Basis of Article J.2 of the Treaty on European Union on the European Union's Contribution to the Promotion of Non-proliferation and Confidence-Building in the South Asian Region (98/606/CFSP)." *Official Journal of the European Communities* 41 (290): 1–2.

———. 2000. "Council Common Position of 13 April 2000 Relating to the 2000 Review Conference of the Parties to the Treaty on the Non-proliferation of Nuclear Weapons (2000/297/CFSP)." *Official Journal of the European Communities* 43 (97): 1–3.

———. 2003a. EU Strategy against Proliferation of Weapons of Mass Destruction as Endorsed by the Council on 9 December 2003. Doc. 15708/03. Brussels: Council of the EU.

———. 2003b. Mainstreaming Non-proliferation Policies into the EU's Wider Relations with Third Countries. Doc. 14997/03. Brussels, November 19.

———. 2003c. *A Secure Europe in a Better World: European Security Strategy*. Brussels, December 12. www.consilium.europa.eu/uedocs/cmsUpload/78367.pdf.

———. 2004a. "Council Joint Action 2004/495/CFSP of 17 May 2004 on Support for IAEA Activities under Its Nuclear Security Programme and in the Framework of the Implementation of the EU Strategy against Proliferation of Weapons of Mass Destruction." *Official Journal of the European Union* 47 (182): 46–50.

———. 2004b. "Council Joint Action 2004/797/CFSP of 22 November 2004 on Support for OPCW Activities in the Framework of the Implementation of the EU Strategy against Proliferation of Weapons of Mass Destruction." *Official Journal of the European Union* 47 (249): 63–69.

———. 2005a. "Council Common Position 2005/329/PESC of 25 April 2005 Relating to the 2005 Review Conference of the Parties to the Treaty on the Non-proliferation of Nuclear Weapons." *Official Journal of the European Union* 48 (106): 32–35.

———. 2005b. "Council Joint Action 2005/913/CFSP of December 12, 2005 on Support for OPCW Activities in the Framework of the Implementation of the EU Strategy against Proliferation of Weapons of Mass Destruction." *Official Journal of the European Union* 48 (331): 34–41.

———. 2006a. "Council Common Position 2006/242/CFSP of 20 March 2006 Relating to the 2006 RevCon of the Biological and Toxin Weapons Convention (BTWC)." *Official Journal of the European Union* 49 (88): 65–67.

———. 2006b. "EU Action Plan on Biological and Toxin Weapons, Complementary to the EU Joint Action in Support of the BTWC (2006/C 57/01)." *Official Journal of the European Union* 49 (C 57): 1–2.

———. 2007a. "Council Common Position 2007/469/CFSP of 28 June 2007 Relating to the 2008 RevCon of the Convention on the Prohibition of the Development, Production, Stockpiling and Use of Chemical Weapons and on Their Destruction (CWC)." *Official Journal of the European Union* 50 (176): 39–41.

———. 2007b. "Council Joint Action 2007/178/CFSP of 19 March 2007 in Support of Chemical Weapons Destruction in the Russian Federation in the Framework of the EU Strategy against Proliferation of Weapons of Mass Destruction." *Official Journal of the European Union* 50 (81): 30–34.

———. 2007c. "G8 Global Partnership." April 13. www.consilium.europa.eu/showPage.aspx?id=1226&lang=en#ftn2.

———. 2008a. Council Conclusions on an EU Contribution for the Establishment of an IAEA Nuclear Fuel Bank as Endorsed by the Council on December 8–9 2008. Doc. 17187/08. Brussels.

———. 2008b. "Council Joint Action 2008/314/CFSP of 14 April 2008 on Support for IAEA Activities in the Areas of Nuclear Security and Verification and in the Framework of the Implementation of the EU Strategy against Proliferation of Weapons of Mass Destruction." *Official Journal of the European Union* 51 (107): 62–69.

———. 2008c. "Council Joint Action 2008/858/CFSP of 10 November 2008 in Support of the Biological and Toxin Weapons Convention (BTWC), in the Framework of the Implementation of the EU Strategy against the Proliferation of Weapons of Mass Destruction." *Official Journal of the European Union* 51 (302): 29–36.

———. 2008d. Six Monthly Progress Report on the Implementation of the EU Strategy against the Proliferation of WMD (2008/I). Doc. 10744/08. Brussels.

———. 2009a. "Council Decision 2009/569/CFSP of 27 July 2009 on Support for OPCW Activities in the Framework of the Implementation of the EU Strategy against Proliferation of Weapons of Mass Destruction." *Official Journal of the European Union* 52 (197): 96–107.

———. 2009b. Six-Monthly Progress Report on the Implementation of the EU Strategy against the Proliferation of WMD (2009/II). Doc. 17387/09. Brussels.

———. 2010a. "Council Decision 2010/212/CFSP of 29 March 2010 Relating to the Position of the European Union for the 2010 Review Conference of the Parties to the Treaty on the Non-proliferation of Nuclear Weapons." *Official Journal of the European Union* 53 (90): 8–14.

———. 2010b. Six-Monthly Progress Report on the Implementation of the EU Strategy against the Proliferation of WMD (2010/I). Doc. 11135/10. Brussels.

———. 2010c. Six-Monthly Progress Report on the Implementation of the EU Strategy against the Proliferation of WMD (2010/II). Doc. 17080/10. Brussels.

———. 2012. "Main Documents." www.consilium.europa.eu/showpage.aspx?id=718&lang=en#Bookmark6a.

Craft, Cassady. 2004. "Challenges of UNSCR 1540: Questions about International Export Controls." *Center for International Trade and Security Issue Briefs*. University of Georgia.

Dando, Malcolm. 2010. "New Blood: Civil Society Helps Shape the 2011 BTWC Review Conference Agenda." *Bulletin of the Atomic Scientists*, Web ed., September 23. www.thebulletin.org/print/web-edition/columnists/malcolm-dando/new-blood-civil-society-helps-shape-the-2011-btwc-review-confer.

Dhanapala, Jayantha. 2005. *Multilateral Diplomacy and the NPT: An Insider's Account*. With Randy Rydell. Geneva: United Nations, UNIDIR.

Diez, Thomas. 2005. "Constructing the Self and Changing Others: Reconsidering 'Normative Power Europe.'" *Millenium* 33 (3): 613–36.

EU (European Union). 2001. Statement by Belgium on Behalf of the EU to the 5th BWC RevCon. Geneva, November 19.

———. 2003. "The Hellenic Republic on Behalf of the European Union: Challenge Inspections; Views of the European Union." Working paper. RC-1/NAT.21. The Hague, May 1.

———.2008. Statement of the EU to the 2nd CWC RevCon. RC-2/NAT.13. The Hague, April 7.

European Council. 1994. "European Council at Corfu: 24–25 June 1994: Presidency Conclusions." Doc. SN 150/1/94. www.europarl.europa.eu/summits/cor1_en.htm.

Feakes, Daniel. 2003. "Global Society and Biological and Chemical Weapons." In *Global Civil Society Yearbook 2003*, edited by Mary Kaldor, Helmut Anheier, and Marlies Glasius, 87–117. Oxford: Oxford University Press.

Findlay, Trevor. 2006. "Lessons of UNSCOM and UNMOVIC for WMD Non-proliferation, Arms Control and Disarmament." In *Arms Control after Iraq: Normative and Operational Challenges*, edited by Waheguru Pal Singh Sidhu and Ramesh Thakur, 140–159. Tokyo: United Nations University Press.

Fisher, Cathleen S. 1999. *Reformation and Resistance: Nongovernmental Organizations and the Future of Nuclear Weapons*. Henry L. Stimson Center Report no. 29. www.stimson.org/images/uploads/research-pdfs/ReformationandResistance.pdf.

Grand, Camille. 2000. *The European Union and the Non-proliferation of Nuclear Weapons*. Chaillot Paper no. 37. Brussels: Western European Union Institute for Security Studies.

Grip, Lina. 2009. *The EU Non-proliferation Clause: A Preliminary Assessment*. SIPRI (Stockholm International Peace Research Institute) Background Paper. Stockholm, November.

Hawkins, Dimity. 2010. "Now We Can: Civil Society and Governments Moving toward a Ban on Nuclear Weapons." *Disarmament Forum* 2010 (4): 39–48.

HRW (Human Rights Watch). 1993. *Landmines: A Deadly Legacy*. New York: Human Rights Watch.

IANSA (International Action Network on Small Arms). 2001. Statement by Non-governmental Organisations, UN Conference on the Illicit Trade in SALW in All Its Aspects. New York, July 16.

———. 2005. *International Action on Small Arms 2005: Examining Implementation of the UN Programme of Action by Biting the Bullet*. PDF e-book, www.international-alert.org/sites/default/files/publications/red_book_2005.pdf.

ICBL (International Campaign to Ban Landmines). 1997. "Report on Activities." Diplomatic Conference on an International Total Ban on Anti-personnel Landmines, Oslo.

ICRC (International Committee of the Red Cross). 1975. *Report on the Conference of Government Experts on the Use of Certain Weapons: Lucerne 1974*. Geneva: ICRC.

Johnson, Rebecca. 2000. "Advocates and Activists: Conflicting Approaches on Nonproliferation and the Test Ban Treaty." In *The Third Force: The Rise of Transnational Civil Society*, edited by Ann M. Florini, 49–82. Washington: Carnegie Endowment for International Peace.

———. 2009. *Unfinished Business: The Negotiations of the CTBT and the End of Nuclear Testing*. Geneva: UNIDIR.

Johnstone, Ian. 2007. "The Secretary-General as Norm Entrepreneur." In Chesterman 2007, 123–38.

Joyner, Daniel H. 2008. *International Law and the Proliferation of Weapons of Mass Destruction*. Oxford: Oxford University Press.

Keck, Margaret E., and Kathryn Sikkink. 1998. *Activists beyond Borders: Advocacy Networks in International Politics*. Ithaca: Cornell University Press.

Knopf, Jeffrey W. 2012. "NGOs, Social Movements and Arms Control." In *Arms Control: History, Theory, and Policy*, edited by Robert E. Williams and Paul R. Viotti, 169–94. Santa Barbara: Praeger.

Kobia, Roland. 2008. "The EU and Non-proliferation: Need for a Quantum Leap?" *Nuclear Law Bulletin* 2008 (1): 31–53.

Krause, Keith. 2002. "Multilateral Diplomacy, Norm Building, and UN Conferences: The Case of Small Arms and Light Weapons." *Global Governance* 8 (2): 247–63.

Kytömäki, Elli, and Valerie Yankey-Wayne. 2003. *Implementing the United Nations Programme of Action on Small Arms and Light Weapons: Analysis of Reports Submitted by States in 2003*. Geneva: United Nations, UNIDIR.

Lindroos, Anja. 1997. "The Role of Euratom in the Non-proliferation Regime." In *The Finnish Yearbook of International Law*, vol. 8, edited by Martti Koskenniemi, 307–35. The Hague: Martinus Nijhoff.

Manners, Ian. 2008. "The Normative Ethics of the European Union." *International Affairs* 84 (1): 45–60.

Martens, Kerstin. 2005. *NGOs and the United Nations: Institutionalization, Professionalization and Adaption*. Basingstoke: Palgrave Macmillan.

Maull, Hans W. 2010. "The European Union as a Civilian Power: Aspirations, Potential, Achievements." In *US-China-EU Relations: Managing the New World Order*, edited by Robert S. Ross, Øystein Tunsjø, and Tuosheng Zhang, 48–74. London: Routledge.

Müller, Harald. 2005. "A Treaty in Troubled Waters: Reflections on the Failed NPT Review Conference." *International Spectator* 40 (3): 33–44.

———. 2010a. "Enforcement of the Rules in a Nuclear Weapon-Free World." In *Cultivating Confidence: Verification, Monitoring, and Enforcement for a World Free of Nuclear Weapons*, edited by Corey Hinderstein, 33–66. Stanford: Hoover Institution Press.

———. 2010b. "The 2010 NPT Review Conference: Some Breathing Space Gained, but No Breakthrough." *International Spectator* 45 (3): 5–18.

Müller, Harald, and Lars van Dassen. 1997. "From Cacophony to Joint Action: Success and Shortcomings of the European Nuclear Non-proliferation Policy." In *Common Foreign and Security Policy: The Record and Reforms*, edited by Martin Holland, 52–72. London: Pinter.

Nixdorff, Kathryn, and Jean Pascal Zanders. 2006. *Enforcing Non-proliferation: The*

European Union and the 2006 BTWC Review Conference, edited by Gustav Lindstrom. Chaillot Paper no. 93. Paris: Western European Union Institute for Security Studies.

NPT (Treaty on the Non-Proliferation of Nuclear Weapons). 2010. Final Document of the 2010 NPT RevCon. NPT/CONF.2010/50 (Vol. 1). New York.

OPCW. 2009. "OPCW Director-General Welcomes Continued EU Support for OPCW Activities." *OPCW News*, December 15. www.opcw.org/nc/news/article/opcw-director-general-welcomes-continued-eu-support-for-opcw-activities.

Otto, Ralf, Ted Paterson, and Vera Bohle. 2010. *Evaluation of EC-Funded Mine Actions, 2002–2007*. Geneva: Geneva International Centre for Humanitarian Demining. PDF e-book.

Parker, Sarah. 2011. "Analysis of National Reports: Implementation of the UN Programme of Action on Small Arms and the International Tracing Instrument in 2009–10." Occasional Paper no. 28. Geneva: Small Arms Survey.

Payne, Roger A. 2001. "Persuasion, Frames and Norm Construction." *European Journal of International Relations* 7 (1): 37–61.

Pearson, Graham S. 2006. "The Biological Weapons Convention Sixth Review Conference." *CBW Conventions Bulletin* 2006 (74): 1–44.

Peterson, M. J. 2009. "General Assembly Majorities on the Preferred Nuclear Order." In Boulden, Thakur, and Weiss 2009a, 52–72.

Piasecki, Edmund, and Tobi Trister Gati. 1993. "The United Nations and Disarmament." In *Encyclopedia of Arms Control and Disarmament*, vol. 2, edited by Richard Dean Burns, 751–70. New York: Scribner.

Price, Richard. 1998. "Reversing the Gun Sights: Transnational Civil Society Targets Land Mines." *International Organization* 52 (3): 613–44.

Regehr, Ernie. 2003. "Non-governmental Organizations Participation in the Nuclear Non-Proliferation Treaty Review Process." Prepared for the International Security Research and Outreach Programme, International Security Bureau. www.international.gc.ca/arms-armes/assets/pdfs/ngo_npt_review_regehr.pdf.

———. 2009. "The Security Council and Nuclear Disarmament." In Boulden, Thakur, and Weiss 2009a, 31–51.

Rissanen, Jenni. 2002. "NGO Perspectives: NGOs at Geneva Negotiations." *Disarmament Forum* 2002 (1): 31–35.

Risse-Kappen, Thomas. 1988. *The Zero Option: INF, West Germany and Arms Control*. Boulder: Westview Press.

Rotblat, Joseph, ed. 1982. *Scientists, the Arms Race and Disarmament: A Unesco/Pugwash Symposium*. London: Taylor and Francis.

———. 1995. *Towards a War-Free World: Annals of the 44th Pugwash Conference, 1994*. Singapore: World Scientific.

Rutherford, Kenneth, R. 2009. "The Anti-personnel Landmine Ban Convention: A

Non-hegemonic Regime." In *Cooperating without America: Theories and Case Studies of Non-hegemonic Regimes*, edited by Stefan Brem and Kendall Stiles, 123–46. London: Routledge.

Rutherford, Kenneth R., Stefan Brem, and Richard A. Matthew, eds. 2003. *Reframing the Agenda: The Impact of NGO and Middle Power Cooperation in International Security Policy*. Westport: Praeger.

Rydell, Randy. 2009. "The Secretary-General and the Secretariat." In Boulden, Thakur, and Weiss 2009a, 73–107.

Safer Rwanda. 2011. "About Us." Safer Rwanda: Building for Peace and Prosperity. www.saferrwanda.org/spip.php?rubrique1.

Sauer, Tom. 2008. "Struggling on the World Scene. An Over-ambitious EU versus a Committed Iran." *European Security* 17 (2): 273–93.

Schrag, Philip G. 1992. *Global Action: Nuclear Test Ban Diplomacy at the End of the Cold War*. Boulder: Westview Press.

Simmons, Beth A., and Lisa L. Martin. 2001. "International Organizations and Institutions." In *Handbook of International Relations*, edited by Walter Carlsnaes, Thomas Risse, and Beth A. Simmons, 192–211. London: Sage.

Simpson, John. 2001. "The 2000 NPT Review Conference." In *SIPRI Yearbook 2001: Armaments, Disarmament and International Security*, 487–502. Oxford: Oxford University Press.

Small Arms Survey, eds. 2002. *Counting the Human Cost*. A Project of the Graduate Institute of International and Development Studies, Geneva. Oxford: Oxford University Press.

Tocha, Monika. 2009. "The EU and Iran's Nuclear Programme: Testing the Limits of Coercive Diplomacy." EU Diplomacy Papers 1/2009. Brussels: College of Europe, Department of EU International Relations and Diplomacy Studies.

Traub, James. 2007. "The Secretary-General's Political Space." In Chesterman 2007, 185–201.

UN (United Nations). 2000. *The United Nations Disarmament Yearbook*. Vol. 25. New York: United Nations.

———. 2002. *The United Nations Disarmament Yearbook*. Vol. 27. New York: United Nations.

———. 2004. "UN Advisory Board on Disarmament Matters, Multilateral Disarmament and Non-proliferation Regimes and the Role of the United Nations: An Evaluation." Contribution to the High-Level Panel on Threats, Challenges and Change. DDA Occasional Paper no. 8. New York, United Nations.

———. 2010. "Working Papers." 2010 Review Conference of the Parties to the Treaty on the Non-Proliferation of Nuclear Weapons. May 3–28. www.un.org/en/conf/npt/2010/workingpapers.shtml.

Ware, Alyn. 2007. "Nuclear Disarmament: Views and Efforts of NGOs." Presentation for the 19th UN Conference on Disarmament Issues, Sapporo, August 27–29.

Wetter, Anna. 2009. *Enforcing European Union Law on Exports of Dual-Use Goods*. Oxford: Oxford University Press.

Wisotzki, Simone. 2008. "Negotiating Human Security at the UN: Transnational Civil Society, Arms Control and Disarmament." In *Transnational Activism in the UN and the EU: A Comparative Study*, edited by Jutta Joachim and Birgit Locher, 74–89. London: Routledge.

———. 2009. *Between Morality and Military Interests: Norm Setting in Humanitarian Arms Control*. PRIF Report no. 92. www.hsfk.de/fileadmin/downloads/PRIF_NO_92hp.pdf.

Wittner, Lawrence S. 1998. *The Struggle against the Bomb*. Vol. 2, *Resisting the Bomb: A History of the World Nuclear Disarmament Movement, 1954–1970*. Stanford: Stanford University Press.

———. 2009. *Confronting the Bomb: A Short History of the World Nuclear Disarmament Movement*. Stanford: Stanford University Press.

Zanders, Jean Pascal. 2006. "The European Union and the 6th Review Conference." In *Enforcing Non-proliferation: The European Union and the 2006 BTWC Review Conference*, edited by Gustav Lindstrom, 99–100. Chaillot Paper no. 93. Western European Union Institute for Security Studies.

CONCLUSION

Agency Is Central

Harald Müller

THE CONCLUDING CHAPTER draws together the results of our empirical investigations with a view to understanding the interaction between the various factors influencing norm evolution or stagnation. It starts with a description of the various modes in which norm change takes place in the regimes (section two). It then considers the impact of norm conflicts, notably those with relation to justice issues, on norm development (section three). Section four explores the ambivalences of technology development by comparing the interplay between technology and regime development. How major international changes in the short, middle, and long term affected multilateral arms control regimes is the subject of section five. In section six, the different types of norm entrepreneurs are revisited with a view to understanding the particular ways in which they react to extrinsic developments and regime conflicts in dealing with norms. The final section discusses the theoretical implications of our findings, notably the relationship between "interests" and justice concerns, and outlines some ideas for further research.

TRAJECTORIES OF NORM DYNAMICS

In what ways have regimes and their norms evolved—or shrunk—in multilateral arms control? We can use as a template the landmark study by Thomas Gehring (1994) on the evolution of environmental regimes. He discovered a general pattern whereby these regimes were created as framework norms that left room for more specific norms, or "rules" in the original definition of regime theory (Krasner 1983). In the follow-up phase, such specifications then were added to the original treaty through a series of protocols, each of which tackled a particular subfield of the larger area that the regime was meant to cover.

In multilateral arms control, there is only one regime following this trajectory: the Convention on Certain Conventional Weapons (CCW), which has been left out of our study as it is usually assigned to the realm of traditional humanitarian law. The CCW was established as a framework that gained its operational political meaning through later protocols. None of our cases follows this pattern. True, we find one case of successful protocol making (the Additional Protocol on enhanced safeguards in the nuclear nonproliferation regime) and one failed attempt at amendment, the BWC. But the only remaining case then, the Additional Protocol, was not originally intended to amend the regime regularly by specific subinstruments to make it operational; instead, NPT parties reacted to a discovery made in Iraq and the impossibility of tackling the challenge of clandestine nuclear programs within the boundaries of the established verification system. And indeed, it was not a protocol to the NPT as such, but to the safeguards agreement NNWS had concluded with the IAEA. While similar in legal form to Gehring's pattern of evolution, in substance it is different.

For the SALW PoA, the situation is reversed: here, the mode of change was similar to Gehring's model in substance, but different in its legal form. Problems that were articulated during the negotiations or addressed in the ensuing PoA review meetings but could not be tackled within the PoA setting itself were delegated to groups of experts that would then work out guidelines or fully fledged legal instruments. Brokerage, marking and tracing, ammunition, and MANPADS were approached in that way. As a consequence, the SALW regime, which is merely a loose, nonlegal agreement, proved fertile ground for instruments to regulate fields with a more restricted scope, but in a stronger form.

Elsewhere, the need to respond to challenges has been a source of regime dynamics. The misgivings of some about weak BWC compliance procedures increased when the confidence building measures proved insufficient; improvements of the NPT verification system and the emergence of the sophisticated CWC verification system made the BWC look outdated; we have a cross-regime effect here. The end of the Cold War offered the opportunity for a new initiative. All these impulses contributed to the failed quest for a compliance protocol in the BWC. The dangerous crisis of the regime after the failure of the protocol negotiations then moved parties to start the new intersessional process. Awareness of the problem served as a catalyst for both the Ottawa Convention and the SALW PoA. Ottawa, so to speak, gave birth to the CCM, which was not established as a protocol to the existing convention but as a separate, freestanding treaty.[1] The CCM closely followed the procedure that had helped establish the MBT; it covered a weapon that had very similar characteristics to antipersonnel land mines. Before the MBT, it would have been impossible to secure impetus for this project in the face of resistance from national air forces. After the precedent provided a reference, progress became a real possibility when the abundance of cluster munitions remnants emerged as a menace equivalent to landmines.

Next, we can make a distinction between incremental, intrinsic evolution and extrinsic evolution by way of strong steps. The CWC is characterized by the first alternative. This regime—with maybe the smallest increment of change after it had been created among all regimes visited in this volume—developed largely along the lines of the instruments and stipulations that the convention itself contained. Some revisiting of chemical technology without groundbreaking consequences, some practical activities in terms of technological cooperation that were initiated partially in response to NAM complaints, universalization and implementation action, the creation of disarmament assistance for CW holders not capable of meeting their deadlines (not foreseen in the original language of the convention), and the initiation of some antiterrorist activities after 9/11 were the developments that we observed after the CWC entered into force. All of them were useful and certainly in harmony with the letter and spirit of the convention, while none was particularly dramatic or momentous.

Complementary norm construction outside the established regime institutions was important in all WMD regimes. This concerns the sharpening of the export control instruments by the NSG and the Australia Group, the installation of PSI as a complement to export controls in case these controls fail, and Security Council Resolution 1540 and successive resolutions as a way to make measures taken by members of the export "clubs" universal with a view to preventing proliferation both to nonstate and to state actors. The fact that the norm entrepreneurs responsible (most notably the United States) chose to transcend the boundaries of the established regimes points to intraregime conflicts that rendered comparable amendments within the regime framework difficult or even impossible; at the same time, this strategy exacerbated existing conflicts in some cases and thus had an ambivalent effect on norm development.

Altogether, we have not observed norm degeneration or decay in our sample. Nevertheless, the risks of this possibility were obvious during the crises of the BWC in 2001, the NPT in 2005, and the SALW PoA in 2006. In each instance, governmental change in the United States or the gallant efforts of pro-norm actors eventually saved the regimes, but the episodes confirmed that the growth or even survival of normative structures cannot be taken for granted.

We have not observed a general cyclic pattern of norm development; norm change takes different forms depending on the context and the constellation of actors (cf. Sandholtz 2007; Sandholtz and Stiles 2009).[2] Equally, the idea of "norms as processes" (Krook and True 2010, 105) suggests a continuity of development that is defied by the irregularity of change: norms may be stagnant for an extended period of time despite contestation (e.g., nuclear disarmament from 1970 to 1995) but then enter innovative change (1995 and beyond); they might undergo considerable change only to fall back into stagnation (as did verification and compliance in the BWC).

JUSTICE CONFLICTS AS DRIVERS OF NORM DYNAMICS

Substantive Issues

Because international norms, embedded in regimes, have distributional effects and also afford the chance to participate in decision making, it is no surprise that issues of justice and fairness appear as salient factors in the development of regimes once one devotes serious study to them.

The three WMD regimes show both similarities and differences concerning the impact of justice issues on their development. As a nondiscriminatory treaty, the BWC does not contain any inherent "injustices." Justice-related claims emerge over its interpretation and the nature of potential additional instruments such as the Australia Group. These claims can be grouped into the categories of distributive justice (regarding equal access to biotechnology and its products) and procedural justice (nondiscriminatory compliance procedures and export control measures or equal chances to determine the agenda). Especially in the first area, normative claims to fair distribution and equal chances of participation mingle with material interests. The CWC case is similar in that it also distributes rights and duties equally among all members. Some NAM states, however, claim cases of procedural and distributive injustice occur in this field too due to club-style export controls, perceived unequal opportunity to reap the benefits of economic and technological cooperation, and what they consider a lack of equitable representation in the Technical Secretariat (e.g., African Group 2008).[3] All this is connected to the notion of past deprivations and results in a collective demand for compensatory justice on the part of the developing countries. In both areas, justice claims have impacted upon the norm dynamics in the regime. At times, they have prompted efforts to address the inequalities such as in the case of a BWC verification system (which failed) or in increasing efforts in recent years to address the concerns of developing countries regarding international cooperation. In other instances, however, perceived injustices have also fueled conflicts (for example, export controls versus technological exchange), thus preventing a strengthening of some regime norms.

The pivotal importance of justice concerns in the NPT (Rathbun 2006; Müller 2010) emerges from its inherent inequality, which can be overcome only by disarmament and universalization. Justice concerns, which were already articulated when the treaty was negotiated, influenced the misgivings of NNWS (the NAM in particular) about the insufficient progress of disarmament. Western nuclear energy users and developing countries resent discrimination concerning peaceful uses of nuclear energy, major NAM and Arab states complain about unequal standards, and developing countries criticize a lack of opportunity to participate in key decision-making procedures. Thus, justice concerns drive norm dynamics in the nuclear nonproliferation regime, a factor not to be underrated, as a closer look at the three most salient conflicts involving justice claims reveals.

The conflict over disarmament has driven norm specification and the imposition of accountability on NWS. It took a long while and the extraordinary opportunity of the 1995 Extension Conference to put this dynamic in place: before that date, all efforts to make the undertaking under Art. VI less vague failed against resistance by the NWS, while the normative precedent set in 1995 facilitated later agreements and failed in 2005 only because of the revolutionary approach of the Bush administration toward arms control multilateralism.

Intra-Western conflicts over peaceful uses have contributed to the development of export control norms, while the conflict between the industrialized world and the NAM in the same issue area has been blocking norm development for a decade. The reason is that the conflict—from the NAM perspective—is aggravated by two additional factors that, for industrialized states, are either nonexistent or less virulent. First, there is the notion that disarmament is the quid pro quo for the renunciation of nuclear weapons; without disarmament, ending nonproliferation is seen, in this perspective, as the most viable and legitimate means to achieve equality. Second, the inequality of burdens that result from nonproliferation measures is perceived as perpetuating the tremendous inequalities from the colonial and imperial periods. Resistance to this is thus very fundamental. What is important here and found in the other regimes as well is that efforts to change norms are not just connected to singular actions or events (see below), but also relate to lasting practices that are challenged by claims for justice. And they involve not only "trial and error" search "in the nexus between theory and practice" (Krook and True 2010, 117), but also strong disputes engaging the metanorm of justice.

In the CWC, the connection between justice and disarmament is of a different quality than in the NPT. The difference between weapon possessors and those who never had chemical weapons did not amount to the same fundamental conflict as within the NPT even though some weapon holders, the two biggest ones included, did not meet their disarmament deadline. The CWC contains specific, binding, and time-bound language concerning the disarmament obligation. There is no doubt that the weapon holders accept this duty and move in that direction. The "coupling" of the issues of disarmament and economic justice thus does not occur. As a result, the disarmament controversy was aggravated no further (despite Iran's best efforts) and resulted in a range of schemes for disarmament assistance rather than blockage, while economic cooperation activities develop that mitigate and may, over time, eliminate the conflict for good; in either aspect the OPCW proved helpful for managing the conflicts. In the BWC, there is no disarmament conflict because no party is supposed to have biological weapons to be disarmed.

While there are thus significant differences in the intensity of the disarmament issue as a root cause of justice conflicts, the peaceful uses/trade/cooperation conflict is virulent in all three WMD regimes. Developing countries are exerting their right to catch up in the use of technologies considered essential for their development. Real-world value resides with civilian biological and chemical technology more than with nuclear technology, inter alia, due to their significance for public health. The high capital and associated costs of nuclear power plants present small and middle-sized developing countries with serious entry barriers and have so far prevented even many major ones from moving forward with civilian nuclear power programs. In real terms, then, the supposed impediments to civilian cooperation in biotechnology and chemical technology are a more serious concern than in the nuclear sector. However, in the NPT, access to civilian nuclear technology is part of the larger justice bargain involving disarmament. This might explain why the controversy is as bitter in the NPT as in the other two regimes, and why the NSG is the target of hardly less resentment than is shown toward the Australia Group.

Conflicts over justice in humanitarian arms control are found at different junctures. They concern, first, issues of sovereignty; this, however, is no North-South issue even though the Southern approach to sovereignty is more justice-loaded because it refers to the principle of equal sovereignty as a matter of status, while major powers are more interested in the instrumental value of freedom of action. The United States is at the head of the sovereignty claimants, as is Russia. This cross-cutting frontline takes much of the heat out of this conflict but, of course, does little to help with the universalization of the related norms.

The second justice conflict in humanitarian arms control concerns distribution of the cost of implementing the agreed norms. This conflict is probably not resolved, but considerably mitigated, by related assistance programs that are even written into the regimes themselves (though not necessarily implemented with the necessary vigor and resources). There is logic behind this treatment of the issue: after all, the regimes were initiated for humanitarian reasons. The distribution-of-the-burden problem, then, is an outgrowth of the humanitarian catastrophe that the regimes are meant to remedy. It is thus only logical that the protagonists of regime creation follow up with some effort to tend to the distribution burden—because otherwise the humanitarian objective could not even come close to being reached despite the norm for which they fought with such zeal. This conflict has thus tended to be fairly benign toward norm development, since it was defined by the actors as a problem to be solved and not as incompatible claims to demand of each other.

The third—muted—justice concern exists between the technological haves and the have-nots; more cheap and rudimentary weaponry could have been prohibited while sophisticated, "intelligent" arms were permitted, favoring the technologically advanced countries. The probability that this could happen was quite high, because this is a US preference that is overdetermined by both a desire (to remain superior by having superior weaponry) and a cultural inclination (to look for technical solutions). This concern has been reduced by the broad scope of the related prohibitions, with only few exceptions. The moral rigor of the like-minded norm entrepreneurs and the watchful guardianship of the NGOs have prevented this problem from escalating into a have/have-not problem on a nuclear scale.

The question of universalization has had only a limited impact on regime development so far. In the CWC this might be due to the fact that there are clear rules for tracing chemicals and related technology that punish those who hold out. That there is no hard evidence for BW possession by holdouts might help to keep the issue "toned down" in the BWC. For both the BWC and the CWC, the fact that leading Arab states and Israel are not states parties prevents the Arab side, the most vocal advocate of universalization in the NPT, from playing this card. There is no *nonmember* position for the PoA, as it does not need to be signed and ratified. In the MBT, the largely norm-observing behavior of the nonparties also helps to keep the potential conflict well contained. Here, as in the CCM, the exception for joint operations with nonmembers (the "NATO clause"), which may imply the use of weapons prohibited under these treaties by outside states, has created some misgivings among the non-allied parties, albeit apparently more for compliance and effectiveness reasons than from concerns about justice. In the NPT regime, one might have expected the trade agreements with nonmember India—against established norms—to have negative ramifications, but the consequences remained limited; expression of concern and some rhetorical lambasting but—so far—no more; probably India's status as an influential NAM member and developing country was helpful. Israel's holdout status, in contrast, was powerfully framed as a justice issue by Arab states with Egypt at the forefront.[4] It proved a norm-driver under the circumstances of 1995, when Arab consent was desired for indefinite extension. Thus emerged the compromise of the "Middle East Resolution" as confirmed in 2000 and specified in 2010, which made the regional issue in the Middle East—other than South and East Asia—a specific concern for the treaty community, which required operational political steps to be taken.

Considerations of Procedural Justice

The longstanding blockage of the CD and the start of negotiations on the MBT and the CCM outside of the official negotiation forums invite an interesting question regarding procedural justice. The formal forums are characterized by unit vetoes. Negotiations cannot be concluded unless all parties agree (the same applies for review conferences). From one perspective, this setting may ultimately seem just: all states have the equal opportunity to prevail with their interest in not having the existing order changed by a new legal or political instrument, independent of their power status. This is a remarkable application of the principle of equal sovereignty, a beacon of justice in the world of states. Yet, by the same token, this procedure prevents all other parties from concluding an agreement that they want to conclude, and that would not bind the vetoing state as long as it decides not to join. The vetoing state, thus, not only applies its right not to be bound to something that it deems incompatible with its interest, but it also prevents all others from concluding, among themselves, something they believe is very much in their interests. From this perspective, all others suffer from injustice. Whether the veto procedure or the inclusive negotiation procedure without a veto is more just is not self-evident. Nevertheless, the high entry hurdles of exclusive negotiation forums have negative effects on the perception of outsiders. This effect is mitigated for the UNSC as this is a legally established institution that still enjoys certain legitimacy. Even so, UN SC/RES/1540 created some irritation among nonpermanent members and even more among nonmembers of the UNSC who had no say in making a norm that affected their domestic decision-making prerogative. It was all the more remarkable then that this norm proved relatively effective and successful. The tension engendered by the exclusive export control bodies, however, clearly had a negative impact on the possibility of forging agreement on export and cooperation issues in all three WMD regimes.

Furthermore, there are misgivings about the core role of the UNSC in WMD norm enforcement. The problem is most acute in the nuclear nonproliferation regime, because the five erstwhile sinners proudly pose as the guardians of the regime tasked to keep others from emulating their own example. It has also led norm-conscious Sweden to push for an alternative enforcement scheme in the BWC where only the UNSC is called upon to address noncompliance issues. The CWC is the regime with the most sophisticated regime-internal enforcement procedure; it may be for this reason that the issue has not become virulent. In the conventional arms regimes, enforcement has not caused conflict so far. Because powerful states such as the United States, Russia, China, and India are not members of either the MBT or the CCM, the idea of "enforcement" would lack realism. The nature of these regimes suggests persuasion and assistance as the appropriate tools for enhancing compliance rather than condemnation, applying sanctions, and the use of force that has been more typical of the WMD areas. Iran has repeatedly articulated the injustice and hypocrisy of UNSC action against its nuclear activity. While the reactions of NAM states to Iran's nuclear program show concern and occasional condemnation, a modicum of solidarity has been preserved by the NAM, a clear reflection of the misgivings about the "aristocratic" character of UNSC decision making.

Another source of tension over procedure is the decisive role of small group negotiations both for establishing a regime and amending it in politically binding form at review conferences. Informal negotiations involving smaller numbers of key countries with a certain kind of regional representation have been used time and again to make breakthroughs when the situation was stalled; agreements reached in such settings provided a suggestive momentum that carried the majority behind it. Inevitably, some of the excluded parties were alienated (while others were glad that the group solved the problem for them). The apparent representation, however, dampened the desire for declaring an exit, and agreements of this kind tend to prevail.

Finally, Western-dominated "clubs," the NSG, the Australia Group, the MTCR, and the Wassenaar Agreement, run arms-control-related export controls. The former two, in particular, have provoked a great deal of resentment and occasional demands for dissolution among non-aligned states. Club members argue with the efficiency objective; the greater emphasis that advanced states put on efficiency is opposed to the priority for justice and equality set by the global South. Only a few countries such as Sweden on the Northern side and South Africa on the Southern side try to reconcile these two objectives. Nevertheless, it is obvious that the "clubs" have been important for norm development in an area that, left to market forces, would probably have witnessed a race to the bottom in export control policy.

Regime Conflicts and Norm Development

The principled indeterminacy of the language in which norms are represented is not the cause of their being disputed but rather offers the opportunity structure for the contest, not only over norm application but also over the very meaning of norms and their relative priorities. The contention itself is, inter alia, triggered by different justice claims. These claims, and emphasis on them, differ with the position, history, cultural background, and experience of the actors (see Krause 1998). Contrary to expectations, disputes about the principles underlying justice claims were not of great importance. Rather, the relative weight of these claims or their justification in a specific situation (was there enough nuclear disarmament?) had an impact. There is also the obvious priority conflict between justice and the common-good norm of regime efficiency, which is notably evident in the establishment of (efficiency-oriented) "clubs" for the implementation of norms and the inevitable protestations of nonmembers against their exclusion.[5]

TECHNOLOGY AND NORM DYNAMICS

Chapter 4 emphasizes the ambivalent effects of technology development as providing both a *challenge* and an *opportunity* for arms control to proceed. This ambivalence reverberates through all regimes investigated.

The CW regime is confronted with rapid technological developments, such as in biochemistry and nanotechnology, but norm development lags behind technological progress, including the area of incapacitants, and so-called non-lethal weapons. Rapid developments in biotechnology have also given rise to concerns about increasing potentials for misuse. Yet, until 2012 the BWC members had not even discussed ways and means to monitor scientific and technological developments relevant to the convention collectively and systematically. While this is changing in the current intersessional process, and while there is a growing awareness among states that scientists need to be educated about the potential risks of their work, at the time of writing it still remains to be seen how effective the new science and technology review process will be.

In the United States, the speed of progress in biotechnology has turned the country against complementing the regime by verification and compliance norms in direct opposition to other members, including, notably, the EU. These members viewed technological development as a reason for strengthening the normative order. The United States, in contrast, saw no possibility to verify the BWC reliably and was concerned about the loss of competition- or security-relevant information through strong verification. In sum, the rapid pace of progress in the chemical and biological fields has changed the perception of challenges facing the regimes; but the regimes, in particular the BWC regime, have been slow to adapt to these changes.

Technology developments had a limited impact in the NPT, too. The emergence of centrifuge enrichment taught suppliers that uranium enrichment had become more accessible to advanced developing countries, while leaving a smaller energy footprint for satellite infrared sensors than gas diffusion technology. Innovative verification schemes (the Hexapartite Agreement) were the response. The recent push for multinational fuel cycle arrangements owes much to this development, too. The strong improvement of measurement and analytical capabilities for verification purposes enabled some features of the Additional Protocol in the first place. Finally, improved resolution by satellite sensors and advances in analytical capabilities based on information technology (IT) have enhanced the likelihood of detecting undeclared facilities and thus thrust the area of compliance and enforcement into the foreground. And it also appears possible to direct technological development toward helping generate the new norm of giving priority to proliferation-resistant technologies.

In humanitarian arms control, technological change proved a mighty temptation to design circumvention technologies to evade the impact of prohibitions on the freedom and flexibility of military action. On the whole, the temptation did not prevail. The humanitarian motivation shown by like-minded governmental and nongovernmental actors was, somehow surprisingly, stronger than the impulses and desires of the military-industrial complexes.

SALIENT EVENTS

Limited Impact: Power Shift and 9/11

The current power shift has so far had little impact on the BW and CW regimes. The importance of several developing and emerging countries for the global chemical industry has increased, and the growth of the biotechnology sector in several developing countries might in the medium term impact (or may already have impacted) their attitude toward transfer controls and international cooperation (Becker 2007; Sims 2009); but this is hardly an example of power transition influence. In addition, these countries are now much more strongly affected by several provisions of the CWC, such as in the area of verification, and will have greater influence in related areas in the future. So far, however, this has had little impact on norm development, and there appears to be no connection between changes in power status of major players and their positions and actions in the regime.

Power shift appears to have had a direct impact only in a limited field of the nuclear nonproliferation regime, export controls. India's rise motivated the United States to embrace the new power and potential ally. The compromises that the United States made to India led to a rollback of the established norm of comprehensive safeguards as a condition of nuclear export and sealed, for the time being, the increasingly illusory objective of achieving universality for the NPT. China's emergence as world power might have made enforcement action more difficult because of the great Chinese skepticism concerning sanctions and other instruments of political pressure, and potential power rivalry motivates hedging policies in nuclear disarmament that, in turn, reinforce the related intraregime conflict in the NPT. Other than that, the power shifts that occurred over recent years have apparently not (yet?) left a decisive imprint on the regimes.

The impact of 9/11 on the regimes was very specific rather than general. The OPCW reacted to the terrorist attack with a series of initiatives for preventing CW attacks by terrorists. Already at the end of 2001, it installed an Open

Ended Working Group on Terrorism, which reviews contributions of the organization to the fight against global terrorism. The OPCW believes that complete implementation of the CWC and its norms is fundamental to this struggle. As in the CWC, 9/11 motivated antiterrorist activities in the IAEA and a number of extra-regime institutions such as the Global Threat Initiative, various G8 programs, or the Washington Security Summit of 2010; all are designed to limit nonstate actor access to fissile material. The pathbreaking initiative, however, long preceded 9/11: the Nunn-Lugar program for helping Russia and other successor states of the Soviet Union to deal with the communist empire's nuclear inheritance started in 1994 and had expended several billion US dollars long before Al Qaida heightened the concern about mass murder terrorism.

The concern about bioterrorism goes back to the early 1990s as well.[6] The attacks of 9/11 and the anthrax letters mailed in the United States shortly afterward, while factually unrelated, acted as a catalyst to place a strong focus on bioterrorism and on national measures to prevent illegitimate access to dangerous biological materials that had superseded the preoccupation with verification on a state-to-state level. This new focus dominated US positions during the Bush years, but it was also taken up in a weaker form by other states. It has induced BWC parties to focus on biosecurity with a view to preventing biological terrorism. Similar efforts have thus been undertaken in all regimes regarding terrorism, while the most important measures in areas such as the G8 Global Security Initiative, PSI, and UN Security Council Resolution 1540 largely evolved outside of the traditional regime institutions (see Craft 2004; Oosthuizen and Wilmshurst 2004; Valencia 2005).

Significant Impact: The End of the Cold War and Intrinsic Regime Events

In contrast to the relatively limited impact of general and global events, two types of "salient events" have exerted a strong influence on the development of international arms control norms. The first event was the end of the Cold War. This global conflict situation had structured international relations in general and, therefore, the arms control component as well. It is thus not surprising that the conclusion of that conflict had momentous effects on arms control (see Krause 1998). Whereas the East-West conflict had prevented the emergence of new norms (such as prohibiting CW and developing humanitarian arms control) or the improvement of old ones (the NPT or the BWC), new openings appeared; the NPT was extended, its verification system overhauled, and related export controls strengthened. The progress on reducing nuclear arsenals paved the way to becoming more specific when it came to what Art. VI could mean in practice. The end of the Cold War led to greater involvement of the UNSC in compliance policy and enforcement efforts (North Korea, Iraq, Iran). These efforts had only limited results and caused frequent controversies among the P5. The BWC parties made a major (though eventually abortive) effort to amend the convention and, failing that, developed the new intersessional process. Contrary to the popular myth that the "loss of control" by the superpowers over their underlings had opened up the Pandora's box of proliferation, there was more of a rollback of existing programs than a stampede of new ones (see Müller and Schmidt 2010). Thus, while power shift had a limited effect and 9/11 a negligible effect on arms control, the end of a world conflict left its mark on it.

The second type of "salient event," different from the extrinsic ones investigated in chapter 5, was *intrinsic events* inside the regimes that persuaded parties to embark on new paths, with ambivalent effects on norm dynamics. We did not list this factor in our considerations at the beginning of this book (and of our project), but our empirical work led us to the conclusion that it is of considerable importance. This was most visible in the development of export controls: chemical warfare in the Iran-Iraq War during the 1980s, combined with the knowledge that Western companies had exported material and precursors to Iraq, led to the creation of a forum with harmonized export control measures, the Australia Group, even before the CWC was negotiated. In response to some cases of BW proliferation that were discovered in the early 1990s, the group expanded their export control guidelines to the biological field. In both fields, these developments contributed to improved export controls, but also to exacerbation of the conflict over international cooperation and technology exchange. The Indian nuclear explosion of 1974 and the discovery of the Iraqi nuclear weapons program after the 1991 war motivated stronger nuclear export controls, and the latter event also led to an improved verification regime for the NPT that relied on progress in verification technologies. Improvement and spread of centrifuge enrichment technology prompted the search for new norms such as fuel guarantees and multinational fuel cycle arrangements in the NPT regime. However, as stated above, the priority conflict concerning nonproliferation versus cooperation and development has compromised the effectiveness of these improvements: they did not become politically binding norms.

The failure of the protocol negotiations and of all attempts to strengthen the

BWC through a legally binding protocol in 2001, largely a result of US policy at that time, was a crucial factor in the subsequent fundamental changes to the regime. For at least ten years, action turned away from traditional modes of arms control and nonproliferation and shifted toward national, voluntary measures to prevent proliferation and terrorism, with some additional issues tackled as secondary area of focus. As a positive corollary, the regime saw an overdue improvement of its institutional setting; the annual meetings established in 2002 were devised to prevent the regime from collapse after the 2001 shock but also provided a useful platform for improved interaction.

The creation of humanitarian arms control and its ensuing evolution (the emergence of special regimes rolling out of SALW, and the CCM being shaped after the model of the MBT) were stimulated by the emergencies of internal conflict and external intervention that caused the calamity of mines, cluster munitions, and abundant small arms for civilian populations. Norm creation and development reacted to the specific problems and dangers created by these weapons in the context of ongoing conflict or postconflict reconstruction. Even though no single events initiated this process, the processes observed fit into the category of specific intrinsic developments as well.

Thus, like regime conflicts, salient events and technological developments had ambivalent effects. They have presented challenges to the regimes whose effects on regime stability were at times severe; some of these effects are lasting and continue to require efforts to be neutralized. But they also led parties to adapt the regime to the challenges and motivated norm entrepreneurs to spring into action. In that, our findings confirm those of Sandholtz and Stiles (2009, chapter 12).

NORM ENTREPRENEURS

The role of norm entrepreneurs differs from the above-mentioned variables that are *structural* factors, partially intrinsic (regime conflicts), partially extrinsic (events impacting upon structure, power shift, technology developments) to the regimes. Norm entrepreneurs, in contrast, represent *agency*. They are transmission belts for transforming structural challenges and changes into political action that results in norm development. The term *transmission belt*, however, suggests mechanics that do not exist. Agency possesses considerable degrees of freedom. How norm entrepreneurs respond to said external stimuli is thus far from predetermined.

The various types of norm entrepreneurs that we have reviewed in the preceding chapters betray quite different motivations, or combinations thereof, respond in different ways to technology changes and external events, and act differently in the regime conflicts. They do so in their own respective manner, with varying effect.

Common Good–Driven Norm Entrepreneurs

"Good international citizens" plus South Africa, nongovernmental organizations, and international organizations—both the UN and the EU—as far as they act in an independent way, pursue a combination of common good, humanitarian, and justice orientations. The common good objective aims at enhancing regime efficiency, as the functioning of the regimes and the smooth implementation of their norms is seen as the prerequisite for a law-based, peaceful international order in which all humans and their governments should be interested. The humanitarian objective takes the individual as the rightful moral claimant entitled to be protected; this explains why this group of entrepreneurs is strongly promoting humanitarian arms control. South Africa is relatively close to the "good citizens." It differs due to its stronger emphasis on collective justice claims but concurs in a NAM-atypical understanding of the common good of cooperative security regimes and the importance of individual justice claims as manifested in its strong support for humanitarian arms control.

Technological developments impact on those actors' behavior in two distinct ways: innovation that offers new types of weaponry or opportunities to circumvent existing restrictions is seen with alarm as provoking dangerous challenges to the existing order and leads to efforts to contain these risks by new or amended norms. NGOs tend to react to such changes with strong expressions of moral revulsion. Innovation promising new possibilities to make controls—such as verification—more efficient is pursued, supported, and promoted. As a developing country, South Africa shares the NAM longing for compensatory assistance in technology development and unimpeded access to civilian technologies required for further development. As a technologically relatively advanced country it has a greater understanding of the risks of unfettered transfer and exchange but still insists that undue constraints must not be allowed. Access to technology for developing countries is the main point of norm entrepreneurship in that regard. The UN organs, notably the Secretariat, tend to promote compromise via norm-based solutions to all these challenges. The same applies to the EU, with a slightly stronger impetus for norm efficiency.

The three types of salient events that we have investigated, two as planned in our research outline and one found inductively, uniformly lead to efforts by these actors either to use opportunities to extend the scope and depth of arms control or to contain the risks that extrinsic shocks and developments may entail for security multilateralism. They all tried to exploit the rapid dismantlement of the East-West conflict for creating regional and global norms that would provide a peace dividend, eliminate the risks of new arms races, and enhance overall stability in the international system. NGOs took the initiative in humanitarian arms control and pushed for nuclear and chemical disarmament. The EU made arms control and multilateralism a key element of its emerging Common Foreign and Security Policy. The UN, with its limited means to set up policy initiatives of its own, was instrumental as a forum for global initiatives and played a key role in the emergence of humanitarian arms control. South Africa, Canada, Germany, and Sweden worked on all fronts to create and strengthen norms. By the same token, when 9/11 occurred, all these actors took the suddenly perceived new threat as the reason to renew efforts for multilateral security cooperation with a view to strengthening existing regimes and utilizing them to prevent the access of nonstate actors to dangerous materials, technologies, and weapons. When the Bush administration, in contrast, took 9/11 as a stimulus to continue with the selective dismantlement of multilateral norms it disliked, they either worked hard to provide for continuity (state actors, EU, UN) or burst out in hostile criticism (NGOs and South Africa). Likewise, the main reaction to indications of a rearrangement of global power relations led them to try to keep the superpower with its unilateral instincts within the bounds of arms control multilateralism and at the same time to bind the rising powers to the same norms while accommodating some of their particular concerns.

The group is divided regarding positions on regime conflicts. NGOs tend to side with reformers and their critique of great powers, pushing moral and justice issues and asking for much quicker progress on all disarmament fronts. The rest positions itself as mediator between great powers and the justice-minded reformers from the NAM, South Africa leaning more toward the NAM side. Taking middle positions and trying to bridge gaps can be said to present a "basic instinct" of good citizens and international organizations with their secretariats for which finding common ground among members is indeed a fundamental *raison d'organisation* as equivalent to the *raison d'état* of nation-states.

So far, so good; but the record is not completely spotless. Good citizens also tend to be trading states, and their economic interests occasionally lead to compromises with the moral high ground as in dubious conventional arms exports or insufficient efforts to curb norm-breaching transfers by private actors of a criminal nature. Germany and Canada, moreover, have to compromise with their nuclear-armed allies in nuclear arms control and with their super-ally United States in the conventional field where the American inclination to accept constraints on conventional arms development and their use is, to put it mildly, strongly limited. It is also remarkable that the degree of proactivism varies with the party in power, at least during the last ten years. In Canada and Sweden neoconservatism and its devastating attitude toward multilateralism have not reached the excesses observed in the United States but have compromised the entrepreneurial role that they fulfilled during the last generation.[7] It is to the credit of foreign office bureaucracies that they have protected a modicum of continuity even without the support and occasionally against the desires of the political leadership.

International organizations are condemned to move close to the lowest possible denominator of their member states and never to trespass the limits of tolerance of the least arms-control-minded member. Secretariat bureaucrats and leaders pursue their own personal ambitions, or those of their departments and offices, as can be presently observed in the EU: continual infighting between the various collective actors under the Lisbon Treaty, the European Commission, the permanent presidency, the European External Action Service (EEAS), the European Council—all working at cross-purposes with a negative impact on the Union's effectiveness.

NGOs, certainly the most moral actors in the field, are also organizations with material interests (in funding) and leaders who, at times, display inflated egos. Battles over turf are not infrequent, and coordination is always a problem. The revival of the nuclear disarmament agenda, for example, has pushed three major global efforts forward—the Nuclear Threat Initiative (NTI), International Campaign to Abolish Nuclear Weapons (ICAN), and Global Zero—whose activities are barely coordinated, and all of which compete for public attention.

However, at the end of the day it is this group of actors that has been responsible for a great deal of progress—and for preventing regression—in multilateral arms control. Advocating and protecting norms and preventing regime conflicts—notably between great powers and non-aligned states—from total degeneration demonstrate the considerable merits of multilateral cooperative security policy in serving the common good.

Conventional Interest-Driven Actors

What dominates the great powers, according to our findings, are status concerns mixed together with a stronger emphasis on national security than that found among the "good citizens." While this motivation complex fits traditional understandings of national interest well, it takes the form of a belief in entitlement to great power status (or the leadership position) the denial of which is perceived as an undeserved injustice.

For the United States this means aversion to proposals that curb military options in order to maintain freedom of military operations worldwide. For the three others (notably Russia and China, to whom the United States presents, in their perception, a security problem) preventing the United States from achieving credible offensive options against their core security limits the readiness to accept arms control proposals that would inhibit their countering such options. The constellation of an "attitudinal race" between superiority ambitions and equal security claims leads to only a small area of overlap in which good citizen proposals, reformer's justice claims, and great power status interests converge on arms control norms.

Consequently, American norm entrepreneurship aims at the effectiveness of regimes in terms of verification (if possible exempting the United States itself), compliance, and enforcement. Increasingly, the United States has promoted norms outside the established international law–based regimes, such as export controls, antiterrorism measures, and the Proliferation Security Initiative. There is aversion on the US side to proposals limiting national options, and this attitude is even stronger among Republicans than it is with Democrats.

Russia and China work as norm entrepreneurs to ensure their status against the US challenge, but they are loathe to accept effective disarmament unless the US concessions were to definitively and decisively surpass their own. As in the American case, economic interests in conventional arms export and—less selectively than the United States—nuclear transfers also compromise their capability to engage in norm entrepreneurship. India is strongly oriented toward China, both in security and in status terms. Apart from far-reaching nuclear disarmament proposals that in the 1990s were somehow no longer voiced and a willingness to comply with the CWC and the BWC, India's contribution to building and maintaining norms has been small.

Technology developments are strictly assessed in terms of their exploitability for enhancing military options (United States) or providing counterbalances (Russia, China). When a technology appears to offer these options, these countries oppose constraints. Russia and China are willing to promote arms control measures against technologies the early utilization of which might reinforce Washington's advantage. Where nonproliferation norms are strengthened by particular technologies, such as for verification, great powers, notably the United States, are leading the way in advancing such technologies.

A similar pattern emerges in how great powers respond to extrinsic events. The Soviet Union/Russia pursued the maintenance of formal equality during the end phase and after the end of the Cold War, though with a considerable orientation toward common global security during the Gorbachev years. The United States, on the other hand, after a brief period of accepting parity, used the demise of its rival for establishing global superiority and then tried desperately to cling to this cherished position. Arms control was subordinated to this overarching objective. China (and possibly India) worked its way into multilateralism according to the speed of its rise. Norms were acceptable only to the extent that they fitted their increasing influence.

After 9/11, China and Russia tried eagerly to maintain as much of the existing multilateral norm network as possible, because it promised constraints on US power, and to oppose new norms that would constrain them (as in the humanitarian sectors). The Bush government took 9/11 as confirmation of its long-held view that multilateral arms control norms were largely useless and should be replaced by ad hoc coalitions to pursue narrowly circumscribed national security gains. Only the combined efforts of the rest of the world could prevent it from damaging existing regimes in an irreversible way. India kept a low profile, pursuing rapprochement with the United States while observing the norms to which it had subscribed (such as the CWC and the BWC), not disturbing the NPT too much, but abstaining from humanitarian arms control as did its great power peers.

Great powers, then, are more oriented to national interests than to the common good (different from the first group of actors) but justify this attitude by identifying the national and the global interest, thereby cloaking their national aspirations in the mantle of global justice. When they put their weight behind norms, it has a most beneficial effect, as the creation of the NPT or the CWC proved. Altogether, however, it is not unfair to say that the glass is half empty instead of half full. And their record on humanitarian arms control is negative, whatever high moral ground they otherwise claim to occupy: petty military advantages outdo compassion for the victims of indiscriminate conventional arms.

In an almost ironical way, the DPRK, arguably the most brittle state in our sample, comes closest to this pattern of great power behavior. For North Korea, the pivotal concern was the intricate combination of regime survival and recognition as a worthy partner. If this double objective were to be achieved in any way, it can be assumed that all normative concerns would quickly dissipate in an airy opportunistic realm.

In Between Plus and Minus: Egypt and Iran

For Iran, a return to the "true" original norms of multilateral arms control would emasculate great power (notably, but not exclusively, American) superiority and restore Iran to its status as a regionally preponderant actor to which the Iranian political class, despite all its divisions, appears to be uniformly devoted. Iran combines the aspiration of leadership, founded upon an ancient culture and the fervor of Shia Islamism, with a deeply felt disdain for the injustice of the existing order (beyond arms control, that is), a disdain that is equally informed by the worldview ingrained in this brand of Islamism. Genuine moral positions (a morality alien to prevailing Western thinking and feeling) combine with a worldly quest for status.

Egypt wants an effective multilateralism with as much disarmament as possible and one that is based on formal sovereign equality. The quest for justice, read as compensation for past injustices, fulfillment of need, and a claim to equality that we can see in profusion in Iranian stances is also tangible in the attitudes and demands of much more moderate Egypt.

For Egypt, regional status and national defense needs are key factors influencing its arms control positions. Its imposing and enduring emphasis on the Middle East in the nuclear regime, and its refusal to accede to the BWC and CWC as long as the regional nuclear asymmetry persists, are consequences of the first factor; its abstention over humanitarian arms control is motivated by the second factor.

As far as Egypt is concerned, technology is more important as a tool of economic development than for either creating military options or strengthening disarmament norms; discriminatory access conditions violate this interest as much as Egypt's equality principle, a position that is taken to an extreme by Iran. Consequently, Egypt, despite no national experience of having been victimized by nuclear export controls, is as adamant an opponent of the NSG as Iran, which has indeed been the target of such export controls. Iran, in turn, has organized its nuclear and arms production sectors in order to exploit technological advances as quickly for security and supposedly military purposes as the level of national competence permits, as soon as the authorities so decide, while Egypt appears to deal with technology issues as an equal-access issue in the first place and shows no significant sign of large-scale military application.

The continuity of Egypt's arms control policies after the end of the East-West conflict is impressive; the decisive change took place much earlier with the coming to power of President Sadat and the opening up to the West—that is, as a consequence of domestic change. Neither the rise of China and India nor the landmark event of 9/11 has led to any reconsideration or change in the thrust of Egyptian efforts. The Bush administration's attempt to break out of the multilateral "straightjacket" met Cairo's resistance, of which the most impressive instance was the blocking strategy at the 2005 NPT Review. Otherwise, Egypt continued with its strong efforts to insert constructively a special regional norm on the Middle East in the nuclear nonproliferation regime.

Conversely, the hardening of the Iranian stance, combined with much higher visibility at the multilateral level after 2004, was less a reaction to external events and more a reflection of the distinctly radical political leadership. Nevertheless, Iran used the rift between the great powers and the relative gain in power of China to bolster its resistance to regime norms that it dislikes; here, the power shift and the underlying conflict between China/Russia and the United States has had clearly negative consequences for norm enforcement.

Iran is a member of all WMD regimes but clearly shows a defiant pattern of noncompliance with the nuclear regime and works as a skillful spoiler in all regimes, based on its preference for a different order; nevertheless, Iran's position is a seismograph for the direction in which a considerable share of the NAM would like the normative setting to move. In contrast to Iran, Egypt has avoided membership in all regimes except the PoA and, significantly, the NPT, and it strictly abides by the rules while using the platform for pursuing tough but constructive norm entrepreneurship with an emphasis on the regional issue.

Comparing Norm Entrepreneurs

The grouping of norm entrepreneurs as a consequence of our empirical work looks slightly different from the initial grouping that informed the division of the related chapters. We have a quite diverse group that is generally supportive of norm development across the board, because legally bound, cooperative security corresponds to their worldview, and working for such an order fits the chosen identity of these actors. The common good orientation is in various ways combined with justice concerns, as is discussed in the next section, but there are clear differences between the strength of these concerns (which are strongest for South Africa and the NGOs) and their relative weight compared with other objectives such as regime efficiency or alliance considerations. The great powers and (curiously) North Korea behave closer to the classical understanding of interest-based statecraft, but nevertheless it appears that interests are wrapped in, and reinforced by, justice claims that relate to the status aspirations that the political elites deem to be rightful entitlements of their countries. Iran and Egypt start from different positions, and both are clearly less norm-obedient than the actors in the first group. But their practices reveal how different consequences can emerge from a similar starting point on the basis of different domestic ideologies (see for similar arguments, albeit restricted to the field of nuclear policy, Hymans 2006; Solingen 2007; Rublee 2009). In the regime on which it focuses, the nuclear one, Egypt is a critical, often difficult, but overall constructive and innovative actor. Iran, pursuing fundamental opposition, is more of an obstructive force. Nevertheless, even Iran is not pursuing norms that common sense would term "bad." Rather, it is taking a "fundamentalist" approach that pretends to change the status quo by returning to the "true" meaning of the established norms by eliminating unjust inequalities.

The Iranian position is clearly related not only to its international ambitions but equally to the prevailing domestic ideology. Given the central position of norm entrepreneurs in shaping norm development, the domestic constellation plays a crucial role. We have noted remarkable shifts in norm policies by several actors. Sweden's and Canada's proactivism has markedly declined under neoconservative governments. While the Bush administration presented the only case of a destructive strategy toward multilateral arms control norms, the degenerative impact could be limited only through the countervailing activities of other players, including US allies. The Russian shift to a more nationalist coalition in power under Putin's leadership turned Moscow's tolerance of multilateral arms control into a much more selective combination of interest-compatible entrepreneurship and stonewalling. In China and Germany, in contrast, we observed a shift to more norm-supportive behavior as the consequence of political learning, and in South Africa a revolutionary leap into a leadership position as the consequence of a domestic revolution.

INTERESTS AND JUSTICE

On the basis of these findings, we can revisit our initial considerations (see the introduction to this volume) on the relationship between interests and justice in the policies of actors and how these policies relate to norm development.

Among the actors, the United States utters justice claims the least frequently. They are at best implicit in the quest for leadership status that permeates Washington's policy and policy statements. Otherwise, US officials are not shy when it comes to articulating national interests, which are frequently intermingled with the notion that US strength serves international stability and world order best.[8] The three other great powers link their interest in status preservation (Russia) or status growth (China, India)—which is related to the military concerns that induce them to promote some norms (such as banning weapons in space or withdrawing substrategic nuclear weapons from foreign territory) or oppose others (such as eliminating substrategic nuclear weapons or enhancing transparency)—to their central justice notion of "equal security," which, in turn, links up with their status claim of world power. Altogether, the justice claims of great powers most closely resemble classic notions of national interest.

Among the rest, North Korea is closest to the way the great powers draw interest and justice together. Regime survival and the call for recognition are so intimately linked that they can hardly be disentangled. Similarly, Iran—which among all actors is maybe the most frequent articulator of the term *justice* and its synonyms—sees higher justice as inexorably dependent upon higher status for the Islamic Republic.

Egypt is similarly status conscious in regional as well as global terms. Its dismay about unequal standards and its insistence on creating equality in the region and equal implementation of regime norms globally are most probably genuine; that Egypt has serious security concerns about Israel's nuclear capacities and feels immediately threatened by the lack of P5 disarmament appears less probable than a real discomfort with the inequality that these asymmetries entail. Egypt appears to be strongly justice oriented, with due regard to its own status, but also to the collective status of Arabs and NAM states. Individualistic justice concerns, in contrast, have a much lesser role, unlike in South Africa. Post-apartheid South Africa has entered the international system as a shining beacon of moral righteousness, notably in the field of nonproliferation and disarmament. The moral call for the elimination of inhumane weapons, both WMD and conventional, and the request for justice in that the nuclear weapon states should eliminate their arsenals and that hapless victims of conflict should be delivered from the scourge of indiscriminatory weapons flow easily from this newly gained moral identity. At the same time, the moral stance serves South Africa's particular profile in international relations. The same might be said of the three "good international citizens." They echo South Africa's security concerns but more softly voiced (at least this is the case for NATO members Canada and Germany). All three have been defining a lawful, multilateral, arms-race free and deproliferated international environment as conducive to their security. Defined in these terms, their arms control policies can be understood as rooted in interests. None of them has suffered the same historical humiliation and repression as the "reformers and revolutionaries" in our sample (though Canada started out as a colony as well). The justice concerns they articulate—apart from the moderate call for nuclear disarmament—are more related to individuals and show humanitarian substance. South Africa and these three are farthest removed from traditional notions of national interest even though, as shown, their positions and policies are not interest free.

The relationship between moral/justice and interest is perhaps most compelling with regard to the defense of sovereignty that is typical of the great powers and the NAM states and least encountered in the coalition of "good citizen" states, NGOs, and IGOs. In the case of the great powers, the defense of sovereignty is intimately connected with their identity and the roles they aspire to in the international system. The responsibility they all claim can be fulfilled only if the freedom of action that goes with a largely unconstrained sovereignty is possible. On the other hand, non-aligned states want sovereignty as a defense against a return to the dark past of colonial suppression and as the shell within which they can unfold their autonomous development just as the industrialized states did from the seventeenth to the twentieth centuries. Interest, morally founded identity positions ("responsibility"), and compensatory justice claims flow together with what is conventionally thought to be "pure" national interest.

The relation of moral and justice, on the one hand, and "interest," on the other, in our investigations has thus confirmed the original expectation that the substantial differences or oppositions between the two are less than the terminological distinction appears to suggest. And it would be less than cautious, on the basis of our findings, to insinuate that moral/justice concerns are just used to cloak pedestrian wants in a noble coat. Normative and moral positions are not mere "hypocrisy" used strategically by actors (Krasner 1999). The most likely interpretation is that many of the moral and justice concerns are genuine and based on strong convictions, deeply enshrined in the belief system of greater and smaller powers, and that their conflation with what we usually call national interest is what political leaders and bureaucrats believe is the right thing to do.

VALUE-ADDED AND OUTLOOK

Our research has revealed new insights in the way multilateral arms control norms evolve. It is a bumpy road; national instincts, particularly but not exclusively on the side of great powers, remain a considerable impediment on the way to a close-knit, norm-based system of global security cooperation.

Current academic fashion likes clear-cut, if possible linear, "causal" laws that connect independent with dependent variables. The world of international politics that we try to understand, however, is not that neat: supposed "independent variables," regime conflicts, technology, and seminal or spectacular extrinsic events are by nature ambivalent. They are significant in offering constraints and opportunities, but by no means do they determine action, interaction, and the trajectory of development that flows from there. Among the actors we investigated, a highly varied group could be identified that is inclined, based on their specific combination of interest, identity, moral, and justice concerns, to make efforts to render the regimes more efficient and more just. We have two other groups that do so much more selectively.

In addition, we would emphasize the following findings as value-added, where our work has enriched our knowledge about norm change:

- Seemingly momentous events outside of the regimes—fundamental change in the international system excluded—exert a surprisingly marginal influence on norm change.
- Great powers do not always get what they want, and norm change (like the specification of the nuclear disarmament norm) can emerge against their preferences.

- Domestic politics can have a strong impact on an actor's policies toward norms and may influence normative change for better (South Africa) or worse (George W. Bush). Normative change that strengthens the regime emerges most likely when like-minded countries bridging the North-South gap commit jointly to positions that recognize both the need to make the regime more effective and the appropriateness of satisfying the South's justice claims.

Further research should undertake the complex task of investigating the intricate interplay of the more traditional notions of national interest and the moral elements with which such interests are interwoven. National policies are bound to emerge as a vector of both components. Particular attention should be paid to the justice problem. Justice is a central value in all cultures and is a strong bond among communities once justice is attained and everybody agrees that it is. Particularist justice claims, based on national or cultural idiosyncrasies, on the other hand, have great potential for generating conflict, and for these conflicts, solutions satisfying all these claims are not always at hand. Justice claims thus have the potential to make regime dynamics more obstructive. That this is not necessarily so is proven by some of the examples we discussed. But it takes skilled and well-disposed actors to develop empathy toward their counterparts and act as mediators between the extreme poles in negotiations. Last but not least, the willingness of great powers, those with the greatest spoiling *and* building potential, to compromise and to recognize the legitimacy of positions deviating from their own is important; alas, such willingness is also a rare commodity.

Because of insuperable limits of available methods, we will never know with full certainty whether what we are confronting is just an example of rhetorical action. But it is fairly probable that such claims are genuine. The fervor that accompanies a justice-based position to which the actor feels deeply entitled is a real factor in negotiations. One has to pay attention to it. Moral concerns can be a decisive driver for norm creation, as the case of humanitarian arms control demonstrates. Contention over justice issues can be fruitful for norm development when parties treat it in a constructive way. The quest for justice, on the other hand, can lead to serious conflict and put a regime into a prolonged stalemate. We are thus well advised to take justice concerns seriously, in research as well as in practice. To ignore or dismiss them might precipitate failure.

Notes

1. It is this curious development of one regime from another that motivated us to include this relatively young regime in our cases; it documents an unexpected way in which regimes develop: namely, by creating "offspring."

2. This difference in the findings of Sandholtz and Stiles might, however, be due to our shorter research period; cf. Sandholtz and Stiles 2009, 18–19.

3. "The proposal, therefore, is not a call on the Australia Group to be desolved [*sic*!], but to be evolved into a truly representative body under the framework of the Convention" (Nasseri 1997, 3).

4. Iran pushed the Israeli issue as well, but its uncompromising hostility prevented constructive norm entrepreneurship in this area.

5. On the relation of justice claims and interests, see below.

6. In the early 1990s, the Japanese sect Aum Shinrikyo carried out several attempts to release biological and chemical agents in Tokyo (Kaplan 2000). The growing concern of BWC states parties over bioterrorism is reflected in statements such as the final declaration of the 1996 RevCon (BWC 1996).

7. Interestingly, there is no neoconservatism in Germany.

8. It should be noted that the United States is more eloquent on justice in other policy areas, such as human rights. Security matters with highly military content, however, appear to be more strongly dominated by functionalist concerns; this approach does not make justice and morals disappear but gives them lower visibility.

References

African Group. 2008. Statement on Behalf of the African Group of States Parties to the 2nd CWC RevCon. The Hague, April 7.

Becker, Una. 2007. *Light at the End of the Tunnel? The Sixth Review Conference of the Biological Weapons Convention*. PRIF Report no. 79. Peace Research Institute Frankfurt. www.hsfk.de/fileadmin/downloads/prif79.pdf.

BWC (Biological Weapons Convention). 1996. Final Document of the 4th BWC RevCon. BWC/CONF.IV/9. Geneva, November 25–December 6.

Craft, Cassady. 2004. "Challenges of UNSCR 1540: Questions about International Export Controls." *Center for International Trade and Security Issue Briefs*.

Gehring, Thomas. 1994. *Dynamic International Regimes: Institutions for International Environmental Governance*. Frankfurt am Main: Lang.

Hymans, Jacques E. C. 2006. *The Psychology of Nuclear Proliferation: Identity, Emotions, and Foreign Policy*. Cambridge: Cambridge University Press.

Kaplan, David A. 2000. "Aum Shinrikyo." In *Toxic Terror: Assessing Terrorist Use of Chemical and Biological Weapons*, edited by Jonathan B. Tucker, 207–26. Cambridge: MIT Press.

Krasner, Stephen D. 1983. *International Regimes*. Ithaca: Cornell University Press.

Krause, Keith R., ed. 1998. "Culture and Security: Multilateralism, Arms Control and Security-Building." Special issue, *Contemporary Security Policy* 19 (1).

Krook, Mona Lena, and Jacqui True. 2010. "Rethinking the Life Cycles of International Norms: The United Nations and the Global Promotion of Gender Equality." *European Journal of International Relations* 18 (1): 103–27.

Müller, Harald. 2010. "Between Power and Justice: Current Problems and Perspectives of the NPT Regime." *Strategic Analysis* 34 (2): 189–201.

Müller, Harald, and Andreas Schmidt. 2010. "The Little-Known Story of Deproliferation: Why States Give Up Nuclear Weapons Activities." In *Forecasting Nuclear Proliferation in the 21st Century*, vol. 1, *The Role of Theory*, edited by William C. Potter and Gaukhar Mukhatzhanova, 124–58. Stanford: Stanford University Press.

Nasseri, Sirous. Iran. 1997. Statement to the 1st Session of the CWC CSP, The Hague, May 8.

Oosthuizen, Gabriel H., and Elizabeth Wilmshurst. 2004. *Terrorism and Weapons of Mass Destruction: United Nations Security Council Resolution 1540*. International Law Programme Briefing Paper 04/01. London: Royal Institute of International Affairs.

Rathbun, Nina Srinivasan. 2006. "The Role of Legitimacy in Strengthening the Nuclear Nonproliferation Regime." *Nonproliferation Review* 13 (2): 227–52.

Rublee, Maria Rost. 2009. *Nonproliferation Norms: Why States Choose Nuclear Restraint*. Athens: University of Georgia Press.

Sandholtz, Wayne. 2007. *Prohibiting Plunder: How Norms Change*. New York: Oxford University Press.

Sandholtz, Wayne, and Kendall W. Stiles. 2009. *International Norms and Cycles of Change*. Oxford: Oxford University Press.

Sims, Nicholas A. 2009. *The Future of Biological Disarmament: Strengthening the Treaty Ban on Weapons*. London: Routledge.

Solingen, Etel. 2007: *Nuclear Logics: Contrasting Paths in East Asia and the Middle East*. Princeton: Princeton University Press.

Valencia, Mark J. 2005. *The Proliferation Security Initiative: Making Waves in Asia*. London: Routledge.

CONTRIBUTORS

UNA BECKER-JAKOB is a research associate at PRIF, where she specializes in constructivist foreign policy analysis, arms control and disarmament, and Canadian and Irish security policy. She publishes in particular on biological weapons control and has regularly attended the meetings of the Biological Weapons Convention as adviser to the German delegation.

ALEXIS BELOW is a project associate at PRIF. His research areas include peace building, security policy, and development cooperation. He has also worked at the Crisis Prevention and Peacekeeping Division of the German Federal Foreign Office and at the international NGO Partners for Democratic Change.

MARCO FEY is a research associate at PRIF. His research focuses on US foreign and security policy. His further research interests are arms control and military sociology.

GIORGIO FRANCESCHINI is a research associate at PRIF and at Darmstadt University of Technology, and a project coordinator within the EU Non-Proliferation Consortium. A physicist by training, he works and has published on the activities of nuclear weapons laboratories in the context of the Comprehensive Test Ban Treaty, as well as on the impact of new nuclear technologies—such as nuclear fusion—on the nonproliferation regime.

ANDREA HELLMANN is a project associate at PRIF. Her current work focuses on Chinese nonproliferation policy and cultural influences on foreign policy decision making.

GREGOR HOFMANN is a research associate at PRIF. His research areas include German foreign policy and arms control, international ethics, and humanitarian intervention.

FRIEDERIKE KLINKE is a project associate at PRIF. Her current work focuses on Eastern Europe, Russia, and Russian identity in international arms control.

DANIEL MÜLLER is a research associate at PRIF. His current work focuses on arms control in the Middle East, Egypt's arms control policy, and normative causes in international and regional conflicts.

DR. HARALD MÜLLER is professor of International Relations at Goethe University Frankfurt and executive director of the Peace Research Institute Frankfurt (PRIF). His research areas include arms control and disarmament, particularly of nuclear weapons. He has been a member of the German delegation to the NPT Review Conferences from 1995 onward, served as a member of the UN Secretary-General's Advisory Board on Disarmament Matters from 1999 until 2005 (chair in 2004) and was a member of the IAEA Expert Group on Multilateral Nuclear Arrangements (2004–5). Since 2011 he has been vice president of the EU Consortium for Non-Proliferation. He has published in *International Security*, *European Journal of International Relations*, *Review of International Studies*, *Security Studies*, *Contemporary Security*, and *Nonproliferation Review*, among other journals. Inter alia, he is co-editor, with Anna Geis and Lothar Brock, of *Democratic Wars: Looking at the Dark Side of Democratic Peace* (Palgrave Macmillan 2006) and, with Anna Geis and Niklas Schörnig, of *The Janus Face of Liberal Democracies: Militant "Forces for Good"* (Cambridge University Press 2013). His most recent book is *Building a New World Order: Sustainable Policies for the Future* (Haus 2009).

FRANZISKA PLÜMMER is a project associate at PRIF. Her research interests are peace research and the role of identity and culture on political conflicts in general and Chinese political culture and its influence on arms control policy in particular.

CARSTEN RAUCH is a research associate at PRIF, where he works on Indian foreign policy and power shifts in the international system. His research interests further include theories of international relations with a focus on power transition theory and realist theories of international politics.

JUDITH REUTER is a project associate at PRIF. She has specialized in the field of South African politics and policy.

ELVIRA ROSERT is a research associate at PRIF Frankfurt and a research associate and lecturer at the Institute for Political Science, Goethe University Frankfurt. Her research interests include international humanitarian law and prohibitions of weapons, in particular cluster munitions.

DR. ANNETTE SCHAPER is a senior research fellow at PRIF. She works on nuclear disarmament and arms control and its technical aspects, including the security of fissile materials, the Comprehensive Test Ban Treaty (CTBT), a Fissile Material Treaty, verification of nuclear disarmament and nonproliferation problems arising from dual-use technology. She was a member of the German delegation to the negotiations on a CTBT from 1994 to 1996 and serves as an adviser to the German government on these issues.

DR. HANS-JOACHIM SCHMIDT is a senior research fellow at PRIF. He works and has published on conventional and nuclear arms control in Europe and on the Korean Peninsula. He is a consultant to the German government and to international institutions on issues of conventional arms control and the Korean Peninsula.

TABEA SEIDLER-DIEKMANN was a research associate at PRIF from 2005 until May 2011. Her research focus centers on chemical weapons control and on Swiss and Austrian arms control policy, on which she has published various articles. She was a member of the German delegation to the Conferences of the States Parties to the Chemical Weapons Convention from 2005 until 2010.

DR. SIMONE WISOTZKI is a senior research fellow at PRIF. Her research areas include international ethics, humanitarian arms control, and gender studies. She was member of the German delegation to the review conference of the United Nations program of action on the illicit trade in small arms and light weapons in all its aspects in 2006. She is a consultant to the German government and parliament.

CARMEN WUNDERLICH is a research associate at PRIF, where she works on the role of norms in international relations and so-called rogue states. Her further research interests include arms control and disarmament, critical constructivist theory, and Swedish foreign and security policy. She was a predoctoral fellow at the Vienna Center for Disarmament and Non-Proliferation in early 2012. She has coauthored an article in *Nonproliferation Review* and is the author of "Moving beyond Neutrality: Sweden's Changing Attitude towards the Military Use of Force" in *The Janus Face of Liberal Democracies: Militant "Forces for Good,"* edited by Harald Müller, Anna Geis, and Niklas Schörnig (Cambridge University Press 2013).

INDEX

Page numbers in italics indicate tables.